The Rhetoric of Law

The Amherst Series in Law, Jurisprudence, and Social Thought

Each work included here in The Amherst Series in Law, Jurisprudence, and Social Thought explores a theme crucial to an understanding of law as it confronts the changing social and intellectual currents of the late twentieth century.

The Rhetoric of Law

Edited by
Austin Sarat and Thomas R. Kearns

Ann Arbor
THE UNIVERSITY OF MICHIGAN PRESS

First paperback edition 1996
Copyright © by the University of Michigan 1994
All rights reserved
Published in the United States of America by
The University of Michigan Press
Manufactured in the United States of America
    Printed on acid-free paper

1999 1998 1997 1996   4 3 2 1

A CIP catalogue record for this book is available from the British Library.

Library of Congress Cataloging-in-Publication Data

The Rhetoric of law / edited by Austin Sarat and Thomas R. Kearns.
    p.   cm. — (The Amherst series in law, jurisprudence, and
social thought)
    Includes bibliographical references and index.
    ISBN 0-472-10525-6 (acid-free paper)
    1. Law — United States — Language. I. Sarat, Austin. II. Kearns,
Thomas R. III. Series.
KF380.R49   1994
349.73'014 — dc20
[347.30014]   94-5693
                                                                      CIP

ISBN 0-472-08386-4 (pbk. : alk. paper)

Acknowledgments

The Rhetoric of Law highlights law's distinctive language, arguments, and hermeneutic practices. These features of law are central to the conception of legal study that animates the work of Amherst College's Department of Law, Jurisprudence, and Social Thought, and they were the subject of a course called "The Rhetoric of Law," which was first taught jointly by Austin Sarat and Lawrence Douglas in the spring of 1992. Students in that course provided invigorating interest and intellectual companionship as many of the issues taken up in the volume were explored. In addition, the editors are grateful for the insights of the group of distinguished scholars whose contributions are included in this volume. Finally, we would like to express special thanks to the Mellon, Keck, Arthur Vining Davis Foundations for their generous financial support, and to Amherst's President, Peter Pouncey, for his friendship and enthusiastic engagement with our work.

Contents

Editorial Introduction

Austin Sarat and Thomas R. Kearns

Dealing in words is dangerous business. . . . Dealing in long,
vague, fuzzy-meaning words is even more dangerous business and
most of the words The Law deals in are long, vague and fuzzy.
—Fred Rodell

The legal process is always the same, an open, though bounded,
forum where forensic battles are contingently and temporarily
won.
—Stanley Fish

Oratory serves . . . to produce the kind of conviction needed in
courts of law . . . and the subject of this kind of conviction is right
and wrong.
—*Gorgias*

"Law," Gerald Wetlaufer claims, "is the very profession of rhetoric."[1]
It is "a profession of words."[2] Once uttered, these descriptions of law
seem commonplace. They conjure up familiar images of obscure legal
jargon and Dickensian evocations of law's sometimes absurd preoccupation with form over substance. At the same time, however, they
unsettle and arouse anxiety among some mainstream social scientists,
traditional jurisprudes, and conventional legal scholars.[3] They remind
all of us that law can never escape the intricacies and imprecisions,

We are grateful for the helpful comments of Adam Thurschwell.
1. See "Rhetoric and Its Denial in Legal Discourse," *Virginia Law Review* 76
(1990): 1545, 1555.
2. David Mellinkoff, *The Language of the Law* (Boston: Little, Brown, 1963), vi.
3. See Fred Rodell, *Woe unto You, Lawyers* (Berkeley and Los Angeles: University of California Press, 1980), 39.

as well as the promise and power, of language itself.[4] Such observations about law's rhetoric seem to let law off too easily by displacing
the question of justice. Shouldn't law after all be a "profession of
justice"? And while law may be a profession of words and of rhetoric,
"the particular rhetoric embraced by law operates through the systematic denial that it is rhetoric."[5] It appears, then, that to insist on
the importance of the rhetoric of law is to highlight an opposition
with law's conception of itself.

Talking about law as a "profession of rhetoric" would seem, at
first glance, to stand in stark contrast to the view that law is a
profession of power, the command of the sovereign backed by sanction,[6] or that law is a profession of rules.[7] Yet both of these ideas
themselves depend on language, on verbal or written utterances.
Commands and rules, though distinct in many different ways,[8] each
is signaled by words—for example, *must, should, ought to*—that
purport to require particular forms of conduct. But recognizing law
as a "profession of rhetoric" means more than noting that it characteristically directs us through language and that its use of language
is calculated to be persuasive. Law is not only profuse in its verbosity;
in addition, it celebrates, and dogmatically insists on, the proper and
precise formulation of human desires in words.[9] It calls on us to keep
in mind the dramatic consequences that often accompany law's peculiar linguistic formulations. As Robert Cover put it, "Legal interpretation plays on a field of pain and death."[10] Law, then, is a stage for
the display of verbal skill, linguistic virtuosity, and persuasive argument in which words take on a seriousness virtually unparalleled in
any other domain of human experience.

To focus on law's language instead of the serious business with
which law is everyday engaged will seem to some frivolous at best

4. See Stanley Fish, "Fish v. Fiss," *Stanford Law Review* 36 (1984): 1325.

5. Wetlaufer, "Rhetoric and Its Denial," 1554. See also Peter Goodrich, *Legal
Discourse: Studies in Linguistics, Rhetoric, and Legal Analysis* (New York: St. Martin's, 1987).

6. John Austin, "Law as the Sovereign's Command," in *The Nature of Law:
Readings in Legal Philosophy*, ed. M. P. Golding (New York: Random House, 1966),
77–98.

7. H. L. A. Hart, *The Concept of Law* (Oxford: Clarendon, 1961).

8. Ibid., chaps. 2 and 4.

9. For a dramatic instance of such insistence see Trident Center v. Connecticut
General Life Insurance, 847 F. 2d 564 (9th Cir. 1988).

10. "Violence and the Word," *Yale Law Journal* 95 (1986): 1601.

and dangerous at worst. It arouses anxiety among law's adherents and its defenders by drawing attention to the unscrupulous, unattractive ways legal processes can be manipulated, for example, by the lawyer who artfully mesmerizes an audience with the sound rather than the substance of his words.[11] Some of law's most ardent defenders claim that justice is its true subject and argue that the scholarly enterprise should be devoted to identifying ways of making law more just rather than to exploring its linguistic artifice.[12] To them, as Anselm Haverkamp puts it, "While it looks as if rhetoric could do almost anything, nothing it actually does seems to be 'right' in itself."[13] For critics of law eager to expose the ways law is complicit in, if not responsible for, maintaining injustice,[14] talk about law's discursive, aesthetic, or persuasive aspects seems to be little more than a disturbing distraction. Yet it may be that attending to the rhetoric of law is a way of attending, albeit from a new and perhaps unrecognized angle, to questions of justice and injustice.[15] It may be that analysis of law's rhetoric is more than aesthetic self-indulgence, but rather is part and parcel of a political and ethical project whose object is the transformation of law in the name of a justice all too rarely spoken about in the profession of law.[16]

The association of rhetoric and law, the recognition of law's "profession of words," despite its unsettling, anxiety-arousing effects, has had a long history.[17] While today it is acceptable, perhaps even fash-

11. See Rodell, *Woe unto You, Lawyers.*
12. See Paul Carrington, "Of Law and the River," *Journal of Legal Education* 34 (1984): 222.
13. See Anselm Haverkamp, "Rhetoric, Law, and the Poetics of Memory," *Cardozo Law Review* 13 (1992): 1639.
14. For example, see Edgar Friedenberg, "The Side Effects of the Legal Process," in *The Rule of Law,* ed. Robert Paul Wolff (New York: Simon and Schuster, 1971).
15. Jacques Derrida, "Force of Law: The 'Mystical Foundation of Authority,'" *Cardozo Law Review* 11 (1990): 919, 935. "One cannot," Derrida argues, "speak *directly* about justice, thematize or objectivize justice, say 'this is just' and even less 'I am just,' without immediately betraying justice." See also Drucilla Cornell, "From the Lighthouse: The Promise of Redemption and the Possibility of Legal Interpretation," *Cardozo Law Review* 11 (1990): 1687, and Haverkamp, "Rhetoric, Law," 1652.
16. Cornell, "From the Lighthouse."
17. Peter Goodrich contends that "[t]he earliest explicit study of legal argument and legal judgment was linguistic; it dates back to the fifth century B.C. and takes the form of technical or forensic manuals associated initially with the work of Coraz and Tisias of Syracuse." "Semiotics, Dialectic, and the Law: Historical Aspects of Legal Interpretation," *Indiana Law Journal* 61 (1986): 331, 349.

ionable,[18] to speak of the two together, and, in so doing, to acknowledge that law is a deeply rhetorical enterprise,[19] a book entitled *The
Rhetoric of Law* would have been understood, in the not too distant
past, as an invitation to contemplate the merely arcane, often parodied, qualities of legal language. Study of the rhetoric of law would
have been thought to involve no more than the examination of the
orator who though he knows "nothing about good or evil undertakes
to persuade a city in the same state of ignorance . . . by recommending
evil as though it were good."[20]

Such understandings would have made recourse to a tradition
dating at least as far back as Plato's *Gorgias*,[21] a tradition in which
rhetoric, as that which "gives [rise to] belief without knowledge,"[22]
exists under a cloud of suspicion, while philosophy is praised because
it "engenders knowledge" and a commitment to justice.[23] Rhetoric,
Socrates contends in the *Gorgias*, is "pandering and base clap-trap."
Philosophy, in contrast, "aims at the edification of the souls of the
citizens and is always striving to say what is best, whether it is
welcome or unwelcome to the ears of the audience."[24]

In this tradition, law can only be worthy to the extent it subjects
rhetoric to a disciplining silence, and to the extent that the rhetorical
life of law is contained and rendered secondary to a deeper com-

---

18. As Stanley Fish says, "[t]he fortunes of rhetorical man are on the upswing,
as in discipline after discipline there is evidence of what has been called the interpretive
turn, the realization . . . that the givens of any field of activity are socially and polit-
ically constructed, are fashioned by man rather than delivered by God or Nature."
*Doing What Comes Naturally: Change, Rhetoric, and the Practice of Theory in
Literary and Legal Studies* (Durham, N.C.: Duke University Press, 1989), 485. See
Jack Getman, "Voices," *Texas Law Review* 66 (1988): 577; and Gregory Leyh, ed.,
Legal Hermeneutics: History, Theory, and Practice (Berkeley and Los Angeles: Uni-
versity of California Press, 1992). For a different view see Michael Moore, "The
Interpretive Turn in Modern Legal Theory: A Turn for the Worse," *Stanford Law
Review*, 41 (1989): 871.

19. See Peter Goodrich, "Rhetoric as Jurisprudence: An Introduction to the
Politics of Legal Language," *Oxford Journal of Legal Studies* 4 (1984): 88. See also
Chaim Perelman, *Justice, Law, and Argument: Essays on Moral and Legal Reasoning*
(Boston: D. Riedel, 1980).

20. Plato, *Phaedrus*, ed. and trans. W. C. Helmbrod and W. G. Rabinowitz
(New York: Macmillan, 1952), 260.

21. Plato, *Gorgias*, ed. and trans. Walter Hamilton (London: Penguin Books,
1960).

22. Ibid., 32.

23. Ibid.

24. Ibid., 110.

mitment to justice.[25] Where law is unable to discipline rhetoric, it is inevitably corrupted by it; "the orator," Socrates says, "does not teach juries and other bodies about right and wrong—he merely persuades them."[26] The rhetoric of law is, in this understanding,

> a magical thing. It transforms things into their opposites. Difficult choices become obvious. Change becomes continuity. Real human suffering vanishes as we conjure up the specter of righteousness. Rhetoric becomes the smooth veneer on the cracked surface of the real and hard choices in law.[27]

In the Platonic tradition, rhetoric is "skill detached from any moral center . . . [and] eloquence is the hard-won creation of a special and technical facility, a facility one acquires by mastering a set of complicated—and morally neutral—rules."[28] Like the traditional opposition of rhetoric and philosophy, a rhetorical analysis of law would have seemed to pose a threat to concerns with justice that lie, at least in theory, at the heart of law's enterprise.

But today, fortunately, times have changed. Though its anxiety-arousing potential is, for some, as great today as ever, one need no longer feel tentative about, or embarrassed by, the pairing of rhetoric with law.[29] To pair rhetoric with law is, as the essays in this volume attest, to invite inquiry about many things at once, about law's literary and linguistic qualities, its interpretive practices and idiosyncracies, its verbal and written productions, the rules that govern who can speak and in what ways in a legal forum; it is also to invite questions about justice.[30] Throughout the legal academy the study of

25. See Ernest Weinrib, "Law as Myth: Reflections on Plato's *Gorgias*," *Iowa Law Review* 74 (1989): 787.

26. Ibid. See James Boyd White, "The Ethics of Argument: Plato's *Gorgias* and the Modern Lawyer," *University of Chicago Law Review* 50 (1983): 849.

27. Thomas Ross, "The Rhetorical Tapestry of Race: White Innocence and Black Abstraction," *William and Mary Law Review* 32 (1990): 1. As Freud said, "Words were originally magic and to this day words have retained much of their ancient magical power." *The Complete Introductory Lectures on Psychoanalysis*, trans. and ed. James Strachey (New York: Norton, 1966), 17.

28. Fish, *Doing What Comes Naturally*, 472.

29. As Wetlaufer argues, "[T]here is, as we all on some level already know, a discipline-specific rhetoric of law, and . . . this rhetoric shapes our advocacy, our judicial opinions, our scholarship, and our teaching." "Rhetoric and Its Denial," 1551.

30. Most often, as we will argue below, the question of justice is taken to be a question of the extent of law's inclusiveness and responsiveness to the community of speakers that it is supposed to serve.

each of these things has, in the face—or perhaps because—of the anxieties it arouses, been rehabilitated.[31] Recognition of, for example, the literary qualities of law as well as the increased emphasis on interpretation have both contributed to and been a by-product of that rehabilitation. Indeed, so powerful has been the embrace of rhetorical analysis that we are already in the throes of a correcting revisionism.[32]

Scholars of all kinds and of varying political commitments now take up the challenge of understanding the way law is spoken to, and spoken about, as well as the way law speaks.[33] This diversity is fully on display in the essays collected for this volume. In these essays one sees the varied and textured influence of literary studies, history, and interpretive social science as well as of feminism and critical theory. While for some of the authors in this book the analysis of the rhetoric of law is a celebratory opening to a hoped-for humanistic revival, or a way of saving law from creeping instrumentalism and a life-destroying emphasis on technique,[34] others, here and elsewhere, seize on rhetorical analysis to open up the question of politics and of law's connection to the world of contingency.[35] As a result, and as the essays included in this collection amply demonstrate, analysis of the rhetoric of law is neither colonized nor owned by any sectarian group. In the hands of a wide range of scholars such analysis provides a bracing reminder of the possibilities as well as the problems of law, of its capacity to engage what is best in human character, and through that to engender deep loyalties, as well as of law's corruptions and the opportunities it provides for cynical manipulation.

For those who now seek to rehabilitate the rhetoric of law as a

---

31. Kathryn Abrams, "Hearing the Call of Stories," *California Law Review* 79 (1991): 971. See also "Symposium: Legal Storytelling," *Michigan Law Review* 87 (1989): 2073, and "Symposium: The Emperor's Old Prose: Reexamining the Language of Law," *Cornell Law Review* 77 (1992): 1233.

32. See Cover, "Violence and the Word"; and Austin Sarat and Thomas R. Kearns, eds., *Law's Violence* (Ann Arbor: University of Michigan Press, 1992).

33. See "Symposium: Legal Storytelling"; Ross, "Rhetorical Tapestry of Race," and "The Rhetoric of Poverty: Their Immorality, Our Helplessness," *Georgetown Law Journal* 79 (1991): 1499.

34. See James Boyd White, "Law as Rhetoric, Rhetoric as Law: The Arts of Cultural and Communal Life," *University of Chicago Law Review* 52 (1985): 684.

35. See Goodrich, *Legal Discourse.* See also William Felstiner and Austin Sarat, "Enactments of Power: Negotiating Reality and Responsibility in Lawyer-Client Interactions," *Cornell Law Review* 77 (1992): 1447.

subject of academic inquiry the classical referents are more likely to
be Aristotelian than Platonic.[36] In the Aristotelian tradition, rhetoric
is defined as a faculty or art whose practice helps us to observe "in
any given case the available means of persuasion."[37] Aristotle suggested that we use persuasion in order to assign meaning to events
and to convince others that the meaning so assigned is reasonable,
if not right.

Thus, as opposed to the Platonic view, in the Aristotelian tradition
rhetoric is not in itself morally iniquitous. It can be used well or badly
by good as well as evil men; "What makes man a 'sophist' is not his
faculty, but his moral purpose."[38] But Aristotle advanced a still
stronger claim on behalf of rhetoric; contra Plato, he suggested that
it was, in fact, an essential aid to the discovery of truth. Rhetoric, he
observed, was always needed "in order that we may see clearly what
the facts are."[39] Thus rhetoric is a "heuristic, helping us not to distort
the facts, but to discover them."[40] Traditional legal analysis, "by
emphasizing the search for the sources of law, discounts its evangelical
element; rhetorical analysis, by contrast, makes this aspect its focus."[41]

Today perhaps the most powerful and eloquent statement of the
Aristotelian view of rhetoric in legal scholarship has been advanced
by James Boyd White.[42] In a series of books and articles dating back
to 1973,[43] White has led the effort to rescue law from the technocrats

36. See, for example, Gerald Frug, "Argument as Character," *Stanford Law Review* 40 (1988): 872.

37. *Rhetoric* (New York: Modern Library, 1984), book 1, 1355, 27.

38. Ibid., 17.

39. Ibid., 28–33.

40. Fish, *Doing What Comes Naturally*, 479.

41. Frug, "Argument as Character," 872.

42. White defines law as the "particular set of resources made available by a culture for speech and argument on those occasions, and by those speakers we think of as legal." "Law as Rhetoric," 689. "To define 'the law' in this way," White suggests, "as a set of resources for thought and argument, is an application of Aristotle's defini- tion of rhetoric, for the law in this sense is one set of those 'means of persuasion' that he said it is the art of rhetoric to discover." For a critical review of White's status as a leading theorist of law's rhetoric, see "Note: The Universe and the Library: A Critique of James Boyd White as Writer and Reader," *Stanford Law Review* 41 (1989): 959.

43. See *The Legal Imagination* (Chicago: University of Chicago Press, 1973); *When Words Lose Their Meaning: The Constitution and Reconstitution of Language, Character, and Community* (Chicago: University of Chicago Press, 1984); *Heracles' Bow: Essays on the Rhetoric and Poetics of Law* (Madison: University of Wisconsin Press, 1985); *Justice as Translation: An Essay in Cultural and Legal Criticism* (Chi- cago: University of Chicago Press, 1990).

and secure for it a place as a humanistic discipline.[44] He has argued consistently and repeatedly that

> law is most usefully seen not, as it is usually seen by academics and philosophers, as a system of rules, but as a branch of rhetoric, and ... the kind of rhetoric of which law is a species is most usefully seen not, as rhetoric usually is either as failed science or as the ignoble art of persuasion, but as the central art by which community and culture are established, maintained, and transformed. So regarded, rhetoric is continuous with law, and like it, has justice as its ultimate aim.[45]

At the center of White's conception of law is the view that law, as Marianne Constable argues, depends on words and, in so doing, avows, or professes, faith in the capacity of language to work in the world.[46] But as a "profession of words" law does more than avow its faith in language; it creates occupations in which rhetorical facility is claimed and cultivated.[47] Law thus provides a "set of resources for thought and argument."[48]

White juxtaposes a conception of law as rhetoric with a conception of law "as a machine acting on the rest of the world."[49] Law is not just, or primarily, a set of commands working their way down from a group of legislators, bureaucrats, and judges to a population "made the objects of manipulation through a series of incentives or disincentives."[50] It is, instead, a "culture of argument perpetually remade by its participants" in which rhetoric is understood as the "art of establishing the probable by arguing from our sense of the possible."[51]

---

44. See also Guido Calabresi, "Introductory Letter," *Yale Journal of Law and the Humanities* 1 (1988): vii, and Owen Fiss, "The Challenge Ahead," *Yale Journal of Law and the Humanities* 1 (1988): viii. For a recent assessment of the success of the humanistic enterprise in legal education see Austin Sarat, "Law's Two Lives: Humanistic Visions and Professional Education," *Yale Journal of Law and the Humanities* 5 (1993): 199.

45. "Law as Rhetoric," 684.

46. See "Discussion Outline: Justice and Power in Language and Discourse," (typescript, 1992).

47. Ibid.

48. White, "Law as Rhetoric," 689.

49. Ibid., 686.

50. Ibid.

51. *Heracles' Bow*, 35, 31.

When a court renders an opinion or an agency makes a ruling, it not only resolves a particular dispute, it validates, in White's view, one way of looking at the world, one way of speaking and thinking. "In rhetorical terms, the court gives itself an ethos, or character, and does the same both for the parties to a case and for the larger audience it addresses. . . . It creates by performance its own character and role and establishes a community with others."[52] Courts speak, and *how* they speak matters independently of what they say. Here White calls attention to three aspects of law as a "profession of words."

First he says that the speaker in a legal setting "must always start by speaking the language of his or her audience, whatever it may be."[53] White notes that lawyers must develop facility in the "technical language of the law" so that they can speak to judges and other lawyers, as well as in some version of "the ordinary English of . . . [their] time and place" so that they can speak to clients or jurors.[54] "Law," White contends, "is in this sense always culture specific. It always starts with an external, empirically discoverable set of cultural resources into which it is an intervention."[55]

Second, law, according to White, also provides the occasion for rhetorical inventiveness and argumentativeness. Lawyers and judges do not just use available cultural resources, they use them for a purpose and, in so doing, modify or rearrange them so as to do the work of persuasion.[56] Lawyers and judges engage in a rhetorical process of remaking and reshaping those resources by being willing to "add or drop a distinction, to admit a new voice, to claim a new source of authority."[57] In this sense, "legal rhetoric is always argumentatively constitutive of the language it employs."[58]

---

52. *Justice as Translation,* 102. See also Robert A. Ferguson, "The Judicial Opinion as Literary Genre," *Yale Journal of Law and the Humanities* 2 (1990): 201.

53. "Law as Rhetoric," 688.

54. Ibid. On speaking to clients see Austin Sarat and William Felstiner, "Law and Strategy in the Divorce Lawyer's Office," *Law and Society Review* 20 (1986): 93. See also Anthony Alfieri, "Reconstructive Poverty Law Practice: Learning Lessons of Client Narrative," *Yale Law Journal* 100 (1991): 2107. On speaking to jurors see Lance Bennett and Martha Feldman, *Reconstructing Reality in the Courtroom* (New Brunswick: Rutgers University Press, 1981).

55. "Law as Rhetoric," 689.

56. See Wetlaufer, "Rhetoric and Its Denial," 1557. See also Ferguson, "Judicial Opinion."

57. "Law as Rhetoric," 690.

58. Ibid.

The third aspect of law as a profession of words is what White calls its "ethical or communal character."[59] The rhetoric of law, he contends, is argumentative not just about results in specific cases but about visions of self and of community that should be encouraged and supported.

> Every time one speaks as a lawyer, one establishes . . . a character—an ethical identity, or what the Greeks called an *ethos*—for oneself, for one's audience, and for those one talks about, and, in addition, one proposes a relation among the characters one defines. One creates, or proposes to create, a community of people talking to and about each other.[60]

Here White analyzes the rhetoric of law in an optimistic spirit, looking to rhetoric as a way of reviving law or of saving it from those who would turn it into a machine.

In contrast to this hopeful emphasis on the community-building, character-displaying qualities of the rhetoric of law, others, including some feminists and critical theorists, have looked to rhetoric as a way of understanding the contingency of law and the way power is exercised in and by law.[61] Such scholars emphasize the rhetorical qualities of law, in particular its linguistic indeterminacy, and the capacity of legal language to mystify and reify social relations.[62] Linguistic indeterminacy makes it possible to generate opposing arguments with equal force and convictions; "[G]iven the play in the logic of justification," Stanley Fish contends, "the facts of a case can, with equal plausibility, be made to generate any number of outcomes, no one of which is deduced from a firm base of principle."[63] Moreover, as Fish continues,

---

59. Ibid.
60. Ibid.
61. See William Joseph Singer, "The Player and the Cards: Critical Legal Studies and Nihilism," *Yale Law Journal* 94 (1984): 997. See also Goodrich, *Legal Discourse*.
62. See Pierre Schlag, "Cannibal Moves," *Stanford Law Review* 40 (1988): 929. See also Jamie Boyle, "The Politics of Reason: Critical Legal Theory and Local Social Thought," *University of Pennsylvania Law Review* 133 (1985): 685; Clare Dalton, "An Essay in the Deconstruction of Contract Doctrine," *Yale Law Journal* 94 (1985): 997.
63. "The Law Wishes to Have a Formal Existence," in *The Fate of Law*, ed. Austin Sarat and Thomas R. Kearns (Ann Arbor: University of Michigan Press, 1991), 194.

One who has learned the lesson of rhetoricity does not thereby escape the condition it names. . . . There is . . . no contradiction here, only a lack of relationship between a truth one might know about discourse in general—that it is ungrounded—and the particular truths to which one is temporally committed and concerning which one can have no doubts.[64]

For scholars like Fish, careful analysis reveals less of a community dedicated to justice through its rhetorical commitments and more of a repetitive series of highly stylized, bootstrap arguments, each of which claims to be grounded in a reality external to language and rhetoric.[65] Legal argument, so these scholars suggest,

consists . . . of a series of shifting appeals to . . . various grounds for decisionmaking, with any particular ground on which the decision is said to rely ultimately resting on yet another ground. An argument built on precedent, for example, may be said to turn on the facts of the case, but the facts themselves are often interpretable only in light of the intention of the parties, which is understandable only through a court's reading of the facts of the case; and which facts are relevant . . . is determined by precedent. In legal argument, this kind of shifting of the basis of decision can continue *ad infinitum* without ever finding an adequately stable place on which the decision can be grounded.[66]

Yet rhetoric is itself also available as a device for disguising the inescapably rhetorical quality of all legal arguments and for lending the appearance of stability to law. As Peter Goodrich argues,

In reading the law, it is constantly necessary to remember the compositional, stylistic and semantic mechanisms which allow legal discourse to deny its historical and social genesis. It is necessary to examine the silences, absences and empirical potential of the legal text, and to dwell upon the means by which it

---

64. Fish, *Doing What Comes Naturally,* 522.
65. See Singer, "Player and the Cards."
66. Frug, "Argument as Character," 871. In *Allegories of Reading,* Paul de Man argued that "rhetoric suspends logic and opens up vertiginous possibilities of referential aberration" (New Haven: Yale University Press, 1979), 10.

appropriates the meaning of other discourses and of social relations themselves, while specifically denying that it is doing so.[67]

Despite its need to appear to do so, law cannot escape its own
rhetoricity.

Law's rhetorical quality is apparent in all of the institutions and
processes that comprise the "space of law," not just in the elaborately
staged legal argument before a jury or in the highly stylized production of an appellate court. It can be observed in the way lawyers
speak to clients and the way they speak to each other; it can be
observed in the places and on the occasions where law empowers
citizens to speak, as in the deliberations of a jury or of a police
citizen review board.[68] In each of these places and on each of these
occasions law regulates and disciplines particular acts of speaking
and defines appropriate modes for the making of persuasive argument.[69] In each, conventions and rules enable and, at the same time,
constrain the opportunities for voice. This is, for example, surely and
purposefully the case with respect to the rules of evidence,[70] and it
is now recognized to be the case in the production of judicial
opinions.[71]

If we think of legal argument as providing an opportunity for
the display of character and the constitution of community, it is also
important to recognize that, in the space of law, not all characters
or voices are welcome and among those that are welcome not all are
equally valued.[72] Feminist theory has made an especially important
contribution in noting that not everything can be spoken and not
everything can be spoken about in every way. This quality of rhetoric

67. *Legal Discourse,* 204.
68. See Martin Shapiro, "On the Regrettable Decline of Law French: or Shapiro
Jette le Brickbat," *Yale Law Journal* 90 (1981): 1198.
69. Clark Cunningham, "The Lawyer as Translator, Representation as Text:
Towards an Ethnography of Legal Discourse," *Cornell Law Review* 77 (1992): 1298.
70. See Lucie White, "Subordination, Rhetorical Survival Skills, and Sunday
Shoes: Notes on the Hearing of Mrs. G.," *Buffalo Law Review* 38 (1990): 1.
71. Ferguson, "Judicial Opinion."
72. As Lucie White argues, "The law governing the use of speech in legal
rituals—the law of evidence—has devised an arsenal of doctrines for guarding against
the voices of women and other subordinated groups. . . . [A] range of evidence suggests
that women and other subordinated groups do not in fact participate in legal proceedings as frequently or as fluently as socially dominant groups." "Subordination,"
9, 20.

opens the way for an inquiry into new questions of justice and for an effort to link the rhetoric of law to its operation as a system of power in which power is defined in terms of what can be spoken and what is silenced.[73] Here we are invited to recognize the fact that law is both a privileged discourse and a discourse of the privileged.

This emphasis on the rhetorical quality of law seems antithetical to the legitimating claims of law itself. "In law, assent is secured through an appeal to reason and logic, through a strong claim to objectivity and certain knowledge, through a voice that claims objectivity and authority."[74] If law is inescapably rhetorical, and if power operates in and through its rhetoric, then what happens to these claims?[75] If law is inescapably rhetorical, is there any basis for judging the correctness of legal arguments and the correctness of legal decisions? The emphasis on the rhetoric of law "increases the level of anxiety because it denies the existence of a basis for legal decisionmaking"[76] while, at the same time, insistently pressing the question of justice. Awakening this contemporary anxiety about law is, despite many ingenious efforts to alleviate it, perhaps the inevitable price that we pay for the rehabilitation of rhetoric as a subject of legal scholarship.

The essays that follow run the risk of provoking such anxiety by providing a panoramic view of the rhetoric of law. They have been chosen to represent the breadth and diversity of scholarship that treats law's rhetoric and its associated linguistic or interpretive characteristics. Some are authored by scholars with long-established points of view, others by those whose views are less well established and less well known.

The essays in *The Rhetoric of Law*, each from its own distinctive disciplinary or theoretical point of view, address three broad questions. First, what is the nature of law's rhetoric and what is its connection to the achievement of justice in and through law? How

---

73. See Kathleen Lahey, "On Silences, Screams, and Scholarship: An Introduction to Feminist Legal Theory," *Canadian Perspectives on Legal Theory* 3 (1991): 319; Lucinda Finley, "Breaking Women's Silence in Law: The Dilemma of the Gendered Nature of Legal Reasoning," *Notre Dame Law Review* 64 (1989): 886.

74. Wetlaufer, "Rhetoric and Its Denial," 1565.

75. See Owen Fiss, "Objectivity and Interpretation," *Stanford Law Review* 34 (1982): 739.

76. Frug, "Argument as Character," 871.

exclusive or inclusive is the rhetorical field on which law operates? What historical forces and linguistic phenomena shape the way law speaks and is spoken to? What possibilities for altering and improving law are made available by careful examination of rhetorical phenomena drawn from fields outside law? These questions are at the heart of the first two essays in this volume, those by James Boyd White and Peter Goodrich.

Second, how does law's rhetoric vary? Does it, in fact, make sense to speak about the rhetoric of law as if it were characterized by a single, consistent style or a uniform set of rules and conventions? To address this question several of the essays (those by Ferguson, Sarat, White, and Douglas) provide careful historical accounts, case studies, and close readings of the rhetoric of particular legal institutions.

Third, what is the status of contemporary scholarship on the rhetoric of law? We include two essays, one by Barbara Johnson and one by Adam Thurschwell, each of which carefully examines the work of one of the major contributors to current debates about the rhetoric of law, namely Patricia Williams and Stanley Fish. These essays provide helpful guides to understanding the discomfort that some scholars experience when confronted with analysis of law's rhetoricity. And, at the same time, each shows how the question of justice is, and can be, addressed by taking seriously law's "profession of words."

James Boyd White opens this collection by asking, "How do we imagine the law? Or, to put it more precisely, what ways of imagining the law do we have, and how do we choose among them?" Following his earlier work, "Imagining the Law" suggests that law is typically thought about as a set of rules and procedures, as a "tool for social control" or "an instrument for achieving social objectives." White invites us instead to another, a different, imagining of law. He suggests that it should be seen as a literary and rhetorical process, "an activity of speech and the imagination."

A literary or rhetorical imagining changes our relationship to law by inviting citizens to take an internal perspective and think about law as a process of argument and persuasion about the "meaning of authoritative texts." Meaning is a domain of rhetoric. Argument and persuasion determine how members of a community regard the subjects of our talk. Law, in turn, "establishes the conditions upon which this special kind of talk goes on, both by defining its places and occasions and by establishing its resources, its terms, and practices—in the largest sense of creating its language."

As White's article points out, much of the rhetorical energy of lawyers, judges, and others involved in the legal process is invested in the reading and rereading of law's authoritative texts. This means that when they draft rules or write opinions, lawyers, judges, and others must imagine themselves as constituting a community of readers whose character is, in turn, imaginatively made present in the written product. As readers, legal actors must "imagine the writer as a person with a certain character inhabiting a certain context and having a certain set of expectations and understandings about the process in which he or she is involved." Thus White contends that imagination is at the center of the rhetorical engagements that are necessarily part of writing and reading law.

Yet White contends that a decent, humane legal order cannot be sustained simply through the recognition of the imaginative dimensions of its rhetorical processes. Such an order must learn from literature to be inclusive in the imaginings it sponsors and those to which it responds. White speaks in the name of a humanistic commitment that, he believes, can renew and revitalize law. He illustrates this commitment by reading a case, *Riverside County v. McLaughlin*,[77] in which the Supreme Court decided that it was constitutional to consolidate probable cause hearings and arraignments even if it could mean that persons would be detained for substantial periods of time without having the validity of their confinement affirmed. He argues that Justice O'Connor's majority opinion "imagines the county of Riverside as a bureaucracy, laboring to do its best with insufficient resources," while Justice Scalia's dissent, in contrast, invests his imaginative energy elsewhere, taking the perspective of the "innocent person who will be discharged when his probable cause determination is heard." As in this case, any court will have available to it many possible imaginings. Thus in making its decision and in putting that decision into language it confronts the "tragic necessity of occluding voices and erasing experiences." Yet, in the end, the quality of law's rhetorical productions can, White believes, be judged by the degree to which they minimize the "violence" of such exclusions. A just legal order keeps alive "competing

77. See 111 S.Ct. 1661 (1991).

ways of imagining the world, in a way that undermines the claims
of absoluteness otherwise at work in the judgment and its
explanation."

Concern for problems of inclusion and exclusion is also central
to Peter Goodrich's "Antirrhesis: Polemical Structures of Common
Law Thought."[78] Inclusion and exclusion, defining the terms of membership, of who counts in the "community of believers" that we call
citizenship, are, Goodrich contends, close to the heart of law's enterprise. Unlike White, however, Goodrich is dubious about humanism
and the possibility of building a more inclusive legal community. His
contribution to *The Rhetoric of Law*, by examining the historical
origins of the common law, helps to explain that dubiety.

The turn to rhetoric in recent legal scholarship, Goodrich contends, is, in fact, itself partially a response to issues of inclusion and
exclusion, as well as to anxiety about the "nihilistic indeterminacies
of interpretation." The practical value of rhetoric to the study of law,
he notes, is "almost universally perceived to be resident in its capacity
to produce agreement," to promise some resolution to the persistent
problem of self and other that gives law its very reason for being.
This is, however, an historically inaccurate understanding of the function of rhetoric in law; its rhetoric has always been linked to "disputation, casuistry, apologetic, proof, and polemic," not to a pacifying
openness to divergent perspectives. Rhetoric, Goodrich suggests, has
a critical and unsettling force because it discerns "behind the self-
conscious use of tropes and figures of speech the unconscious structures of institutional reason."

In law, Goodrich argues, these structures have historically been
oppositional; they have been used to exclude rather than include, to
justify domination rather than to build community. Law's rhetoric is
more often the rhetoric of denunciation than of welcoming. This is
the case because the rhetorical structure of the common law has
historically borrowed heavily from the rhetoric of theology. In both
"each tenet of doctrine or of creed is matched against a figure of
heretical exclusion or excommunication." As a result, the common
law was, during the Renaissance, developed against the "image of
other laws," against "other traditions and foreign histories," against

---

78. Goodrich defines antirrhesis as a form of speech by which speakers reject
"the authority, opinion, or sentence of some person" for the "error or wickedness of
it."

"the fantasy, imagination, or 'dreams' of other disciplines," and, most especially, against "the threat of feminine succession."

Goodrich concludes his article by arguing that there is a deep structure to legal rhetoric, a structure of conflict and opposition, which defeats even the most sustained and well thought out efforts to use law in projects of reconciliation and harmony. This structure

> subsists over the long term of common law history, in the language and categories of a legal reason that long outlives the impermanent and tendentious forms of merely positive laws. Without an appreciation of those essentially antithetic rhetorical structures and their persistent semiotic force, the critique of contemporary legal forms . . . [and here White's critique of the undue exclusiveness of law would be a prime example] is doomed to the status of a repetitious and ineffective play upon institutional surfaces that history and dogma will soon consume and forget.

The question of inclusion and exclusion is made literal in the rhetoric of particular legal processes, perhaps none more vivid than the criminal trial. The next two papers, by Robert Ferguson and Austin Sarat, each provides close readings of such rhetoric, the former in the context of the well-known treason trial of Benedict Arnold, the latter in a contemporary capital trial.

Ferguson's "Becoming American: High Treason and Low Invective in the Republic of Laws" amply demonstrates the fact that trial transcripts provide a treasure trove for the student of law's rhetoric. Such transcripts, though less frequently the object of attention than the appellate court opinion, "register . . . conflict in the advocacy system in ways that a judicial decision ignores," "reveal . . . the real preoccupations in the flow of legal argument," and supply a "better perspective for understanding the formulation of [the] story that lies at the center of all courtroom proceedings." Trial transcripts display the full range of the available rhetorical resources of a community and its historical epoch; they enable us to understand the central argumentative preoccupations of a culture as well as the limits on what can be spoken about within law's ambit. This, Ferguson argues, is never truer than in moments of crisis.

Thus Ferguson presents an analysis of a single trial that took place at a moment of profound crisis in the formation of the American

Republic, namely the treason trial of Benedict Arnold. How could one speak about treason, how could one name an act as treasonous, at a revolutionary moment when the specter of treason hung as an accusation against those who themselves accused Arnold of treason? Was it indeed possible to be guilty of treason against those who themselves were guilty of their own brand of treason?

As Ferguson reminds us, the trial of Benedict Arnold is as much a misnomer as is the so-called Rodney King trial, since Arnold had successfully escaped capture and was thus never brought to justice. Arnold's treason was, however, vicariously on trial during the trial of his less fortunate British collaborator, John Andre. The substitution of Andre for Arnold mirrors the larger avoidance of treason as a subject in revolutionary America.

The rhetorical structure of Andre's trial was epistolary, revealed in a series of letters that surrounded it. The trial transcript, Ferguson notes, was mostly a composite of some seventeen such letters. Andre's correspondence, which plays an important role in the trial, is replete with the "circumlocutions, abstractions, and archness of the eighteenth-century epistolary style." It is an ingenious and artful effort to "gloss admitted duplicity in the principles of virtue and honor, proper station and disinterestedness." Nevertheless, the rhetorical structure of the correspondence contained in the trial transcript "fulfills the needs of narrative." It displays the persons of the major actors, their conflicting agendas, and strategies for realizing their objectives. And as in every criminal trial, "the disruption of crime yields to the discursive reenactment of order through language."

Reenacting that order is accomplished in part by defining the deed, in this case the crime of treason, as the deed of an "other," someone who by his acts removed himself from the community. It is also accomplished by the structure of epistolary exchanges itself. Here Ferguson notes that Arnold as well as Andre wrote several letters to George Washington, but that Washington never responded to any of them. Whereas

> trial advocacy gives each participant a place in the ceremony of the trial . . . , [s]ilence banishes Arnold from the realms of honor and virtue that Washington symbolizes, and, in the process, the abstractions of republican identity begin to register on a new or

personal level. In the trial transcript Arnold begins to assume a hapless role: he is permanent prodigal to the father of his country.

Washington's silence suggests that the purpose of the treason trial is precisely not to "understand the culprit," to include his perspective and his imaginings in the moral community, as James Boyd White advocates. Benedict Arnold served, as Goodrich would have predicted, as "a lightning rod for negative commentary," as a symbolic other against which the "ritual of the courtroom" articulates and "reinforces a national faith."

Washington's silence also prepared the way for the final ignominy of Andre's treason trial: his execution by hanging rather than firing squad. That silence stood firm against the entreaties of Arnold and Andre to allow him to die in the way officers and gentlemen die, and against their insistent effort to make Andre's prospective death the center of law's rhetorical preoccupation.

Sarat's "Speaking of Death: Narratives of Violence in Capital Trials" argues that this unwillingness to put the question of law's own violence into discourse characterizes a less sensational capital trial in the contemporary United States, the trial of William Brooks for the rape and murder of Janine Galloway. In this paper, Sarat, following Elaine Scarry,[79] suggests that law is not unique in facing the problem of figuring out how to put violence into discourse. Sarat employs the techniques of interpretive social science to suggest that "[a]s pervasive as is the relationship of law and violence, it is nonetheless difficult to speak about that relationship, or to know precisely what one is talking about when one speaks about law's violence." Sarat contends, again following Scarry, that trials are "occasions for lawyers to 'invent' languages of violence and pain . . . [but] that in law, as elsewhere, the languages that can be invented are quite limited." Violence, he suggests, is put into discourse by speaking of its instrumentalities (weapons) and its effects (wounds).

In the Brooks trial, while concerted efforts were made vividly to portray the weapons and wounds that took the life of Janine Galloway, no comparable effort was made to represent the prospective violence law wished to inflict on her killer. In this way the rhetoric

---

79. *The Body in Pain* (New York: Oxford University Press, 1985).

of law "seeks to do a double deed. *First*, it strains to instantiate and vividly portray the violence that exists just beyond law's
boundary.... *Second*, it works to mute other kinds of violence ... [including] the violence of law itself. This is done," Sarat
contends, "in the hope of affirming the social value of law, of
reassuring citizens that its use of violence is somehow different from
and better than illegal violence."

Reading the rhetoric of the Brooks trial suggests that these two
linguistic gestures, in fact, coexist, but that their coexistence is an
uneasy one. Other tropes must be mobilized to legitimate law's violence, a violence that is as silent in this trial as it was in Washington's
nonresponse to Andre. Here race and racialized images play an important role. By portraying Brooks, a black man who raped and murdered a white woman, as a racialized other, as someone who would
use an innocent human for his own pleasure and then cruelly dispose
of her, Brooks and his act are portrayed as "'inexplicably alien,
horrendous and inhuman.'" This invites us to banish his perspective
from the rhetorical construction of "our" community. "We," the prosecutor claimed without needing to say who is included in that "we,"
"'have a right ... to be vindicated and protected'" from a "them"
who also need not be named.

Even on those other occasions when law tries to expand its
rhetorical field and include a wide range of perspectives and points
of view, it may face substantial, if not insurmountable, barriers.
This is one lesson that can be drawn from Lucie White's "Ordering
Voice: Rhetoric and Democracy in Project Head Start." White treats
Head Start as an effort to expand the range of law's discursive
community and the variety of rhetorics to which it must respond.
Such apparent inclusiveness was mandated in the authorizing legislation; that statute required that Head Start be "'developed, conducted, and administered with the maximum feasible participation
of ... members of the groups served.'" In addition, implementing
regulations required that Head Start projects provide the "'channels
through which such participation ... can be provided for and
enriched.'"

White describes the "performances, from sequences of speech
acts," that such a structuring of rhetorical possibility engenders. Her
project, White notes, "immerses itself in ... sites where the law has

authorized its subjects to get together for a specific kind of talk." The site of White's own work, a project Head Start parent council in central North Carolina, is subject to an extensive ethnographic examination and rhetorical analysis.

White documents the parts played by three staff members and nine parents in a single parent council meeting, the agenda of which was to elect a new chair for the group. She carefully analyzes the roles played and the rhetorical moves made by the various participants. As a result, she is able to show how the effort to include the perspectives and desires of the parents mandated in legislation and regulation is frustrated in minute, almost unnoticeable ways, including the subtle but powerful effects of race and gender. She listens as parents explain that as "black people" they "feel there are things that we're not supposed to do . . . [I]t's that plantation mentality. . . . It comes from way back. . . . [I]t's just that the whites will do it better." For such people, "social power seldom feels as fluid and multidirectional as postmodern political theorists maintain."

Law's inclusive aspirations fail, White argues, echoing the insights of feminism and critical theory, because the rhetorical opportunities it affords subordinate groups always occur "in the very heartlands of domination. They convene in those settings where power has long been marshaled, in countless routine ways, to maintain historic patterns of domination." While law may make bold gestures to include new perspectives, its "rhetorical grammar . . . short-circuits whatever transformative passion that its imagery might call forth." Nevertheless, White cautions that the experience of the people to whom that effort was addressed cannot be read monolithically. Each drew multiple meanings from his or her encounter with law; given the opportunity to participate, an opportunity not fully realized, each subverted "the law's pretense to authorize social and political order in the community that it constitutes among them."

Apparently subversive rhetorical gestures, this time emanating from a more familiar and recognizable site of law's rhetorical production, namely the United States Supreme Court, play an important part in the next contribution to this volume, Lawrence Douglas's "Constitutional Discourse and Its Discontents: An Essay on the Rhetoric of Judicial Review." The apparently subversive gesture that draws Douglas's attention is Justice Jackson's famous dictum describing the

Supreme Court itself: "We are not final because we are infallible, but
we are infallible only because we are final."[80] Opinions like Jackson's,
Douglas contends, far from undermining the Court's claims to legitimacy, "lie at the heart of" those claims.

Douglas reads Jackson's gesture, and others like it (such as the
rhetorical dancing of Justice Marshall's famous opinion in *Marbury
v. Madison* and the opinions of Justices Black and Frankfurter in
Adamson v. California) as a particular kind of rhetorical move, "an
attempt to resolve the tensions between interpretation and legitimation not by an act of mystification or fetishization, but by an even
more provocative move: by an act of confession." In this move the
right to read authoritatively is itself authorized by an open admission
of "radical uncertainty about its very possibility." "An expression of
the impossibility of justifying the discourse," Douglas argues, "is thus
a chief feature of the discourse itself."

Jackson is the true child of Marshall, as well as of Black and
Frankfurter, and of each of their efforts to resolve the problem of
legitimacy through acts of reading. Each of those justices tried to
make a case for the Court's interpretive authority "through reading"
and to render the Constitution "interpretively legible." Marshall
attempted to legitimate the Court's role in our constitutional system
by conjuring an image of the "textual fecundity" of the Constitution
that, Douglas argues, undercuts the very effort at legitimation by
challenging forever "the coherence of any hermeneutic that claims to
be able to read the deep rhetoric of 'We, the people.'" Such textual
fecundity keeps the Supreme Court in business as the final, and
therefore authoritative, reader of legal texts, even as it reveals "the
close connection between discourse and doctrine," and "the Court's
intense preoccupation with its own anomalous position within the
American system of governance."

Douglas calls attention to Jackson's statement because it seems,
at first glance, to expose and disavow the longstanding effort of the
Court to resolve Alexander Bickel's "countermajoritarian difficulty"
by claiming that its interpretations and rulings are grounded in objective readings of the constitutional text or in "neutral principles." As
Douglas argues,

---

80. See Brown v. Allen, 344 U.S. 443, 540 (1953).

One would expect a Supreme Court justice writing in an official opinion to attempt to engage in a Bickelian effort at legitimation. Jackson's statement, however, merely restates, indeed exacerbates, the problems about judicial review that so preoccupied Bickel. Indeed, Jackson seems to assume that the Court's powers of constitutional exposition cannot be grounded.

Jackson, Douglas contends, seems to have "revealed the deep artifice of the Court's power to read the Constitution."

Yet Douglas shows in this essay that Jackson's gesture was neither so debunking nor so subversive as it would initially seem. He focuses on two cases, *Marbury v. Madison* and *Adamson v. California*, for what they reveal about the Court's own "response to its problematic role as constitutional expositor" and for what that in turn reveals about the Court's own "rhetoric of reading in which the instabilities within the Court's own hermeneutic project are ceaselessly concealed, revealed, displaced, and disclaimed." The Court's authority, though not its finality, will be perpetually under suspicion.

The final two essays in *The Rhetoric of Law* direct our attention to another kind of textual fecundity, namely the richness of recent scholarly explorations of legal rhetoric. These essays both provide extended meditations on single pieces of scholarship, scholarship that itself has called attention to rhetoric's connection to justice by high-lighting its inclusions and exclusions.

Barbara Johnson's "The Alchemy of Style and Law" starts with the assertion that to understand the rhetoric of law one must understand the rhetorical constitution of what she calls the "impersonal book" and its connection to "madness." She sees these themes as being central to the exploration of legal rhetoric in Patricia Williams's *The Alchemy of Race and Rights.*[81] That book, Johnson argues, amply illustrates how law privileges a particular rhetorical position—the impersonal and objective—all the while denying that there is anything contingent or political in this act.

Johnson argues that such a position and the ideology of style it engenders is a "powerful reinforcer of hierarchy" and, in the case of law, a contributor to the "intractability of racial misunderstanding"

81. Cambridge: Harvard University Press, 1991.

that frustrates law's self-proclaimed efforts at inclusion. She shows how Williams herself, an African-American woman law professor, understood the linkage between style and the exclusion of particular voices from law's "profession of words." Johnson recounts Williams's experience in trying to publish an essay describing how she was kept out of a Benetton's in New York City by a white sales clerk who would not open the door for her. In the process of confronting law's stylistic conventions, all the aspects of the encounter that made it meaningful to Williams were progressively edited out in the name of impersonality and objectivity, including most particularly all mention of her race.[82] "'This is just a matter of style,' she was told." And, Johnson argues, that was exactly right. For Johnson, however, style, including the style of law, is never just style; there is always an overdetermination at work, and the style of law is rarely "just" in what it condones or accepts.

Johnson admires Williams's book precisely because it is concerned with the justice of style. Moreover, Johnson argues that Williams comes close to doing justice to style precisely by "complicating, demystifying, confounding, rethinking" the polarities that law presents as its way of organizing the world. Johnson describes how such an effort arouses anxiety among the official guardians of law's rhetoric and those who police its style. As she puts it,

> If academic writing or legal codes are defined through their exclusions and disconnections, then what Patricia Williams does is to find, explore, elaborate, and restore the connections among the bill of sale for her great-great-grandmother, the lawyer who bought her and impregnated her, the contemporary homeless man on the street, the advertising industry, the academic conference circuit, a basketball camp in Hanover, New Hampshire, Christmas shopping, the Critical Legal Studies movement, and the United States Constitution.

---

82. Williams is, of course, by no means the first to feel the oppressive bite of law review style, nor is she the first to comment critically on it. For an earlier example see Fred Rodell, "Goodbye to Law Reviews," *Virginia Law Review* 23 (1936): 38. As Rodell put it, commenting on what law reviews typically publish, "There are two things wrong with almost all legal writing. One is its style. The other is its content." See also George Gopen, "The State of Legal Writing: *Res Ipsa Loquitur*," *Michigan Law Review* 86 (1987): 333.

In so doing, Johnson argues, she reveals the way "the madness of juxtaposition mimes the structure of the social text."

Williams's writing is, according to Johnson, an instruction in the way law's rhetoric manages to exclude, while proclaiming its inclusiveness. She "repeatedly documents the revisions, erasures, and displacements her writing undergoes in its encounters with the rules of legal style and citation." One way in which Williams's writing challenges such revisions and erasures is by insisting that "subject position is everything in my analysis of law." This Johnson insists is not a Justice Jackson–like confession; it is instead a way of confronting the constraining conventions of law itself, conventions that demand distance and objectivity and insist on maintaining a rigid distinction between rhetoric and reality.

Williams, Johnson insists, "lays bare the network of constraints and censorships that attempt to produce 'plain, readable prose.'" When Williams talks about subject position she is, quite intentionally, displaying herself as the constructed object of a rhetoric controlled by others. In so doing, she exposes, at the level of rhetoric, law's maddening, objectifying, impersonal terms of inclusion and the continuing reality of its exclusions.

The final essay in this volume, Adam Thurschwell's "Reading the Law," asks whether, in the end, we may not have made too much of the practices and consequences of law's rhetoric. The question, which an analysis of the rhetoric of law must ultimately address, is whether "*poetics*—that is, the theory and practice of literary reading—might not make something happen within the sphere of law and legal practice." By pressing this question Thurschwell reminds us of James Boyd White's optimistic insistence on a positive answer. But Thurschwell concentrates his own reading on Stanley Fish rather than White. He does so because he believes that Fish is

> among the most successful in synthesizing a global theory of literary interpretation with a similarly broad (and deep) perspective on the law. In a remarkable balancing act, Fish manages both to endorse White's affirmative view of the law as rhetorically constitutive of community *and* CLS's critical demonstration of the ideological nature of the law's claims to a (more than rhetorical) foundation.

In the end, Thurschwell argues, Fish provides the most extended and challenging refutation of the view that "a self-consciously literary and rhetorical theory of law can (or should) 'make something happen' within law's practical sphere."

Thurschwell reads Fish by way of Paul de Man and deconstruction, and he suggests that Fish has capitulated to the story that law tells about itself. Fish does so by exposing and yet celebrating law's legitimating formalism. For Fish, the fact that "'law is at once thoroughly rhetorical and engaged in the effacing of its own rhetoricity' is as much a sign of the law's genius as of its duplicity." He holds fast to the claim that no theory, legal or otherwise, can inform or alter practice. Yet Thurschwell claims that Fish's argument itself depends on the sturdiness of a rhetorical distinction between legal practice and theories of reading that Fish's own rhetoric helps to deconstruct. In addition, Thurschwell argues that Fish himself gives evidence of a form of the very thing he so persistently denounces, namely "anti-foundationalist theory hope."

Fish can only sustain his position by forgetting law's relationship to justice. Law's "impulse toward realizing itself as justice" raises a doubt that Fish does not entertain, namely that law is more than a rhetorically constituted and rhetorically effacing process of resolving disputes and exercising authority. As a result, Fish, against his own intentions, seems committed to the very positivism that his rhetorical reading of law is intended to expose and question.

Thurschwell credits Fish with noting with "great precision" the process by which law's connection to justice is forgotten, yet he shows how Fish attributes those acts to law rather than to his own interpretation of this process.

> Identifying law's "primary business" and "goals" with "winning an argument or crafting an opinion," rather than with the . . . achievement of a just world, demarcates law as a set of technical and formal rhetorical practices without regard to the meaning of these practices outside the sphere of their conventional usage.

But escaping such an entrapment is precisely the task of rhetorical readings and rhetorical understandings of an institution which denies its own rhetoricity. Fish fails to take advantage of the escape that his own powerful readings make available to him (a failure that Thurschwell at the same time suggests is inevitable). On Thurschwell's reading, Fish's neopragmatic philosophical bias "equates antifoun-dationalism with historicism" and in so doing pulls his work toward a "rhetorical privileging of *present* interests and beliefs . . . and away from the insight into the structural excess of act over meaning" in which law's aspirations to justice are to be found.

Law's promise of justice is, according to Thurschwell, exemplary of a utopian moment that inheres in all linguistic acts, a moment that rescues law from its own self-privileging positivism. This promise "is never fulfilled . . . but by that same token must be made again and again, each time a legal decision is rendered." Fish loses touch with the connection of law and justice because he unduly concentrates on law's "violent positing of a fictional present and its fictional history masquerading as truth." He accords, in Thurschwell's view, undue attention to law's own official story. In so doing, Thurschwell contends Fish fails to take full advantage of the promise of a rhetorical analysis of law, the promise of keeping alive anxiety about the adequacy of that story and, at the same time, making space for a continuing insistence that law be as attentive to its exclusions as it is insistent on its inclusiveness. This, Thurschwell claims, is the unfulfilled prom-ise of justice.

Thus, *The Rhetoric of Law* ends where it began, by asking its readers to consider various styles and types of rhetorical readings of law and give attention to its rhetorical structure. Doing so is one way of opposing the tendency of law itself to insist that its profession is simply power patterned through rules. This book ends by sug-gesting that those who, in the name of justice, are made anxious by attentiveness to law's rhetoric, may take some comfort in that which, at least until recently, has seemed to them frivolous and strange. It ends with the hope that seeing law as a "profession of rhetoric" may, through its insistent attention to questions of inclusion and exclusion, keep alive law's as yet unredeemed promise of justice.

Imagining the Law

James Boyd White

My aim in this paper is to trace out a certain line of thought about what it might mean to think of law rhetorically.[1] In doing this I shall be resisting the impulse, quite common in our culture, to see the law from the outside, as a kind of intellectual and social bureaucracy; rather I am interested in seeing it from the inside, as it appears to one who is practicing or teaching it. Throughout I shall conceive of the law as a system of discourse that the lawyer and judge must learn and use, and of which we can ask what meanings it creates— or enables us to create—for our individual and collective lives.

Ways of Imagining the World

I wish to begin with the basic point that as human beings we perpetually imagine and reimagine the world and reflect what we imagine in the ways we talk. If I start to talk or write about an academic institution, for example—about Amherst College, say, or the University of Michigan—I will immediately begin to define that institution in a certain way: as a place where classes are given, or where

---

The discussion of the poetry of Robert Frost is drawn in part from my book, *"This Book of Starres": Learning to Read George Herbert* (Ann Arbor: University of Michigan Press, 1994).

1. For especially valuable work on the way we imagine the world, see Kenneth Boulding, *The Image: Knowledge in Life and Society* (Ann Arbor: University of Michigan Press, 1956), and Northrop Frye, *The Educated Imagination* (Bloomington: University of Indiana Press, 1964). For a fuller statement of my general views on rhetoric and law, see "Rhetoric and Law: The Arts of Cultural and Communal Life," in James Boyd White, *Heracles' Bow: Essays on the Rhetoric and Poetics of Law* (Madison: University of Wisconsin Press, 1986), chap. 2.

young people complete their growing up, or as a competitor with other institutions, athletically or intellectually, or as the grantor of certain credentials. I cannot help imagining a past, as well as a future, for actors such as these—the roots of Amherst College in a nineteenth-century reaction to the godless unitarianism of Harvard, for example, or of the University of Michigan in its early commitment to a new idea of the possibilities of graduate education. Often, of course, I will be unaware that the way I talk reflects a particular way of imagining. Usually I just talk, as though the world were the way I imagined it, and there were nothing problematic in my speech. But whatever we may consciously think, in fact all of us are constantly imagining the world.

It is also true, though perhaps less obviously so, that when we talk or write we imagine both our audience and ourselves, and again this is so whether or not we are aware of it. I think of myself as simply giving a lecture, for example, or teaching a class, my students as simply attending one, as if all this were instantly comprehensible, not in the least odd nor the proper object of critical attention; yet these are in fact peculiar social practices, which people differently situated from us might find most odd.

Despite our usual inattention to them it is possible to make our ways of imagining the world, and our action within it, the object of reflection. In fact, one of the functions of great literature, and I shall argue of the law as well, is to do just this, to make conscious, and thus render the object of critical examination, the ways in which our speech imagines at once a larger world that we claim to inhabit and an immediate world we create with our audiences.

Consider for example this brief poem by Robert Frost:

Range-Finding

The battle rent a cobweb diamond-strung
And cut a flower beside a ground bird's nest
Before it stained a single human breast.
The stricken flower bent double and so hung.
And still the bird revisited her young.
A butterfly its fall had dispossessed
A moment sought in air his flower of rest,
Then lightly stooped to it and fluttering clung.

On the bare upland pasture there had spread
O'ernight 'twixt mullein stalks a wheel of thread
And straining cables wet with silver dew.
A sudden passing bullet shook it dry.
The indwelling spider ran to greet the fly,
But finding nothing, sullenly withdrew.

Many things happen in this poem, of course, but among them the speaker of the poem imagines the world a certain way, or finds himself wanting to do so: he wants to think of the flower, and the bird, and the butterfly as being like him, as actors with feelings with which he can identify—feelings of safety, danger, sympathy with others, feelings that will confirm the reality and importance of his own. He tries, that is, to imagine nature as a world of fellow feeling.

As he does this he finds himself imagining the world in another way as well: the bird, it turns out, is wholly indifferent to the fate of the flower, as is the butterfly too, and to neither has the stained human breast any significance at all. This is not a universe of creatures like us, then, full of the capacity for sympathy and themselves the proper objects of our sympathies, but one of mysterious actors, each driven by its own needs.

But the poem does not stop here. It goes on to suggest that this way of imagining may be wrong as well: perhaps these animals and plants are like us after all, but not benign, as the speaker at first imagines it, but malign: think of the spider running to "greet the fly." The poem thus first imagines a world of significant and sympathetic action, then throws that way of imagining life into doubt, and does this in two ways, seeing its actors first as inscrutable, then as malign. In doing so it makes its real subject the process of imagining the world itself: it is the competing imaginings that become the topic of thought and feeling.

This is frequent in Frost: think of the white-tailed bird that the narrator pursues in "The Woodpile," and to which he attributes the vanity of taking "everything said as personal to himself"; or of the two voices countering one another in "West Running Brook"—hers playful, full of fun and imagination, his ponderous, sententious, and self-important; or of the two actors in "Mending Wall," one committed to one reiterated sentence—"something there is that doesn't love a wall"—the other to another, "good fences make good neighbors." In each of these poems different ways of imagining the world are contrasted with each other and thus made the object of critical reflection and ultimate uncertainty.

Or think of Emily Dickinson's poem, "A Narrow Fellow." As you remember, this poem begins with the speaker imagining the snake running through the grass as a kind of social being, a friendly chap:

> A narrow Fellow in the Grass
> Occasionally rides —
> You may have met Him — did you not
> His notice sudden is —

But by the end of the poem the speaker's efforts to domesticate and familiarize this experience have failed:

> Several of Nature's People
> I know, and they know me —
> I feel for them a transport
> Of cordiality —
>
> But never met this Fellow
> Attended, or alone
> Without a tighter breathing
> And Zero at the Bone —

How does each of these writers imagine herself or himself, the reader, and the kind of relation between them that the poem creates? Each poem defines its writer as a person partly captured by the ways of imagining the world implicit in the languages, in the verbal gestures, by which he or she has learned to negotiate the world; yet also as one interested in bringing this circumstance to consciousness. The reader too is defined as one who imagines the world and wants to come to terms with the implications of the ways in which he or she does so.

The Law as Machine

I mean all this as a way of defining the question implied in my title, How do we imagine the law? Or, to put it more precisely, what ways of imagining the law do we have, and how do we choose among them? With this question goes a second: In imagining the law in one way or another, how do we imagine ourselves and our audience and the relation between us? I am trying to think, that is, of all speech as a kind of imagining, and this in two dimensions, as we imagine the larger world, and as we imagine the immediate world in which our language is a form of action.

My impression is that law is usually imagined, by those outside of it, and by many of those who teach it as well, as a machine: a machine that is part of another machine, the Government, which in turn is part of another machine, Society, which is part of another machine, Nature, until we get to the greatest machine of all, the Universe. Sometimes this image is used rather explicitly, when we speak of law as a "tool for social control" or "an instrument for achieving social objectives," sometimes less so. But very often, at least, I think that what is imagined is a set of parts that function in interrelationship, by cause and effect. To think of something as a machine—whether society, law, or the natural world—is to imagine it as in principle wholly comprehensible by human intelligence and subject to human control. Machines, after all, are made by people; if they do not work correctly, they can be remade, or refashioned.

In this vision the law is the set of rules that govern a part of the social machine; they could in theory govern all of it, but for reasons of practicality or principle they govern only part. So imagined, the law works by establishing a set of prohibitions and commands, enforced by incentives and disincentives. Of course there are imperfections in the process by which they function, but these defects arise from our temporary want of knowledge, from the inherent defectiveness of the language in which the law's commands are cast (for it cannot be perfectly precise), or from the defectiveness of human beings themselves. They are not inherent in the idea of law as machine, and they can be minimized.

The fact that the natural world and the social world, the individual actor and the law, and language itself, are all imagined as machines gives an extraordinary coherence to this vision of the world. In particular, it makes it natural to think that the mode of reasoning by which it works is a form of universal rationality: namely, reasoning as the maker of the machine does reason, in terms of the specification of ends to be obtained and the means by which they are to be accomplished. True reasoning meets the standards of an intellectual machine. Its parts fit together to work in ways that can be rendered wholly explicit in language, which is of course another machine. Other forms of mental life and expression—for example, poems or novels or music—are not "reasoning," but something less, or different. On this view the principal question for the lawyer or the student of law is what policies should be adopted, that is, what value choices should be made and how they should be put into effect, given our various constraints. Once a choice of value is made, law is simply a system of implementation. Laws are rules that work, or don't work; the main issue is compliance, and here is the role for legal expertise, namely how to secure it, or how to evade it. Lawyers are either architects or engineers for a social machine.

This image of the world, and of the law, is so deeply seated in our culture—it was promoted by the politics of the New Deal, and is still advanced by forces within the social sciences, from sociology to economics—that it is often hard to recognize that it is, after all, just one way of imagining among many. I do not mean that one ought never imagine the law this way: important conversations can be based upon it and we would be worse off if we never talked this way. But I do mean that this is only one way of talking among several, and that it actually has rather less to do with what lawyers and judges— and citizens—do in the world than one might think.

What is more, it has a serious internal difficulty, namely that, however powerful this vision may be for everything else, it cannot account for itself. For how can this vision account for our own thought and speech? Are we machines too? It certainly does not feel like it; and whenever we talk we make claims for attention, for the value and meaning of what we say, that are radically inconsistent with any conception either of us or of our audience as machines. If "we" are outside the machine we observe, how are we imagined: as analyzers, makers, and designers of machines? Where do we come from? If we are to have a vision that claims to be global it had better be one that includes us.

The Law as Rhetoric

How else might one imagine the law? My suggestion is that it can be imagined as a rhetorical and literary process, as an activity of speech and the imagination that takes place in a social world that can be imagined that way too—including our own performances with language and each other, including indeed this very paper.

It may help the reader who is not a lawyer to see how this might be done if you were to imagine yourself not outside the law, observing it, but inside it, doing what lawyers and judges and legislators actually do. Think, to begin with, of what you would expect to learn if you went to law school. You might imagine that the law consists of a set of rules, to be found in the books and applied to facts as they come up, in lawyers' offices or in judges' courts. If so, the function of law school would be to attain a comprehensive knowledge of those rules.

This is in fact part of what happens in law school and in the law, but rather a small part. Sometimes of course a person will be told by a lawyer simply what the law requires; in such a case it may make sense to imagine her as simply functioning as a part of a social machine, doing what some external authority commands. But actually very little of the lawyer's life consists of this kind of work. In any real case there may be dozens or hundreds of rules, or other authoritative texts, that arguably bear upon it. Some of them will be too clear for argument, but many others will not, and it is upon these— upon the uncertainties in the authoritative texts that bear upon a case—that the lawyer's attention is largely devoted.

Think, for example, of the First Amendment, which says: "Congress shall make no law . . . abridging the freedom of speech or of the press." Does this mean that laws punishing libel, or conspiracy, or incitement to murder, or pornography, or racial insults—which could all be seen as forms of speech—are invalid? The word "interpretation" hardly does justice to what is called for here: a process of thought and argument not only about words and context, but about the meaning of a nearly infinite variety of human activities.

The lawyer's task is not just to apply rules in a mechanical way, then, but to learn how to think and argue about their meaning, not simply as words but as texts given significance by their contexts. What the lawyer is to learn in law school is not merely a structure of rules—in fact that is a very small part of what she learns—but how to engage in argument of a certain sort, especially in argument about the meaning of a set of authoritative texts: constitutions, statutes, judicial opinions, regulations, contracts, and any other text that may be called upon as legally authoritative in a case.

Why do I speak of "authoritative" texts? Because one characteristic of legal thought is that in every legal case the lawyers invoke
authorities external to themselves as the ground upon which it should
be resolved. Of course policy choices must be made by judges and
others, but this is always done in the context of a process in which
the decider looks outside of herself for her source of authority. In
deciding a case, that is, the judge looks not simply to her sense of
what would be best, but to what is called for by a text external to
her: a constitution, or a statute, or a contract written by the parties.
Formally speaking, at least, this is always true. Even where judges
ultimately conclude that a particular matter is open for their choice,
they traditionally think of that choice not as wholly free, but as
shaped by guides and constraints external to them, in the law or
culture, not by their personal preferences, say, or by drawing lots.
At its heart the law is a system of textual authority.[2] This is what
we mean both by the rule of law and by a Constitution that separates
the powers it creates.

For the lawyer, all this is a radically rhetorical process, in precisely the sense in which Aristotle defines the term in his treatise on
rhetoric: It is the art of "finding out the available means of persuasion
in a given case." What is to count as a means of persuasion is to be
determined not by "logic" but by knowledge of the relevant audience
and its culture. This too Aristotle knew, and much of his treatise is
devoted to a catalogue of the argumentative claims that were, in his
judgment, effective in his world. The lawyer, therefore, must learn
the ways in which lawyers and judges think, so that he can speak
to them effectively. This is what law school is about.

These brief words about legal education reflect a way of imagining
the law not as a machine but as a set of people talking. The law

---

2. With legislators it works somewhat differently: they do look to the United
States Constitution to see if they are within their competence to act, and, if they
are state legislators, they will look at their own constitution and federal legislation
as well, much as judges do. But if they are within their competence they may, with
few exceptions, act on any ground they choose, and in any event need not explain
themselves to any one. This is what the writers of the Federalist Papers meant when
they said that legislation is a matter of will, adjudication of judgment. Thus in arguing
to a legislature the lawyer will address an audience less constrained by texts external
to it; in arguing to a court, the constraints provide the terms in which argument
proceeds.

establishes the conditions upon which this special kind of talk goes on, both by defining its places and occasions and by establishing its resources, its terms, and its practices—in the largest sense creating its language. Much of the life of the law is the reading of prior texts claimed to be authoritative, listening to arguments about those claims and about the meaning of those texts, and making arguments of both kinds oneself. This is itself not a scientific process, nor readily describable in scientific terms, but a rhetorical and literary one.

One of the effects of this process, indeed I think one of the aims we can attribute to it, is the maintenance of the language or discourse in which the process itself proceeds. When two lawyers represent opposing parties in a particular case, each undertakes to say everything that can be said, or can persuasively be said, on his or her side; the result is that between them the lawyers mark out the possibilities for speech in this situation. The lawyers disagree, of course—that is the point—but they cannot disagree about everything. Some things are unsayable in any language; some claims cannot be made in the language of the law. In thus articulating and prosecuting their disagreements, the lawyers perform their agreement to everything else, including the language in which their disagreement is defined. In this sense one social function of the practice of law is the maintenance of a culture, a culture of argument.

In the process, the language is not merely maintained, it is both criticized and transformed. Both the lawyers and their audiences are led to become at least somewhat self-conscious about the nature of the languages they speak, of the language games they engage in, and they find themselves forced to make judgments about their propriety as well.

In this way the law works rather as poetry does—at least the poetry of Frost or Dickinson—to make conscious, and thus the object of critical thought, the languages we use. And since the language of law is in principle subject to modification and transformation, no particular mode of thought is taken as absolutely valid or authoritative. It is all open to question and reexamination. This means, among other things, that there is no stable or fixed language in which bureaucratic "ends" can unquestionably be stated.

To imagine law as rhetorical, then, is to think of it not as a machinelike process of cause and effect, driven by a rationality that is fundamentally instrumental in kind, but as a discourse maintained

by the processes of persuasion and argument. These processes work
not simply by ends-means rationality but by all the movements of
mind and feeling that lawyers and judges display. One of the ends
and effects of the law is the simultaneous maintenance and transformation of the culture it defines.

But there is more to it even than this. For while the law works
as a system of discourse, this does not happen in isolation but in
interaction with the other systems of discourse that make up our
world. Law is a language that must establish relations with virtually
all of the other languages spoken in our world: scientific and technical
talk, psychological and sociological language, the speech habits of
the parties and the witnesses, and so forth. The relationship is one
of translation, for each of these other discourses is translated into
the law. This is itself an activity calling for the highest sort of art,
by which the law must maintain its character as a meeting ground
for other systems of speech.

Finally, it is not merely a language that the law maintains, but
an entire social and dramatic system, a set of speakers and actors.
Indeed one feature of legal thought is that the power to decide is
allocated among various actors, each of whom has a particular and
limited role, no one of whom has plenary power. Thus the judge, or
regulator, or private citizen, or legislator, or governor or president,
must all ask when facing a particular legal question—about the validity of a law prohibiting abortions, say—not only what they think
of the question in the abstract but whether, under our system, the
question is one for them to decide at all, and if so under what
standards. This set of questions, institutional and procedural in kind,
is at work, though sometimes only implicitly, in every legal conversation. The authoritative legal text in this way creates a social universe
that works at once competitively and cooperatively.

I mean the term "rhetoric," then, to call attention to four features
of legal discourse: that its modes are not those of scientific reasoning;
that it works by persuasion; that it maintains and transforms its
culture; and that it is socially and institutionally constitutive.[3]

---

3. In *Heracles' Bow* I say that the study of "constitutive rhetoric" is the study
of "the ways we constitute ourselves as individuals, as communities, and as cultures,
whenever we speak.... The law is an art of persuasion that creates the objects of its
persuasion, for it constitutes both the community and the culture it commends" (35).

The Rhetoric of Writing Law

The rhetorical structure of legal discourse might be summed up this simple way: in a legal proceeding a rule (or other prior text) must be selected, read, and applied to the case. Two key features are therefore the composition of the rule (or other authoritative text) and the reading of it, both of which are open to argument. At the end of the process other texts will be created: settlement agreements, judicial opinions, administrative orders, which in turn become authoritative texts. From time to time the legislature too adds its texts to those that already speak.

To think of the law this way will affect one's sense of what is called for at every stage of the legal process. One can start with the writing that a lawyer does, and in its most lawlike form: the making of rules. On the view suggested here the rule will be conceived of less as a command that is to be obeyed or disobeyed than as a way of establishing and guiding the conditions of other people's rhetorical activities. Like every text the rule requires for its operation the cooperation of others, and the task for the writer of such a text is how to secure it. The image of obedience and disobedience is far too simple for a process of such complexity, and this is true whether one is writing contracts as a lawyer, opinions as a judge, or rules or regulations as a legislator or administrator.[4]

We might think of this, for example, in connection with the composition of a marital separation agreement, that is, a contract between divorcing parties that, subject to judicial approval, will regulate their relations after the divorce decree. This agreement normally governs all aspects of the dissolution, including property transfers— who gets the house? What about her accrued pension benefits?—as well as alimony, child support, custody, and the like. It may provide that insurance be maintained on life or property, require one side or the other to pay orthodonture bills, school and college tuition, and

---

4. One might think that one could eliminate the difficulties of interpretation by publishing a guide to the interpretation of one's statute or contract. But, apart from all other difficulties, a moment's thought shows that the guide will itself require interpretation—and how is that to be done? In accordance with a second guide or a third? What is inescapable is that the drafting of rules or other authoritative texts is a challenge for an art, and not reducible to a kind of intellectual technology.

so forth. It is a charter, or constitution, governing the relation between two people who no longer want to have anything to do with each other, but who must.

How are we to imagine what we are doing when we draft such an instrument? Do we want, for example, simply to get the most we can for our client? Not in the usual sense, for both sides have a great interest in the workability of the arrangement. If he is impoverished by the burdens placed upon him, she starved by the inadequacy of support, or vice versa, they will be back in court, with great costs to each other and the children. And even if they do not go to court, serious inequities will affect the children's judgment of both parents, and, even where there are no children, still affect the actors' judgments of themselves and each other. The first step, after trying to bring your client to face the fact that in the real world he is going to get less than he wants—and that you will not be used to carry on pointless warfare—may be to try to get him to see that essential fairness is important to both sides.

One will then face the question how fully the agreement should resolve every issue: for example, shall exceptions to the visitation arrangements be spelled out in detail—specifying funerals, college visits, doctors' appointments, visits from distant relatives, and so forth? Or should a general standard of reasonableness be employed? To do the former perfectly is intellectually impossible—you cannot imagine every contingency—but equally important, undesirable as an ethical or constitutive matter. Too detailed a code invites rule-bound thought and argument; it defines the husband and wife as legalistic and creates the circumstances that make it likely for that definition to be realized. More general language, by contrast, requires them to have more confidence in their capacity to negotiate and work things out. It defines them as reasonable people, capable of mutual adjustment, and creates conditions that invite the realization of that definition as well.

Of course, language alone does not automatically work as we wish, or all separation agreements would be quite general in character. We, and the parties, must judge whether they can stand the responsibilities that more general language brings, or whether, by contrast, they need the specificity of a more legalistic code, at least with respect to certain issues.

The separation agreement can thus be seen not simply as a set

of rules to be obeyed or disobeyed but as a constitution for a relationship: it creates roles for husband and wife, sometimes even gives
them lines to say, and these may be wise or foolish. And what is so
vivid here as hardly to require comment is also true of other texts,
where it might be harder to see: for example, of a statute establishing
an administrative agency, say the Securities Exchange Commission
or National Labor Relations Board, or of a Supreme Court opinion
regulating police conduct, or of a business contract. How will the
text define the various actors it speaks about and what relation among
them will it create? Will the text specify every contingency, or will
it grant lawmaking and fact-finding power subject to general standards? What are the consequences of one form over another? How
indeed will the text try to see to it that the parties continue to regard
it as the relevant authority? For all of the provisions of the document
are wasted unless they are consulted.

The person doing a good job of drafting the document engages
in an activity of the dramatic imagination, asking herself how her
language might be used, or abused, by one of the parties or another,
how it will function as a charter for this set of human relations. To
do this well brings one to the awareness of the limits of language,
or of any one particular language, and defines one's art as a way of
living with that fact.

The Rhetoric of Reading Law

Much the same kind of thing can be said of the other main stage of
the process, the reading of the rule or other text. Like writing, this
is an art that cannot be reduced to rules or techniques. Of the many
things that might be said about the process of interpretation, I want
to focus on only one: that just as the writing of such a text entails
the imagining of the world in a certain way, so does its reading. For
example, in reading a statute or constitutional provision, one must
imagine the writer as a person with a certain character inhabiting a
certain context and having a certain set of expectations and understandings about the process in which he or she is involved. This
would obviously be true in the case of the separation agreement
discussed above, but the same thing is true throughout the law. Think,
for example, of the construction of the United States Constitution.
Are we to imagine this document as a set of authoritarian commands,

issued in 1787 or 1791, on the assumption that they wholly and perfectly state something we think of as the wishes of the Framers? This would be a highly legalistic and time-bound way to think of this document and, in an extreme form, utterly impossible to live with. Or are we to imagine the framers of the Constitution as creating a document full of ambiguity and uncertainty, in the confidence that other people—those given roles, places, and occasions of speech by this document—will later resolve the meaning of this language wisely? Or some third way?

Two competing possibilities of somewhat different kinds, strenuously argued for in the early years of our national life, were to conceive of the Constitution as a contract among the states, to be read as a set of compromises among actors who are still present on the scene; or as a kind of mystical document, composed not as a matter of political compromise by still existing states, but as a unified expression of political wisdom by the Framers, of sanctified memory, who spoke for a momentarily unified people.[5]

The reading of such a text is thus inherently an act of the imagination. We often seek to deny this, however, by claiming either that the meaning of the authoritative language is plain or that the reading we give it is justified by the intention of the document or its framers. Actually, part of the meaning of any text is its way of imagining the world and its actors, present and future; and part of the reading of that text is the imagining both of it and of the context out of which it emerged.

A Poet's Reading

But there is more to it than this, and to suggest how that is so I want now to turn to another poem, this one in part about the process of reading. My hope is that this will both illuminate what reading a text involves and suggest possible standards we might bring to the reading of legal texts.

5. Perhaps the most explicit example of this conception of the Constitution appears in Chief Justice Marshall's opinion in *McCulloch v. Maryland*, where he justifies an extremely generous reading by reference to the character he attributes to the instrument. For elaboration of this point see James Boyd White, *When Words Lose Their Meaning: Constitutions and Reconstitutions of Language, Character, and Community* (Chicago: University of Chicago Press, 1984), chap. 9.

The poem I have in mind is John Keats's "Ode on a Grecian Urn":

Thou still unravished bride of quietness,
    Thou foster-child of Silence and slow Time,
Sylvan historian, who canst thus express
    A flowery tale more sweetly than our rhyme:
What leaf-fringed legend haunts about thy shape
    Of deities or mortals, or of both,
        In Tempe or the dales of Arcady?
    What men or gods are these? What maidens loth?
What mad pursuit? What struggle to escape?
        What pipes and timbrels? What wild ecstasy?

Heard melodies are sweet, but those unheard
    Are sweeter; therefore, ye soft pipes, play on;
Not to the sensual ear, but, more endeared,
    Pipe to the spirit ditties of no tone:
Fair youth, beneath the trees, thou canst not leave
    Thy song, nor ever can those trees be bare;
        Bold Lover, never, never canst thou kiss,
Though winning near the goal—yet, do not grieve;
        She cannot fade, though thou hast not thy bliss,
For ever wilt thou love, and she be fair!

Ah, happy, happy boughs! that cannot shed
    Your leaves, nor ever bid the Spring adieu;
And, happy melodist, unwearied,
    For ever piping songs for ever new;
More happy love! more happy, happy love!
    For ever warm and still to be enjoyed,
        For ever panting and for ever young;
All breathing human passion far above,
    That leaves a heart high-sorrowful and cloyed,
        A burning forehead, and a parching tongue.

Who are these coming to the sacrifice?
    To what green altar, O mysterious priest,

Lead'st thou that heifer lowing at the skies,
  And all her silken flanks with garlands drest?
What little town by river or sea-shore,
  Or mountain-built with peaceful citadel,
    Is emptied of this folk, this pious morn?
And, little town, thy streets for evermore
  Will silent be; and not a soul, to tell
    Why thou art desolate, can e'er return.

O Attic shape! fair attitude! with brede
  Of marble men and maidens overwrought,
With forest branches and the trodden weed;
  Thou, silent form! dost tease us out of thought
As doth eternity. Cold Pastoral!
  When old age shall this generation waste,
  Thou shalt remain, in midst of other woe
Than ours, a friend to man, to whom thou sayst,
  "Beauty is truth, truth beauty,—that is all
    Ye know on earth, and all ye need to know."

Here the speaker addresses a Grecian urn, imagined to be directly in front of him, in a series of ways that can be taken as establishing a set of possibilities for the response to any text or other work of art.[6] He first defines the urn, for example, as a storyteller: "Sylvan historian, who canst thus express / A flowery tale more sweetly than our rhyme." On this view, the urn is a kind of historian (as well as a competitor); the speaker's response to its work is to ask questions of it, a bit as if he were in training to become a professor or a museum guide. "What leaf-fringed legend haunts about thy shape / Of deities or mortals, or of both, / In Tempe or the dales of Arcady?" These questions are apparently asked on the assumption that they have answers of a kind an expert might give; and on the additional assumption that the answers, when given, will enable the speaker to locate, and thus in a sense dispose of, the work of art itself.

    The speaker seems to contemplate, that is, something like this: that we might learn that the "legend" is that of the sacrifice of Iphi-

---

6. My reading is much indebted to Helen Vendler, *The Odes of John Keats* (Cambridge, Mass.: Harvard University Press, 1983).

genia or the judgment of Paris; if so, we would know all that we needed to know. We could display our knowledge as we walked through the museum, placing this object, as we did others, in its pigeonhole. This is a way of responding to the uncertainty and anxiety that any work of art generates in its observer. Here the response is the assertion of the organizing and categorizing mind, the mind that will locate something on a grid and claim thus to understand it. The impulse is to evade and dominate the force of the mysterious by placing it in frameworks of our own. We all have it; professors build their careers upon it.

But by the end of the first stanza the speaker's tone and emphasis shift. He goes on: "What mad pursuit? What struggle to escape? / What pipes and timbrels? What wild ecstasy?" Although his expressions still have the form of questions, they are of a different kind. No longer do they seem to imply an answer that will enable him to categorize and thus dispose of the work; instead they express the beginning of a kind of merger with the work, a way of imagining himself into its world.

This is the second kind of response enacted by the speaker. He allows himself to envy the imagined actors in this world, attributing to them feelings and a condition that he wished he shared: "For ever wilt thou love, and she be fair!" As he goes on he becomes increasingly enraptured by this possibility: "More happy love! more happy, happy love! / For ever warm and still to be enjoy'd, / For ever panting and for ever young." He thus finds in the world represented in the urn what he thinks of as an ideal experience, more blissful than any he can have, and seeks to escape to it.

But the very way he characterizes this world unwittingly undercuts his claim about it: he tells the fair youth that "thou canst not leave / Thy song," not a wholly favorable condition to say the least; and goes on to say "never, never canst thou kiss." What he actually describes is an impossible state for any life we can recognize as human; if it were possible it would not in any sense of the word be bliss, but a kind of perpetual frustration. Human life, with its hopes and fears and memories and despairs, would on such condition of frozenness be entirely impossible. Although the speaker makes these things plain, he does not see them himself, or at least not consciously, so swept up is he in his use of this image as a way of separating himself from aspects of his own life, a fact he reveals at the end of the third stanza when he makes reference to his own experience of the human passion "That leaves a heart high-sorrowful and cloyed, / A burning forehead, and a parching tongue."

If the first response is to dominate the work of art by a professorial inquisition, the second is to imagine it meeting the peculiar emotional needs of the viewer—here to make it serve as a fantasy object for escape—and to do so against the very realities the work insists upon and makes apparent even to the speaker himself.

A third mode of response is represented in stanza four:

> Who are these coming to the sacrifice?
>   To what green altar, O mysterious priest,
> Lead'st thou that heifer lowing at the skies,
>   And all her silken flanks with garlands drest?
> What little town by river or sea-shore,
>   Or mountain-built with peaceful citadel,
>   Is emptied of this folk, this pious morn?
> And, little town, thy streets for evermore
>   Will silent be; and not a soul, to tell
>   Why thou art desolate, can e'er return.

Here the speaker is asking questions, but not questions that might have professorial answers. The questions are addressed to the actors themselves, and they ask about the meaning of their experience to them. Instead of assuming and asserting what the experience "must mean," as in stanzas two and three, that is, the speaker here acknowledges the limits of his knowledge. This acknowledgment of limit enables him to engage in accurate description—see how much clearer the scene is than the earlier ones—and at the same time to show realistic and genuine sympathy with someone else, for he can now see the imagined figures indeed as "other," and not as a solution to his own problems. This poem may remind us of "Range-Finding," where two different ways of characterizing the same experience were put before us in such a way as to make us feel at the same time their inconsistency and their mutual dependency.

The speaker now knows that his questions never will be answered, and he accordingly assumes the responsibility of responding to the scene as he has come to it. He achieves, that is, a state in which he is simultaneously respecting three things: the reality of that which is before him; the limits of his own knowledge; and the necessity of his asserting his own judgment and mind on these conditions. In this he is acting as I have elsewhere suggested a good translator acts, creating a world in which both self and other receive recognition, and I wish to suggest now that this is the way a good judge acts too.

Two Judicial Readings

I now turn to an actual case decided by the Supreme Court, which I shall look at as I have suggested law ought to be looked at, as a world of people talking rather than as a machine. I mean to ask how we can evaluate the way in which these people talk. To what extent do the poems by Frost and Keats help to establish standards or models that we can employ in making this evaluation? Can our judges, that is, recognize that they are both imagining the world in which the events they describe took place and, as readers of texts, imagining those texts and their authors too? Can they recognize that the ways in which they, and others, imagine these things have deep inconsistencies, and perhaps interdependencies as well? Will they compose a text that brings us to see these things? And, finally, will a way of imagining the law as itself an imaginative process enable them—or us—to discipline the mind and feelings in such a way as to attain a kind of realistic and genuine sympathy that our modes of discourse usually prevent?

The case is *Riverside County v. McLaughlin*, decided by the Supreme Court in 1991, which I have chosen in part for its relative obscurity. This is not a famous case, but the kind of work the Supreme Court does all the time.

Riverside addressed the validity of the way in which Riverside County, California, treats arrested people. In most jurisdictions an arrested person is entitled to be brought promptly before a judge, who will decide whether the arrest was valid—in technical terms, whether it was supported by "probable cause." Such a hearing is called a "probable cause determination." If the judge finds probable cause to exist the suspect can be detained further; if not, he or she must be discharged. In Riverside, however, this hearing is not held right away but can be delayed up to two full days, not counting weekends or holidays. This means, the Supreme Court tells us, that a person "arrested without a warrant late in the week may in some cases be held for as long as five days before receiving a probable cause determination."

Riverside has this system not simply for the sake of delay, however, but in order to consolidate the probable cause hearing with another stage of the criminal process, the arraignment, in which the defendant is formally charged with a crime and given a chance to plead guilty or not guilty. The question is whether this consolidation is permissible if it means that a person can be held in jail several days merely upon the officer's judgment that he has probably committed a crime. To raise it, a suit was brought by individuals who had been held in jail for a substantial period without a probable cause hearing.

In addressing a question of this sort the Supreme Court does not, of course, simply ask itself whether it thinks the Riverside procedure wise or salutary, for under our arrangements it does not sit to address such questions. It can only act as if in its view the procedure violates a federal statutory or constitutional provision. In this case there is no relevant statute and the question therefore becomes a constitutional one, specifically whether this procedure works an "unreasonable seizure" of the person of the suspect in violation of the Fourth Amendment, which reads in relevant part: "The right of the people to be secure in their persons, houses, papers, and effects against unreasonable searches and seizures shall not be violated, and no warrants shall issue but upon probable cause, particularly describing the place to be searched and the persons or things to be seized."

The question then becomes: Does the Riverside procedure involve an "unreasonable seizure" of the arrested persons? To begin to think about this question, the lawyers and judges must imagine many things: the experience of arrested persons held in jail, unable to present their case to a judge; the experience of police officers and minor judicial officials, trying to process arrested defendants in an expeditious manner; the Fourth Amendment itself, as a text addressed from one point of time to another; the Constitution that it is part of, and the role of the Supreme Court in interpreting it; and earlier decisions by that same Supreme Court addressing related issues.

To begin with the meaning of the Fourth Amendment as an authoritative text: I said above that whenever people disagree about one thing they must simultaneously affirm their agreement about others, and in this case that is what happens. All the participants in the legal argument conceived of the "reasonable seizure" language of the Fourth Amendment as insisting upon judicial control of what police officers do. This can take place either beforehand, when a warrant for arrest or search is issued, or afterwards, in a probable cause hearing (or in the case of illegally seized evidence, in a motion to suppress). The language of the amendment does not require this result, but earlier decisions, age-old practice, and the language about "warrants" in the Fourth Amendment itself all support it.

This kind of judicial control of the police is in fact one of the most important safeguards in the Constitution, doing much to distinguish us from totalitarian regimes. The law is brought to bear by one agency of government, the judiciary, against another, the executive. Perhaps no constitutional protection is more important than the right to have the decision of the police to arrest someone subjected to judicial review, with all that that means, including the presence of counsel and the press. This is a constitutionalization of the ancient principles of habeas corpus. All the speakers agree on this much, and in making these claims they are collectively engaged in imagining the world a certain way—as including competitive and dangerous police; neutral and fair judges; competent lawyers; and a diligent press—though of course a wholly different act of imagining might, for some regimes at least, be far more accurate.

How then do the two sides in this case differ? The writer of one of the two Supreme Court opinions, Justice O'Connor, believes that the two-day delay is permissible, although she recognizes that even within two days there might be examples of delay that she would hold "unreasonable": "delays for the purpose of gathering additional evidence to justify the arrest, a delay motivated by ill will against the arrested individual, or delay for delay's sake." What Justice O'Connor has at the center of her imaginary visual screen is the question whether the government is behaving reasonably or unreasonably, given all the burdens and constraints to which it is subject. She imagines the county of Riverside as a bureaucracy, laboring to do its best with insufficient resources, and subject to the constraint that if it is to provide more judges, at more hours of the day or night, in order to make probable cause determinations, this will force the county either to allocate tax dollars to this activity, away from some other presumptively valuable one, or to raise taxes.

The opinion on the other side, by Justice Scalia, imagines the situation very differently, from the point of view of the arrested person, and particularly of the innocent person who will be discharged when his probable cause determination is heard. Of course in a great many cases, in all probability the huge majority, the probable cause determination will simply result in affirmation of the police judgment and the continued detention of the suspect. But this opinion focuses not on this general bureaucratic likelihood, but on the plight of the wrongly arrested suspect, who is kept in jail longer than he otherwise would be by virtue of this practice.[7]

Justice O'Connor puts the competing issues this way:

On the one hand, states have a strong interest in protecting public safety by taking into custody those persons who are reasonably suspected of having engaged in criminal activity, even when there has been no opportunity for a prior judicial determination of probable cause. On the other hand, prolonged detention based on incorrect or unfounded suspicion may unjustly "imperil [a] suspect's job, interrupt his source of income, and impair his family relationships."

This language represents an imaginative choice to which the suspect might respond not by denying the public interest as it is here stated, that of detaining people "reasonably" suspected of crime, but by saying that this interest of the county should be conceived of very differently, namely as an interest in failing to provide prompt determinations of the propriety of an arrest. Likewise, the suspect would find the characterization of his own interest, and the impact of jail on him, woefully understated by this language, which fails to put any value at all on the deprivation of liberty as such, or the humiliation and danger of life in a jail.

There is another question on which the two sides divide, and that is how to read an earlier text, Gerstein v. Pugh, 420 U.S. 103 (1975), which both regard as a central precedent. In this case the Court invalidated Florida procedures under which arrested persons "could remain in police custody for 30 days or more without a judicial

---

7. Of course even for the correctly arrested person it is important that this judgment be reviewed promptly, for the meaning of the detention is very different after the police judgment has been judicially affirmed.

determination of probable cause." The Court held that the states "must provide a fair and reliable determination of probable cause as a condition for any significant pre-trial restraint of liberty, and this determination must be made by a judicial officer either before or"— the key language—"promptly after arrest." The Court was in effect saying that arrests, unlike searches, could generally be valid without prior judicial warrant—a rule justified by the likelihood that in many cases the opportunity to make the arrest would disappear if the policeman left the scene in order to obtain a warrant—but that the judicial judgment must be made "promptly" after the arrest.

The textual question thus becomes: What does the word "promptly" in this opinion mean? One way to think of *Gerstein* is that it creates, or validates, for arrests, an exception to a general principle that police intrusions must be justified to judicial officers before they occur, through the warrant mechanism. In this event, one would think that "promptly" meant as soon as an officer could find a magistrate after the arrest.

But there is language in *Gerstein* that supports a different way of thinking of it, in which the Court speaks about its sensitivity to its own role and its reluctance to impose a single model of criminal procedure on the states:

> There is no single preferred pre-trial procedure, and the nature of the probable cause determination usually will be shaped to accord with the state's pre-trial procedure viewed as a whole. . . . [W]e recognize the desirability of flexibility in experimentation by the States.

The Court goes on to give examples: one state might establish the probable cause determination as a separate proceeding, another might incorporate it into the procedure for setting bail, another might choose another mechanism. This is a way of imagining the Court not simply as an interpreter of the requirements of the Fourth Amendment, but as an actor in a constitutional system, one of whose great merits is variety and diversity of result, charged with the duty of articulating the general standards to which a wide variety of systems will be held.

In *Riverside* Justice O'Connor focuses upon this second way of conceiving of the Court, finds authority for it in *Gerstein*, and holds the *Riverside* procedure valid, as one among many permissible forms of experimentation. She justifies this in part because the *Riverside* procedure integrates two stages of the criminal process—the probable cause determination and the arraignment—as specifically contemplated in *Gerstein*. Justice Scalia sees as the salient points in *Gerstein* the requirement of judicial supervision, the acknowledgment of continuing harm while incarceration continues, and the presumption that there should be a judicial determination before the harm is inflicted. Under this way of imagining things "promptly" means right away, not when bureaucratically feasible.[8]

My point is not to suggest that one way of imagining and acting is right, the other wrong, but that in the process of legal argument— and in a good opinion—two ways of imagining the world are both present, in tension with and opposition to each other, much as the various ways of imagining the world are present, in tension and opposition, in the poems we have read. This implies a standard for judging an opinion—that it reflect what can be said the other way— and suggests as well that for the law as for poetry truth lies not in any set of propositions but in the tensions that exist among competing versions of the world.

The task of the lawyers in this case is to present alternative and coherent ways of imagining at least the following things: the transaction to which it speaks (the delayed incarceration of suspects by Riverside County); the Fourth Amendment, which speaks to that; its historical context; earlier cases (of which I have in fact selected only one); and the role of the Supreme Court itself. When they have finished, they have articulated differing possibilities for thought and speech in this context, in the course of which they have of necessity affirmed much about which they do not and cannot disagree. The effect is to give the Court competing ways of envisioning this event,

---

8. There is still another level at which the two sides imagine the world differently, and that has to do with the relevance of legal practice at the time the Constitution was framed. Under the common law it was the general rule that a person must be brought before a magistrate very quickly indeed, or as soon as possible, after his arrest. The side favoring the suspect sees this practice as deeply influencing the meaning that should be given to the Fourth Amendment. The other side sees this practice as pretty much irrelevant. For them the Fourth Amendment articulates standards of a general sort that are to be applied in new particular circumstances without special regard for the practices of what are now bygone eras.

and their own role in it; when the Court acts, if it does not do so unanimously, it will articulate these competing ways itself, making them—both of them—part of the law.

The role of the Court in this rhetorical and literary system is to fuse reading and writing, and both as imaginative activities: first in the reading of the texts of the law—constitutional, statutory, and judicial—that bear upon the case; and then in the composition of a text that will connect that reading with the events of the world, as these are imagined too: the experience of suspects and officers both, the relation between the state and federal systems, and so forth. At every point the Court is faced with a choice of language, and its choices in the end cannot be harmonized. One way of imagining and speaking will be chosen over another. The activity of law thus entails the tragic necessity of occluding voices and erasing experiences. It is unavoidable. Yet in a case like *Riverside* the dissent may answer the opinion of the majority in such a way as to give their joint work— the work of the whole Court—a quality missing in either opinion standing alone, the tension between different ways of imagining the world that brings both of them to the surface of attention.

In what spirit, by what art, is this to be done? Here too the poet can perhaps help us, showing how to make a text that includes competing languages, competing ways of imagining the world, in a way that undermines the claims of absoluteness otherwise at work in the judgment and its explanation. One test of judicial quality would then be inclusion, acknowledgment of loss and cost; another, humility, the degree to which the court recognizes its own intellectual and imaginative limits. Perhaps the best way to think of the good judge is as a good translator, as one who mediates between inconsistent ways of talking and tries to give each a place in his text, even as he recognizes that, to reach a decision at all, one of them must be accorded priority. The life of the mind that does this is not so different, after all, from the life of "Range-Finding" or "A Narrow Fellow."

Or, using Keats, we might ask if the judge can attain something like the balance achieved in the last stages of that poem: if he can see the litigants as different from him and from each other; as people about whose experience he can ask questions, but always with the knowledge that they will never be fully answered, and that the barrier between his mind and theirs will thus never entirely dissolve; as those

with whom he can thus have a real and disciplined sympathy; yet
recognize as well that he must describe their experience, and do so
in language; and that whatever language he uses will exclude another.
The art of mind and judgment called for, then, is one in which
opposing accounts and feelings and terms are held in the mind, or
in the text, at once, each limiting the other.

If so, there may be seen—as Owen Barfield in particular has
said[9]—a deep harmony in structure between the legal and the poetic process, the legal process enacting slowly, explicitly, and self-
consciously, what the poem achieves much more quickly, namely a
sense that against one way of conceiving of the world and functioning
within it is always posed another. Just as Robert Frost's way of
thinking of the spider and the flower and the butterfly was first
asserted, and then challenged, or Emily Dickinson's way of thinking
of the snake, so too in the law one way of imagining a piece of the
world, including individual persons, public institutions, and great
documents from the past, is poised against another.

Imagination and Power

Does this way of looking at law disregard the fact that the law is a
medium through which power is exercised, by one person over
another, or by one group or class over another? I think not; indeed
it is precisely because the law does involve the exercise of power that
it is so important how it is written, how it is read, and how it is
imagined. In every society power is exercised by some people over
others; but one can distinguish among these societies and among the
institutions through which that is done. There are significant differences, for example, between the rule of law, even in the imperfect
form in which we know it, and rule by the Imperial Guard, say, or
the Red Army, or the Mafia. What matters is not that all forms of
government are species of power, but what differentiates them. My
own interest here is in beginning to work out a way to analyze and
evaluate particular exercises of power by judges.

The claim that the law is power, nothing but power, is as false

---

9. Owen Barfield, "Poetic Diction and Legal Fiction," in *The Rediscovery
of Meaning and Other Essays* (Middletown, Conn.: Wesleyan University Press,
1977), 45.

as the opposed claim, that the law—or the judiciary—is perfectly just or perfectly neutral, which is of course impossible. A system by which human beings decide matters of deep importance to other people will always be one in which the deciders bring their own values and experiences of life to the process; they will always function out of particular cultural places, out of particular psychological and emotional structures, which will do much to shape how they work. But these exercises of power will be expressed and enacted in different ways by different minds; they will be given much of their meaning by the cultural forces through which they work; and the critical analysis of these expressions and forms is a central element of legal thought.

To imagine the law as a rhetorical and literary process may help us to see each moment in the law differently: the composition of rules and authoritative texts; their construction by others; and the process of legal thought and argument itself. It leads to a different conception of the teaching of law and may help the practitioner conceive of its practice differently too. It defines the lawyer's life as involving a perpetual interaction both between language and reality, and among languages as well, for law is a language into which other languages must continually be translated. In the practice of law, so conceived, there is the perpetual interplay of the particular and the general, of theory and practice; and one can imagine as well a continuity with the rest of life.

I said at the beginning that I was interested in the way in which we imagine law. I have suggested that we imagine the law as a process of imagination itself, as a set of occasions on which people imagine their world into being. In this it can be connected with what we do in the rest of life; and the poems by Frost, Dickinson, and Keats do much to suggest standards by which we might learn to do this better.

Antirrhesis:
Polemical Structures of
Common Law Thought

Peter Goodrich

There is the future, in that past which you never wanted.
—Luce Irigaray, *Marine Lover*

The call for a return to the method, style, and goals of rhetoric within contemporary legal studies has been marked by a certain conformity of purpose. While rhetoric is appropriately and variously understood to be a discipline concerned with argumentation (dialectic), persuasion, and action, its practical value to the study of law is almost universally perceived to be resident in its capacity to produce agreement. For Chaim Perelman, the pioneer of the new rhetorics of law, the function of the revival of the study of oratory was to facilitate communication, to identify specific messages, and to align legal orator and legal audience.[1] More recent studies vary little in their reformative

I am happy to record my thanks here to a number of perceptive commentators on earlier versions of this article. David Caudill, Neil Duxbury, Yifat Hachamovitch, Alan Hunt, Lester Mazor, Tim Murphy, Austin Sarat, Jeanne Schroeder, and Marty Slaughter all took me to task in varying degrees for overexpansive claims. I have benefited from their sobriety. I have also benefited financially from the support of the Nuffield Foundation and the British Academy who funded differing stages of the research upon which this paper is based.
    1. Chaim Perelman and Obrechts Tyteca, *The New Rhetoric: A Treatise on Argumentation* (Notre Dame, Ind.: Notre Dame University Press, 1969) formulates the goal of rhetorically successful speech in terms of "intellectual contact" that "establishes a sense of communion centred around particular values recognised by the audience" and held in common by them (14). See also Chaim Perelman, *Logique*

goals. Rhetoric will return language to nature,[2] eloquence to the institution,[3] and community to law.[4] Rhetoric will not only save law from the specter of nihilistic indeterminacies of interpretation[5] but will equally return the art of judgment to its proper ethical parameters as a genre of civic speech.[6] In its latter formulation, rhetoric not only

Juridique, Nouvelle Rhétorique (Paris: Dalloz, 1976), where the reciprocal desire of speech is formulated in terms of "a desire to realise and maintain contact of minds; a desire, in the head (*chef*) of the orator to persuade, and in that of the audience, a willingness to listen" (108). For analysis of Perelman's work, see Peter Goodrich, "Rhetoric as Jurisprudence: An Introduction to the Politics of Legal Language," *Oxford Journal of Legal Studies* 4 (1984):122.

2. This claim, which is found classically in Isocrates and Longinus particularly, is made most stridently in Brian Vickers, *In Defence of Rhetoric* (Oxford: Oxford University Press, 1988) as for example: "the lore of rhetorical figures [can] be seen as deriving originally from life. It was mimetic, an attempt to classify emotional states and their resulting speech forms . . . the eloquence of rhetoric is merely a systematisation of natural eloquence" (296). For discussion and criticism of that view, see Ernesto Grassi, *Rhetoric as Philosophy* (Philadelphia: University of Pennsylvania Press, 1980), chaps. 1–2; Thomas Cole, *The Origins of Rhetoric in Ancient Greece* (Baltimore: Johns Hopkins University Press, 1991), chap. 2; Peter Goodrich, "We Orators," *Modern Law Review* 53 (1990):546. For criticism, in broader terms, that links the nature in rhetoric to the heliotropism of Western metaphysics, see Jacques Derrida, *Margins of Philosophy* (Brighton: Harvester Press, 1983), 207ff.

3. See Kenneth Burke, *A Rhetoric of Motives* (Berkeley and Los Angeles: University of California Press, 1969), 90–102; James Boyd White, *Justice as Translation: An Essay in Cultural and Legal Criticism* (Chicago: University of Chicago Press, 1990), chap. 3; Vickers, *In Defence of Rhetoric*, 7–9, 236–38.

4. White, *Heracles' Bow: Essays on the Rhetoric and Poetics of Law* (Madison: University of Wisconsin Press, 1985), chap. 3; White, *Justice as Translation*, 36: "Part of maintaining a community is maintaining the agreement not to speak or ask about the ways in which its language means differently for different members"; or "to speak and act like a lawyer, as one learns to do at law school, is to commit oneself to a certain community and discourse, to enact a view of language and the world that entails an ethics and politics of its own, even to give oneself a certain character" (215).

5. See, for example, Gerald Frug, "Argument as Character," *Stanford Law Review* 40 (1988):869, 871–72: "I reject the notion that the only alternative to finding a way to ground legal argument is nihilism. In my view, we should abandon the traditional search for the basis of legal argument because no such basis can be found, and we should replace such a search with a focus on legal argument's effects, in particular, on its attempts to persuade. I suggest, in other words, that we look at legal argument as an example of rhetoric."

6. See Jürgen Habermas, *The Structural Transformation of the Public Sphere: An Inquiry into a Category of Bourgeois Society,* trans. Thomas Burger with the assistance of Frederick Lawrence (Cambridge: MIT Press, 1989), and *The Philosophical Discourse of Modernity: Twelve Lectures,* trans. Frederick G. Lawrence (Cambridge: MIT Press, 1987). For more classically rhetorical accounts of this position, see Michael Mooney, *Vico in the Tradition of Rhetoric* (Princeton, N.J.: Prince-

undoes the evil of theory—of speech without limits—but returns the study of legal argument to the safety of literature.[7] In opposition to this communitarian revivalism the present essay will argue in considerable historical detail that the rhetorical form of legal doctrinal rhetoric is derived from the theological model of discourses against heresy and specifically against iconoclasm. The genre of doctrine is marked indelibly by the sign or more properly figure of *antirrhesis,* a figure described significantly by Peacham as "a form of speech by which the orator rejecteth the authority, opinion or sentence of some person: for error or wickedness of it . . . this form of speech doth especially belong to confutation and is most apt to repell errors and heresies and to reject evil counsel and lewd perversions."[8] Among the classical examples of such discourse Peacham lists those of Christ against Satan, the apostle Paul against the Epicureans, and Job against his wife. Each example has a peculiar significance.

While the contemporary revivals and defenses of rhetoric have significant political implications for the institutional legitimacy of law, it will be argued here that they are of little heuristic value, and further, that they are historically ill informed. Through a detailed analysis of a series of Renaissance texts on rhetoric and the interpretation of law it will be argued that the form of legal rhetoric complies with the adversarial form of all doctrinal discourse and is best understood as a form of antirrhetic or discourse of defense and denunciation.

---

ton University Press, 1985); John Schaeffer, *Sensus Communis: Vico, Rhetoric and the Limits of Relativism* (Durham, N.C.: Duke University Press, 1990). For a historical view, see Paul Kristeller, "Rhetoric in Medieval and Renaissance Culture," and Marc Fulmaroli, "Rhetoric, Politics and Society," both in *Renaissance Eloquence,* ed. James J. Murphy (Berkeley and Los Angeles: University of California Press, 1983).

7. See Stanley Fish, "Dennis Martinez and the Uses of Theory," in *Doing What Comes Naturally: Change, Rhetoric, and the Practice of Theory in Literary and Legal Studies* (Oxford: Oxford University Press, 1990); see also the very strong attack on theory in White, *Justice as Translation,* 8–12; White refers to "bureaucratic and theoretical modes of thought [that] have so nearly captured law" and placed its future in doubt (267). The reference of the revival of rhetoric in America is almost exclusively literary in the Anglo-American authors cited. See, for an explicit example, Richard Posner, *Law and Literature: A Misunderstood Relation* (Cambridge: Harvard University Press, 1980), 270ff. For broadly corrective views, see George Kennedy, *Classical Rhetoric and Its Christian and Secular Tradition from Ancient to Modern Times* (London: Croom Helm, 1979); Peter Goodrich, *Reading the Law* (Oxford: Blackwell, 1986), chap. 6.

8. In Renaissance rhetorical manuals this is, as far as I am aware, the only extant definition of *antirrhesis.* It comes from Henry Peacham, *The Garden of Eloquence* (London: H. Jackson, 1593), sig. N iv b–N v a.

The use of rhetoric in law was always a specific and distinctively sophistic genre.[9] While in certain formulations, associated particularly with Cicero and Vico, the method and ethos of rhetoric was deemed relevant to civic virtue and political stability or *sensus communis*, the practice of legal oratory was unambiguously associated not so much with the felicitous use of speech as with disputation, casuistry, apologetic, proof, and polemic. In a superficial sense, the contemporary revival of forensic rhetoric is flawed by a failure to recognize that the figure of revival or defense—*apologia*—is itself a distinctive and antithetical genre of discourse. In a more comprehensive and historically sensitive sense it will be argued that the critical force of rhetoric is epistemological and semiotic.[10] The study of legal rhetoric is most incisive, powerful, and historically appropriate where it discerns behind the self-conscious use of tropes and figures of speech the unconscious structures of institutional reason, the norms and the antagonisms, the dogmas and the polemical forces, whereby subjectivity is successfully captured by the value of law. In this sense, rhetoric is a means of reading legal language use as a sign or index of repressed narrative structures and of the various adversarial, conflictual, and antithetical discursive forms that constitute both the history and the structure of legal reason. In the most obvious of senses, that reason is in rhetorical terms the reason of judgment, the residue of conflict, the memorial of an agonistic practice.

The argument will proceed in three stages. By way of tracing the shared antithetical structure or antirrhetic at the basis of theology

---

9. Plato, *Theaetetus*, 172e–173b argues that the legal orator, subject to the constraints of time and adversary circumstance, "is a slave disputing about a fellow slave before a master sitting in judgment with some definite plea in his hand." The rhetorician as lawyer "acquires a tense and bitter shrewdness . . . his mind is narrow and crooked. An apprenticeship in slavery has dwarfed and twisted his growth and robbed him of his free spirit." Tacitus also associates legal rhetoric with decadence and decay. *Dialogus* (London: Loeb Classical Library, 1911), 127–31.

10. For an important essay on this sense of the semiotic as decipherment, diagnostic, and prognostic, see Carlo Ginsberg, *Myths, Emblems, Clues* (London: Radius, 1990), 96–125. An early example of such a semiotic view of rhetoric can be found in Richard Sherry, *A Treatise of Schemes and Tropes* (London: J. Day, 1550), sig. E viii a–b, discussing rhetorical proof in terms of *symeia* or signs: "they be called signs properly, which rising of the thing itself that is in question come under the senses of men, as threatenings, which be of the time that is past, crying heard out of a place which is of time present, paleness of him which is axed of the murder, which is of the time following, or the blood lept out of the body lately slain, when he came that did the murder."

and jurisprudence, the argument begins by examining the apologetic rhetorical practice of both doctrinal discourses during the Renaissance. In synoptic terms, it will be argued that the history of these institutional discourses is dogmatic and destructive, that their principal figure or rhetorical force has been antirrhetical or denunciatory, that the exemplary discourses of social foundation in either God, nature, or law have taken the form of *apologia* within which each tenet of doctrine or of creed is matched against a figure of heretical exclusion or excommunication. The second phase of the argument is deconstructive. The antithetical structure of legal and religious rhetoric will be evoked in the substantive terms of the common lawyer's historical discourse of origins and of foundation. In specific historical terms, the analysis will take the form of a reading of a series of Renaissance legal texts—the earliest systematic legal treatises within the common law tradition—in terms of their polemical oppositions. Legal doctrine, it will be argued, was rhetorically structured according to a logic, or more properly a dialectic of antinomy: common law was pronounced *against* the image of other laws, its legitimacy was defined *against* other traditions and foreign histories, its reason was enunciated *against* the fantasy, imagination, or "dreams" of other disciplines, and, perhaps most surprisingly, its genealogy was spelled out *against* the threat of feminine succession. The concluding stage of the argument will suggest that for all the discontinuity that separates the classic Renaissance legal *apologia* from the concerns of contemporary jurisprudence and its critics, there are striking rhetorical as well as historical continuities. The concept of rhetorical structure or, in semiotic terms, of narrative grammar[11] allows an ambitious conclusion. The antirrhetic capture of legal subjectivity, or the simple persistence of the dogmatic forms of the legal institution, is the product of a rhetorical order of thought or division (disposition) of reality that subsists over the long term of common law history, in the language and categories of a legal reason that long outlives the impermanent and tendentious forms of merely positive laws. Without an appreciation of those essentially antithetic rhetorical structures and

---

11. The notion of narrative grammar is spelled out most clearly in Algirdas Greimas, *Of Meaning* (London: Pinter, 1987) and is developed in relation to the analysis of a legal text in Greimas, *Semiotics and Social Science* (London: Pinter, 1990). For commentary on that analysis, see Bernard S. Jackson, *Semiotics and Legal Theory* (London: Routledge, 1985).

their persistent semiotic force, the critique of contemporary legal forms, whether in ethical, feminist, literary, or sociological terms, is doomed to the status of a repetitious and ineffective play upon institutional surfaces that history and dogma will soon consume and forget.[12]

Antirrhesis, Apologia, and Antithesis

The defence of faith or doctine, creed or rule, belongs to the rhetorical genre of apologia "and signifies defence, not with arms, but with reason, answer in defence, excuse, purgation or clearing of that one is charged with . . . in every apology or excuse, three things meet together, the plaintiff or accuser, the defendant and the crime objected [which is] schism, heresy, and breach of unity."[13] Within the Western legal tradition, the apology has tended to take a strongly antithetical and frequently ad hominem character. Its most explicit and antagonistic form is theological and legal. On one side, the faith or true

---

12. For an interesting elaboration of this argument in terms of the ineradicably mythical basis of stable human groupings, see Régis Debray, *Critique of Political Reason* (London: New Left Books, 1983), 116ff. For a more extended discussion, see Pierre Legendre, *Le Désir Politique de Dieu: Etude sur les Montages de l'Etat et du Droit* (Paris: Fayard, 1989). For an introduction to Legendre's work, see Peter Goodrich, *Languages of Law* (London: Weidenfeld and Nicolson, 1990), chap. 7.

13. Thomas Harding, *A Confutacyon of a Booke Intituled an Apologie of the Church of England* (Antwerp: J. Laet, 1565), fol. 1 a. While it is necessary to refer to certain earlier traditions and works of apology, the period and genre that will be delineated here is that of the Reformation and Renaissance defense of ecclesiastical and secular law. The synoptic account offered here draws on diverse religious and legal polemics. As an indication of vitriolic theological style, see John Jewell, *Apologia Ecclesiae Anglicanae* (London: n.p., 1562); replied to in Thomas Harding, *Confutacyon*. The response to the response comes in John Jewell, *A Defence of the Apologie of the Churche of England* (London: Fleetstreet, 1567), to which the most striking response is Thomas Stapleton, *A Returne of Untruthes upon M. Jewell* (Antwerp: J. Latius, 1566). There is also the original interlocutor's reply, Thomas Harding, *An Answere to Mr. Jewells Challenge* (Antwerp, 1565). See, finally, for a classically positive apology, Thomas Stapleton, *A Fortresse of the Faith* (Antwerp: J. Laet, 1565). In terms of secular legal apologetics, the classic work is John Fortescue, *De Laudibus Legum Angliae* (1470; London: Selden Society, 1737). In addition to works cited subsequently, see Christopher St. German, *Doctor and Student* (1528; London: Selden Society, 1538) (defending common law); St. German, *A Treatise Concerning the Division between the Spirituality and the Temporality* (London: Redman, 1534) (a polemic against church abuses and ecclesiastical usurpation of the common law jurisdiction). Sir Thomas More responded to St. German, in *The Apologye of Sir Thomas More Knyght* (London: Rastell, 1533).

doctrine is expounded in eulogistic terms of authorities, axioms, and the unity of tradition. The positivity of Christian dogma and canon law is identified with the community of the faithful and the laws of ecclesiastical polity are aligned to nature and to immemorial usage, the "titles of antiquity." On the other side, false doctrine, heresy, or heterodoxy is denounced and the disorder and novelty of the schismatic are aligned to evil, idolatry, error, or ignorance. In structural terms, it should be observed that heresy or heterodoxy are not incidental aspects of doctrine but are rather an inevitable implication of the positivity of creed, constitution, or law.[14] Doctrine could not establish itself in any other way than through a self-definition that opposed the age of the law to the youthfulness of its critics, the universality of the institution or established church to the local and particular character of reformation, the iconic truth of Christian vision to the dissimulating blindness of its idolatrous and polluted opponents.

There are two relatively obvious features of the apology that deserve initial emphasis. The apology is a foundational work that establishes doctrine either in the formative period of an institution or during a period of crisis and reform. In both cases the apologetic treatise has a constitutive didactic character and is a normative or exemplary statement of its subject. That the rhetorical structure of such dispositive dogmatic works should be strongly antithetical, that the exposition of institutions should be necessarily illustrated by their opposites,[15] is properly and necessarily paradoxical. The relation at

---

14. For an analysis of the interrelation of orthodoxy and heterodoxy, doctrine and heresy, truth and error, see Michel Foucault, "The Discourse on Language," in *The Archaeology of Knowledge*, trans. A. Sheridan Smith (New York: Pantheon Books, 1982), 220. In the introduction to Michel Foucault, *The Order of Things*, trans. A. Sheridan Smith (London: Tavistock, 1970) a similarly antithetical conception of doctrine is applied to the development of science in terms of a "positive unconscious" that eludes scientific consciousness, yet is part of it: "the influences that affected it, the implicit philosophies that were subjacent to it, the unformulated thematics, the unseen obstacles . . . the unconscious of science. This unconscious is always the negative side of science—that which resists it, deflects it, disturbs it. What I would like to do, however, is to reveal a positive unconscious of knowledge: a level that eludes the scientist and yet is part of scientific discourse." In structural terms, heresy is thus a necessary aspect or part of doctrine, it is *internal* to the creed or code, but in a repressed or pathological form.

15. Antithesis is classically defined as a figure of comparison, whose argumentative function is to amplify or diminish the *comparata*. It is thus grouped by Peacham with *similitudo* (likeness), *dissimilitudo* (dissimilarity), and *syncrisis* (comparison of

stake is that between truth and error, and the antithetical relation between the two has always been self-definitional: error subsists within truth as that element which must constantly be distanced, repressed, or kept at bay. The universality of truth also paradoxically entails that error or falsehood is resident within its territory, and it is only through the repression of such error, through the constant fight against evil, that truth triumphs.[16] It is thus only in an institutional and not in a logical sense that heresy or unorthodoxy exist outside the church or that the devil, the face (*prosopopoeia*) of evil, is thrown onto the outside (*diabolikos*). Drawing upon psychoanalytic theories of symptom and repression, it is relatively easy to observe that the structure of conflict is both intrinsic and constant: where the antithetical or conflictual character of a doctrinal work is least evident, it is deepest repressed.[17] In the words of one sixteenth-century

---

contrary things in the same sentence). See Peacham, *Garden of Eloquence*, sig. Y iii b. He comments that it is "of great use in persuading by reason, for the parts of the comparison being brought together, their likeness or unlikeness, their equality or inequality, is as plainly discerned." For further discussion of the analogical value of antithesis, see, for example, Thomas Wilson, *The Arte of Rhetorique* (1533; New York: Garland, 1982), 64–68, 201–7, 411–13; George Puttenham, *The Arte of English Poesie* (London: R. Field, 1589), 175 (on *antitheton*); Thomas Farnaby, *Index Rhetoricus scholis et institutioni tenerioris aetatis accommodatus* (London: R. Allot, 1633), 55–58; for a somewhat later example, see John Smith, *The Mysterie of Rhetorique Unveil'd* (London: E. Cotes, 1657), sig. M. 6 b. It should further be emphasized that the logical force of antithesis is an important element in depictions of logical argument, for which see, Thomas Wilson, *The Rule of Reason, conteyning the Arte of Logique* (London: n.p., 1533) fol. 50 a–60 b; Ralph Lever, *The Arte of Reason, rightly termed witcraft* (London: Bynneman, 1573), 99: "a reason is a compounded showsay, proving that which lyeth in controversie by knowne and graunted sayings." See also Peter Ramus, *The Logike* (London: Vautroullier, 1574), 42–50.

    16. For a striking rhetorical example of the logical entailments of paradox, see Anthony Munday, *The Defence of Contraries: Paradoxes against common opinion, debated in the forme of declamations in place of publicke censure* (London: J. Winder, 1593). On the figure of *paradoxon*, see Peacham, *Garden of Eloquence* sig. I iv b. It may be noted also that contemporary works of logic assumed an equally polemical and reformist style, most notably Ramus, *Logike*. For commentary on this work, see Donald Kelley, "Horizons of Intellectual History: Retrospect, Circumspect, Prospect," *Journal of the History of Ideas* 48 (1987):143.

    17. This argument is central to Pierre Legendre, *L'Inestimable Objet de la Transmission* (Paris: Fayard, 1985); it is equally important to Jacques Derrida, *Of Grammatology*, trans. Gayatri Chokravorty Spivak (Baltimore: Johns Hopkins University Press, 1976). For a recent analysis of the role of paradox, see Matthew Kramer, *Legal Theory, Political Theory, and Deconstruction* (Bloomington: Indiana University Press, 1991), chap. 1. In a psychoanalytic sense, of course, repression drives within and conflict is least observed when deepest repressed, on which see J. Derrida, *Writing*

treatise on logic, we here "follow the precept of Solomon, to confute
[opponents of the art of logic] with silence."[18]

The second observation to be made is hermeneutic. The apology
is initially a defense of faith—of Christian doctrine—and only sec-
ondarily a eulogy of law. Faith itself, however, is an object of law,
of the Christian "government of the soul" in an age when polity and
person are explicitly both civil and ecclesiastical.[19] The form that the
apology takes in secular treatises is thus to be interpreted according
to a model that is most explicit, and frequently most violent in its
religious archetype. The terms of apologetic argument are structured
around an exemplary or more accurately prototypical, anagogical,
or mystical state, within which place the word, idea, image, and icon
have their exemplary—continuous and unitary—meaning. The word
is the real presence of the Father in the Son, and, for the Catholics,
of God in the sacrament. It is a reference or direction to a mystical
and invisible state, to the truth either figured consubstantially or
really present transubstantially. For present purposes it is sufficient
to advert to the concept of language itself as a sign, more or less
distant, of an invisible and divine world. In this context, rhetoric is
most usually an adversarial form of speech; it is at best a more or
less accurate image of true speech and the written word of Scripture.
The rhetorical word suffers the need for interpretation and is in consequence ever dangerous, ever legalistic and not yet the truth, which
is without interpretation.[20] For the apologist, rhetoric is thus always

---

and Difference, trans. Alan Bass (New York: Routledge, 1978), 196: "repression, not
forgetting; repression, not exclusion. Repression, as Freud says, neither repels, nor
flees, nor excludes an exterior force; it contains an interior representation, laying out
within itself a space of repression." For a more detailed analysis, see Gilles Deleuze,
Différence et Répétition (Paris: Presses Universitaires de France, 1968).

18. Dudley Fenner, The Artes of Logike and Rhetorike (Middleburg: n.p., 1584),
sig. A 1 a. Logic is subsequently explicitly defined by Fenner as a sword and more
generally as a weapon, sig. A 2 b.

19. In terms of the development of English law, the most important work on
the conjunction of the two polities (reflecting the theology of the unity of two natures,
of Father and Son), is Richard Hooker, Of the Lawes of Ecclesiastical Politie (1593–
97; London: R. Scott, 1676); see also Sir Thomas Ridley, A View of the Civille and
Ecclesiasticall Law (1607; Oxford: H. Hall, 1676); Calybute Downing, A Discourse
of the State Ecclesiasticall of this Kingdome, in Relation to the Civill (1586; Oxford:
Torner, 1633). On the concept of a dual state, expressly developed in the legal
definition of the corpus mysticum of the Crown, see Ernst Kantorowicz, The King's
Two Bodies (Princeton, N.J.: Princeton University Press, 1958).

20. T. Stapleton, Returne of Untruthes, fol. 107b: "he that speaks with tongues,

potentially a form of heresy, a corporeal, human, representation—a painted word—that is likely to confuse the mundane sign with true reason. Thus images are termed the "devil's rhetoric,"[21] figures without substance, while rhetorical reason is the armory of heresy: of he

> who endeavours to prove his false doctrine *versutis disputation-ibus*, with subtle and crafty reasonings. . . . Beware that no man spoil you through philosophy and vain deceit . . . for these heretics put all the force of their poisons in logike, or dialectical disputation, which by the opinion of philosophers is defined not to have power to prove, but an earnest desire to destroy and disprove.[22]

Doctrine opposes rhetoric—"vain eloquence or painted words"[23] —but it does so, ironically, in the most vehement of rhetorical forms, that of the antirrhetic. The attribution of heresy to orators, to eloquence, and to rhetoric or crafty reason has a very specific and vehement figurative form. It is indeed formulaic and the rhetorical structure of that formula can be recuperated by briefly examining the specific history of antirrhetic in the patristic tradition. While antir-

---

speaks not with men, but unto God, for no man hears him . . . *spiritus autem loquitur mysteria*, the spirit speaks mysterie, and *spiritu licet mysteria loquatur*, in the spirit mysteries speak."

21. James Calfhill, *An Answere to the Treatise of the Cross* (London: Denham, 1565), fol. 172 a.

22. Harding, *Confutacyon*, fol. 33 b.

23. Jewell, *Defence of the Apologie*, sig. A iv b. He continues: "a simple eye is soon beguiled . . . it is a desperate cause, that with words, and eloquence may not be smoothed. Be not deceived. Remember, of what matters and adversaries thou has to deal . . . let reason lead thee: let authority move thee: let truth enforce thee." See also Nicholas Sander, *A Treatise of the Images of Christ and of his Saints* (Omers: J. Heigham, 1624), 161, who defends the image against rhetoric in comparable terms:

the image is by so much in the better case to be honoured [than the orator], by how much it has more affinity with my inward image, than the orators words had. For it serves me both in the whole stead of the orator, and also in part of the stead of forming the inward image, because it gives me the very express form and figure already made, which my understanding must conceive: whereas if I learned the matter by words, I must have taken the pain to have changed the shape of those words into another form, and therefore to have formed a visiable image.

He subsequently cites Exodus 20 to the effect that when "God gave the ten commandments to the children of Israel, his words were not only heard, but even visibly seen . . . the whole people saw the words (*videbat voces*)" (162).

rhesis gains passing mention in the Attic orators as speech directed toward outcasts,[24] those who have "betrayed their friends and kinsmen,"[25] and is associated with a vehemence appropriate to the denunciation of sworn and deadly adversaries, the exemplary antirrhetic is that of Nicephorus, author of the *Apologeticus Major* and three *Antirrhetici* against the iconoclastic Emperor Constantine V.[26] Written as a response to questions posed by Constantine V, the *Antirrhetici* have the internal stucture and tripartite logic of a denunciation. While the object of that denunciation is iconclastic doctrine, it should also be briefly observed that the antirrhetic is also an attack upon rhetoric: the etymology of antirrhetic implies both "words against" and "against words."

Nicephorus defends the icon as the model of an immediate relation between the visible and the invisible, the present and the absent, divinity and its visible form. The icon represents the archetype, and it alone can direct the human eye from material forms to incorporeal truth: "the icon is the counterpart (reflection) of the archetype, in it is found imprinted in visible form that of which it is the imprint . . . it is not distinct from its model save for the essential difference of its substance."[27] The icon is enigmatic,[28] it directs the eye from the symbolic to the imaginary, from symptom to cause,[29] from creation

---

24. Hermogenes, *On Types of Style* (Chapel Hill: University of North Carolina Press, 1987), bk 1.8.52 (on vehemence).

25. Polybius, *Histories* (Harmondsworth: Penguin, 1977), 22.8.

26. References are to the French edition of the texts, *Discours contre les Iconoclastes*, ed. Marie-José Mondzain-Baudinet (Paris: Klincksieck, 1989). For further commentary on the specific context of the *Antirrhetici*, see particularly, Marie-José Mondzain-Baudinet, "Visage du Christ, forme de l'Eglise," in *Du Visage*, ed. Mondzain-Baudinet (Lille: Presse Universitaire de Lille, 1982); George Florovsky, "Origen, Eusebius, and the Iconoclastic Controversy," *Church History* 19 (1950):77; Gerhardt Ladner, "Origin and Significance of the Byzantine Iconoclastic Controversy," *Mediaeval Studies* 2 (1940):127; G. Ladner, "The Concept of the Image in the Greek Fathers and the Byzantine Iconoclastic Controversy," *Dumbarton Oaks Papers* 7 (1950):1; Edward J. Martin, *A History of the Iconoclastic Controversy* (London: SPCK, 1930).

27. *Antirrhetic I*, 276 D. For a further example, see Calfhill, *Answere*, fol. 169 a: "The world itself is a certain spectacle of things invisible, for that the order and frame of it, is a glass to behold the secret working and hidden grace of God. The heavenly creatures and spheres above, have a greater mark of his divinity, more evident to the world's eye, than either can be unknown or dissembled."

28. The basis of the icon of Christ lies in "the knowledge of the invisible and absolutely incomprehensible character of a unity of two natures." Ibid., 309 C.

29. For an excellent analysis of the image as symptom, see Georges Didi-Huberman, *Devant l'Image* (Paris: Editions de Minuit, 1988), 218-31. The structural

to creator. The virtue of this speculary direction of faith, as against rhetorical persuasion, is threefold. The iconic inscription is immediate, it is the homonym of that which it reflects, whereas the word is heterogeneous and can at best refer to images. Second, it is continuous, it does not change over time, whereas language is both mutable and refutable: whereas the icon is beyond discourse, speech implies disputation and interpretation. It is, finally, unitary and addresses all universally through sight, whereas (after Babel) speech is diverse and particular to nations and places.

It is the virtue of the icon that it founds the visible world; it makes nature possible, and without it—without circumscription and without icon—"the universe in its entirety would disappear."[30] The icon thus dispenses equally with the need for the poison of logic, the cunning of reason, and the play of interpretation. The icon founds nature, and to defend it is thus to impugn the enemies of nature, the enemies of reason, and the enemies of sanctity, of the institution as such. If iconoclasm threatens, quite literally, to destroy the world, to cast the visibility of nature into the limitless (uncircumscribed) void of formless matter, these iconomachs are the prototype of the nihilist, idolators of nothing, heretics who have severed all relation to the visible world and who are in consequence without civility, filiation, or legitimacy.[31] In a strict philosophic sense, they are not, or are no longer, human. The antirrhetic wherein their crimes are denounced and repelled is thus the strongest of rhetorics, the archetype of apologia, and the norm or exemplar of all other defenses of doctrine, faith, and law in the antiportrait of the iconoclast.

The iconoclast is first sacrilegious; he steals from the person of God and of the saints. He mocks all that is venerable, all consecration and piety: "he transgresses the written and unwritten law, he destroys tradition, and respects nothing."[32] There are two aspects to sacrilege:

---

exemplar of the icon is the *archiropoietic* image, the image—such as the Turin shroud—that is made by the direct imprint of divinity and without the mediation of human hands. See further *Antirrhetic I*, 260 A–260 C.

30. *Antirrhetic I*, 244D.

31. For the development of this concept of filiation, see Legendre, *L'Inestimable Objet* (depicting genealogy as the inscription of power in the order of succession), and Alexandra Papageorgiou-Legendre, *Filiation* (Paris: Fayard, 1990). See also G. Ladner, "Medieval and Modern Understanding of Symbolism," *Speculum* 54(1979):239.

32. Nicephorus, *Discours contre les Iconoclastes*, 19.

one positive and one negative. It is "a sin above all others," the sin of Satan, because it invades the person of the Deity: in its positive formulation, sacrilege arrogates divine knowledge of good and evil to human beings. In destroying the visible world the powers of creation are transferred into the realm of darkness, of the formless and limitless substance of nothingness, of a world without sight or the direction of vision. In legal terms, we thus find sacrilege listed as a crime alongside "blasphemers, sorcerers, witches and inchanters," crimes that steal from the divinity so as to create other images and so other worlds.[33] In its negative variation, sacrilege is straightforwardly destructive: it pollutes and so destroys holy places, sacred books, relics, and other sacral objects. It destroys the sites and tools, the architecture, of tradition and transmission at the same time that it pollutes the aura that authorizes knowledge.[34] It is first and foremost unclean, and among the figures or emblems of that "shameless uncleanness" the most frequent and conventional is that of femininity: the sacrilegious image is variously a woman, an adulteress, a harlot, a witch, and her polluted faith a nameless and "inchaunting void."[35]

The reason of the iconoclast is that of delirium and dream; it is unreason manifest, a private language without either logic or audience. The iconoclast speaks the language of Babylon, and precisely in placing his faith in language rather than icons, in "building a

33. Sir Henry Spelman, *The History and Fate of Sacrilege* (1632; London: Hartley, 1698), 2. On the detail of these crimes, see, for example, the writs of abjuration listed in William West, *Symbolaeography* (1598; London: Society of Stationers, 1603). For relevant legislation, see W. Rastall, *A Collection in English, of the Statutes now in Force* (London: T. Wright, 1603), fol. 65 d, Against Conjurations, Enchantments and Witchcraft (5 Eliz., 1 cap. 16, 1563). The crime is the worse for its effectivity: the dead are summoned (magic), new likenesses are formed (enchantment), the lost is found (divining), the future is foretold (witchcraft), the unseen is seen (sorcery). The legislation referred to punishes according to the effects of the practises: where witchcraft killed or maimed the penalty was most severe.

34. *Antirrhetic III*, 480 C et seq.; Spelman, *Sacrilege*, 23.

35. Robert Parker, *A Scholasticall Discourse Against Symbolizing with Antichrist in Ceremonies* (London: private circulation, 1607), 7. The idol is an instrument of witchcraft and of fornication: "for the image is an harlot, and man is no otherwise bent to the worshipping of it than he is bent on fornication in the company of a strumpet" (137). Henry Hammond, *Of Idolatry* (Oxford: H. Hall, 1646) talks of idolatry as prostitution and idol worship as "pollution, inversion of nature, disorder of marriage, adultery, and shameless uncleanness . . . the beginning, cause and end of evil" (7–8).

Name for himself on earth," his punishment is confusion, dispersion, babel, and noncommunication.[36] Without the power to communicate, deprived of all rules of logic and expression, locked in the private madness of analphabetic speech, "he resembles an old illiterate and senile woman" with whom communication is no longer possible.[37] Private language banishes all possibility of certainty; it threatens the institutions of meaning and denies any potential for agreement or commonality, respect, or obedience. The demise of tradition and culture is also, finally, the death of nature: the iconoclast is a monster, a homosexual, an illegitimate being without similarity or resemblance to anything known. Antinature is in one sense simply that which lacks resemblance: in Selden's definition, "[O]ne not like his parents is, in some sort monstrous, that is, not like him that got him, nor any other of the ascending or transverse line."[38] In a broader sense, the nihilistic unreason of the iconoclast brings with it a madness of nature, in which those who deny the relation of the icon to its model refuse all the fecundity of semblance and of similitude; they are sterile, obscene, and unproductive, "excluded from nature itself which lets loose earthquakes, famines, epidemics, cataclysms of all sorts, to express its suffering before such hatred towards God."[39] The conclusion of the *Antirrhetici* is thus the threat of perdition and damnation, of a world that is unknown and unknowable, a world populated by the damned, by nomads, lepers, nihilists, and other untouchables. There, in short, is what nature, reason, and law must be defended against.

Law and Dissimulation

The art of law, which included the science or practice of legislation, had always been associated in some measure with dissimulation,[40]

---

36. Henry Spelman, *Sacrilege*, 10–11. The reference is to the Tower of Babel (Genesis 11.4). For commentary, see Jacques Derrida, "Des Tours de Babel," in *Psyché* (Paris: Galilee, 1987).

37. Nichephorus, *Discours contre les Iconoclastes*, 19.

38. John Selden, *Titles of Honour* (London: Stansby, 1614), sig. b 4 a.

39. Nichephorus, *Discours contre les Iconoclastes*, 20.

40. "Qui nescit dissimulare nescit regnare." (He who knows how to dissimulate knows how to rule.) The statement is attributed to an unnamed king of France by William Harrison, in *An Historical Description of the Island of Britain* (London: n.p., 1586), fol. 115a. G. Puttenham, *Arte of English Poesie*, 155, cites the aphorism as a definition of the "courtly figure of *allegoria*."

manipulation, pretense, and apologetics. Law was in this respect an arm or weapon of government and its use was generically polemical. The apologetic character of early legal doctrinal writing is most evident in explicitly polemical works, in dialogues and exchanges between Sir John Fortescue and William Hakewill, St. German and Sir Thomas More, Reginald Pole and Sir Thomas Lupset, Sir Edward Coke, Sir John Davies, and Sir Henry Spelman, to take but the most obvious examples.[41] The immediate context of, and model for, such apologetic writing was theological. Reformation polemics as to the proper form of law, polity, and representation not only provided the rhetorical terms for the defense of the legal institution but also lent the means for the common lawyers' dismissal of popular resistance to law.[42] The historical and jurisdictional context of these apologetic forms cannot be entered into here save to offer a loose synoptic overview of the adversaries or antiportraits of common law and its burgeoning profession.[43] The depiction will follow the order of the

---

41. Fortescue, *De Laudibus Legum Angliae*; William Hakewill, *The Antiquity of the Laws of this Island* (1604; London: Richardson, 1771); Edith Starkey, ed., *A Dialogue between Reginald Pole and Sir Thomas Lupset* (1535; London: Chatto and Windus, 1935); St. German, *Doctor and Student*; the anonymous *Replication of a Serjaunte at the Lawes of England*, in Francis Hargrave, ed. *A Collection of Tracts relative to the Law of England* (Dublin: E. Lynch, 1787); Christopher St. German, *Salem and Bizance* (London: Bertheleti, 1533); More, *Apologye*; Sir Thomas More, *Deballacyon of Salem and Bizance* (London: Rastell, 1533); Sir Edward Coke, *Reports* (London: Rivington, 1777); Sir John Davies, *A Discourse of Law and Lawyers* (Dublin: Frankton, 1615); Sir Henry Spelman, *Of the Original of the Four Law Terms of the Year* (1614; London: Gillyflower, 1684).

42. For an indicative guide to that literature, see Thomas Wilson, *The State of England, Anno Domini 1600* (1601; London: Camden Miscellany, 1936); Walter Carey, *The Present State of England* (1627); John Hare, *St Edward's Ghost or Anti-Normanism* (1642); and John Warr, *The Corruption and Deficiency of the Laws of England* (1649), all reprinted in the *Harleian Miscellany* (London: Dutton, 1810). A good survey of the literature is given in John H. Baker, *Spelman's Reports* (London: Selden Society, 1978).

43. On the historical issue of resistance to law in Europe, see Gerald Strauss, *Law, Resistance, and the State* (Princeton, N.J.: Princeton University Press, 1986). On the adversaries of common law, see Christopher W. Brooks, *Pettyfoggers and Vipers of the Commonwealth* (Cambridge: Cambridge University Press, 1986); Peter Goodrich, "*Ars Bablativa*: Rhetoric, Ramism, and the Genealogy of English Jurisprudence" in *Legal Hermeneutics: History, Theory, and Practice*, ed. Gregory Leyh, (Berkeley and Los Angeles: University of California Press, 1991); Peter Goodrich, "Critical Legal Studies in England: Prospective Histories," *Oxford Journal of Legal Studies* 12 (1992): 195.

antirrhetic and move from the categories of sanctity or authority to those of reason and nature.

In theological terms the Reformation in England had led early and uniquely to the arrogation of the powers of the spiritual to the Crown. From the Act of Supremacy onward, the English constitution was an explicit marriage of ecclesiastical and secular, spiritual and temporal laws.[44] The secular state had thus to defend itself against Rome, to justify its refusal of the universal authority of the Roman Catholic church while at the same time establishing a distinctive constitution that rejected an equally universal Roman law. In terms of positive law, the defense of common law against the logic and power of Rome took the form of a war of jurisdictions in which the ecclesiastical courts and civilian law were eventually subjugated to the prerogative and will of the king's courts.[45] In dialectical terms, the most significant facet of this exchange lay in the development of an Anglican state in which the English church and spiritual law became an integrated, or at least subordinate, aspect of both royal and judicial prerogatives and jurisdictions.[46] The ecclesiastical titles of antiquity and continuity united "one law and the other" (*utrumque ius*) in a prerogative shared between the trinity of monarch, parliament, and judiciary.[47] The spiritual state modeled the unwritten constitution and its hierarchical system of authority and obedience,

44. 28 Hen. 8, cap 1 (1534), in Rastall, *Collection*, fol. 404 a.

45. For striking examples of this polemic, see St. German, *Treatise Concerning the Division*; More, *Deballacyon*. More generally, see Ridley, *View*; W. Fulbecke, *A Parallele or Conference of the Civil Law, the Canon Law and the Common Law of this Realme of Englande* (1602; London: Society of Stationers, 1618); Francis Bacon, *The Elements of the Common Lawes of England* (London: I. More, 1630); John Cowell, *The Institutes of the Lawes of England, Digested into the Method of the Civill or Imperiall Institutions* (1605; London: Roycroft, 1651). For a good general discussion, see Brian Levack, *The Civil Lawyers in England 1603–1641* (Oxford: Oxford University Press, 1973).

46. See particularly, John Cowell, *The Interpreter, or Booke Containing the Signification of Words* (Cambridge: n.p., 1607) (*sub prerogativa*): the prerogative power was *iura sublimia*, an absolute and perpetual power, unbound by law, while "our lawyers *sub prerogativa regis* do comprise also, that absolute height of power that the civilians call *majestatem vel potestatem*"; John Cooke, *Juridica Trium Quaestionum ad Majestatem Pertinentium Determinatio* (Oxford, 1608); John Hayward, *Of Supremacie in Affairs of Religion* (London: J. Bilt, 1624), 9–11.

47. For an important discussion of the concept of *utrumque ius*, see Pierre Legendre, *Ecrits Juridiques du Moyen Age Occidental* (London: Variorum, 1988). See also Yifat Hachamovitch, "One Law on the Other," *International Journal for the Semiotics of Law* 3 (1990): 188.

property and faith: in Sir Thomas Smith's influential description of
the law of the land (*lex terrae*), "[N]o man holds land simply free
in England, but he or she that holds the Crown of England: all others
hold their land in *fee* . . . or *feoda*, which is as much as to say in *fide*
or *fiducia*, that is upon a faith or trust, that he shall be true to the
Lord of whom he holds it."[48] Irrespective of the historical fate of that
faith, the rhetorically significant implication concerns the dual form
of property and commonwealth, of a land held both spiritually and
temporally, visibly and invisibly, of one law and the other.

The defense of the legal authority and sacral prerogative of the
Crown institutes a particular order and specific places of public or
legal reason. In one sense, it establishes tradition, the "unwritten"
authority of institutional sources of law and judicially approved custom and opinion, as the ever-present mystery, the logic and truth, of
an immemorial and invisible law. The judges take the role of custo-
dians of a peculiar and antique "spirit of the law," of the *arcana iuris*,
which is to be defended as axiom, maxim, and judicial declaration,
against all secular, imperite, or vernacular forms of knowledge. Legal
reason, in short, is conjoined with judicial power, tradition with
authority, source with truth: "it is the great lesson of legal history
that the power and authority of reason are one and the same."[49] The
reason of law shares in the two natures of the ecclesiastical and civil
polity; it is explicitly a knowledge of things divine and human; it is
necessarily a language unto itself;[50] it is incapable of error save through

---

48. Sir Thomas Smith, *De Republica Anglorum* (1565; London: Middleton,
1584), 111. See further Abraham Fraunce, *Lawiers Logike* (London: Howe, 1588),
fol. 54 b; West, *Symbolaeography*, I s. 235; Sir Henry Finch, *Law, or a Discourse
Therof in Foure Bookes* (London: Society of Stationers, 1627), fol. 143.

49. Legendre, *L'Inestimable Objet*, 38. See further Pierre Legendre, *L'Empire de
la Verité* (Paris: Fayard, 1983).

50. Sir John Doderidge, *The English Lawyer* (1629; London: I. More 1631), 29:
(paraphrasing the *Digest*): "knowledge of the law is affirmed to be *rerum divinarum
humanarumque scientia*—it contains the knowledge of all things divine and human."
See also Fortescue, *De Laudibus Legum Angliae*, 4, who cites biblical sources to
associate law with a "filial" fear of God: "be pleased to know then, that not only the
Deuteronomical, but also all Human laws are sacred; the definition of a law being
thus, it is an holy sanction, commanding whatever is honest, and forbidding the
contrary." Sir Edward Coke, *The First Part of the Institutes of the Laws of England*
(London: I. More, 129) sig. c 6 a, argues against the use of the vernacular, referring
to law French as *vocabula artis*, which was "so apt and significant to express the true
sense of the laws, and so woven into the laws themselves, as it is in a manner impossible
to change them." See further Coke, *Reports*, part 3, sig. c 6 b. Doderidge, *English*

human failing or the interference of those unlearned in law.[51] To the other time and distinctive place of legal reason as the logic of an always already established law should be added certain observations as to the specific character of that reason as an expression of the genealogy of English institutions. The learned character of legal reason, its artificial quality, is a construction directed against all other possible forms of legal reason, be that those of civil law, the scholarship of other disciplines, or the more popular logic of resistance to or reform of common law.[52] What is staked out in the defense of legal reason is a legitimacy that belongs to the mythical antiquity of specifically English, common law sources and forms, a lineage, a blood, a law whose rationality belongs to the immemorial authority of its source. Its logic is thus that of inheritance,[53] its order is that of succession,[54] its power and virtue is that of the fathers.[55]

Lawyer, 51 refers to a language of memorials and not of speech; William Fulbecke, *Direction or Preparative to the Study of Law* (London: Clarke, 1599) refers to "words of the law [which] may be compared to certain images called *sileni Alcibiades*, whose outward feature was deformed and ugly, but within they were full of jewels and precious stones" (55–56). For further discussion see Goodrich, *Languages of Law*, chap. 3.

51. Thus Coke, *Reports*, part 2, sig. A 5 a: "if you observe any diversities of opinions amongst the professors of the laws, content you, to be learned in your profession, and you will find, that is *hominis vitium non professionis*. And to say the truth, the greatest questions arise not upon any of the rules of the common law, but sometimes upon conveyances and instruments made by men unlearned, many times upon wills intricately, absurdly and repugnantly set down, by parsons, scriveners and other such imperites." See, further, Davies, *Discourse*, 253.

52. For examples of scholarly resistance and demand for reform, see Fraunce, *Lawiers Logike;* Thomas Elyot, *The Boke Named the Governour* (1531; London: Dent, 1835); Thomas Powell, *The Attourney's Academy* (London: Fisher, 1610). The curricula rhetorical tradition also provides numerous powerful examples of criticism of the poor scholarship of lawyers, as for example in Leonard Cox, *The Arte or Crafte of Rhetoryke* (1530; Chicago: University of Chicago Press, 1899); Richard Rainholde, *A Booke Called the Foundacion of Rhetorike* (1563; London: Scholars Facsimiles, 1945); Wilson, *Arte of Rhetorique*. For popular criticism, see John Day, *Law Tricks* (1608; Oxford: Malone Society, 1950); James Earle, *Micro-Cosmographie* (London: RB, 1628); Ruggles, *Ignoramus or the English Lawyer* (1621; London, 1736); and somewhat later, Richard Head, *Proteus Redivivus* (London: WD, 1675).

53. Sir Edward Coke, *Magna Charta with short but necessary observations* (London: Atkins, 1680) sig. A 2 a: "The best inheritance a subject has is the laws of the realm."

54. See particularly, T. Smith, *De Republica Anglorum*, referring to the importance in royal succession of "the right and honour of the blood," for the "quietness and surety of the realm" (20). See further, on the principle of succession, John Ferne, *The Blazon of Gentrie* (London: Winder, 1586); James Bossewell, *Workes of Armorie* (London: Totell, 1572).

55. Thus Selden, *Titles of Honour*, sig. B 4 b. See further, William Wryley,

Reason and nature join in the origin of a common law conceived to be "connaturall" with the people of England.[56] The time of the origin and of the ancestors of law is that of a natural governance instituted according to the model of a divine order of all visible forms. Nature is the zero point of the genealogical line; it is not only the first model of all subsequent reproduction, but also the mediate historical source of positive law: "among the learned in English law, this is called the law of reason, which natural reason has established among all men . . . a sign, possessed naturally, which is indicative of the right reason of God" and from which positive law "is derived as a thing which is necessarily and probably following of the law of reason and the law of God for the due end of human nature."[57] There are, in other words, two laws, one natural or "native," inscribed, "unchangeable and perpetual," without writing, in the heart of men; the other a replica or derivation from the former.[58] The relation between natural and positive law, between model and replica, primary and secondary, was not, however, simply a conceptual correlation; it was also a genealogical claim. The antiquity of the common law, its excessive age, was not only an argument directed against the claims of Roman law, it was also a positive statement of the historical proximity of England's unwritten law to nature itself: "this customary law is the most perfect, and most excellent, and without comparison the best, to make and preserve a common-wealth . . . as coming nearest to the law of nature, which is the root and touchstone of all good laws."[59] The immemorial and unwritten character of common law allowed its origin to be placed, beyond memory, in the realm of nature and not of man. The last defense of law was thus to be a natural law conceived as the order of things: "for by an order we are born, by an order we live and by an order we make our end.

The True Use of Armorie (London: I. Jackson, 1592), 3–4; Henry Spelman, *Aspilogia* (1610; London: Martin and Allestry, 1654), 4–5; and the slightly later William Bird, *A Treatise of the Nobilitie of the Realme collected out of the body of the Common Law* (London: Walbanke, 1642), 8–10.

56. Davies, *Discourse*, 255.

57. St. German, *Doctor and Student*, 13, 27.

58. Finch, *Law*, fol. 2. Finch explicitly distinguishes law of nature and law of reason as respectively primitive and secondary, *noeticum* and *dianoeticum*.

59. Davies, *Discourse*, 252–53.

By an order one ruleth as head and others obey as members. By an order realms stand and laws take their force."[60]

The outline description provided above of a foundational order, of a common law tradition in which "reason, justice and law do stand together,"[61] should already indicate much of the likely content and form of the specific legal order that the Renaissance apologetics sought to institute and defend. At the somewhat recondite level of the theory of the sources of law, the elements of antirrhetic and antiportrait are already evident: those that oppose or even simply question the order of common law and the professional or esoteric status of legal knowledge were not simply fools or *imperites* but were also, and by definition, likely to be accounted as harbingers and companions of the godless, the disordered, the irrational, the mad, and the unnatural. They were at the very least irreverent, unlearned, and prey to dreams and other fantastical imaginings. The antithetic character of the statement and defense of common law can be rendered more explicit, however, by invoking elements of the substantive content of the definition of the new "old English order" of custom and judge-made law. While the examples which follow are illustrative, I believe, of a more general rhetorical form, they are not intended as anything approaching a comprehensive survey.

Antitheton: Strangers, Foreigners, Nomads, and Others

The first allegory or dissimulation of common law is that of its identity. The system of common law developed by the early doctrinal writers, Coke's sages and the Renaissance treatises, is based upon the elaboration of a myth of an origin that precedes historical time and so lends an identity to a tradition that is otherwise and self-evidently polyglot, partial, and impermanent. The origin of common law is an obsessive object of doctrinal description, and the first law of England is variously depicted as being Samothean, Albion, Druidic, Greek, Trojan, and Arthurian.[62] What is sought in these repeated

---

60. Wilson, *Arte of Rhetorique,* 17–18.
61. Fulbecke, *Direction or Preparative,* 3. See also Finch, *Law,* fol 1 a, who defines law as an amalgam of three laws: *"lex veritatus, lex iusticiae, lex sapientia."*
62. For examples of these statements of origin of law, see Coke, *Reports,* refer-

returns to the originary, to a past that was never present, is an emblem of ancestral identity, a character of Englishness, an insular nature that preexists and will outlive the crisis and criticism of an illogical and historically haphazard system of case-made law. As with any genealogy, the essential question is that of legitimacy, of the proper constitution of the social family, its image and its fate. If the depiction of family and familiarity, of legitimacy and line, is analyzed in terms of its explicit figures of antithesis, an antinomic structure can be elicited, one that opposes the myth of imagined community or of belonging to the histories of law, nation to alienation, antiquity to novelty, familiarity to strangeness, permanence to transience, and the Island of Ceres to its continental Gallic forebears.[63]

The primary task of the Reformation defenses of English law lay in finding some method of explaining the legitimacy of a newly united civil and ecclesiastical commonwealth that had left the universal church, the family of Rome, to become an independent constitution under the English crown. The reformers, almost without exception, embarked upon the extreme endeavor of opposing truth to history. In its most extreme version, represented among others by Bishop Aylmer's "counterblast" against the Roman Antichrist, we find a marginal note stating, "God is English," followed in panegyric form: "oh England, England, thou knowest not thine own wealth: because thou seest not other countries penury . . . for first you have God, and all his army of angels on your side: you have right and truth, and seek not to do them wrong, but to defend your right. Think not that God will suffer you to be soiled at their hands, for your fall is his dishonour."[64] In words later cited unacknowledged by Edward Coke, Aylmer proceeds to depict a time of origin and antiquity, of God's

---

ring variously to Brutus, the Trojans, Romulus and Remus, and King Arthur; Spelman, *Four Law Terms*, who refers to Druids, Moses, and Lycurgus of Sparta; William Lambard, *Archeion or Discourse upon the High Courts of Justice in England* (1591; London: Seile, 1635) refers to Moses, the Greeks, and the Druids; John Selden, *Jani Anglorum Facies Altera* (1610; London: T. Bassett, 1683) refers to the Samothes, as well as the Druids; William Dugdale, *Origines Juridiciales, or Historical Memorials of the English Laws* (1666; Savoy: Newcomb, 1671) refers to the Druids.

63. William Camden, *Britannia sive florentissimorum regnorum, Angliae, Scotiae, Hiberniae chorographica descriptio* (1586; London: Collins, 1695), fol. iii–iv.

64. Bishop Aylmer, *An Harborowe for Faithfull and Trewe Subjectes against the late blowne blaste* (Strasborowe, 1559), sig. P iii a, and P iv b.

presence in England, which story is explicitly "the witness of time, the candle of truth, the life of memory, the Lady of life and the register of antiquity."[65]

In constitutional terms the legitimacy of papal authority in all matters of ecclesiastical law and government, consequent upon the historical conversion of England to Christianity by the Pope's envoy Augustine, can be challenged by reference to royal rights of ecclesiastical government that descend directly from God and so precede and supersede the Roman presence in England. According to Dr. Fulke, "[T]he protestants are returned to the ancient faith which was in the land before Augustine came from Rome, which was not so much good in planting faith where it was not, as in corrupting the sincerity of faith where it was before he came."[66] It was the law of the "primitive faith" in England, that the Crown, the "civill magistrate," had supreme authority over all persons and causes ecclesiastical.[67] Henry VIII, in declaring the supremacy of the Crown, "resumed the ecclesiastical power of the King . . . and so the statutes [of supremacy] . . . are not laws inductory of a new, but declaratory of the ancient authority of our prince, with the solemn signification of their reassumption."[68] The English family had returned to its own, the natural law of *patria potestas* was to be complemented again by *regia potestas*—"the extension of the former to many families"—and the power of the Crown could thus be conceived as the constitutional equivalent in natural and civil law of the absolute power of the father.[69]

While the major force of Anglican ecclesiastical polemic was directed against the sophistries, lies, and errors, the idolatry and false doctrine of the papal Antichrist, the more secular legal treatises developed a comparable rhetoric against the threat and treachery of foreign law. If the English Crown was the authorizing source of national custom, and as such of all tradition, it followed naturally that English

---

65. Ibid., sig. E iv b. Coke, *Reports*, part 1, sig. A 4 a, part 3, sig. B 1 a and B 5 a (the citation is originally from Cicero, *De Oratore*, book 2).

66. W. Fulke, *T. Stapleton and Martiall (two popish heretics) Confuted and of their Particular Heresies Detected* (London: Middleton, 1580), 14.

67. Ibid., 13. See, for further examples, Jewell, *Defense of the Apologie*, sig. A. iii a–A iv b; Downing, *Discourse*, 63–69 on the Crown's *iure positivo pontificio*, and *iure divino apostolico*; J. Selden, *Jani Anglorum Facies Altera*), 72.

68. Downing, *Discourse*, 66.

69. Ibid., 64.

law was a secondary derivation or replica of that native sovereign power.[70] Leaving aside the specific question of the legal form of the *regia potestas*, and the indicative irony of its Latin title and Roman law sources, constitutional theory had first to depict a uniquely English populace whose character would find expression in England's antique customary law, that law that Davies described as connatural with the land. The lawyer needed some image or emblem of the Englishness of common law that would both support the assertion of its antiquity and repel the threat of reformation by evidencing a unity to the tradition, a unity and particularism that could override the history of foreign conquest, alien monarchs, continental languages, and borrowed laws.

Who then are the English? or by their generic name the Britains? The received wisdom on the continent was that the British were Gauls, the island having been once occupied and once conquered from France. Worse than that, according to Bodin and Hotman, English law was in procedure and institution a borrowing from local French customary law.[71] According to the English historian William Harrison, Britain received from the Gauls "some use of logike and rhetorike, such as it was which our lawiers practised in their pleas and common causes. . . . Howbeit as they taught us logike and rhetorike, so we had also some sophistrie from them; but in the worst sense: for from France is all kind of forgerie, corruption of manners, and crafty behaviour not so often transported into England."[72] In an exhaustive survey of theories of origin, William Camden could find nothing more distinctive as a national characteristic of the British than a philological slip or phonetic synecdoche that applied the ancient British custom of painting the body with woad to the island itself:

---

70. While Coke and others on occasion challenged the power of Crown and Parliament, they did so only on the basis that such power absolute should be vested in the judiciary, and not on the basis of the illegitimacy of that power as such. See further on this point Phillip Allott, "The Courts and Parliament: Who Whom?" *Cambridge Law Journal* 38 (1979): 79; Goodrich, "Critical Legal Studies in England."

71. Jean Bodin, *De Republica* (1580; London: Knollers, 1606), 559; François Hotman, *Franco-Gallia or, an account of the ancient free state of France* (1574; London: Goodwin, 1711).

72. William Harrison, *An Historicall Description of the Island of Britaine, with a brief rehersall of the nature and qualities of the people of England* (London: n.p., 1586) fol. 20 a–b.

it was the general custom of all nations, to apply to themselves
such names as had a respect to something wherein they either
excelled, or were distinguished from the rest . . . what, then, if I
should suppose, that our Britons took that denomination from
their painted bodies; for the word Brith, in the ancient language
of this island, signifies any thing that is painted and coloured
over. . . . Nor can any man in reason censure this, as either an
absurd or over-strained etymology . . . the name (which is as it
were the picture of the thing) expresses the thing itself.[73]

As Camden recognized, and as the legal antiquarians John Selden
and Henry Spelman confirmed, there was very little distinctive about
antique England: its people, its language, and its laws were all of
foreign provenance and could well be greatly reformed by conceptual
systematization or codification according to the logic of their source.[74]
    It is a principle of apologetics that the most vehement and antag-
onistic defense is reserved for the weakest arguments. In exemplary
style, Coke determines that the historical and philological questioning
of English origins defames the self-evidence of legal truth, profanes
the due reverence owed to common law, and is in constitutional terms
as seditious and treacherous as consorting with the enemy and with
Rome. The answer to such "seditious cavilling" is to keep historians
and philologists away from the study of law and simultaneously to
reassert the national peculiarity, excellence, and antiquity of the common law and of its lawyers. The national distinctiveness of common
law extended beyond the reach of any other national history, while
the correlative excellence of that law identified it closely with a populace that was itself not simply pure in its lineage—the island was
inhabited before all others[75]—but superior in its quality: "I am con-

---

73. Camden, *Britannia*, xxix.
74. On the need for systematization, see Fraunce, *Lawiers Logike*; Bacon, *Elements of the Common Law*, Cowell, *Institutes*; Fulbecke, *Parallele or Conference*,
fol. 2 a: "The common law cannot otherwise be divided from the civil and canon
laws than the flower from the root and stalk." See further Sir Robert Wiseman, *The
Law of Laws: or the Excellency of the Civil Law* (London: Royston, 1664); Arthur
Duck, *De Usu et Autoritate Juris Civilis Romanorum in Dominiis Principum Chris-
tianorum* (London: n.p., 1679).
75. See Fortescue, *De Laudibus Legum Angliae*, 32–33; Coke, *Reports*, part 6,
sig. Z 2 a–b; Davies, *Discourse*, 253–54; Finch, *Law*, 75.

vinced that the laws of England eminently excel all other countries"
and particularly those of the Romans and of the French.[76] As if simple
denunciation of those other and inferior laws were not sufficient, it
remains to point out a more insidious and general antagonism toward
all aspects of things foreign, strange, or unfamiliar.

Despite the title of Inns of Court (*hospitii curiae*),[77] the first rule
of apprenticeship to the law was that of the exclusion of all strangers,
"of foraigners, discontinuers, strangers or other not of the society . . .
nor common attorney or sollicitor."[78] Like any family, the legal profession was to be defined by blood and an exclusory membership:
"it is an error to think that the sons of Graziers, farmers, merchants,
tradesmen, and artificers can be made a gentleman by their attendance
or matriculation . . . at an Inne of Court, for no man can be made a
gentleman but by his father . . . because it is a matter of race, and of
blood and descent," and in consequence the ungentle were to be
excluded or weeded out.[79] What was true of the legal community
and of the Inns as the training place or nursery of lawyers, of *appren-
ticii nobiliores*,[80] was equally the case on a broader political or constitutional stage. It was not enough simply to exclude foreigners and
strangers, but in over twenty enactments of the sixteenth century it
was legislated that no one was to appear like a foreigner or stranger.
In legislation of 1509,[81] for example, it was forbidden for any subject
of the realm to "weare in any part of his apparell any wollen cloth
made out of this realm of Englande," and by legislation of 1511 it

76. Fortescue, *De Laudibus Legum Angliae*, 89 (mentioning the Romans and
Venetians); Davies, *Discourse*, 278: "doth she [the profession] not register and keep
in memory the best antiquities of our nation? Doth she not preserve our ancient
customs and forms of government, wherein the wisdom of our ancestors doth shine
above the policy of other kingdoms." Coke, *Reports*, part 3, sig. B 3 b: "hereby as
I think it is sufficiently proved that the laws of England are of much greater antiquity
than they are reported to be, and than any constitutions or laws imperial of Roman
emperors."

77. See Cowell, *Interpreter*, sig. Q 3 a; Sir George Buc, *The Third Universitie
of England* (London: n.p., 1615), fol. 969 b (defining the Inn as a Hostelry or
Diversoria).

78. Legislation from the Middle Temple, cited in Dugdale, *Origines Juridiciales*,
fol. 192 a.

79. Buc, *Third Universitie*, 968–69; see also Ferne, *Blazon of Gentrie*, 58–59.

80. Dugdale, *Origines Juridiciales*, fol. 142 a.

81. *For Reformation of apparell* (1 Hen. 8, cap. 14), in Rastall, *Collection*, fol.
13 a.

was ordered that "there be no cappes or hats made and readie wrought in any part beyond the sea."[82] Further legislation was directed against strangers, against Egyptians, and against vagabonds in any part of the realm and including native dwellers who took up with or appeared to be traveling people.[83] French fashions of dress were a constant object of legislation and vilification, as too were foreign colors and materials, which, according to Harrison, tranformed the populace into "monsters." The Englishman was to be known by "his cloth. . . . without any such cuts and garrish colours as are worn . . . by the French."[84] The Inns of Court introduced additional legislation to ban French dress and styles: "for, even as his apparell doth show him to be, even so shall he be esteemed among them."[85] Idolatrous dress would threaten the identity of the citizen and encourage a foreign presence within the realm. Judging by the extent and scope of the legislation, foreign clothes would betray a foreigner within, the external model an internal decadence.

Paradoxon: Public Laws and Private Reasons

In many respects the enemy without the polity—the foreigner, the alien, the French, the Roman, and the Egyptian—is matched by the enemy within. The construction of a negative national identity, of an English character that exists only by virtue of its definition against an external threat, is replicated at an internal level by the formulation of a constitution defined against the subject and the subjectivity of reason. The Crown's arrogation of supreme authority over the ecclesiastical realm succeeded, in external terms, in constituting an independent kingdom as against the former position in which England was a province of the papal jurisdiction.[86] In internal terms, the

---

82. 3 Hen. 8, cap. 15.

83. 22 Hen. VIII cap 10, outlawing "divers and outlandish people . . . using no craft nor seat of merchandise [who] by great subtlety and crafty means do deceive the people, bearing them in hand that they by palmistry could tell men's and women's fortunes." By 1 and 2 P and M cap 4 the offence of being an Egyptian is extended to natives "who shall be seen within this realm of England or Wales, in any company or fellowship of vagabonds, commonly called, or calling themselves Egyptians, or counterfeiting, transporting, or disguising themselves by their apparell, speech or other behaviour, like unto such vagabonds."

84. Harrison, *Historicall Description*, 172 b.

85. Dugdale, *Origines*, fol. 144 a–149b, 192 a–193b.

86. Downing, *Discourse*, 6–7.

expansion of the monarchical jurisdiction or *regia potestas* was to transfer the "government of the soul" to the civil magistrate. In place of the confused idolatry of earlier times and authorities, the civil subject was now properly reflected in the mirror of the constitution. The icon of the Crown and the spiritual unity of secular authority formed a model in which the subject could narcissistically see his or her own face, a law in which the subject was himself mystically present and so could only ever obey. Such presence was structured by a logic of transubstantial representation that denied the possibility of any disjunction between appearance and substance: the social body, the icon and model of civility, included and annexed the subject. Its art, the art of law, held the subject fascinated, magnetized, or bound to an already established law from which the only escape would be into madness: it was the logic of the mirror, of mimetic duplication, of the mask.

The establishment of an identity, the constitution of a community, and the capture of subjectivity are first a matter of establishing a collective or national identity whose virtue will be matched only by the evil of those who do not belong to it. In the same sense that the Church is the spouse of Christ, the civil polity is a marriage—the most holy and exemplary of unions—between the individual families that make up the populace and the Crown that heads them.[87] In accordance with the spiritual character of any marriage, the social family is joined in a mystical union in which the relation between the elements of the union is subject to the transcendental imperative of the union as such. It is a relation that breaks the boundaries of the individual will and specifically subordinates the weaker party to the desire of the stronger: Christian marriage is defined legally by *patria potestas* and socially by the subordination of the woman and the children. The absolute dominion of the father of the social and political realm, *regia potestas*, is the logical extension and correlate of the metaphor of marriage. The prerogative power is variously described as *sacra sacrorum, sacra regni, iura sublimia,* and *majestatem potestatem.*[88] The common lawyers directly applied the Roman

---

87. See Hooker, *Ecclesiastical Politie,* 441–43; and Downing, *Discourse,* 9–13, 64–65.

88. For striking examples, see Hooker, *Ecclesiastical Politie,* 443–45; Sir John Hayward, *Of Supremacie in Affairs of Religion* (London: J. Bilt, 1624), 9–11; Downing, *Discourse,* 91–92.

definition of royal sovereignty[89] to the English Crown and thus identified the polity with the absolute will of its head: "what pleases the
prince, has the force of law," his will being "an absolute and perpetual
power, to exercise the highest actions in some certain state."[90] The
Crown is the icon of social presence and the subjects of the realm
are the elements of that presence or mystic body. In constitutional
terms the dual nature of the Crown, as both natural and political
(mystic) body, is the explicit model for the dual nature of legal being,
for an impossible subjectivity: "one and the same multitude may in
such sort be both [spiritual and secular], and is so with us, that no
person appertaining to the one can be denied to be also of the other."[91]
Such membership of the spiritual or mystic realm binds the subject
of law to an absolute and foreign will of which he or she is inescapably
an element or part.

The Crown is the icon or model of political and legal subjectivity,
but it is not its representation, they are not like it, nor is it their
similitude. The prerogative of the Crown asserts an absolute power
whose social representation or symbolic presence is found in the unity
of three elements that make up the legal sovereign. Here again the
people are married to a higher order, authority, and reason that both
define and annex them. Parliament represents the polity, and thus in
Sir Thomas Smith's definition: "Parliament represents and has the
power of the whole realm both the head and the body. For every
Englishman is entended to be there present, either in person or by
procuration and attornies. . . . And the consent of Parliament is taken
to be every man's consent."[92] Selden adds a musical metaphor by way
of explanation of this definition of subjective consent, suggesting that
the Parliament of *Pananglium* (all England) resembles a composition:
"so of the highest, middlemost and lowermost states shuffled together,
like different sounds, by fair proportion doth a city agree by the

---

89. The earliest source of such a borrowing is Glanvill, *Treatise on the Laws
and Customs of the Kingdom of England* (London: Nelson, 1187/1965), 1. (citing
Justinian's *Institutes* I.1.)

90. *Digest* 1.4.1 (*quod principi placuit, habet vigorem legis*) in *Fleta* (*Com-
mentarii Juris Anglicani*), cited in Dugdale, *Origines*, fol. 3 b. Similarly, William
Staunford, *An Exposition of the King's Prerogative* (London: Society of Stationers,
1607), fol. 5 a; William Noy, *A Treatise of the Rights of the Crown* (London: Lintoth,
1634/1715), 54.

91. Hooker, *Ecclesiastical Politie*, 438.

92. Smith, *De Republica Anglorum*, 35.

consent of persons most unlike [and unlikely]; and that which by
musicians in singing is called harmony; that in a city is called concord,
the straightest and surest bond of safety in every commonwealth."[93]
For Hooker, the appropriate metaphor for the power and dual presence
of "the body of the whole realm" is that of a triangle: "as in a figure
of a triangle, the base doth differ from the sides thereof, and yet one
and the self same line is both base and also a side; a side simply, a
base if it chance to be the bottom and under-ly the rest."[94]

Among the qualities of the realm stressed by such metaphors of
perfection are those of unity, exclusivity, and an irreal and so natural
or perfect presence. The trinity of estates represented in Parliament
is not only deemed to contain the whole realm but also to constitute
a site of annunciation: it is the sacred place of law, and when the
whole realm speaks it must necessarily do so as the authoritative
public voice of a unitary reason. In short it speaks for "us" and it
speaks as "us," that is, as the oracular and incontestable voice of the
whole. There is an absolute force to the word of the law as the
expression of the totality, a marriage of authority and reason that
precludes from the very start the possibility of any member challenging or even legitimately questioning the reason of the whole.
Public reason defines a private being that only has a legitimate existence within the public sphere of its representation. In short, public
reason envelopes and determines or possesses private reason: there
is no private reason outside of that which is always already incorporated in the public sphere and acts as a part or *representamen* of
the whole. In Hooker's depiction, the impossibility of any disjunction
between the whole and its parts, between representative and represented, is spelled out at two levels. At a conceptual level the unity
of the whole binds the part or member both temporally and logically:

> although we be not personally ourselves present, notwithstanding
> our assent is by reason of other agents there in our behalf. And
> what we do by others, no reason but it should stand as our
> Deed, no less effectually to bind us, than if our selves had done
> it in person. In many things assent is given, they that give it,

---

93. Selden, *Jani Anglorum*, 94.
94. Hooker, *Ecclesiastical Politie*, 438. The same metaphor is used in Bodin,
De Republica, 757.

not imagining they do so, because the manner of their assenting
is not apparent.[95]

At a pragmatic level, what is essential, for Hooker, is faith in authority, "in him whom he hath sent," not least because "easier a great
deal it is for men by law, to be taught what they ought to do, than
instructed how to judge as they should do of law; the one being a
thing which belongs generally unto all, the other, such as none but
the wiser and more judicious sort can perform."[96]
     In rhetorical terms, the image or icon is a figure that represents.[97]
Here reason is represented as the figure of the whole; it embraces
the unity of public and private, and specifically of a private fixated
or held in the gaze of the whole. It remains, however, to be observed
that the unity of reason is antithetically directed against the possibility of its fracture or fragmentation. The concept of a totality
cannot avoid the implication of an outside, of a space of the unfaith-
ful, disordered, seditious, or satanic. That space is occupied in legal
doctrine by those who would judge for themselves or who "would
follow the law of private reason, where the law of public should
take place."[98] Thomas More, Richard Hooker, and Edward Coke are
the most vehement exponents of the view that the authority of law
in general and of the judges in particular is predicated upon a concept of law as the proper form of public reason that is paradoxically
neither accessible to the public nor open to public dispute.[99] Hooker
is again most expansive in his delineation of the errors of unlearned
judgments of law. Law is a matter for our "Directors" and not for the
"vulgar sort." Those that challenge the institutions of public reason,
even if only by means of discourse, are variously referred to as
contentious, divisive, juvenile, academic, tedious, opinionated, perverse, strange, disturbing, superstitious, fantastical, zealous, diseased,

        95. Hooker, *Ecclesiastical Politie*, 87.
        96. Ibid., 94, 100.
        97. See, for example, the definition in Sherry, *Schemes and Tropes*, sig. F vi
b; Puttenham, *Arte of English Poesie*, 201; John Susenbrotus, *Epitome Troporum ac
Schematum et Grammaticorum et Rhetorum* (London: G. Dewes, 1562), sig. G 6 b.
        98. Ibid., 102.
        99. On the mysterious truth, opaque language, and inaccessible technicality of
common law, see Thomas More, *The Confutacyon of Tyndales Answere* (London:
Rastell, 1532), 272; idem, *Deballacyon*, sig. F ii b, M vi a–b, U ii a; Coke, *Institutes
I*, sig. C 6 a; idem, *Reports*, part 3, sig. C 6 b.

foreign, extreme, overconfident, and dissolute.[100] For Coke they are ignorant, superficial, and stupid, "and I will not sharpen the nib of my pen against them."[101]

The order of public reason is an institutional one connoting both temporal obedience and spiritual observance: "the subjection which we owe unto lawful powers, doth not only import that we should be under them by order of our state, but that we show all submission towards them both by honour and obedience."[102] External or visible conformity should be matched by a discursive submission, an inner tranquillity and compliance, "for they that seek a reason in all things, do utterly overthrow reason."[103] The legal person, in other words, is a member of two polities, subject to two laws and to the hierarchy that appertains between them. The body is prisoner of the soul. The logic of such a dual law is that of inheritance and possession, tradition and compliance, belonging and identification. It establishes a constitution, a public order of lawful reason that can admit only of a binary and antithetically defined classification of those that belong and those that are excluded, those that listen and those that speak back. It is an institutional reason, a logic of communal membership, an isomorphism of truth and power. Its antiportrait depicts an obverse or outside of reason in specifically denunciatory and exclusory terms; those that do not belong to reason and the institution exist in the twilight and spectral zone of idols, fantasies, and dreams: the outsider inhabits a world of the half living and of the dead; she is both a nihilist and an augur of an apocalyptic fate.

Reason is an expression of belonging to the institution. Its figures and tropes are those of legitimacy, of family membership and purity of origin and line. In terms of origin and source, the most explicit correlation between rationality and group membership is found in the earliest depictions of lawful foundation. For the common lawyers the first signs of law were those of common sacrifice and communal eating.[104] Among the discourses on the origins of common law, the

---

100. Exemplary passages can be found in Hooker, *Ecclesiastical Politie*, 54, 55, 57, 87, 193.

101. Coke, *Reports*, part 10, sig. A a 1 b.

102. Hooker, *Ecclesiastical Politie*, 469–70.

103. Ibid., 82.

104. On the significance of food and sacrifice, see George Bataille, *The Accursed Share* (New York: Zone Books, 1988); and on legal rites, see Peter Goodrich, "Eat-

druidic past of the British polity is one of the most persistent. These first judges reserved the punishment of exclusion from sacrifice and common food for the worst offences: "whosoever he is, that obeys not their sentence, they forbid him their sacrifices, which is amongst them the most grievous of punishments; for they who are thus interdicted, are accounted in the number of the most impious and wicked, all people shunning them, and refusing their conversation, lest they should receive damage by the infection [*contagione*] thereby."[105] Exclusion from the ceremony of sacrifice (*sacrificiis interdicunt*) deprives the interdicted both of membership of the abstract community of those that through sacrifice communicate with God and deprives the expelled subject of all speech. With the demise of the druidic religion, the sacrificial interdiction becomes incorporated into ecclesiastical excommunication and secular writs of outlawry. As regards the latter, Bracton's definition of outlawry replicates the earlier form:

> he forfeits his country and the realm [*patriam et regnum*], and he is made an exile, and the English call such a person an outlaw, and of ancient times he was accustomed to be called a friendless man, and so it seems he forfeits his friends, and hence if anyone has knowingly fed such a person after his outlawry and expulsion, and received and held communication with him in any way, or harboured or concealed him, he ought to be punished with the same punishment.[106]

The outlaw is deprived of legitimacy, of social family and community, including that of food and speech. The emblem of reason is that of a community bonded by blood in the dual sense both of inheritance or succession and of sacrifice, the one being natural and the other ceremonial. The sacrifice transports social collectivity into natural

---

ing Law: Commons, Common Land, Common Law," *Journal of Legal History* 12 (1992):246.

105. Dugdale, *Origines Juridiciales*, fol. 96 b–97 a. Dugdale's source is Caesar and is found as well in Fortescue, *De Laudibus Legum Angliae*, 29–33; Lambard, *Archeion*, 5–7; Harrison, *Historicall Description*, fol. 24 a–b.

106. Bracton, *De Legibus Angliae* (London: Longman, 1879), 2:321. See further John Rastell, *An Exposition of Certaine Difficult and Obscure Words, and Termes of the Lawes of this Realme* (1566; London: T. Wright, 1602), fol. 193 b–194 a; Cowell, *Interpreter*, under *utlagaria*. For a specimen of a bull of excommunication, see Ridley, *View*, 245–49.

order and its antithesis must be antinature and destruction. Such a person is unclean.

Aporia: Contingency and the Government of Women

The metaphoric use of femininity as a synonym of uncleanness and of the void or of nothing is one of the most common elements of Reformation polemics.[107] The rhetorical figure of woman represented the sins of the flesh and of lust as against the law of the spirit. Sacrilege, the first sin of theft from the Deity, was the sin of "a weak woman,"[108] and all subsequent or lesser sins of appearance, contact, and infidelity, respectively idolatry, fornication or adultery, and superstition, are depicted as being essentially feminine in character. In short, femininity is the sin or crime of contingency—of *contingencia*, of contact or touch—and where the cross, images, vestments, or ceremonies are attacked as heretical, their fault, like that of the harlot or the witch, is that of diverting the spirit from the incorporeal nature of truth. At one level, the sins of contact and of the flesh are literally aligned to feminine pollution, shame, uncleanness, vanity, and hypocrisy, to a "soul confused with sense."[109] At a deeper level, women serve other Gods: the feminity of false (material) signs of divinity lies not only in their power to distract, but also in their reference to a monstrous world "of nothing, that has no being," a world of fantasy and imaginations.[110] It is important to stress that the imaginary or fantastical quality of these feminine representations is not a matter of their ontology, their existence or being; they are morally nothing, they have no ethical being but are nonetheless real in the sense of appearing. The feminine is in this respect above all else immoral and unconscionable, it transgresses the boundaries of the sensible and the spiritual and conflates the world of appearance with the realm of invisible powers: fantasy becomes reality and reality fantasy. What should remain unseen is rendered visible. It is not, however, the reality or unreality of this transgression that is at issue but rather its ethics,

---

107. See particularly Robert Parker, *Scholasticall Discourse*; Sander, *Treatise of the Images*; Hammond, *Of Idolatry*, 1–3; Hammond, *Of Conscience, Scandall, Will-Worship and Superstition* (Oxford: H. Hall, 1644), 13.
108. Spelman, *Sacrilege*, 3.
109. Parker, *Scholasticall Discourse*, 138.
110. Hammond, *Of Idolatry*, 1.

and it is this ethical question that underlies the legal debate as to the
exclusion of women from public office.

This generic depiction or antiportrait of women and the antithetic
semantic field associated with femininity is, if nothing else, rhetorically indicative both of the threat constituted by the feminine and
also of a certain aporia associated with women. In legal terms, Sir
John Fortescue, in a work entitled *De Natura Legis Naturae*, written
around 1460, had devoted an entire book to the question of whether
or not women had a right to public office or succession.[111] While his
dialogue is clearly slanted in favor of its male protagonists and his
conclusion unequivocally decides the issue in favor of the traditional
civilian exclusion of women from public office on the ground that
"nature hath excluded women,"[112] what is significant is that the issue
merited such extensive coverage. Fortescue resorts ultimately to biblical arguments in rejecting the lengthily canvased claim of women
to political office and concludes in terms of the subordination of
women to men by virtue of their lack of moral sensibility and of the
higher faculties of reason more generally. It should be observed further that Fortescue's deliberations depend heavily upon Roman Catholic doctrines and upon their elaboration in civilian law. In the most
obvious of terms it should be observed that the Reformation and the
establishment of an Anglican constitution not only allowed priests
to be married but was also in large measure the product of a female
monarch, it being Queen Elizabeth I who presided most successfully
over the English settlement. The constitutional writers thus needed
to give some account of the place of women: it was, after all, Roman
law that denied the right of feminine succession, whereas English
municipal law might legitimately differ.[113] Several arguments of considerable significance were made out variously by Smith, Aylmer,
and Selden, in particular, in defense of feminine right and in support
of a view of an origin of common law that explicitly recognized the
equality and heritage of women. The importance of such texts lies

111. J. Fortescue, *De Natura Legis Naturae* (London: Private Circulation, 1869).
For a later expression of similar arguments, see Lodowick Lloyd, *A Briefe Conference
of Divers Lawes* (London: Creede, 1602), esp. 67–88.

112. Ibid., 252.

113. Bodin, *De Republica*, 746–54 gives the most extended account of the civilian
arguments against female succession. Aylmer, *Harborowe*, is subtitled *concerning the
government of women* and gives the most extended English defense of feminine
succession.

not so much in their subsequent obscurity but in their polemical or dialectical relation to foundational doctrinal treatises that were forced to denounce women precisely because antithetic views of femininity were possible and indeed stated.

In contradistinction to French and Roman law, English law knew no originary ban upon women's inheritance or dignity.[114] According to Selden, female government was the norm in antique England: the original Celtic colonies were ruled by *semnotheai*, goddesses of justice, whose name derives from the Greek Furies, also termed Themis. *Semnai theai* means venerable Goddess, to which Selden adds both a description of their awful powers and the comment "nor let it be any hindrance, that so splendid and so manly a name is taken from the weaker sex, to wit, the Goddesses."[115] Selden and Camden both find further proof of feminine rule in altar inscriptions of the words *Deis Matribus*, to the mother-goddesses, whose referent is for Selden at least the *semnotheai* of antique England.[116] After referring to English queens, such as Martia of Mercia, Selden returns again to the dignities of women by asserting the role of women in druidic war councils and citing Ovid to the effect that "virtue herself, however it came / is Female both in dress and name."[117] Against Bodin, and indeed Aristotle, Selden concludes with quantitative arguments to the effect that there were more "she-Gods" than "he-Gods" and that history equally shows a greater number of women monarchs than kings. The arguments against women are "mad rude expressions . . . not unfit for a professor in Bedlam College," for "virtue shuts no door against anybody, any sex, but freely admits all." Conscience thus dictates that both "Dame Nature" and it might be added "our Lady the Common Law" should logically impose respect for the suffrage and right of women.[118]

Selden's argument for feminine succession and dignity is in part historical or at least concerned with originary constitutions and laws.

114. Hotman, *Franco-Gallia*, 55–58 provides the most detailed historical account of the prohibition of women's succession in Gallic law.

115. Selden, *Jani Anglorum Facies Altera*, 4. Hotman, *Franco-Gallia*, 125 refers to the traditional equality of women within the English constitution, and his text is in many respects the source and object of Selden's remarks.

116. Ibid., 5.

117. Ibid., 18–19. The Ovid text is *ipsa quoque et cultu est, et nomine femina Virtus.*

118. Ibid., 20–21.

He suggests that superstition, bad manners, and weak reason alone could account for their exclusion. In a similar, though expanded argument, Aylmer exhaustively rebuts the fallacies of those who would argue against the right of women to inherit kingdoms and to govern and guide the same. His argument begins with an important though familiar assertion of the distinctiveness of the English constitution: "I say therefore that this matter belongs not to the civil law, but to the municipal law of England, for like as every field brings not forth all fruits: so is not one law mete for all countries."[119] In synoptic terms, the principal arguments against women's rule were that it was against nature, against Scripture, and against civil law. The argument from nature states that women are the weaker sex, are not equipped to govern, and are by nature and law subject to their husbands. These arguments are respectively vitiated by fallacies of consequence, accident, and category mistake. That women are weaker does not prove any inability to govern, for otherwise elderly male monarchs would be precluded from ruling. Secondly, that certain women had faults as rulers is an accident of history that cannot lead to any universal conclusion. Natural law, which alone is universal, is proved by the histories of all societies and such history provides adequate testimony of female rule. Finally, the subordination of women to their husbands does not preclude women from ruling over men in other respects; the two categories are not comparable.

The arguments proposed by Aylmer depend upon an assertion of alternative genealogies, of older and so truer or more natural laws, coincident with and coeval to the origin of English common law. The argument that Scripture precludes female government is thus rebutted by resorting to histories that are either older than the Bible or omitted from it, for "all antiquities of time, all histories and monuments, cannot be contained in so little room" as the Bible.[120] The "ancient stories" dictate the right of women to rule, as also does the antique law of England, which, in this as in many other respects, differs from the law of Rome. The principles of distributive justice require that English law be applied in England "because it best agrees with our country,"[121] and the tradition of our country is that there should be no differentiation between the sexes in matters of inheritance of office

119. Aylmer, *Harborowe*, sig. K iv a.
120. Aylmer, *Harborowe*, sig. E 4 b.
121. Ibid., sig. K 4 b.

or government. No argument, however, is offered as to the status of
patria potestas, and both authors appear to accept the civilian definition of the father's powers in domestic matters. The rule of women
is thus exclusively a question of public law right, a view confirmed
by Sir Thomas Smith, who sets out Aristotle's conception of domestic
hierarchy as the natural law of relations between male and female.[122]
Women cannot be freemen but are rather to be taken as the equivalent
of bondmen,

> who can bear no rule or jurisdiction over freemen, as they who
> be taken but as instruments and goods, and possessions of others.
> In which consideration also we do reject women, as those whom
> nature hath made to keep home and nourish their family and
> children, and not to meddle with matters abroad, nor to bear
> office in a city or commonwealth no more than children and
> infants.[123]

The only exception to this principle of feminine disability is genealogical and obtains "in such cases as the authority is annexed to the
blood and progeny, as the crown, a dutchy or an earldom, for there
the blood is respected, not the age nor the sex." Only in such cases
of succession "upon whom by right of the blood that title is
descended" can sex be ignored. In such cases, the woman could take
the place of a man, and while she did so in her own right, by
implication of descent or blood, it should always be recalled that the
system of legitimacy that accorded her such a place was defined by
a male right of succession and of property holding.

Selden's argument for the legal right of women to succeed ends
by stating, "[N]or could I forbear out of conscience with my suffrage,
to assist as far as I could, that sex, which is so great and comfortable
an importance to mankind, so sweet a refreshment amidst our sharp-
est toils, and the vicissitudes of life."[124] The context of a limited
suffrage is that of the exception. More than that, the foundational
discourses place women within an antithetic structure in which the
figure of woman or of femininity is polarized between harmony and

---

122. T. Smith, *De Republica Anglorum*, 12–13.
123. Ibid., 19.
124. Selden, *Jani Anglorum Facies Altera*, 21.

dissonance, family and chaos, succession and illegitimacy. While it is of considerable significance that feminine suffrage constituted an aporia within constitutional discourse, the foundational logic of legitimacy was structurally incapable of according women anything more than a parallel but secondary right. In philosophical terms the legal conception of community was founded upon an antithetical relation between mind and matter, spirit and body, form and substance, in which the former abstract categories were correlated with truth and with the perfect community or emblematic society established by sacrifice, sacrament, or judgment. Precisely as flesh, as contingency, contact, or touch, the feminine would destabilize the universality of law and the abstract character of homosocial community as a relation of certainty paradoxically predicated upon the incertitude of paternity. At a jurisprudential level, the metaphysical character of truth and the abstraction of lawful community were instituted in concepts of familial and social legitimacy that derived from a patristic form of power: the father was present in the son, or else the son was monstrous.[125] The two laws, spiritual and temporal, were reflected in two families, domestic and social, and in two powers, the paternal and the monarchical. More than that, the reason of law obeyed a principle of legitimacy that was inseparable from the foundation of its authority: so long as the logic and validity of law was to be constructed genealogically, according to origin and inheritance, sources and their repetition, it would necessarily replicate a model of patristic power and paternal forms of judgment. The law was dependent upon a principle of blood mythologically rooted in the soil of England and expressed in purely abstract terms in the law of the land, a law of succession or inheritance of legitimacy in which the resemblance of father to son, of imitation or *imitatio dei*, was always already a principle of exclusion of feminine right.

For the Reformation theology of Anglican community and constitution, femininity represented another sense of blood, namely that of the contingency and materiality of flesh, the immediacy of contact as flesh and as blood, as a pollutant of the purity of the line. Conceived by the reformers as image, materiality, or body, the feminine was not simply a distraction or lure away from the abstraction and

---

125. Selden, *Titles of Honour*, sig. b 4 a: "For one not like his parents is, in some sort, a Monster, that is, not like him that got him."

invisibility of the object of faith, it was a potent threat in the form of the image or counterfeit representation of other worlds and suprahuman powers. For Perkins, the power of the feminine is evident in the reality of its creations: "that witches may and do work wonders, is evidently proved . . . and the wonders wrought by them are not properly and simply miracles, but works of wonder, because they exceed the ordinary powers and capacity of men, especially such as are ignorant of Satan's hability, and the hidden causes in nature, whereby things are brought to pass."[126] The work of the feminine witch is not damnable for being unreal—"they were works truly done and effected"—but for being immoral. Works of wonder, of divination and soothsaying, are deceitful only by virtue of the "evil end and purpose in working them, which is to lie unto men" as to the hidden nature of their causes.[127] A law that borrowed substantially from the Anglican conception of a dual polity could not avoid confronting and excluding the feminine principle in antirrhetical terms. The feminine was representative not simply of another blood opposed to the invisible lineage of legal legitimacy, but its purposes were immoral and its reality defective. The feminine existed only as an antiportrait, a figure of the misappropriation of divine power, and as such it had to be excised. Such were structural constraints upon the constitution, rhetorical forms of a foundation of law that could not conceive of contact or contingency precisely because its conception of legitimacy depended upon an indefinite time of origin, or originary present that was never present. In terms of the symbolization of community and of law, the homosociality of the legal community was expressed directly in the depiction of a system of reason whose symbol was appropriately that of a woman rendered blind, *Justitia* with her face erased.[128]

Conclusion: Penitus Amputare, Inner Incisions

The rhetoric of foundation, of origins and sources, of constitution and community, is in large measure a discourse of symptoms. The

126. William Perkins, *A Discourse of the Damned Art of Witchcraft*, fol. 6 a–b.

127. Ibid., 27–28.

128. For discussion of the iconography of Justice, see David Curtis and Jean Resnik, "Images of Justice," *Yale Law Journal* 96 (1986):1727; Goodrich, "Critical Legal Studies in England"; Emmanuel Levinas, *Totality and Infinity* (Pittsburgh: Dusquene University Press, 1969).

plastic image, the trope, or the textual figure are alike signs for the
direction of vision both in a literal sense and also in an anagogic or
internal sense: the "mind's eye" or inward image is to be directed
toward a hidden grace, an invisible and imaginary source. The symbol is in Reformation terms always a monument; it moves the mind
(*movet mentum*), legitimately or falsely, from form to substance,
sense to spirit, and from body to soul. The symbolic is therefore no
more than the medium that evokes or refers to the imaginary, the
perfect community or model of relation, of which the symbol (image
or word) is a distant replica. In this respect it is interesting to consider
the disputed status of "aereall" or vanishing signs. The question posed
was that of whether the sign of the cross made on the forehead, in
the air or with water, could be idolatrous. Such signs vanished almost
immediately; their materiality was transient, and it would in many
senses be hard to conceive of such spectral signs being in themselves
objects of false worship or *latria*. For the reformers, however, the
vanishing sign was the exemplary idol by virtue of being that much
closer to the model it replicated: "but if there be any odds between
the material and the mystical [aereall] cross, it is the mystical that
hath the start . . . for the cross aereall hath more need to be abolished
than the material . . . as in the mother, so in the daughter. Provided
that the cross aereall be acknowledged the mother of the material."[129]
The material sign is in this logic a monument of the mystical, the
more evanescent or the less material the form of signification "so
much the quicker is the passage *ab imagine ad rem significatem.*"[130]

The dispute as to vanishing signs is a dispute as to the permissible
forms of the signs of the invisible. In the reformer's argument the
proper form of signification of invisibility or perfection was the word,
and in its purest form that word was spoken: God was heard but
never seen, his voice was known but not his face. The word was the
"image of the soul," and a faith that was heard came consequently
by the word, by tradition, and by text.[131] The emphasis upon the
Scriptures was thus secondary to a conception of an oratorical word
that was in its strictest sense the presence of the father in the son:

---

129. Parker, *Scholasticall Discourse*, 47–48.
130. Ibid., 49 (by means of imagination/pictures to the thing signified). See also
Calfhill, *Answere*, fol. 24 a, 29 a–b, on the power of the air.
131. Calfhill, *Answere*, fol. 64 b, also 22 a–24 a.

writing was in this respect artificial memory, a visual image—though a permitted one—of a precedent sound or speech.[132] The dual nature of all signs was thus transmitted from the visual to verbal, from the imagistic to the rhetorical and graphic, but the structure of seeing and reading were analogous. The inversion or reversal that took place was not at the level of the structure or hierarchy of reference but rather at that of the lawfulness of specific types of sign: whereas the image had previously been the mark of memory, the book of the illiterate, the symptom or model of presence, that role was now to be taken by the word, and the image was, by the same process of inversion or reversal, to be subordinated to the word. Allowing that in the age of print the text was the principal type of the word, Scripture the first source of faith, it follows that the image became an aspect of, and internal to, the text. Where in civil law the image previously took the place of knowing how to read (*pro lectione pictura est*), the text now took the place of knowing how to see: "we have not images of their bodies, but of their souls, for those things which are spoken . . . are images of their souls [and] the written lives of holy men are printed unto us, as certain lively images."[133] Rhetoric became an art of seeing well or vividly through words, through graphic signs and oral disputations, through texts and speech.[134]

The assertion of the word as the primary legitimate form of knowing became the basic method of science in the age of print.[135]

132. It is this structure of priority and reference which contemporary philosophy, and Derrida in particular, has so consistently endeavoured to deconstruct. See Derrida, *Of Grammatology*.

133. Calfhill, *Answere*, fol. 65 a.

134. The history of the rhetorical figures of vision has yet to be written. In addition to Derrida, *Margins of Philosophy*, 110ff and Deleuze, *Différence et Répétition*; see David Summers, *The Judgement of Sense* (Cambridge: Cambridge University Press, 1987); Margaret Aston, *England's Iconoclasts*, vol. 1 (Oxford: Oxford University Press, 1987); Mary Carruthers, *The Book of Memory* (Cambridge: Cambridge University Press, 1980) on the use of images in rhetoric. For more general discussion, see Serge Gruzinski, *La Guerre des Images* (Paris: Fayard, 1990); Legendre, *Désir Politique*; Michelle Le Doeuff, *The Philosophical Imaginary* (Stanford: Stanford University Press, 1989); Peter Goodrich, "Specula Laws: Image, Aesthetic and Common Law," *Law and Critique* 2 (1991):233.

135. The conventional wisdom is that print inaugurated the restraint, if not the death, of rhetoric. Thus, most notably, Roland Barthes, "L'Ancienne Rhétorique," *Communications* 16 (1970):172; and Gerard Genette, "La Rhetorique Restreinte," *Communications* 16 (1970):158; Tzetvan Todorov, *Theories of the Symbol* (Oxford:

It displaced rhetoric but did not alter its object or function, namely
that of construing a truth of which language was only ever the model,
figure, or replica. The image had come to be perceived as too worldly,
too sensual, too contingent, or too close and was replaced by the
word: the image was a false model, it represented nothing, it was
transparent, a simulacrum.[136] This transference was not without its
cost. By the same token that the text became the principal form for
the direction of vision, it became a dissimulation, an image that
forgot (repressed) that it was an image, a sign that hid its dual function
in the abstract linguistic claim that it was no more than a medium,
a transparent means of reference. It is possible to cite a double cost,
two moments of repression. The first reduced the image to language,
while the second associated imagistic or figurative language with
rhetoric and for that reason subordinated rhetoric to logic as the
proper method of science and of law.[137] In short, the rhetorical, fig-

---

Basil Blackwell, 1982). The same argument is expounded somewhat repetitively in
Vickers, *In Defence of Rhetoric*, chaps. 3 and 4. On the visual character of print,
see Walter Ong, *Ramus: Method and the Decay of Dialogue* (Cambridge: Harvard
University Press, 1958); Elizabeth Eisenstein, *The Printing Press as an Agent
of Change* (Cambridge: Cambridge University Press, 1980); Ramus, *Logike*; H.-J.
Martin, *Histoire et Pouvoirs de l'Ecrit* (Paris: Perrin, 1988); Roger Chartrier and
Henri J. Martin, eds., *Histoire de l'Edition Français I* (Paris: Fayard, 1989).

136. The relevant reforming maxim is taken from Lactantius, *ut religio nulla
sit, ubi simulachrum est*, there is no religion where there is an image. For a similar
and curiously puritanical view of the image, see Jean Baudrillard, *Simulations* (New
York: Semiotext, 1983), and even more explicitly, *La Transparence du Mal* (Paris:
Galilée, 1990), where a comparable argument is made out in relation to the simulations
of ultramodernity, as for example:

> in the style of the baroque, we are the unrestrained creators of images, but
> secretly we are iconoclasts. We are not, however, those that destroy images,
> but those that create a profusion of images *in which there is nothing to be seen*
> [*ou il n'y a rien a voir*]. The majority of contemporary images, video, painting,
> plastic arts, audiovisual, are synthetic images, literally images in which there
> is nothing to be seen, images without traces, without shadows, without
> consequences. . . . They are nothing other than the trace of something which has
> disappeared. (25)

137. The development of this repression can be traced in terms of the use of
rhetorical categories and divisions in the vernacular logics of the reformation period.
Ramus published a rhetoric to accompany the logic, and organised the *Logike* itself
rhetorically, according to dialectic (argument) and disposition (judgment); see Ramus,
Logike, 17–18, 71–72. Lever, *Arte of Reason*, organized his "witcraft" according to
topics (commonplaces), invention, figures, and memory; Fenner, *Logike and Rhetorike*, divides logic into invention and judgment; Wilson, *Rule of Reason*, divides
reason into topics, invention, division, style, and disputation. For a similar development in legal logics, see Fraunce, *Lawiers Logike*; Doderidge, *English Lawyer*,

urative, and imagistic levels of the text became the "positive unconscious" of the sign, the marks of language's long term, the history
(trauma) that tradition and its associated forms of repetition endeav-
ored—indeed existed—to forget.[138]

The full implications of the repression of rhetoric as a discipline
associated with images, with the signs of nothing, cannot be inves-
tigated here. It remains, however, to link the repression of the discipline to the rhetorical or antirrhetic structure of legal argument.
The antirrhetic was explicitly a discourse of foundations; its stake
was the delineation of a reality that would exist against or overcome all others. Its unity was thus forged against dispersion, its
nature against human artifice, its reason against sophistry and feminine deceit, its authority against irreverence or illegitimate signs. The
antirrhetic as genre thus established a specific structure of antagonism,
of prosecution or threat, a rhetorical structure that was most evident
and accessible through its characteristically antithetic figures of diction, its tropes and other incidents or accidents of expression. The
semiotic force of rhetorical study lies precisely in the ability of rhetoric
to read critically against such figures, to reconstruct the accidents or
intentions of the text in terms of a discursive structure that transcends
the apparent significance of textual image and verbal diction and so
allows a comprehension of both the stake and force of the antirrhetic
as genre. Two concluding remarks seem appropriate.

The first observation is hermeneutic. Contemporary revivals of
legal or forensic rhetoric have tended to concentrate upon that aspect
of the classical discipline which promotes argument or dialectic as
the appropriate or ethical means of institutional action. Rhetoric will
found community upon probable reasons, upon a communitarian
dialogue or dialectic in which the force or felicity of argument will
determine appropriate legal outcomes. The opposite is more likely
to be the case. Understood historically the antirrhetic character of

---

148ff. It was in a sense rhetoric's finest postclassical hour. For elements of this view,
set out in philosophical rather than historical terms, see Friedrich Nietzsche, *On
Language and Rhetoric*, trans. S. Gilman, C. Blair, and D. Parent (1873; Oxford:
Oxford University Press, 1989), 21–27.

138. This sense of positive unconscious is taken from Foucault, *Order of Things*,
ix. On the historical significance of the unconscious in history or in the *longue
durée*, see Lucien Febvre, *A New Kind of History* (Princeton: Princeton University
Press, 1978), 38–42; Fernand Braudel, *On History* (Chicago: Chicago University Press,
1980), part 2.

oratory aligned rhetoric with the adversarial fate or defense of institutions: while the discipline certainly had a function in guarding the
great theological, legal, and political orthodoxies of the institution,
it did so by dividing and opposing elements of community, by constituting hierarchies of belief, authority, and reason.[139] While the
return to rhetoric may well have the advantage of translating antagonism into discourse, it cannot plausibly be viewed as anything other
than a return to a fundamentally antithetic dispute as to the character,
foundation, and reason of the institution. Its object is difference, while
its figure, image, or emblem is most properly that of dispersion.
Language, as the very term antirrhetic implies, is the sign of plurality
and of confusion; it marks the difference of peoples and the separation
or distance that is the object of law.

At a substantive level the lesson of rhetoric's history is that the
institutional sites of oratorical and polemical practice are both the-
atrical and affective: it is the function of rhetoric to persuade and to
possess. The recurrent crises of images, as well as of words, figures,
and ornaments of speech and of law, are testimony to a dramatic
institutional stake, that of reproduction. The history of rhetoric thus
plays itself out in relation to the defense of institutional genealogies:
the question of the authority of truth and of law is answered by
establishing its lineage, by inventing or evoking a source that will
resolve what truth is, by indicating from whence it came. The legitimacy of institutions and offices, of persons and laws, is thus played
out in relation to their lineage and their rights of succession: it is
lineage or genealogy as the source of authority that is at stake in the
questioning and defense, the antirrhetic, of legal forms or institutional
traditions. When the antirrhetic figures of sanctity, nature, and reason
are repeated in the discourse or defense of law, they mask and repress
the restatement of truth as a question of blood, a question of a
legitimacy that rests upon genealogical principles, upon lineage and
its representation of a social filiation or legal constitution predicated
upon a shared father or common origin and source. In a less technical
vocabulary, it is myth, the fictions of truth and community, that
rhetoric existed to dispute and defend. To challenge the form, authority, or the reason of law is to question the order of reproduction to

---

139. For an interesting, though perhaps unconscious, exemplification of this
argument, see Gillian Rose, *Dialectic of Nihilism: Post-Structuralism and Law*
(Oxford: Basil Blackwell, 1984), 11–49.

which they belong. It is also to invoke the antirrhetic, to invoke the discourse of foundations, to question the nature of rhetoric in the rhetoric of nature. It is for this reason, to take a contemporary example, that when critical legal studies or feminist legal theory question the character and legitimacy of legal judgment they are met with the full, though unconscious, rhetorical force of the antirrhetic. The critics of doctrinal forms are nihilists,[140] they lack both decency and respect,[141] they are faithless and their reason is that of confusion and dispersion,[142] their fate is properly that of expulsion and their best expression would be silence. Critics of doctrine and of patriarchy have tended to avoid the terms and substance of this antirrhetical discourse of nature, belonging, and reason as irrational or mythological and thus inappropriate to the rational dialogue of civility and its constitutional forms. This essay has attempted to suggest that far from being extrinsic or accidental, the figures of the antirrhetic are the explicit and repeated signs of the discursive structure of foundation and constitution. They are the deep or sedimented form that the institution takes over the long term, and criticism or eulogy that endeavors to engage with questions of the history or form of law cannot avoid directly addressing the nature, sanctity, and reason; the unity, faith, and authority that is the stake of such discourse and the reality of its institution.

In more mundane jurisprudential terms, the history and recovery of the antirrhetic provides an important corrective to the rhetorical analysis of doctrinal discourse. The foundational character of doctrine and specifically of constitutional writings lies precisely in their polemical form. The treatise, the primary form of legal doctrinal writing

---

140. The contemporary aspersion of nihilism dates back to responses to American legal realism and is generally utilized in a pejorative rather than a philosophical sense. See, for discussion, Kramer, *Legal Theory*, 23–25, 240–41; Goodrich, *Reading the Law*, chap. 7; Neil Duxbury, "Some Radicalism about Realism?" *Oxford Journal of Legal Studies* 10 (1990):11. For a much-cited example, see Paul Carrington, "Of Law and the River," *Journal of Legal Education* 34 (1984):222.

141. As, for example, Charles Fried, "Jurisprudential Responses to Realism," *Cornell Law Review* 73 (1988): 331; Patrick S. Atiyah, "Correspondence," *Modern Law Review* 50 (1987):227; Robert Post, "Post-Modernism and the Law," *London Review of Books*, February, 1991.

142. As, for example, White, *Justice as Translation*, 263–64, 267. Also on closure rules, see Fish, *Doing What Comes Naturally*, 392–98. See also D. Neil MacCormick, "Reconstruction after Deconstruction: A Response to CLS," *Oxford Journal of Legal Studies* 10 (1990):539.

that develops from the Renaissance statements of the Anglican form
of civil and ecclesiastical polity, does not escape the rhetorical marks
of the antirrhetic. In its positive formulation, the treatise asserts an
identity and community that is both fictitious (imaginary) and exclusory. In specifying the demonstrative character of its reasoning and
the comprehensiveness of its jurisdiction, the treatise may not need
to invoke explicitly the antiportrait of its opponents. In its modern
positivised form the legal treatise is most usually content to "refute
by silence." Its silence, however, is not without the traces of its
polemical motives or origins. In one sense the pure or normative
character of the treatise as a statement of a system of positive rules
of law is necessarily iconic: its normativity expresses its distance from
the sociality that it both constitutes and regulates. In this respect,
its iconic character opposes it to the diversity and contingency of the
social: the unity of the normative order is purchased at the price of
dissimulation; its coherence is the mask of the diversity of its object.
It is constituted against the social and against the historical particularity of the subjects of law. In more classical terms, it defines itself
against contingency (antinature), private reason, and imagination. A
demonstrative style is in this sense no more than a figure or image
of proof, and the treatise, in being the exemplary work of demonstration, is also the strongest form of figuration: it represents or
imagines a purity of reason, an ideal that legal practice can never
achieve. In a secondary sense, the treatise can be read symptomat-
ically in terms of the explicit traces of the antirrhetic that reside in
the inessential and marginal characteristics of the treatise. Refutation
by silence or the demonstration that proves or "shows"[143] the truth
of that which lies in controversy cannot escape the polemical necessity
of policing the boundaries of the treatise. Precisely as doctrine, as
teaching, it has to persuade, and that persuasion, in its own terms,
transmits a language and forms of argument that developed over the
long term of an agonistic and adversarial legal practice. The polemical
form of that practice gains expression at a higher level of abstraction
in terms of categorial distinctions in which doctrinal writing separates
itself from questions of political and ethical judgment, from questions
of justice and of social change, as well as from any explicit expression
of its own epistemic properties or rhetorical style.

---

143. Lever, *Arte of Reason*, 99.

Becoming American: High Treason and Low Invective in the Republic of Laws

Robert A. Ferguson

The trial transcript deserves to receive some of the same attention that the judicial decision currently enjoys in rhetorical analysis.[1] If transcripts are decidedly more opaque, less accessible, and less dramatic than final opinions, they are richer in the range of commentary that they include, and they tell us much about the choices made in a final opinion. As complete records of court proceedings, transcripts register the conflict in the advocacy system in ways that a judicial decision ignores in the name of judgment. The unavoidable redundancies in courtroom presentation can be tiresome for the transcript reader, but they also reveal, as nothing else quite can, the real preoccupations in the flow of legal argument. The repetition in courtroom exchange also supplies a better perspective for understanding the formulation of story that lies at the center of all courtroom proceedings.

Every trial presents at least two conflicting stories, sometimes many more, in its approach to the events that are subject to determination. The court decision is invariably a gloss on these stories if just because one of its purposes is to choose between them. The

1. For just a few recent examples of rhetorical analyses of judicial opinions, see Richard A. Posner, *Law and Literature: A Misunderstood Relation* (Cambridge: Harvard University Press, 1988); James Boyd White, *Justice as Translation: An Essay in Cultural and Legal Criticism* (Chicago: University of Chicago Press, 1990); Richard Weisberg, *Poethics: and Other Strategies of Law and Literature* (New York: Columbia University Press, 1992); and Robert A. Ferguson, "The Judicial Opinion as Literary Genre," *Yale Journal of Law and the Humanities* 2 (Winter 1990): 201.

transcript, by way of contrast, conveys the making of stories and, in the moment, sudden realizations of either the limitation or the power of language. To the extent that the stories in trials deal with aberrant or at least mysterious behavior—behavior requiring comprehension and demarcation—the transcript is an ideal source of cultural realization. What story can a community tell itself? What is the nature of the community that listens? What explanation is it ready to hear?

Only the fullest record of the attempt to speak can answer these questions. As the complete chronicle of a courtroom event, the spontaneous writing down of everything that is said there, the trial transcript comes closer to evoking the overall range of communal pressures than the crafted conclusion of a presiding judge, and it is especially illuminating for what it does *not* contain. There is no better historical artifact of choices not made. Faced as it is with the disruption and perhaps even the threat of uncertain conduct, the community in a courtroom seeks resolution, but the very nature of that disruption can cut across the desire for ultimate explanations. Trials are often the social circumstances that force a community to rearticulate its values, but the uncertain give-and-take of courtroom debate also demonstrates that articulation can be a threat. A community engages only in that narrative of events that it is ready to receive. For all of these reasons, trial transcripts are particularly useful cultural barometers in moments of crisis.

This essay takes such a moment of crisis to show the value of trial transcripts in a cultural analysis. The American Revolution supplies an obvious context for examining a community in a time of rearticulation, and the year 1780 marks a particularly difficult moment in that endeavour. The Continental Army has reached a low point in 1780, suffering even worse that January and February than it had two years before at Valley Forge. Disasters in the southern theater— the surrender of Charleston to the British in May and the defeat of the army at Camden in August—have left Americans groaning under the reality of unending war and doubting the patriotic cause.[2] Hard upon these catastrophes comes a conspiracy to betray West Point,

---

2. Charles Royster has traced these difficulties and the overall loss of patriotic spirit in 1780 in "'The Nature of Treason': Revolutionary Virtue and American Reactions to Benedict Arnold," *William and Mary Quarterly*, 3d series, 36 (April 1979): 163.

the most important fort and arsenal in America, into British hands. When the conspiracy is exposed in late September 1780, the charge of treason reaches to the very center of George Washington's command, and it grips the new nation like no other event of the times.

This cry of treason is particularly volatile in a national community that is just forming. Since the act of becoming American in the Revolution requires rebellion, the language of community and the specific accusation of treason double back upon themselves. Meanwhile, the whole framework of debate in eighteenth-century America labors under another, more philosophical, division. Scholars long have noted conflicting patterns between "the Age of Reason and the Age of Enthusiasm" in the formation of American character. This "war between reason and emotion" plays itself out between the largely secular notions of the Enlightenment and the religious explanations of an older order.[3] Of course, courtrooms are the secular symbol of the modern republic of laws in this conflict. But if treason is a crime for determination in those courts, it is also an ancient transgression couched in religious explanation and divine sanction.

Not surprisingly, then, the uncertainties of 1780 force Americans toward an orchestration of competing discourses. The republic of laws and the Bible culture of reform Protestantism unite here in ways both uneasy and natural. Unfortunately, strict separation of church and state in post-Revolutionary culture has kept us from seeing either the power or the cultural necessity of this juncture. Voluminous records left in the wake of any major trial in American culture allow one to see competing discourses at every level, and the narratives around the trial of 1780 are expressly valuable in this regard. They demonstrate, among other things, a complicated truth about eighteenth-century American culture: if becoming a citizen in 1776 is predicated upon the idea of innate reason, the attempt to understand the new nation requires a faith beyond itself.

In the spread of the Enlightenment, treason remains a medieval crime. John Locke, in defending natural rights, makes it the greatest offense one can commit in the English world; a traitor should be treated as "the common Enemy and Pest of Mankind."[4] Punishment for treason,

---

3. For a typical example, used here, see Henry F. May, *The Enlightenment in America* (New York: Oxford University Press, 1976), 42–65.

4. John Locke, "The Second Treatise of Government: An Essay Concerning the

perhaps in consequence, continues to rely on the most appalling and rigid of ancient forms—forms that in themselves reach back to atavistic rituals. As late as 1769, within the steady narrative pace of Blackstone's *Commentaries*, encompassing reason and order suddenly give way to something "solemn and terrible," something decidedly primitive, namely:

1. That the offender be drawn to the gallows, and not be carried or walk; though usually a sledge or hurdle is allowed, to preserve the offender from the extreme torment of being dragged on the ground or pavement. 2. That he be hanged by the neck, and then cut down alive. 3. That his entrails be taken out, and burned, while he is yet alive. 4. That his head be cut off. 5. That his body be divided into four parts. 6. That his head and quarters be at the King's disposal.

Nor does official punishment end in death. Attainder, forfeiture, and corruption of blood in the traitor's line—all part of a judgment of treason—generate "future incapacities of inheritance even to the twentieth generation."[5]

Both the gravity of the offense and the corresponding horror in punishment take on an added significance in Revolutionary America.[6] When Benjamin Franklin supposedly tells the other members of the Second Continental Congress in 1776 that "we must, indeed, all hang together, or most assuredly we shall all hang separately," he is reminding them of their treason in the eyes of the British Empire.[7] The

---

True Original, Extent, and End of Civil Government," *Two Treatises of Government*, ed. Peter Laslett (1690; Cambridge: Cambridge University Press, 1988), 418, sec. 230.

5. William Blackstone, *Commentaries on the Laws of England*, 4 vols. (Oxford: Clarendon Press, 1765–69), 4:92, 370, 374, 380–81. Blackstone does note "an almost general mitigation of such part of these judgments as savour of torture or cruelty" in modern times to the extent of "there being very few instances (and those accidental or by negligence) of any person's being embowelled or burned, *till previously deprived of sensation by strangling*" (Emphasis added).

6. For confirmation that "the American law of treason was the law of England transferred to a new home," see Bradley Chapin, *The American Law of Treason: Revolutionary and Early National Origins* (Seattle: University of Washington Press, 1964), 3–9. Chapin concludes that "what was old far outweighed what was new."

7. Jared Sparks, ed., *The Works of Benjamin Franklin*, 10 vols. (Boston: Hilliard, Gracy and Co., 1836–40), 1:408.

warning is part of a cultural refrain, one that goes to the very essence of being American in colonial and early republican society.

From the moment that a rhetoric of opposition even implies the separate possibility of revolution, treason is the impossible problem in Anglo-American exchange. Already in 1721, Jeremiah Dummer, in *A Defence of the New-England Charters*, can in one breath insist on a response to the "Unnatural insult" in British denial of American rights and in the next reject as ludicrous all thought of unlawful resistance. Writes Dummer, "[I]t would not be more absurd to place two of his Majesty's Beef-Eaters to watch an Infant in the Cradle, that it don't rise and cuts its Father's Throat, then to guard these weak infant Colonies, to prevent their shaking off the *British* Yoke."[8] And yet Dummer's metaphors belie the surface of their meanings, and these discrepancies suggest why John Adams later refers to *A Defence of the New-England Charters* as a handbook of the Revolution.[9] To the extent that British rule is a "yoke," it implies the possibility of being thrown off. An infant cannot commit parricide, but, later and often enough, children do revolt against their parents. By 1750, Jonathan Mayhew's sermon *A Discourse Concerning Unlimited Submission and Nonresistance to the Higher Powers* has built these contradictions into an involved dialectic of how Americans must simultaneously "learn to be *free* and to be *loyal*."[10]

In the ensuing continuum of radical pamphleteering, rebellion is the most abominable of crimes. An endless flow of questions about the true nature of loyalty seeks to qualify the stigma of traitor. Assurances of loyalty compete with discussions of a legitimate right of resistance. In part, the very horror of treason dictates the separate possibility, in Locke's words, that "all resisting of *Princes* is not Rebellion."[11] In part, too, Americans recognize their right of resistance

8. Jeremiah Dummer, *A Defense of the New-England Charters* (Boston: B. Green and Company, 1745), 22, 32.

9. For one of the most detailed of John Adams's several statements concerning the importance of Dummer's *Defence of the New-England Charters*, see John Adams to William Tudor, 11 August 1818, in *The Works of John Adams, Second President of the United States*, ed. Charles Francis Adams, 10 vols. (1850–56; New York: Books for Libraries Press, 1960), 10:343.

10. Jonathan Mayhew, *A Discourse Concerning Unlimited Submission And No-Resistance to the Higher Powers: With Some Reflections on the Resistance made to King Charles I, And on the Anniversary of his Death* (Boston: D. Fowle and D. Gookin, 1750), 54.

11. Locke, *Two Treatises of Government*, 419, sec. 232.

only in the loyalty that guarantees their continuing prerogatives as Englishmen. To resist encroachment is to celebrate those prerogatives rooted in common law and English custom from time out of memory. To rebel, quite the contrary, signifies a break from the British Empire; it means the desertion of rights rather than the exercise of them.

The chasm between legitimate resistance and outrageous rebellion helps to explain Patrick Henry's famous exchange with other members of the Virginia House of Burgesses in the Stamp Act crisis of 1765. When Henry proclaims that "Caesar had his Brutus, Charles the First his Cromwell, and George the Third—" the sequence prompts interrupting cries of "*TREASON!*" in the House. "And George the Third," counters Henry above the din, "may profit by their example—if this be treason, make the most of it."[12] The exchange, at least on Henry's part, is deliberately contrapuntal. The juxtaposition of perceived connotations (a cautionary note for his king versus the implied threat of revolt) increases the whole by "making the most" of opposition. At the same time, "treason" shatters every limit in legitimate opposition, and Henry himself must apologize immediately for the overall effect, saying "that if he had affronted the Speaker, or the house, he was ready to ask pardon, and he would show his loyalty to his majesty King George the third at the expense of the last drop of his blood."[13] Henry's words and reaction to them in the House of Burgesses typify a struggle to think the unthinkable in eighteenth-century America. They also occur at exactly that moment in time, 1765, when colonists begin to refer to themselves as Americans more frequently than as Englishmen.[14]

The shift toward a separate identity takes place in a spirit of opposition that nonetheless resists ultimate transgression. No eighteenth-century American embraces the title of traitor. To do so would mean to reject the most basic communal premises of the time. In the most influential colonial writing of the 1760s, John Dickinson explains both the problem and the overlapping parameters in American identity

---

12. For an account of Henry's words and their context, see Norine Dickson Campbell, *Patrick Henry: Patriot and Statesman* (Old Greenwich, Conn.: Devin-Adair, 1969), 56–61.

13. Merrill Jensen, *The Founding of a Nation: A History of the American Revolution 1763–1776* (New York: Oxford University Press, 1968), 103–4.

14. Evidence for this shift is based on content analyses of newspapers cited by Charles S. Hyneman and Donald S. Lutz in *American Political Writing during the Founding Era 1760–1805*, 2 vols. (Indianapolis: Liberty Press, 1983), 1:656.

when he observes that "it will be impossible to determine whether an *American's* character is most distinguishable, for his loyalty to his Sovereign, his duty to his mother country, his love of freedom, or his affection for his native soil."[15] The pain and the craft in Revolutionary rhetoric come in the necessity of making just that impossible determination.

Faced with the preconditions of loyalty and love of freedom as increasingly contradictory bases of identity, American ideologists fashion rhetorical strategies that separate treason from the Revolutionary cause. In legal terms, protecting the people against arbitrary power ceases to be rebellion and becomes a natural right of defense.[16] In religious terms, in the motto that Franklin and Jefferson make famous, "Rebellion to Tyrants is Obedience to God."[17] As natural law justifies opposition, so divine law brings resistance into the higher realm of piety, but neither frame of reference welcomes the extreme of treason, and accusations of treason flourish on every side in Anglo-American politics. The result is a reversal of implications that heightens the crime.

In effect, rebellion and loyalty change places in the cultural formation of national identity. By 1774, even as the British navy closes the ports of Massachusetts, Nathaniel Niles, preaching in Newbury-port, decides that anyone "who infringes on liberty rebels against good government, and ought to be treated as a rebel. It matters not what station he fills; he is a traitor."[18] In 1775, the Reverend John Cleaveland of Ipswich applies this logic when he consigns Thomas

---

15. John Dickinson, "Letter III," *Letters from a Farmer in Pennsylvania*, in *Empire and Nation*, ed. Forrest McDonald (Englewood Cliffs, N.J.: Prentice-Hall, 1962), 17. The *Letters* first appear as a series of newspaper articles between December 2, 1767 and February 15, 1768 and are reissued as a complete work immediately thereafter.

16. The right of resistance through doctrines of natural law is everywhere in American pamphleteering after it is raised in 1750 by Jonathan Mayhew in *Discourse Concerning Unlimited Submission*, 29–30, 38–40, 44–45. Reaching back to the Puritan revolution of the 1640s, Mayhew decides that "it was not [rebellion]; but a most righteous and glorious stand made in defense of the natural and legal rights of the people against the unnatural and illegal encroachments of arbitrary power."

17. The motto so often employed by Franklin and Jefferson also reaches back to the Puritan revolution, where John Bradshaw, the regicide judge, first uses it against Charles I in the legal proceedings against him. See George Earlie Shankle, *American Mottoes and Slogans* (New York: H. W. Wilson, 1941), 146.

18. Nathaniel Niles, *Two Discourses on Liberty*, in Hyneman and Lutz, *American Political Writing*, 1:271.

Gage, governor of Massachusetts and commander of the British armies, straight to hell. As Cleaveland tells Gage, "[Y]ou are not only a robber, a murderer, a usurper, but a wicked Rebel: A rebel against the authority of truth, law, equity the English constitution of government, these colony states, and humanity itself."[19] These inversions reach their logical conclusion in 1776 with Thomas Paine and *Common Sense.* Paine warns against a state of affairs in which "there is no such thing as treason; wherefore every one thinks himself at liberty to act as he pleases." Obviously, treason must be relocated. "A line of distinction should be drawn," Paine argues, "between English soldiers taken in battle, and inhabitants of America taken in arms. The first are prisoners, but the latter traitors. The one forfeits his liberty, the other his head."[20] Loyalty and treason really have switched places in America, and they magnify each other in the process.

Americans, then and now, are obsessed with the notion of treason because they come to their own original identity through the concept. Every eighteenth-century American faces the accusation one way or the other, and the solidarity of initial union, as Franklin points out, depends on the awful price of failure. It is clearly foreseen by both radical Whigs and loyalists that those who lose the Revolution must suffer the designation of traitor and the consequences. Inevitably, if everyone is guilty of treason, then no one can be. Paine captures the essence of that paradox when he claims in 1776 "there is no such thing as treason."

Several things follow from this tangled state of affairs. First, Americans are curiously vulnerable, politically and psychologically, to a charge of treason leveled either at themselves or others. Second, a new definition of treason with appropriate controls is crucial to the evolution of the republic of laws that begins in 1776. Third, the testing of that definition necessarily takes place in the courtroom, where the procedures of indictment, trial, and punishment must somehow handle the volatile emotional and political lines of force that enter into and sometimes shape legal decisions. Fourth, the American

---

19. *Essex Gazette*, 13 July 1775. See also Philip Davidson, *Propaganda and the American Revolution 1763–1783* (Chapel Hill: University of North Carolina Press, 1941), 22–23.

20. Philip S. Foner, ed., *The Complete Writings of Thomas Paine*, 2 vols. (New York: Citadel Press, 1945), 1:43–44.

courtroom, already an obvious gauge of identity in the republic of laws, is an especially powerful barometer of thought and cultural understanding when it considers an indictment for treason, the ultimate crime against community.

A hard fact helps to illuminate the importance of these assumptions. If Americans remain in doubt about charges of treason and if they rather too promiscuously level such charges against each other, finding hidden enemies within and abroad, they do so in part because of their certainty, their conviction, that treason *has* been committed; the terms of the Revolutionary struggle decree this much. Moreover, in all of the turmoil of the Revolution, there is one person in the course of events that every member of the English-speaking world can safely call a traitor. That person is Benedict Arnold.

Rhetorically, the example of Benedict Arnold thrives on a compound negative. For while Arnold goes unpunished for his treason and remains unrepentant, his British collaborator, Major John André, is caught, tried, convicted, and executed as a spy in a way that troubles his captors; they are left wishing that their own inexorable machinery of military law might be stopped. No other episode of the Revolutionary War receives such frequent dramatic treatment as the execution of Major André.[21] Certainly, no other produces a more remarkable emotional response among wartime participants. "Never, perhaps, did any man suffer death with more justice, or deserve it less," writes Alexander Hamilton of André.[22] As George Washington's

21. For an extended analysis of just this point, see Brander Matthews's introductory essay in William Dunlap, *André; A Tragedy in Five Acts*, ed. Brander Matthews (New York: Dunlap Society, 1887), vii–xxiv. For one of the earliest formal recognitions of the unique literary possibilities of the André-Arnold conspiracy in Revolutionary lore, see William Gilmore Simms, "Benedict Arnold as a Subject for Fictitious Story," *Southern and Western Magazine* 1 (April 1845): 257. In Simms's words, "no other series of events, in all that history, seem more naturally to group themselves in the form of story." See also Simms, *Views and Reviews in American Literature, History and Fiction*, ed. C. Hugh Holman (Cambridge, Mass.: Harvard University Press, 1962), 64.

22. Lieutenant-Colonel Alexander Hamilton to Lieutenant-Colonel John Laurens, October 1780, in *Papers concerning The Capture And Detention of Major John André*, ed. Henry B. Dawson (Yonkers: The Gazette, 1866), 101. Where possible, all references to primary materials are to the Dawson edition because of its relatively complete collection of both official and popular materials on the event. Hamilton's letter to Laurens, one of the great set pieces of the affair, appears in print shortly after the execution of André on 2 October 1780 in the *Pennsylvania Gazette*, 25 October 1780.

aide-de-camp, Hamilton is directly involved in the proceedings, but he also writes that "every thing that is amiable in virtue, in fortitude, in delicate sentiment, and accomplished manners, pleads for him. . . . I reverenced his merit." "My feelings," he will later confess, "were never put to so severe a trial."[23] "I became so deeply attached to Major André," writes another important senior officer, "that I can remember no instance where my affections were so fully absorbed in any man. . . . All the spectators seemed to be overwhelmed by the affecting spectacle [of André's execution], and many were suffused in tears."[24] A medical observer confirms the accuracy of this description: "the spot was consecrated by the tears of thousands."[25]

Why should seasoned leaders and veteran soldiers of many campaigns be moved so profoundly by an enemy whose personal treachery and ungentlemanly engagement in espionage threatened their very existence? It is true enough that André dies bravely, that his situation depicts "an ancient story of guilt, sacrifice, and betrayal," and that, as the head of British Military intelligence in North America, his sudden fall from a great height partakes of tragedy—all arguments regularly presented to explain his final appeal—but more is at stake in American reactions.[26]

The overall situation touches the vulnerabilities and the needs of a still-fragile American identity in very specific terms. Together, André and Arnold summarize an American predicament, and Hamilton sees better than he knows when he writes of André, "[T]here was, in truth, no way of saving him. Arnold, or he, must have been the victim: the former was out of our power."[27] Benedict Arnold is indeed beyond the power of Revolutionary America to determine or control—he is the ungraspable phantom of an ideological nightmare. George Washington, never a fanciful man, blurts out that nightmare in the instant of discovery. "Arnold has betrayed us!" he cries out to Hamilton and

23. Alexander Hamilton to Elizabeth Schuyler, 2 October 1780, and Alexander Hamilton to John Laurens, in Dawson, Papers, 94, 95.
24. Major Benjamin Tallmadge, "Narrative of the Detention of Major André," in Dawson, Papers, 12–13.
25. "Narrative of Dr. James Thacher, of the Army of the Revolution, Concerning The Execution of Major André," in Dawson, Papers.
26. For the best overall account of these elements and their appeal as well as the quotation in this sentence, see Robert D. Arner, "The Death of Major André: Some Eighteenth-Century Views," Early American Literature 9 (Spring 1976): 52.
27. Dawson, Papers, 105–6.

the Marquis de Lafayette on the afternoon of 24 September 1780. "Whom can we trust now?"[28]

The surfaces in that betrayal can be summarized quickly.[29] In the fall of 1780, Benedict Arnold, a major general and a legitimate hero in three earlier campaigns of the American army (Quebec, Valcour, and Saratoga), contrives to betray the critical fortress and arsenal of West Point into British hands in exchange for substantial monetary rewards, the promise of a later pension, immediate commanding rank in the British Army of North America, and a per capita bounty for captured Americans, including possibly General Washington himself. Negotiations between Arnold and high-ranking British officers extend across two years, starting in 1778, and Arnold as commander of American troops in Philadelphia must first maneuver with Washington to obtain command of West Point, gateway to the Hudson River and the line of forts along it. The conspiracy, as such, depends on the conviction of Sir Henry Clinton, then commander of British forces, that the capture of West Point would split American forces in a decisive fashion. "Had it succeeded," Clinton later writes, "all agree it would have ended the rebellion."[30] Minimally, the capture of West Point would have given control of the Hudson River to the British navy and its banks to the British army.

If historians now question General Clinton's expectations of total victory, no less a participant than General Lafayette concedes that all might have been "consequently lost." Lafayette, a special confidant of Washington on the occasion, writes that West Point would have fallen but for "an almost incredible combination of accidents" that beset the conspirators; "the plot," he concludes, "was within an ace of succeeding."[31] It fails because André is caught out of uniform

28. James Thomas Flexner, *Washington, the Indispensable Man* (Boston: Little, Brown, 1969), 145. The Marquis de Lafayette confirms both Washington's reaction and the general atmosphere in his own account of the event: "Gloom and distrust seemed to pervade every mind, and I have never seen General Washington so affected by any circumstance," quoted in James Thomas Flexner, *The Traitor and the Spy: Benedict Arnold and John André* (1953; Boston: Little, Brown, 1975), 372.

29. My account, unless otherwise indicated, is summarized from Frances Vivian, "The Capture and Death of Major André," *History Today* 12 (December 1957): 813; Flexner, *Traitor and Spy*; and J. E. Morpurgo, *Treason at West Point: The Arnold-André Conspiracy* (New York: Mason/Charter Publishing, 1975).

30. Quoted from Noemie Emery, *Washington: A Biography* (New York: Putnam's Sons, 1976), 266.

31. "Narrative of General LaFayette," Marquis de Lafayette to the Chevalier de

behind American lines on 23 September 1780 with incriminating
documents about the defenses of West Point—documents in Arnold's
own hand; the two conspirators have just met in secret rendezvous
to insure Arnold's resolve. Even then, Washington infers that André
would have eluded final capture but for "an unaccountable deprivation of presence of mind in a man of first abilities."[32] Arnold, for
his part, escapes by a hairsbreadth when he receives word of André's
capture.

The contrasts in André and Arnold go well beyond mere presence
of mind. The behavior of each supports a radically different line of
understanding in Revolutionary American culture, and the perspective on André is the easiest to explain. Though English, André typifies
the danger to every American of chance identification in the ever-
shifting neutral territory of a bloody civil war—so much so that it
is André and not Nathan Hale who dominates the spy legend in
American literature.[33] Neither courage nor intelligence is wanting in
André; failure comes, rather, in the lack of a certain low cunning,
in the major's unwillingness to compromise his honor or presumed
consistency through disguise. When captured, André's military car-
riage and gentlemanly bearing give him away before his words do,
a point James Fenimore Cooper will later emphasize in his fictional
rendition of the André story, *The Spy: A Tale of the Neutral Ground*
(1821), the first important American novel on the Revolution.[34]

Sincerity of character—a trait of almost obsessive importance to
Americans engaged in rebellion—and the assumption of honor that
forms the foundation of that sincerity are the captured André's most

la Luzerne, 26 September 1780, Lafayette to Madame de Sesse, 4 October 1780,
Lafayette to Madame de Lafayette, 8 October 1780, in Dawson, *Papers*, 204–9.

32. Quoted in Vivian, "Capture and Death," 813.

33. For a previous analysis that raises this point, see Arner, "Death of Major
André," 62–63.

34. The presiding officer of the troops who capture André, Major Benjamin
Talmadge, observes in his own narrative of the event that "as soon as I saw Anderson
[André's alias], and especially after I saw him walk across the floor, I became
impressed with the belief that he had been *bred to arms*." Almost immediately after,
André asks for pen and ink and voluntarily "disclosed his true character to be '*Major
John André, Adjutant-General to the British army*'" (Dawson, *Papers*, 9–10). In
Cooper's novel, the British officer Henry Wharton in disguise represents these char-
acteristics in André. The equally disguised figure of Washington, Mr. Harper, immediately penetrates Wharton's mask. See James Fenimore Cooper, *The Spy: A Tale of
the Neutral Ground*, ed. James H. Pickering (Schenectady, N.Y.: New College and
University Press, 1971), 54, 68, chaps. 2 and 4.

apparent traits. As important, however, is the way that sincerity and honor must recover from an even more apparent unseemliness. All of these traits dominate the first paragraphs of André's letter to Washington on the day after his capture:

> What I have as yet said concerning myself was in the justifiable attempt to be extricated; I am too little accustomed to duplicity to have succeeded.
> I beg your Excellency will be persuaded that no alteration in the temper of my mind, or apprehension for my safety, induces me to take the step of addressing you, but that it is to secure myself from an imputation of having assumed a mean character, for treacherous purposes or self-interest—as conduct incompatible with the principles that actuated me, as well as with my condition in life.[35]

The circumlocutions, abstractions, and archness of the eighteenth-century epistolary style try to gloss admitted duplicity in the principles of virtue and honor, proper station and disinterestedness. They represent higher forms of "extrication" and response to the "imputation of having assumed a mean character." In short, André's embarrassment in the charge of espionage parallels Revolutionary Americans' comparable rhetorical problem in the charge of rebellion. As gentlemen do not spy, so citizens do not rebel. The rest of André's letter to Washington records the circumstances of necessity that have "betrayed" him into "the vile condition of an enemy in disguise." He writes as one "involuntarily an impostor" and "to vindicate my fame . . . not to solicit security." Four of the last eight sentences dwell on the idea of honor. Their thrust is to prove "that though unfortunate, I am branded with nothing dishonorable." The American officers identify with this logic and their captive because his rhetoric is also theirs. A similar pattern of conscious elevation "impels" the

---

35. Major John André to Commander George Washington, 24 September 1780, in *Proceedings of a Board of General Officers Held By Order of His Excellency Gen. Washington, Commander in Chief of the Army of the United States of America, Respecting Major John André, Adjutant General of the British Army, September 29, 1780* (Philadelphia: Francis Bailey, 1780) as reprinted in Dawson, *Papers*, 20–22. All further references to the trial transcript will be to this source, hereinafter referred to as *Proceedings*.

Declaration of Independence. Americans know and identify with the measured calm, the reluctance in negative circumstance, the claim of betrayal, the need for a higher extrication, above all, the concern for world opinion and for sacred honor.

Another homology exists between Major André's proud sense of decorum and the controlling tones of the published proceedings of the Board of General Officers who adjudge him guilty of spying and arrange for his execution. Trials that grip the communal imagination tend to formalize ideological paradoxes, and the narratives about them attempt to resolve the predicament of conflict in a moment of decision by subsuming contending voices into that decision. Major André's measured calm and resignation are just what Washington, his assigned court of officers, and, for that matter, the federal government need in a dangerous situation. Washington wants "a careful examination . . . as speedily as possible." André's many acknowledgments of propriety during that examination "evince that the proceedings against him were not guided by passion or resentment."[36] In the reimposition of decorum all previous disruption, jeopardy, and unpleasantness can be relegated to the past. Significantly, Congress arranges for immediate general publication of the transcript of André's trial and designates a day of national thanksgiving to celebrate the narrow escape from peril.

George Washington and to a lesser extent the federal government must rectify impressions generated by the treason at West Point. Their published transcript of the court of inquiry supplies the means. Washington, after all, has kept Arnold in command at Philadelphia despite evidence of administrative and financial malfeasance; he has continued to sustain Arnold over repeated congressional objection; he has given Arnold command of West Point against his own better judgment; and he has allowed Arnold to slip away into the opposing camp, where, as an extremely able British general, the traitor will prove a nuisance for the rest of the war. Washington needs answers that will minimize his own vulnerabilities and that will calm the nation's fears. Accordingly, his narrative of Major André's trial has the effect of reducing Arnold and treason to scale by making André and espionage the appropriate subject of decision.

A substitution of type rather than a comparison in degree is

36. *Proceedings*, 20, 41.

what is needed. When one of his own officers, Lieutenant Colonel John Laurens, indulges in a comparison, imagining that "Arnold must undergo a punishment comparatively more severe [than André's] in the permanent, increasing torment of a mental hell," Washington resists the inference. "I am mistaken if, at *this* time 'Arnold is undergoing the torment of a mental Hell,'" he responds. "He [Arnold] wants feeling. From some traits of his character, which have lately come to my knowledge, he seems to have been so hackneyed in villainy, and so lost to all sense of honor and shame, that, while his faculties will enable him to continue his sordid pursuits, there will be no time for remorse."[37] But this response raises its own question. How could such a complete villain escape his own commander's detection and for so long? Major André is a special kind of surrogate for the unrepentant Arnold, and Washington's aide-de-camp Hamilton recognizes the connection on the day of execution. "Poor André suffers to-day," Hamilton explains to his fiancée, "hard-hearted policy calls for a sacrifice. He must die."[38]

How André dies, how he fills the role of sacrifice, is a function of the trial transcript. Two letters from Washington as commander in chief to Congress open the court record, and they carefully situate and control the narrative of André from start to finish. The first communication explains that the capture of André *enables* the escape of Arnold; the second announces the execution of André in formal closure of the very subject under investigation.

The transcript itself is a curious document. The proceedings of the court of inquiry occupy just five pages in a twenty-four page record, and half of these pages are given over to reiterated lists of the officers present; the court's formal reasoning and judgment require fewer than two hundred words.[39] The rest of the transcript is a composite of seventeen letters exchanged during the event: the earliest is a letter from André to Arnold proving the former's plan of disguise; three are from Washington to Congress and his judicial board of inquiry; two come from André to Washington; six involve formal

---

37. John Laurens to George Washington, 4 October 1780, and George Washington to John Laurens, 13 October 1780, quoted in Saul K. Padover, ed., *The Washington Papers: Basic Selections from the Public and Private Writings of George Washington* (New York; Grosset and Dunlap, 1955), 367.

38. Hamilton to Elizabeth Schuyler, 2 October 1780, in Dawson, *Papers*, 94.

39. *Proceedings*, 17–41, esp. 19–20, 22–26, 29–30.

exchanges between the heads of the two armies; four, and the longest, come from the pen of Benedict Arnold (three to Washington, one to Clinton); and one letter, the most affecting, is from André to his British commander, Sir Henry Clinton, absolving Clinton of all responsibility for André's fate.

The generic dominance of the epistolary form encourages a predictable difference of views with André, Arnold, and the British commanders, Sir Henry Clinton and James Robertson, contesting formal American proceedings against Major André as a spy. Yet genre also oversees and thereby governs that conflict in views. The form and its constraints allow for a similarity of diction and a quiescence of tone among gentlemen of letters that dignify the ceremonial proceedings against André and enter into its conclusion "that Major André, Adjutant-General to the British army, ought to be considered as a spy from the enemy, and that agreeable to the law and usage of nations, it is their opinion he ought to suffer death."[40]

The sequence of letters fulfills the needs of narrative in the same manner that similar patterns inform the epistolary novel. Each separate voice, recognizable within the whole, participates in a similarity of modes and situation within conflict. When the narrative ends, the story is closed. In their polished punctiliousness, these aspects of the trial transcript also convey the sense of reintegration and balance that Washington and Congress desire. As in every accepted judicial decision, the disruption of crime yields to the discursive reenactment of order through language. The words themselves help signify to a governing elite—in this case the Revolutionary Army and by extension Congress—that it is, in fact, governing.

One element, though, resists these integrative tendencies. The prisoner's cooperation in the highest level of procedural decorum underscores a discrepancy in the mode of his punishment, one that vexes every major account of the trial and execution. André, "buoyed above the terror of death" on the day before his execution, writes a second letter to Washington asking to be shot as a soldier and not hanged as a spy. "Sympathy towards a soldier," he pleads, "will surely induce your Excellency and a military tribunal to adapt the mode of my death to the feelings of a man of honor." André adds that he and Washington together can hope to put all resentment behind them

---

40. *Proceedings*, 29-30.

only "by being informed that I am not to die on a gibbet."[41] This
letter boosts the epistolary form of the trial transcript to the level of
sentimental fiction, where emotion is distilled and appreciated in
writer, recipient, and the later reader as a vicarious participant. But
Washington breaks that mold by refusing to respond in any fashion.
Notably, every eyewitness description of the execution lingers over
André's revulsion on first sighting the hangman's noose.[42]

This part of the event spawns a dilemma in the hagiographical
tradition of George Washington. Alexander Hamilton in full identification with André expresses his own scorn on the spot:

> I urged a compliance with André's request to be shot; and I do
> not think it would have had an ill effect: but some people are
> only sensible to motives of policy, and sometimes, from a narrow
> disposition, mistake it. When André's tale comes to be told, and
> present resentment is over: the refusing him the privilege of
> choosing the manner of his death will be branded with too much
> obstinacy.

Hamilton will have made his own moving version of that tale public
within the month, but like so many tales, this one only seems to
have increased the teller's "present resentment." Soon after, the need
to "brand" Washington will lead Hamilton to break with his commander in chief.[43]

Why *does* Washington resist André's request? From the first, the
American leader holds to the difference between spy and soldier. "I
would not wish Mr. André to be treated with insult; but he does not
appear to stand upon the footing of a common prisoner of war,"

---

41. John André to George Washington, 1 October 1780, *Proceedings*, 40.

42. For the single most dramatic reworking of this theme, see William Dunlap,
*André; A Tragedy in Five Acts: As Performed by the Old American Company, New-
York, March 30, 1798* (New York: T. and J. Swords, 1798), but every major eyewitness
account also raises the matter in excruciating detail, including those of Alexander
Hamilton in both public and private renditions, and of Major Benjamin Tallmadge
and Dr. James Thacher. See Dawson, *Papers*, 94, 103, 112, 132.

43. Alexander Hamilton to Elizabeth Schuyler, 2 October 1780, in Dawson,
Papers, 94. Hamilton's public version of the André affair appears in the *Pennsylvania
Gazette* on 25 October 1780. For his break with Washington in early 1781, see
Alexander Hamilton to Philip Schuyler, 18 February 1781, *The Works of Alexander
Hamilton*, ed. Henry Cabot Lodge, 12 vols. (New York: Putnam, 1904), 9:232–36.

observes Washington the day after André's capture, "and therefore
he is not entitled to the usual indulgences, which they receive."[44]
Biographers have embellished the distinction by suggesting that any
deviation from the prescribed method of punishment for espionage
would have fueled additional British protest by suggesting an American inconsistency. Even so, the argument from policy does not reach
the seeming cruelty or insensitivity of allowing André to remain
uncertain until the time of execution. Washington's only answer on
the occasion comes when André, expecting a firing squad, actually
sees the gallows.[45]

Lost in these discussions is the intricate role of George
Washington as commander in chief of the Army of the United States
of America in the act of discovering treason. As Cincinnatus, Washington stands for Roman discipline as well as civic virtue, and that
sense of discipline calls at times for brutal punishment. Washington's
general orders to the Army commonly level the threat. As he tells
his soldiers, "an Army without Order, Regularity and Discipline, is
no better than a Commission'd Mob." "Three things," he adds to
Congress, "prompt Men to a regular discharge of their Duty in time
of Action: natural bravery, hope of reward, and fear of punishment.
The two first are common to the untutor'd and the Disciplin'd Soldiers; but the latter, most obviously distinguishes the one from the
other." Washington, the owner of slaves, has known the need to
chastise insubordination all of his life. Floggings for relatively minor
offenses, even to a hundred lashes with washings of salt and water
in between, are permitted and conducted in the Revolutionary Army.[46]

---

44. George Washington to Lieutenant-Colonel James Jameson, 25 September
1780, in Dawson, *Papers*, 74.

45. The debate over this issue is an extensive one. See Flexner, *Washington, the
Indispensable Man*, 147–48, and Flexner, *Traitor and Spy*, 386–93, for arguments that
"Washington had no choice." But see, as well, Morpurgo, *Treason at West Point*,
134–46, 158–60, and Vivian, "Capture and Death," 818, for comments that, in Vivian's
words, "Washington, perhaps, in ignoring the young man's request went too far."

46. For a complete working out of the Cincinnatus image in Washington, see
Garry Wills, *Cincinnatus: George Washington and the Enlightenment* (Garden City,
N.Y.: Doubleday and Co., 1984). Washington's comments are contained in "General
Orders, Headquarters, January 1, 1776," "General Orders, Headquarters, July 2,
1776," and "To the President of Congress, February 9, 1776," all in *George Washington, A Collection*, ed. W. B. Allen (Indianapolis: Liberty Classics, 1988), 55, 71–
72, 63. For a more general comment on discipline in the Revolutionary Army and
on Washington's belief in its efficacy, see Jensen, *Founding of a Nation*, 634–38.

The Arnold treason has shaken a weak American military to its foundations—enough for the aloof, usually stern, and always unbending Washington to have found in it an occasion for punishment of the severest kind. Since the penalty for espionage, hanging, tallies with the sentence for treason, the chance to convey a double lesson in the execution of André would not have been lost on the disciplinarian. And behind this official need are subtler claims. The young Washington laboriously listed 110 rules "of civility and decent behavior in company and conversation" and learned to accept the overriding importance of correct conduct. How to behave in the unprecedented crisis of the Revolution dominates the commander's concern for his officers and men, and much of the decorum that he enforces on himself and others has to do with instilling basic expectations even in unexpected times.[47] In Washington's eyes, André is well and properly hanged. The spy's peculiar contribution to the uncertainty of events dooms him to a certain and fixed death.

This disciplinarian has been submerged in subsequent ideological needs. The fabricated Washington of later national formations cannot be allowed to make the same assumptions about André.[48] In William Dunlap's play *André; A Tragedy in Five Acts* (1798), the figure of Washington agonizes until the "cruel mockery" of a British execution of an American officer eliminates all further need for hesitation.[49] In Cooper's novel *The Spy: A Tale of the Neutral Ground*, Washington even works secretly to free a falsely accused British spy. Incognito and out of uniform in neutral territory, this version of Washington could be convicted as a spy himself. Appropriately, Cooper's protagonist, Harvey Birch, is a double agent hunted by all sides, and it

---

47. "The Rules of Civility and Decent Behavior In Company And Conversation," in Allen, *Washington, A Collection*, 6–13. Most of these rules emphasize duties and obligations in hierarchical situations. For a good analysis of Washington's overall character and concern with duty, see Edmund S. Morgan, "George Washington," *The Meaning of Independence: John Adams, Thomas Jefferson, George Washington* (1976; New York: W. W. Norton, 1978), 29–55.

48. This inability to comprehend Washington the disciplinarian is part of what Edmund S. Morgan calls "the story of how the American Revolution transformed some of the least lovable traits of a seemingly ordinary man into national assets," Morgan, *Meaning of Independence*, 30. See, as well, Michael Kammen, *A Season of Youth: The American Revolution and the Historical Imagination* (1978; New York: Oxford University Press, 1980), 105–6, 118.

49. Dunlap, *André; A Tragedy in Five Acts*, ed. Matthews, 67. "My heart is torn in twain," cries Washington in the ultimate moment.

is this last character who delivers the lines that Jacksonian Americans want to believe of their first founder. "No-no-no," cries Birch, "Washington can see beyond the hollow views of pretended patriots. . . . No-no-no, Washington would never say, 'Lead him to a gallows.'" *The Spy*, in this sense, is a bizarre response to those who, in Cooper's words, "affected to believe this execution had sullied the fair character of Washington."[50] Meanwhile, the single most popular work on the subject, "The Ballad of Major André," eliminates the problem altogether by excising all mention of Washington from the decision to hang André.[51]

These recontextualizations of Washington are one more indication that the early Republic is an imagined community, one more proof, if one is needed, that the American experience is distinctive in "the degree to which what is and what should be are identified one with the other."[52] Aspiration and reality come together in patriotic rhetoric at the expense of reality, and never more so than when the subject is treason. Clearly, the conspiracy at West Point stimulates acts of imagination from all concerned, one more reason to pay close attention to the actual language of the event.

The trial transcript of Washington's board of inquiry tells a story. It seeks to establish the separate high-mindedness of the American Army, acting "in such a manner upon the occasion as does them the highest honor, and proves them to be men of great virtue" against "the private and secret manner," the "feigned name," and the

---

50. Cooper, *The Spy*, 221 (chap. 17), 337 (chap. 26), 356 (chap. 28), 383–88 (chap. 30). See also James Fenimore Cooper, *Notions of the Americans: Picked Up by a Travelling Bachelor*, 2 vols. (1828; New York: Frederick Ungar, 1963), 1:217–22.

51. "The Ballad of Major André," in Dawson, *Papers*, 236–39. The ballad does capture both the essential emotive power and underlying wish among observers of the execution:

It mov'd each eye with pity
Caus'd every heart to bleed
And everyone wished him releas'd
And Arnold in his stead.

52. On nationalism, particularly Revolutionary nationalism, as an imagined political community, see Benedict Anderson, "Introduction," *Imagined Communities: Reflections on the Origin and Spread of Nationalism* (London: Verso, 1983), 11–16. The quotation in this sentence and the exceptionalist notion of an American community that is peculiarly concerned with merging aspiration and reality are from the conclusion of Paul M. Sniderman, *A Question of Loyalty* (Berkeley and Los Angeles: University of California Press, 1981), 166–70.

"disguised habit" of "a spy from the enemy."[53] In this narrative, decorum can notice and even sympathize with Major André across the formal divide of friend against enemy, but any such acknowledgment breaks down once treason replaces espionage as subject. Benedict Arnold is himself a pivotal member of that noble army, and the celebration of American virtue in the trial narrative crumbles when he comes to mind.

The substitution of André for Arnold in the formal investigation of the conspiracy and, hence, in the trial transcript mirrors the larger evasion of treason as subject in Revolutionary America. What is to be done about Benedict Arnold? Although Arnold's own letters, published in the transcript, substantiate the truth and scope of his treachery, no part of that transcript ever mentions the word *treason*. André alone uses the words "betrayal" and "treachery," and they apply to his personal situation. Outside of the courtroom, the shift in propaganda terms is immediate and extreme. Arnold the Revolutionary hero instantly turns into "the most loathed name in American history." In the eighteenth-century understanding of character, absolute integrity has acceded to the utter lack thereof.[54] And yet the worst vituperation heaped on Arnold, and the amount is incalculable, cannot come to grips with the overall phenomenon of Arnold's actions.

Tellingly, Arnold uses his own access to the André trial proceedings to resist the notion of metamorphosis in himself. From the safety of a British sloop of war in the Hudson, *The Vulture*, he claims a consistent rectitude and warns against mistaken acts of vengeance. "I have ever acted from a principle of love to my country, since the commencement of the present unhappy contest between Great Britain and the Colonies; the same principle of love to my country actuates my present conduct," he writes Washington. Patiently, Arnold reiterates the point in other letters to Washington, each of which finds its place in the trial transcript: "my attachment to the true interest of my country is invariable . . . I am actuated by the *same principle* which has ever been the governing rule of my conduct, in this unhappy contest."[55] Arnold, in fact, so convinces himself of invariable

---

53. *Proceedings*, 18, 29–30.

54. See on this subject Morpurgo, *Treason at West Point*, 165, and Kammen, *A Season of Youth*, 133–34.

55. Benedict Arnold to George Washington, 25 September 1780, and Arnold to Washington, 1 October 1780, in *Proceedings*, 26, 36.

consistency and, by extension, of still applicable principle that he
will ask the United States for back pay after he has defected![56]

Four related points should be noted about Arnold's claim of
consistency. First, in reaction, neither Revolutionary nor post-
Revolutionary rhetoric can grant Arnold the uniformity that he claims
except in the assumption of an unmitigated knavery. Rhetorically,
there can be no middle ground for the traitor. Either Arnold has been
a complete villain from the beginning or in 1780 he has undergone
an utter transformation into one. These patterns of dismissal already
have been glimpsed in Washington's description of an Arnold incapable of remorse and lost to all sense of honor and shame. But
dismissal also forecloses explanation. Even if the patriotic projection
of wickedness is true, its rhetorical vehemence precludes other avenues
of explanation. Arnold, in consequence, is the absent presence in
Revolutionary history. The alarm and the righteousness in Revolutionary rhetoric leave him in a single, static dimension. Furthermore,
the rhetorical reduction is deliberate: Arnold's authentic complexity
contains a cultural threat of fundamental proportions.

The second aspect of Arnold's claim of consistency explains some
of the alarm over him. He *is* without remorse. Where André sadly
confesses that he is "too little accustomed to duplicity to have succeeded," Arnold stipulates a heart "conscious of its own rectitude."
He refuses to compromise his understanding of events in any way.
Far from it, Arnold carries his belligerence in correspondence to
eventual threats of retaliation in the name of "every tie of duty and
honor"—ties that he summons "heaven and earth to witness" and
that are placed next to Washington's own sense of honor and love of
justice.[57]

Both the obdurate spirit and the skill of appropriation in these
terms are arresting. There is no concession or contrition in Arnold's
language; only challenge and his own assumption of equal station.
By affecting the exterior tone of the gentleman in these exchanges,
he exacts a presumption of the character within. Language creates
character rather than the other way around. Here and elsewhere, the
figure behind the language is a remarkable type for Tom Paine's
greatest fear expressed four years before in *Common Sense*. Benedict

56. See Morpurgo, *Treason at West Point*, 163–64.
57. John André to George Washington, 24 September 1780, and Benedict Arnold
to George Washington, 1 October 1780, *Proceedings*, 20–21, 38–40.

Arnold stands for the proposition that "[n]othing is criminal; there is no such thing as treason."[58] Moreover, the very nature of Arnold's realization, the license to disobey, is ideologically based in ways that reach toward a third point.

Arnold finds his own consistency in a Revolutionary American inconsistency. The self-confidence in his stance relies on a culturewide slippage in conceptions of loyalty. If the original colonial Englishman's devotion to king and country resonates between the personal and the abstract, the rebellion of republican citizens in 1776 diffuses that emotion in the generality of country. The eighteenth-century duty to one's king is a concrete, fixed obligation that brooks little equivocation or room for disobedience. All of that is changed by the more intangible standards of honor and virtue, the hallmarks of enlightened republican participation and favorite terms in Washington's control of the American army.

Whatever the strength of their appeal, honor and virtue are more nebulous or internalized signposts for guiding political action, and they allow for a more flexible range in interpreting personal behavior, particularly where the external code of the gentleman is a linguistic convention rather than an embodiment of character. Benedict Arnold shows how easily these terms can be turned back against their source in an atmosphere where the newly confederated states have few ideological props and little authority for preventing the inversion. The reasoned anger of rebellion in 1776 unleashes an emotional permissiveness in deciding the question of allegiance. Arnold, rebellious by nature, capitalizes on its possibilities, and there is no easy intellectual answer to his challenge.

One outcome is a strange narrative imbalance between Washington and Arnold in the transcript of André's trial. Nineteenth-century commentators on the conspiracy all have celebrated Washington's natural and consummate ascendancy over the treacherous subaltern, Arnold.[59] Without questioning the cultural hegemony of these

---

58. Thomas Paine, *Common Sense*, in *Complete Writings*, 1:43.

59. The most famous and influential of these treatments are those of James Fenimore Cooper in 1828 in *Notions of the Americans*, 1:208–23, and Simms, "Benedict Arnold." See Simms, *Views and Reviews*, 55–75. In Simms's understanding, the whole event is a conflict for ascendancy between "the rival stars of Washington and Arnold," and "the star of Washington rises, and gathers hourly increasing lustre, in due degree as [Arnold's] declines . . . waning away, under a cruel destiny, in mockery of all his merits and all his achievements."

accounts, we can still find a more problematic historicity in primary records. Trial transcripts inscribe proximate actions, and, in their spontaneous generation, they stand on their own as political and literary texts. Viewed in this manner, the transcript relation of Washington and Arnold in the André case takes a curious turn. In the contrapuntal epistolary exchanges of that transcript, Washington's decision *not* to answer Major André has obscured a more subtle resolution to ignore Arnold.

Arnold's dogged persistence makes the absence of all rebuttal from Washington especially interesting. Even André receives an answer of sorts to his request in the machinery of trial procedures, and they are duly noted in the transcript. "The practice and usage of war were against his [André's] request," runs the last line of the transcript on André's request for a firing squad, "and made the indulgence he solicited, circumstanced as he was, inadmissable."[60] Arnold, on the other hand, is left in a narrative void without closure or circumstance of any kind, and his marginalization should be understood against another centrality. Not the subject of André's trial, Arnold is nonetheless pivotal to it, and he contributes more words to the transcript of proceedings than any other single figure, including Washington. Nor is Arnold at a loss when it comes to wielding the creative modes of sentimental fiction. Fearing that his wife and coconspirator, Peggy Shippen Arnold, may suffer when he leaves her behind in the American camp, the traitor takes the first opportunity to remind Washington that "she is as good and as innocent as an angel, and is incapable of doing wrong."[61] Benedict Arnold, in sum, is a formidable adversary in rhetorical terms. Like so many of his fictional counterparts, he secures an advantage in wielding the station of the gentleman without the character.

---

60. *Proceedings*, 41.

61. Arnold to Washington, 25 September 1780, in, Dawson, *Papers*, 117–18. Most commentators on the conspiracy assume that Peggy Shippen Arnold, a leading socialite in Philadelphia during the British occupation of that city and a personal friend of John André at that time, at least knew of Arnold's plans, and they suggest that her ensuing hysterics in Washington's presence immediately after her husband's escape were part of a calculated and successful plan of evasion. Successful it was. Alexander Hamilton writes to his fiancée that "her sufferings were so eloquent, that I wished myself her brother, to have a right to become her defender." Hamilton to Elizabeth Schuyler, 25 September 1780, in Dawson, *Papers*, 92–93. Washington, against all of the facts, enters into Arnold's sentimental narrative when he automatically assumes and accepts Peggy Arnold's innocence.

Washington's silence seems at once fortuitous and planned. How do we know that Arnold is a criminal from a transcript that never mentions his crime? Silence is a double convenience born of the aloofness allowed superior status and of the commander's embarrassment in having to confront his own trusted major general, but it also lends itself to deeper purposes. The theory of give-and-take in trial advocacy gives each participant a place in the ceremony of the trial. The worst defendant or witness is still given the dignity of official standing. Washington's decision to ignore Arnold strips him of standing and leaves him without caste. Thus, if in Revolutionary America the costs of betrayal are no longer personalized in the punishment that a king visits on a subject, they take on another significance in the more abstract ritual of patriotic dismissal. Silence banishes Arnold from the realms of honor and virtue that Washington symbolizes, and, in the process, the abstractions of republican identity begin to register on a new or personal level. In the trial transcript Arnold begins to assume a hapless role: he is permanent prodigal to the father of his country.

This strategy of moral exile makes it easier to forget that Benedict Arnold has been an intrinsic component in Revolutionary practice— not an aberration, not a discrepancy. It is Arnold's crime that requires the perception of a contradiction. His temperamental consistency is precisely what Revolutionary ideology cannot tolerate in 1780, and the ultimate basis of that consistency should be clear. Arnold has been more than an individual hero, he has been part of the fighting heart of Washington's army, "a genius at leading men" and its greatest combat general.[62] Arnold's career from a dissolute apothecary's apprentice in Norwich, Connecticut to the exalted station of Major General in the Revolutionary Army can be read as one long, turbulent, and successful battle against civil authority. Combativeness and social mobility explain him. Made for crisis when he is not creating one, he thrives on the disruption of rebellion and brings a

---

62. Flexner, *Washington, The Indispensable Man,* 141. For the facts on Benedict Arnold in this paragraph and the next, I rely on Flexner, *Traitor and Spy,* and Morpurgo, *Treason at West Point,* 48–86. Morpurgo accurately presents "the hastiness and violence of his nature," traits that make him a pre-Revolutionary "leader of the wilder sort who preferred abusive words and ruthless actions to negotiation," and "in New Haven the most eager and, as always, the noisiest of the radicals." Later, in battle, "the British knew him as 'the most enterprising man among the rebels.'"

powerful and useful characterological anger to every enterprise in it. Manifestly, the Revolution cannot succeed without his type in place, and Washington cannily recognizes the need in guiding Arnold's rapid promotions through tangled military and political channels.

But governing Arnold's anger in the new routinization of authority is difficult even for Washington, and the task is immeasurably complicated by the economic side of the picture. Of a respected but downwardly mobile Connecticut family, Arnold always lives beyond his means and can never rest within the occasional prosperity that he finds. From the beginning, he lacks the stable base and social standing to accept the terms of disinterested service that Washington and the republican ideal expect. At the same time, Revolutionary success enhances Arnold's economic problems by increasing his expectations and his corresponding need for expensive display. Embezzlement charges and other accusations of malfeasance follow him everywhere. Arnold's requests for money define his military career almost as much as his capacity to take risks, and these traits will form their own combination in the act of betrayal.

Arnold and his predicament are unusual only in the last step of treason that has come to define him totally. In social terms, he is one of the many "new men" struggling for place and importance in the flux of Revolutionary times. Indeed, one motive of the later invective against Arnold will be to lift the regular circumstances of the conventional man, one of many, to the extraordinary level of the lonely traitor, where the dangerous energy and resentments of early republicans can be held in place by the contrary example. The negative contrast in Arnold's solitary treason dignifies the presumed power of reason and virtue in every other location. When Washington cuts off Arnold in the trial transcript, leaving his adversary in narrative limbo, he makes it all the easier for others to reconfigure the traitor as the symbol of every imagined republican ill.

The purpose of an invective against treason is never to understand the culprit. Understanding in this context is a positive danger; it invites potential sympathy for the betrayer and, worse, the prospect of further betrayal. As the one figure in the Revolution that all Englishmen and Americans (whether Tory or Whig, republican or loyalist) can identify as a traitor to their cause, Benedict Arnold is a lightning rod for negative commentary. Inevitably, these commentaries tell us more about the sources than the subject, and some interpretations are almost calculatedly perverse. General "Mad" Anthony Wayne, not settling for the truism "that honour and true virtue were strangers to [Arnold's] soul," actually concludes that "[Arnold] never possessed genuine fortitude or personal bravery."[63] Benjamin Franklin terms Arnold a "miserable bargainer." "Judas sold one man, Arnold 3,000,000," Franklin writes Lafayette. "Judas got for his one man 30 pieces of silver, Arnold not halfpenny a head."[64] The differences in these accounts do not prevent them from being characteristic. The soldier and the entrepreneur each finds what he most abhors in his own world.

Why Americans must think the way they do in the situation of treason is as relevant as what they think. Colonel Alexander Scammell, who reads the death sentence at André's execution and who thinks of André as "perhaps the most accomplished officer of the age," has much to ponder in this event. His description of the army's reaction to Arnold illustrates a crucial dynamic at work in the culture at large:

> we were all astonishment each peeping at his next neighbor to see if any treason was hanging about him; nay, we even descended to a critical examination of ourselves. This surprise soon settled down into a fixed detestation and abhorrence of Arnold, which can receive no addition. His treason has unmasked him the veriest villain of centuries past and set him in true colors.[65]

In this passage, an isolating anxiety alleviates itself in a new collective aversion. Just as important is the conclusive nature of the second emotion the instant it has been fully conceived ("settled down," "fixed," "can receive no addition," "set"). The purpose of redundancy in such a short passage is to eliminate all further need for reflection. Repetitive insistence on a permanent position ("abhorrence of Arnold") is the means for recovering a solidarity lost in the actual

---

63. Letter of General Anthony Wayne, 27 September 1780, in Dawson, *Papers*, 69.

64. Quoted in Morpurgo, *Treason at West Point*, 164.

65. See Flexner, *Traitor and Spy*, 392, and Colonel Alexander Scammell to Colonel Peabody, 3 October 1780, in Dawson, *Papers*, 66–67.

contemplation of treason ("we even descended to a critical examination of ourselves"). Here, again, we see the convenience of making
the traitor—not treason—the locus of attention.

The realization of awfulness in treason leads to an explosion in
the scope of the Arnold conspiracy rather than an analysis of it. Is
Arnold really, in Colonel Scammel's terms, "the veriest villain of
centuries past"? Already on 30 September 1780, an editorial from
the *Pennsylvania Packet, or, the General Advertiser* believes that
Arnold's corruption "exceeds all description" and relates "such a scene
of baseness and prostitution of office and character, as it is hoped
this new world cannot parallel."[66] Arnold is a monster that cannot
be described in normal terms, and the image of monstrosity also
draws attention from the act to the figure of treason—from the possibility of conspiracy to the fallen Arnold. "I took up my pen with
an intent to shew a reflective glass, wherein you might at one view
behold your actions," runs a direct address to Arnold from the *Pennsylvania Packet*,

> but soon found such a horrid ugly deformity in the outlines of
> your picture, that I was frightened at the sight, so the mirrour
> dropped and broke to pieces! each of this discovered you to be
> a gigantick overgrown monster, of such a variety of shapes, all
> over ulcerated, that it is in vain to attempt to describe them.[67]

The ability to censure eliminates the need to explain in such passages.
Outrage replaces comprehension by accepting distortion as the handy
and relevant norm.

Since deformity, monstrosity, and distortion translate immediately into conceptions of the satanic in the early American mind,
demonic imagery easily dominates eighteenth-century descriptions
of Arnold.[68] His treason, by managing to "astonish the people of
America," inspires accounts that reach beyond this world. In recording
this shock and amazement, another description from the *Pennsyl-*

---

66. Editorial from *The Pennsylvania Packet, Or, The General Advertiser*, Philadelphia, 30 September 1780, in Dawson, *Papers*, 228.
67. *Pennsylvania Packet*, 25 September 1781, quoted in Royster, "Nature of
Treason," 186–87.
68. For the most complete catalogue of these demonic images, see Royster,
"Nature of Treason," 163–93.

vania Packet declares that Arnold "has improved on the blackest treachery and the most consummate impudence, in a manner that would cause the infernals [to] blush, were they to be charged with it."[69] More seriously and typically, Colonel Scammell in camp at West Point is caught between explanations of "actual transgressions" and "original sin."[70]

A thoroughly secular person, Arnold the traitor grows meaningful in the spiritual domain. Starting with General Nathanael Greene's general orders to the Army the day after Arnold escapes, Americans leave the ultimate discovery and explanation of this event in divine hands. Greene's words help to create a convention of the times: "happily this treason has been timely discover'd, to prevent the fatal misfortune [of a deadly wound]—The providential train of Circumstances which lead to it, affords the most convincing proof, that the Liberties of America, is the object of Divine protection."[71] That proof is soon on every leader's lips. "The remarkable interposition of Providence to frustrate the diabolical conspiracy, will inspire every virtuous American with sincere gratitude to the great Arbiter of all events," intones Governor William Livingston of New Jersey, in writing to George Washington. "[W]e were, by the peculiar guardianship of Heaven, rescued from the very brink of destruction." Few events in the Revolution match the escape from Arnold's treachery in expressions, assurances, and celebrations of a guiding providence.[72]

The difficulty with providential explanations, however, is that they eliminate the need for secular interpretation. The proper place for such an interpretation is the trial transcript or court proceeding, but the admittedly indirect transcript of the André trial carefully evades that assignment for the many reasons already noted. Early republicans, like colonial Americans, are not yet ready to take on

69. From *The Pennsylvania Packet, or, the General Advertiser*, Philadelphia, 30 September 1780, in Dawson, *Papers*, 91.

70. Colonel Alexander Scammell to Colonel Peabody, 3 October 1780, in Dawson, *Papers*, 66.

71. General Orders to the Army, Headquarters Orange Town, September 26, 1780, in Dawson, *Papers*, 64.

72. William Livingston to George Washington, 7 October 1780, in Dawson, *Papers*, 83. See, as well, Abigail Adams to John Adams, 15 October 1780, where she insists that in the discovery of the plot, no matter what "the modern wits" might say, "the virtuous mind will look up and acknowledge the great First Cause," in *Letters of Mrs. Adams, The Wife of John Adams*, ed. Charles Francis Adams, 4th edition (Boston: Wilkins, Carter, 1848), 119.

the concept of treason as a formal intellectual exercise or form of cultural understanding. Not for the last time the trauma of treason encourages an emotional appeal rather than a clarifying investigation, and the community that faces that trauma is as much a Bible culture as it is a republic of laws.

Later, the Federal Convention of 1787 will see the need for clarification when it recognizes that there can be no safety in government without a careful and circumscribed definition of treason. As a measure of their concern, the framers will write down treason and make it the one crime to receive a separate section in the new and wholly secular Constitution. Even then, the proper test of that section will not come until 1807 when another Revolutionary hero, Aaron Burr, will face the charge directly in a court of law with Chief Justice John Marshall presiding.

The similarities in the treatment of Benedict Arnold and Aaron Burr across a quarter of a century are striking. Burr will encounter treason in very different circumstances than Arnold, but his trial will stimulate another round of demonizing commentary on the figure of the traitor. Soldier, leading lawyer, vice president under Thomas Jefferson, western adventurer, and the gentleman duelist who kills Alexander Hamilton, Burr, like Arnold, plays a thoroughly secular role on the American scene, but he is also the grandson of Jonathan Edwards, and his relation to the great revivalist stimulates powerful theological lines of force around him.[73]

Nineteenth-century Americans will never be shy about converting those religious lines into political and historical explanation. When they find Aaron Burr technically innocent of treason, they still regard him as the satanic figure in the American garden.[74] Thereafter, and

---

73. One of the most intriguing emphases of the Edwardsian legacy in Aaron Burr's political career comes in John Adams's insistence that Thomas Jefferson would not have won the election of 1800 over Adams but for the fact that "Aaron Burr had 100,000 Votes from the single Circumstance of his descent from President Burr and President Edwards," John Adams to Thomas Jefferson, 15 November 1813, in *The Adams-Jefferson Letters: The Complete Correspondence between Thomas Jefferson and Abigail and John Adams*, ed. Lester J. Cappon, 2 vols. (Chapel Hill: University of North Carolina Press, 1959), 2:399. Burr, of course, was Jefferson's vice-presidential running mate in what Jefferson always called "the Revolution of 1800." Burr's father and grandfather were presidents of the College of New Jersey (Princeton University); hence, the titles in Adams's designations.

74. See David Robertson, *Reports Of The Trials of Colonel Aaron Burr In The Circuit Court of the United States, Summer Term, 1807*, 2 vols. (Philadelphia:

in many rearticulations, the subject of treason will continue to accommodate a religious strain of explanation—a strain that often gives meaning to an otherwise incoherent narrative of monstrosity. The invective against treason always looks for more than crime. It partakes of an American civil religion where crimes against community are also sins against humanity and where the ritual of the courtroom reinforces a national faith.[75]

Hopkins and Earle, 1808), 2:95–101. Here, in prosecuting attorney William Wirt's summary of the alleged Burr conspiracy, America and Burr are as "the state of Eden when the serpent entered its bowers." For a complete record of the ensuing demonization of Aaron Burr, see Charles F. Nolan, Jr., *Aaron Burr and the American Literary Imagination* (Westport, Conn.: Greenwood Press, 1980).

75. See, for example, the connection between ritual, faith, and national identity in Conrad Cherry, *God's New Israel: Religious Interpretations of American Destiny* (Englewood Cliffs, N.J.: Prentice-Hall, 1971), 6–13.

Speaking of Death: Narratives of Violence in Capital Trials

Austin Sarat

Let's do it.

—Gary Gilmore

Let's get on with it.

—Chief Justice William Rehnquist

At 8:30 A.M. on 15 July 1977, William Brooks accosted Janine Galloway at gunpoint and forced her to drive to a wooded area behind a neighborhood school. There Brooks raped her and shot her to death. Eventually Brooks was arrested, tried, and convicted of kidnapping, robbery, rape, and murder; he received two life terms in prison plus twenty years, and a death sentence. On appeal the murder conviction and death sentence were overturned, though his other convictions were unaffected.

In January 1991 I traveled to Madison, Georgia, a small town approximately sixty miles northeast of Atlanta, to attend the retrial of William Brooks. The sole object of this retrial was to reinstate both his murder conviction and death sentence. This trial provides one vehicle through which to consider the complex relationship of law, language, and violence and one opportunity to observe the ways

An earlier version of this essay appeared in *Law and Society Review* 27, no. 1. Reprinted by permission of the Law and Society Association. I am grateful for the helpful comments of Robert Burt, Marianne Constable, Lawrence Douglas, Tom Dumm, Joel Handler, Frank Munger, and Stephanie Sandler.

in which the rhetoric of law is shaped by what Robert Cover called the "field of pain and death" on which law acts.[1] In that trial and others like it violence is put into discourse, and distinctions between the violence of law and violence outside the law are richly marked. As a result, capital trials, though rare, are enormously important moments in the rhetorical life of the law.[2]

Violence, as both a linguistic and physical phenomena, as fact and metaphor,[3] is integral to the constitution of modern law.[4] As Cover argues, "[L]egal interpretation is a practice incomplete without violence . . . [I]t depends upon the social practice of violence for its efficiency."[5] Modern law is built on representations of aggression, force, and disruption,[6] of aggressive acts like the rape and murder of Janine Galloway. And, once built, law traffics in violence every day, using its own force to deter and punish acts it brands illegal. The proximity of law to, and its dependence on, violence raises a

---

1. "Violence and the Word," *Yale Law Journal* 95 (1986): 1601.

2. Ibid., 1622–23.

3. Drucilla Cornell suggests that the violent "foundation" of law is allegorical rather than metaphorical: "The Law of Law is only 'present' in its absolute absence. The 'never has been' of an unrecoverable past is understood as the lack of origin 'presentable' only as allegory. The Law of Law, in other words, is the figure of an initial fragmentation, the loss of the Good. But this allegory is inescapable because the lack of origin is the fundamental truth." "From the Lighthouse: The Promise of Redemption and the Possibility of Legal Interpretation," *Cardozo Law Review* 11 (1990): 1687, 1689.

4. See Thomas Hobbes, *Leviathan*, ed. C. B. MacPherson (New York: Penguin Books, 1986). See also Hans Kelsen, *General Theory of Law and the State*, trans. Anders Wedberg (New York: Russell and Russell, 1945); Noberto Bobbio, "Law and Force," *Monist* 48 (1965): 321; Walter Benjamin, "Critique of Violence," in *Reflections*, trans. Edmund Jepchott (New York: Harcourt, Brace, 1978); Peter Fitzpatrick, "Violence and Legal Subjection" (typescript, 1991).

5. Cover, "Violence and the Word," 1601. Cover insisted, even at the price of doing linguistic violence, that "the violence . . . [of law] is utterly real—in need of no interpretation, no critic to reveal it—a naive but immediate reality. Take a short trip to your local prison and see." The coercive character of law is central to law, systematic, and quite unlike the "psychoanalytic violence of literature or the metaphorical characterization of literary critics and philosophers." Cover thus invited us to imagine and construct a jurisprudence of violence, and to theorize about law by attending to its pain-imposing, death-dealing acts. See "The Bonds of Constitutional Interpretation: Of the Word, the Deed, and the Role," *Georgia Law Review* 20 (1986): 818.

6. Austin Sarat and Thomas R. Kearns, "A Journey through Forgetting: Toward a Jurisprudence of Violence," in *The Fate of Law*, ed. Austin Sarat and Thomas R. Kearns (Ann Arbor: University of Michigan Press, 1991).

nagging question and a persistent doubt about whether law can ever be more than violence or whether law's violence is truly different from and preferable to what lurks beyond its boundaries.[7] To answer that question and to quiet that doubt is for law a continuing necessity. It is achieved, to the extent it is achieved at all, in the representational practices and rhetoric deployed to speak about violence inside and outside law, to distinguish capital punishment from murder in the situated moments—capital trials—when both are spoken about at once.

As pervasive as is the relationship of law and violence, it is nonetheless difficult to speak about that relationship, or to know precisely what one is talking about when one speaks about law's violence.[8] This difficulty arises because law is violent in many ways— in the ways it uses language and in its representational practices,[9] in the silencing of perspectives and the denial of experience,[10] and in

---

7. See Benjamin, "Critique of Violence"; and Jacques Derrida, "Force of Law: The 'Mystical Foundation of Authority,'" *Cardozo Law Review* 11 (1990): 925.

8. As Ronald Dworkin argues,

Day in and day out we send people to jail, or take money away from them, or make them do things they do not want to do, under coercion of force, and we justify all this by speaking of such persons as having broken the law or having failed to meet their legal obligations. . . . Even in clear cases . . . , when we are confident that someone had a legal obligation and broke it, we are not able to give a satisfactory account of what that means or why it entitles the state to punish or coerce him. We may feel confident that what we are doing is proper, but until we can identify the principles we are following we cannot be sure they are sufficient. . . . In less clear cases, . . . the pitch of these nagging questions rises, and our responsibility to find answers deepens."

Taking Rights Seriously (Cambridge: Harvard University Press, 1977), 15.

Another version of this difficulty is described by Samuel Weber. As he says, "To render impure, literally; to 'touch with' (something foreign, alien), is also to violate. And to violate something is to do violence to it. Inversely, it is difficult to conceive of violence without violation, so much so that the latter might well be a criterion of the former: no violence without violation, hence, no violence without a certain contamination." See "Deconstruction before the Name: Some [Very] Preliminary Remarks on Deconstruction and Violence" (typescript, 1990), 2.

9. See Catharine MacKinnon, *Feminism Unmodified* (Cambridge: Harvard University Press, 1987). For an interesting treatment of representation as violence in a nonlegal context see Nancy Armstrong and Leonard Tennenhouse, eds., *The Violence of Representation: Literature and the History of Violence* (London: Routledge, 1989).

10. See Martha Minow, *Making All the Difference* (Ithaca: Cornell University Press, 1989). Also see Joan Scott, "The Evidence of Experience," *Critical Inquiry* 17 (1991): 773; and Teresa de Lauretis, "The Violence of Rhetoric: Considerations on

its objectifying epistemology.[11] It arises from the fact that the linguistic, representational violence of the law (as seen in capital trials)
is inseparable from its literal, physical violence (capital punishment).
As Peter Fitzpatrick suggests,

> In its narrow perhaps popular sense, violence is equated with
> unrestrained physical violence. . . . A standard history of the West
> would connect a decline in violence with an increase in civility.
> Others would see civility itself as a transformed violence, as a
> constraining even if not immediately coercive discipline. . . . The
> dissipation of simple meaning is heightened in recent sensibilities
> where violence is discerned in the denial of the uniqueness or
> even existence of the "other." . . . These expansions of the idea of
> violence import a transcendent ordering—an organizing, shaping
> force coming to bear on situations from outside of them and
> essentially unaffected by them.[12]

The difficulty of talking about violence is, however, a difficulty
not just for scholars seeking to understand the constitution of modern
law. It is, in addition, a continuing problem for law itself. Legal
discourse, like all discursive forms, confronts the limits of language
and representation when it speaks, as it must in capital trials, about
physical violence and physical pain. However, the limits confronted
in representing violence would seem, at first glance, to be the opposite
of those confronted in representing pain. Violence is visible and vivid.
It speaks loudly, arouses indignation, and, as a result, its representation threatens to overwhelm reason. Thus the problem of representing violence would seem to be one of taming and disciplining its
representations.

Pain, on the other hand, is invisible. As Elaine Scarry argues,

> Physical pain has no voice. . . . When one hears about another's
> physical pain, the events happening within the interior of that

---

Representation and Gender," in Armstrong and Tennenhouse, *Violence of
Representation*.
   11. Robin West, "Disciplines, Subjectivity, and Law," in Sarat and Kearns, *Fate
of Law*.
   12. "Violence and Legal Subjection," 1. Also Robert Paul Wolff, "Violence and
the Law," in *The Rule of Law*, ed. Robert Paul Wolff (New York: Simon and Schuster,
1971), 55.

person's body may seem to have the remote character of some deep subterranean fact, belonging to an invisible geography that, however portentous, has no reality because it has not yet manifested itself on the visible surface of the earth.[13]

Pain is, according to Scarry,

> [V]aguely alarming yet unreal, laden with consequence yet evaporating before the mind because not available to sensory confirmation, unseeable classes of objects such as subterranean plates, Seyfert galaxies, and the pains occurring in other people's bodies flicker before the mind, then disappear. . . . [Pain] achieves . . . its aversiveness in part by bringing about, even within the radius of several feet, this absolute split between one's sense of one's own reality and the reality of other persons. . . . Whatever pain achieves, it achieves in part through its unsharability, and it ensures this unsharability through its resistance to language.[14]

Yet violence and its linguistic representation is inseparable from pain and its representation. We know its full measure only through the pain it inflicts; the indignation that we experience in the presence of violence is, in large part, a function of our imaginings of the hurt it inflicts. In this sense, the problem of putting violence and pain into discourse is one problem rather than two.

It is the business of law in general and capital trials in particular to know violence and pain, and to find the means of overcoming their resistances to language and representation. Scarry herself suggests that the courtroom and the discourse of the trial provide one particularly important site to observe the way violence and pain "enter language."[15] In that discourse the problem of putting violence and pain into language is compounded by the fact that

> it is not immediately apparent in exactly what way the verbal act of expressing pain . . . helps to eliminate the physical fact of pain. Furthermore, built into the very structure of the case is a dispute

---

13. See *The Body in Pain* (New York: Oxford University Press, 1985), 3.
14. Ibid., 4.
15. Ibid., 10.

about the correspondence between language and material reality: the accuracy of the descriptions of suffering given by the plaintiff's lawyer may be contested by the defendant's lawyer. . . . For the moment it is enough to notice that, whatever else is true, . . . [a trial] provides a situation that once again requires that the impediments to expressing pain be overcome. Under the pressure of this requirement, the lawyer too, becomes an inventor of language, one who speaks on behalf of another person . . . and attempts to communicate the reality of that person's physical pain to people who are not themselves in pain (the jurors).[16]

Scarry invites us to consider trials as occasions for lawyers to "invent" languages of violence and pain.[17] However, she suggests that in law, as elsewhere, the languages that can be invented are quite limited.[18] "As physical pain is monolithically consistent in its assault on language," Scarry writes, "so the verbal strategies for overcoming the assault are very small in number and reappear consistently as one looks at the words of the patient, physician, Amnesty worker, lawyer, artist."[19] Those verbal strategies "revolve [first] around the verbal sign of the weapon."[20] We know violence and pain, in the first instance, through its instrumentalities. Second, we know them through their effects. Here violence and pain are represented in the "wound," that is, "the bodily damage that is pictured as accompanying pain."[21]

As violence and pain are put into language, we may be tempted to forget that their metaphorical representation as weapons and wounds cannot truly capture the meaning of violence and pain themselves.[22] And, in the process of putting those things into language, some kinds of violence and pain, those engendered by particular weapons and those which leave visible marks on the body, may be more easily available to us,[23] whereas more diffuse, systemic violence

---

16. Ibid.
17. For an important examination of these processes see Kristin Bumiller, "Real Violence/Body Fictions" (typescript, 1991).
18. Scarry, Body in Pain, 13.
19. Ibid.
20. Ibid.
21. Ibid., 15.
22. Ibid.
23. See Bumiller, "Real Violence/Body Fictions"; and Sara Cobb, "The Domes-

that leaves no visible marks or scars—the violence of racism, poverty, and despair—will be less easily represented and understood as violence and pain. "A great deal is at stake," Scarry herself suggests, "in the attempt to invent linguistic structures that will reach and accommodate this area of experience normally so inaccessible to language."[24]

My analysis of the Brooks case focuses on the representation of violence in capital trials and the ways lawyers use linguistic structures to represent different kinds of violence. How does law overcome the resistance of violence and pain to language? How is the direct, physical violence done by William Brooks to Janine Galloway, the violence of kidnapping, rape, and murder, the violence that extinguished a life, put into discourse? How is the more diffuse violence that pervaded Brooks's life from childhood onward known and understood?

But the discourse of capital trials involves more than the representation of violence beyond law's boundaries. In such trials the specter of law's own violence is real and immediate. It too must be put into language, and it must be put into language in a way that reassures us that law's violence is different from and preferable to the violence it is used to punish and deter. As Cover suggests,

> Because in capital punishment the action or deed is extreme and irrevocable, there is pressure placed on the word—the interpretation that establishes the legal justification for the act. At the same time, the fact that capital punishment constitutes the most plain, the most deliberate, and the most thoughtful manifestation of legal interpretation as violence makes the imposition of the sentence an especially powerful test of the faith and commitment of the interpreters. . . . Capital cases, thus, disclose far more of the structure of judicial interpretation than do other cases.[25]

In this article I describe the ways law's own violence is brought into discourse and how, in that discourse, boundaries are constructed between it and the other forms of violence (e.g., murder and abuse)

---

tication of Violence in Mediation: The Social Construction of Disciplinary Power in Law" (typescript, 1992).

24. Scarry, *Body in Pain*, 6.

25. "Violence and the Word," 1622–23.

with which it traffics.[26] In capital trials, law seeks to distinguish the killings that it opposes and avenges from the force that expresses its opposition and through which its avenging work is done. In such trials violence of the kind done to Janine Galloway is juxtaposed to the "legitimate force" the state seeks to apply to her killer.

Here I will pay particular attention to the way law's violence is transformed rhetorically into such "legitimate force"[27] and distinguished from "the violence that one always deems unjust."[28] In this way law denies the violence of its origins,[29] as well as the continuing disorder engendered by its own violent ordering and peacemaking efforts.[30] As Robert Paul Wolff argues, violence is, in the eyes of the law, *the illegitimate or unauthorized use of force to effect decisions against the will or desire of others. Thus murder is an act of violence, but capital punishment by a legitimate state is not.*"[31]

26. Some suggest that there is no real difference between capital punishment and murder. See Albert Camus, "Reflections on the Guillotine," in Albert Camus and Arthur Koestler, *Reflections sur la Peine Capitale* (Paris: Calmann-Levy, 1957). Others note that the law's reliance on violence erodes its capacity to transform/reform those who disobey its commands. "[W]e must not underestimate the extent to which the criminal is prevented, by the very witnessing of the legal process, from regarding his deed as intrinsically evil. He sees the very same actions performed in the service of justice with perfectly clear conscience and general approbation: . . . the cold-blooded legal practices of despoiling, insulting, torturing, murdering the victim." Friedrich Nietzsche, *The Birth of Tragedy and the Genealogy of Morals*, trans. F. Golffing (Garden City, N.Y.: Doubleday, 1956).

27. Sarat and Kearns, "Journey through Forgetting."

28. Derrida, "Force of Law," 927; see also Edgar Friedenberg, "The Side Effects of the Legal Process," in Wolff, *Rule of Law*, 43. Friedenberg argues that "[i]f by violence one means injurious attacks on persons or destruction of valuable inanimate objects . . . then nearly all the violence done in the world is done by legitimate authority, or at least by the agents of legitimate authority engaged in official business. . . . Yet their actions are not deemed to be violence." Legitimacy is thus one way of charting the boundaries of law's violence. It is also the minimal answer to skeptical questions about the ways law's violence differs from the turmoil and disorder law is allegedly brought into being to conquer. See Wolff, "Violence and the Law."

29. Derrida, "Force of Law," 983–84.

30. See "Violence and the Law." See also Bernhard Waldenfels, "The Limits of Legitimation and the Question of Violence," in *Justice, Law, and Violence*, ed. James Brady and Newton Garver (Philadelphia: Temple University Press, 1991). For a classic discussion of legitimacy see Max Weber, *Max Weber on Law in Economy and Society*, ed. Max Rheinstein, trans. Edward Shils and Max Rheinstein (Cambridge: Harvard University Press, 1954). An important study of the production of legal legitimacy is provided by Douglas Hay, "Property, Authority, and the Criminal Law," in *Albion's Fatal Tree: Crime and Society in Eighteenth-Century England* by Douglas Hay et al. (New York: Pantheon Books, 1975).

31. Wolff, "Violence and the Law," 59. Friedenberg contends that "[t]he police

In capital trials the violence of law is inscribed in struggles to put violence into discourse and to control its discursive representation. Here the rhetoric of law becomes, at the one and the same time, the medium of law's violent expression and of its reassuring restraint. That rhetoric seeks to do a double deed. *First*, it strains to instantiate and vividly portray the violence that exists just beyond law's boundary—the killing of Janine Galloway—that brings pain to the innocent, that merits condemnation. *Second*, it works to mute other kinds of violence, the violence of racial injustice, poverty, and abuse, as well as the violence of law itself. This is done in the hope of affirming the social value of law, of reassuring citizens that its use of violence is somehow different from and better than illegal violence,[32] of alleviating anxiety about law by identifying a more terrifying other,[33] and, in so doing, of overcoming inhibitions against the conscious, willful use of violence and infliction of pain as an instrument of law itself. In capital trials those two rhetorical gestures coexist, but their coexistence is, I argue, an uneasy one. It is uneasy because, in the Brooks trial and others like it, both gestures are replete with racial symbols.[34] The narratives of violence and

often slay; but they are seldom socially defined as murderers. Students who block the entrances to buildings or occupy a vacant lot and attempt to build a park in it are defined as not merely being disorderly but violent; the law enforcement officials who gas and club them into submission are perceived as restorers of order, as, indeed, they are of the *status quo ante* which was orderly by definition." See "Side Effects," 43. As Fitzpatrick puts it, "[T]his association of law with order, security and regularity rapidly became general and obvious, the violence associated with the establishment of law and order assuming insignificance in the immeasurability of the violence and disorder of savagery." "Violence and Legal Subjection," 15.

32. As Weisberg argues, "The criminal trial is . . . a representational medium that . . . serves as a grammar of social symbols. . . . The criminal trial is a 'miracle play' of government in which we carry out our inarticulate beliefs about crime and criminals within the reassuring formal structure of disinterested due process." Robert Weisberg, "Deregulating Death," *Supreme Court Review* (1983): 385.

33. See Thomas L. Dumm, "Fear of Law," *Studies in Law, Politics & Society* 10 (1990): 29. As Dumm puts it, "In the face of the law that makes people persons, people need to fear. Yet people also need law to protect them. . . . Hence fear is a political value that is valuable because it is critical of value, a way of establishing difference that enables uncertainty in the face of danger." Ibid., 54.

34. In addition to my observation of the Brooks trial I read the trial transcripts of twelve other capital cases that reached the penalty phase. The themes of race, law, and violence so vividly exemplified in the Brooks trial are found in most of those other trials as well. One important difference was the quality of Brooks's defense team. In many death penalty cases defendants have inexperienced, underqualified

victimization that appear in capital trials frequently are racially charged;[35] they chart the boundaries between law and nonlaw along a racial divide of us-versus-them, order-versus-disorder, reason against the mob.[36]

Because Galloway was a young white woman, from a respectable Christian family, and Brooks was an unemployed, drug-using, young black male, the juxtaposition of images in the Brooks trial was, as it is in many other capital trials, racialized. The Brooks trial (re)enacted a familiar story of race and law[37] in which legal violence is authorized as a response to imagined racial savagery.[38] The juxtaposition of the images of Galloway and Brooks told a story of lost innocence and racial danger. Thus even as we are reassured about the legitimacy of law's violence and its difference from violence outside the law, the racialization of that difference arouses other fears that themselves motivate an acceptance, if not a warm embrace, of law's violence as a necessary tool in a struggle between "us" and "them."[39]

lawyers. See "Fatal Defense," *National Law Journal*, 11 June 1990, 30. Brooks's lawyers, in contrast, were highly regarded death penalty specialists. Throughout this paper I refer to the lead counsel as Brooks's lawyer.

35. For a similar argument in another context see Bumiller, "Real Violence/ Body Fictions."

36. Gary Peller, "Reason and the Mob," *Tikkun* 2 (1987): 28.

37. See Patricia Williams, *The Alchemy of Race and Rights* (Cambridge: Harvard University Press, 1991). See also Charles Lawrence, "The Id, the Ego, and Equal Protection: Reckoning with Unconscious Racism," *Stanford Law Review* 39 (1987): 317; and Stephen Carter, "When Victims Happen to Be Black," *Yale Law Journal* 97 (1988): 420.

38. Peter Fitzpatrick argues that in the construction of law,
Law and order were constantly combined not just in opposition to but as a means of subduing the 'disordered and riotous' savages in their state of lawless 'anarchy.' . . . [T]his association of law with order, security and regularity rapidly became general and obvious, the violence associated with the establishment of law and order assuming insignificance in the immeasurability of the violence and disorder of savagery. "Violence and Legal Subjection," 14–15.
According to Barbara Omolade, "For the West, the mythic power of skin color determines good and evil, guilt and innocence, ignorance and knowledge in the real lives of black and white people, "Black Codes: Then and Now: The Central Park Jogger Case and Multiple Representations" (typescript, 1991), 2.

39. Omolade, "Black Codes," 16. Here, of course, the first trial of the police officers who beat Rodney King provides a vivid example of the way law's violence is portrayed as an acceptable tool in a racial struggle. See Thomas L. Dumm, "The New Enclosures: Racism in the Normalized Community," in *Reading Rodney King/ Reading Urban Uprising*, ed. Robert Gooding-Williams (New York: Routledge, 1993); also Patricia Williams, "The Rules of the Game," *Village Voice*, 12 May 1992, 32.

In this essay I use the Brooks trial to examine the rhetorical practices through which violence and pain are put into legal discourse. I examine the explicit and implicit ways law draws distinctions among the various kinds of violence with which it traffics—the violence done to the victim, the violence that allegedly shaped the life of her killer, and the violence of law itself. Throughout, I show the racial content of the different images of violence and pain that appear in the Brooks case and illustrate how race provides a way of interpreting the relationship of law and violence.

Putting Violence into Discourse in the Trial of William Brooks: The Life and Death of Janine Galloway

An Innocent Life: Racial Purity and the Attack on Innocence

Perhaps not surprisingly, the Brooks trial revealed few details about the life of the victim, Janine Galloway. She, after all, was not on trial. At the center of the first, or guilt, phase of the trial was, instead, a narrative about the lawless violence that Brooks perpetrated and that Galloway endured. Indeed as the trial unfolded, Janine's white, female body and the attack on it became a symbol for what the prosecutor called "the body of mankind." The violence unleashed against her body was, at the same time, unleashed against a body that was not her own, the disembodied body of "everyone." Her death became a trope in a Hobbesian tale of anomic violence against a supposedly universal body.[40]

Yet the displacement of Janine and her life story could not be and was not complete. That story was the story of a special life, a life of innocence, purity, and virtue.[41] Throughout the trial it was the innocence of Janine's body that provided the context for the discursive representation of the violence and pain that she suffered. Her innocence became the true measure of her worth and of the

---

40. See Hobbes, *Leviathan.*
41. Unlike the rape trial that Bumiller described, in the Brooks trial the defense did not contest or call into question the victim's innocence. See Kristin Bumiller, "Fallen Angels: The Representation of Violence against Women in Legal Culture," *International Journal of the Sociology of Law* 18 (1990): 125.

horror of her body's violation. It was the white, good Janine who was slain by the black, evil Brooks; it was good that was assaulted and sullied by evil. Though the prosecutor denied the significance of race ("This isn't black versus white") the imagery on which he consistently relied was a racial imagery.[42] Sometimes the imagery was overt, as in his repeated references to the fact that Brooks had led his life in "dark places"; sometimes it was more indirect, as in the contrast between those, like Janine, who embrace the "American way, play by the rules, and work hard" and those, like Brooks, who are "mean and lazy." For him, and he hoped for the jury, the trial was an opportunity to vindicate, if not restore, Janine's fallen innocence, to assert the value of white life against the devaluing acts of black men.[43] As Brooks's defense lawyer said to me in an interview after the case was completed, "It was a classic sort of race case with the young white woman, a virgin according to the newspapers, who was taken from her home by a black man. Your classic southern death penalty case is the rape of a white woman by a young, black man."

The image of Janine's innocence and of the value of her white life was constructed by calling attention to particular facets of her life and emphasizing certain of her attributes, the first of which involved her place as the "child" in a loving family, the second her virginity. In 1977, she was a twenty-three-year-old piano teacher at a local music store and engaged to be married to Harold "Bob" Murray, though she still lived at home with her parents, Earl and Heddie. On the day of Janine's death Heddie, who worked for an optometrist, was home on vacation. Janine went out the door at 8:30 A.M. to meet her friend, Ann Overton, for breakfast. As Heddie put it in her testimony,

> Janine went out to the carport. I was beginning to relax after breakfast, and I put the chain on the door because I was alone in the house. I looked out the window and saw Janine's car with the door to the driver's side open. . . .

---

42. "The law in its majestic neutrality takes no official note of the race of the victim. . . . Yet our public insistence that race be divorced from debate over crime does not match the activities of our institutions. At the level of private fears, private categorizations, the link between race and crime is an intimate one." Carter, "When Victims," 440.

43. For similar arguments in other contexts see Carter, "When Victims"; and Omolade, "Black Codes."

Q: At that time did you see anyone?

No. I didn't see anyone. I opened the kitchen door and went outside. I called to her, but no one answered. So I went back into the house to see if she was there. And then I walked back out to the carport. That's when I heard her say "I'm in here." Her voice came from the utility room.

Q: Where is this?

The utility room is just off to the left of the kitchen door. I heard a voice say "I'm in here." And I said, "What are you doing in there?" She said, "I'm just looking for something." She said, "Go back in the house. When I find what I'm looking for I'll let you know." So I went in the house and called my neighbor. I knew something was wrong, but nobody answered. Then I went outside again. The door to the utility room was closed. I started to go back in the house again and the phone rang. I picked it up and it was Ann Overton wanting to know where Janine was and whether she was coming to breakfast. I told her that someone had her in the utility room and I said she should come over here fast. As soon as we hung up I tried my neighbor again. Then I heard the car start up and I ran to the door.

Q: What did you see?

I saw her in her car with a black man on the passenger side. I'd never seen him before. I looked inside the car and I got very close to it. She began to back down the driveway. I walked along as she backed out, and I kept my eyes on him. I called out to her to "Please wait." "No" she said, "I'll be back. Don't worry."

There is something nightmarish and terrifying in this testimony of the mother's witnessing of Janine's kidnapping and her excruciating inability to stop it. Both prefigure and foretell the murder to come. It is as if the violence done to Janine was already present, symbolically displaced, and expressed in Heddie's disbelief of Janine's reassurances. Heddie is here imaged as if in a terrible dream in which she is forced to look at the living corpse of her daughter.

In Heddie's testimony race makes a prominent appearance. What is noticed and recounted is the race of the man in the car next to Janine. The danger that first appears as a disruption of domestic routine is thus a racial danger. At an early stage in the trial, in the voice of the victim's mother, a portrait of the violence on the other side of law's boundary and of its association with race begins to emerge.

Lawless violence invades the unworried, safe space of home and family. Yet that space is a bit less unworried than it might first appear. Even where there has been, as yet, no invasion, the specter of violence is already present. Mrs. Galloway's testimony contained a stark reminder of our collective anxieties about violence. She was herself sufficiently aware of its possibility and its presence that she chained the door to protect herself. Hers was a diffuse anxiety about the particular vulnerability of the woman alone. Her response was to lock the world out so she could "relax."

In addition, the awareness of and anxiety about criminal violence was sufficiently part of Janine's life that, according to the testimony of her fiancé, she "went to seminars about what to do if you are raped." For Janine lawless violence could not be locked out; hers was a life in which neither law nor locks could provide security or certainty. Yet in her world of innocence, preparation to meet such lawless violence seemed to some to be nearly incomprehensible. As her fiancé explained to the court, "I couldn't understand why she went [to the seminars on rape]. I treated it lightly."

Beyond law's boundaries is a violence so bold and powerful that no preparation is adequate. It is so bold and powerful that it takes the innocent daughter literally right out from under her mother's eyes. Thus Heddie watched helplessly as Janine drove away with an unidentifiable "black man" beside her, and as a nightmare of racial victimization was played out before her eyes.[44] Implicit in the testi-

---

44. "The black male suspect's guilt or innocence of raping the white woman . . . can not be accurately assessed within a society of believers in racial mythologies and who thirst for hanging black flesh. . . . If the men are innocent of the rape, then they have been guilty of the crime of being black and male which takes precedence over legal innocence. If they are guilty of rape who can separate the guilt associated with their race and gender from their guilt for the crime. . . . [B]lack men are always guilty of raping white women because of who they are."
Omolade, "Black Codes," 15–16.

mony about this nightmare is a contrast between the description of
domestic routine and the known, but unspoken, soon-to-be-realized
fate of Janine Galloway.[45]

Not only was Janine's innocence the innocence of a dutiful daughter, it was, in addition, a virginal innocence. The fact of Janine's
virginity was admitted into evidence over the strenuous objection of
the defense, who contended that it was irrelevant and inadmissable,
that it went to no material issue in the case. The prosecution
responded that the fact of her virginity went to the issue of noncon-
sent; it showed that there "was no consent to the crime of intercourse."

Once admitted, Janine's virginity would quickly become quite an
important fact in the discursive representation of the violence done
to her. It became an essential part of the story of the "wounds" that
the prosecutor would use to bring Brooks's violence and Janine's pain
into discourse. Once admitted, virginity helped to racialize the narrative of Janine's rape. It became the quite unsubtle symbol of her
innocence and worth, and Brooks's crime became the paradigm of
the racial attack on white womanhood.[46]

In a statement given to the police at the time of his arrest Brooks
said that after he had intercourse with Janine he asked her, "Was it
your first time?" and that she had responded that it was. On Brooks's
own account, he "didn't believe her." Against his disbelief the trial
provided the occasion for an affirmation of the truth of what she had
uttered as if her virginity were itself on trial.[47]

The Violence That Knows No Law

If the story of Janine's life was a rather linear narrative of a racial innocence and a gendered purity, the story of her violation was quite complex. From the beginning of the trial the prosecution painted a picture
of the violence committed against Janine Galloway as gruesome,

---

45. But her testimony is equally potent in conveying an image of Janine's effort
to distance her mother from danger and to calm her, "I'll be back. Don't worry."
The daughter, in her own moment of danger, heroically becomes the mother to her
mother.

46. For a vivid exemplification of the fear of such an attack see McQuirter v.
State, 63 So. 2d 388 (1953).

47. That affirmation came in the testimony of the medical examiner who had
conducted the autopsy on Janine. It was his testimony that Janine "was a virgin prior
to the attack."

wanton, cruel, and unnecessary. In the words of the prosecutor, "Janine died a horrible death. . . . She did nothing to deserve to die."

With these words the prosecutor presented an implicit contrast
between the violence outside the law that is visited upon the deserving
and the undeserving alike and respects neither innocence nor virtue,
and law's own violence, which is reserved for those who by their
guilty acts deserve it.[48] Unlike the indiscriminant use of violence
against the innocent Janine, law provides elaborate procedures (in
Brooks's case, a trial, an extended process of review and appeal, and
now a retrial) and uses them to insure that its violence is visited only
on the guilty. What is unspoken here is that unlike Janine, Brooks
has done something to deserve death, and that the death to which
Brooks might be subjected at the hands of the law will be neither
wanton, nor cruel, nor unnecessary.

Throughout the trial the prosecutor referred to the irrationality
of the crime committed against Janine Galloway and tried to describe
the full measure of the pain that she endured. He returned again and
again to the issue of her blamelessness. "What did she do?" he asked
repeatedly. "She just went outside her home. She was not running
around in skimpy clothes, and she was taken from her home." In his
effort to describe the senseless horror of Brooks's crime, the prosecutor
used the behavior of other rape victims whose dress, he seems to
suggest, invites the crime as a foil to highlight Janine's innocence.[49]
Thus Janine's virtue became a standard against which the flaws of
other women, less pure and innocent than she, could be measured.

In his opening statement the prosecutor told the jury that
Janine was

> accosted by the defendant at gunpoint. She was forced to drive
> with him to the woods behind Dawson school. There she was
> forced at gunpoint to disrobe. She was raped. And then she was
> shot in the neck at a downward angle. Some time later she died
> from the gunshot and the fact that she received no medical
> attention. . . . Behind the school at gunpoint the defendant had
> Janine strip and then he raped her. She was begging "Let me go."

---

48. Herbert Morris, "Persons and Punishment," in *Human Rights*, ed. A. I.
Meldren (Belmont, Calif.: Wadsworth, 1970).
49. Bumiller, "Fallen Angels."

But he taunted her about her virginity. And then he shot her in the neck because she was screaming and she wouldn't shut up.

With these words, the prosecutor sought to make violence and pain speak,[50] though he acknowledges to the jury that "it is not easy for us to appreciate the horror" of Janine's suffering. "Shot in the neck at a downward angle," and "begging 'let me go'" suggest that Janine was on her knees when she was shot. The violence unleashed by the shot was designed to silence its victim who was by then so degraded and desperate that she could only beg for a mercy that was not forthcoming.

The violence that Brooks inflicted on Janine Galloway was, in the prosecutor's description,

done in the course of rape, in the course of armed robbery, in the course of kidnapping with injury. Kidnapping is horrible but this involved an injury to the breast and vaginal area. This was a crime of torture. The defendant wasn't content with just the physical act. He taunted her with his cruel question about her lack of sexual experience.

The prosecutor told the jury that Janine had been shot at close range and that the medical examiner had "found that she had been raped and had been torn up in her private parts. Her panties were very bloody, and on her breast were bite marks. She bled to death over an extended period of time." Violence and pain are put into discourse as a description of wounds and their aftermath.

In the effort to bring violence into discourse and to represent pain as wounds on the body, Janine's body was partialized, objectified, and marked in discrete ways.[51] Brooks's lawless violence is attached to particular parts of her body. It is inscribed as a hole in the neck, bite marks on the breast, blood from "her private parts." As Bumiller argues about rape trials: "the harm to the victim is verified by making visible pain and pleasure; the 'truth' of the women's violation is located in its visibility."[52]

50. Scarry, *Body in Pain.*
51. Bumiller, "Real Violence/Body Fictions."
52. Ibid., 5.

But it is not vision and visibility that dominate in the recreation of the lawless violence done to Janine Galloway. It is speech that carries the burden of representing violence. Three speech acts were central to the narrative of Janine's suffering. First is the statement of Brooks himself, given to the police at the time of his arrest. Second, is Janine's speech as well as her silence. Third, is the testimony of the medical examiner, Dr. Weber.

Brooks's statement became the interpretable text on which much of the narrative of Janine's suffering was written. While he did not testify in his own defense, it was his statement that set the scene and the action of the crime.

> We drove down the dirt road by the Dawson School into the woods. When we got there I told her to stop the car and get out. She asked me to let her go, but I told her to take her clothes off. Then I had sex with her. When we got done I told her to get dressed. I asked her if it was her first time, and she said yes. I told her that I didn't believe her, and she started to scream. I pointed the gun at her and told her to be quiet. I cocked the gun and it went off. She fell. She was still screaming but I couldn't hear her.

On this account Janine's own movement from silence to speech occasioned the violence of her death. She was unable or unwilling to silently endure, to acquiesce in Brooks's demand for silence in the face of his disbelief in her lost innocence. She spoke in the only way she could, first in an audible then in a quickly silenced scream.

Her silence was, throughout the trial, treated as a kind of heroism, even as its end marked the end of her life. As the prosecutor put it,

> [T]he defendant came up to her, but she didn't scream. She was scared to death but she didn't scream. She had taken a course, but she didn't scream. The defendant hid Janine when her mother came outside looking for her. She wanted to say "Momma save me," but she didn't because she knew what would happen. She didn't scream when she was forced to strip naked as a baby or when she was forced to lay down in the woods or when she was penetrated and her body was torn. Still she didn't scream. Then

he taunted her about her virginity. It was only then, only when she saw her death in his eyes that she screamed. And then he killed her.

A third speech act played an important, if unusual role, in representing the lawless violence of William Brooks and in giving a language to Janine's pain by describing the wounds on her body. This was the testimony of the deceased Dr. Weber, the medical examiner who testified at Brooks's first trial. In a strange reenactment of that testimony a member of the prosecution team took the stand equipped with the transcript of the first trial. As if from beyond the grave, Weber became an embodied speaker. Another prosecutor asked the same questions as had been asked in the first trial, and Weber's answers were read verbatim. Those answers suggested that death had been caused by a bullet fired from a short range that entered the base of the neck, "tore away the trachea, hit a rib and the spinal column, lacerated a lung and exited between the third and fourth rib."

Weber stated that Galloway had not died quickly; in his opinion she lived for between one-half hour and two hours after being shot. During this time, he suggested, she had endured a great deal of suffering. In addition, Weber indicated that he found "teeth marks on the left nipple, injuries to the vagina including a lacerated hymen . . . , and hemorrhaging around the pelvis." He noted that Janine was a virgin prior to the assault and that her injuries were "associated with violent sexual activity." In his account virginity becomes the context for understanding the overt marks of violence and pain. Here again violence and pain speak, as Scarry argues they must, through their visible effects—lacerations and hemorrhaging.[53]

The context of a capital trial insures, as Scarry notes,[54] that the difficulty of putting violence and pain into discourse is compounded because at every turn, "the accuracy of the descriptions of suffering" given by one lawyer will be "contested" by the other. This is exemplified in the way the defense reacted to the testimony of Dr. Weber and his representations of Janine's pain. The response was, in fact, to call another medical examiner as an expert witness to contest those representations.

53. *Body in Pain.*
54. Ibid., 10.

That witness put the words of Dr. Weber on trial; he called particular attention to the language of Weber's autopsy report and his testimony. "Dr. Weber," the expert contended, "used words in his report that I would never use and that I've never seen before. He didn't use the standard scientific terms to describe what he was seeing. He talked about rips and tears. As a result, I don't know what he actually saw. . . . And while he described the hymen as virginal, you can't ever tell that."

On cross-examination, this witness persisted for a time in his analysis of Weber's language.

Q: Have you ever found rape in a murder victim?

I prefer to call it sexual battery not rape. The presence of sperm in and of itself doesn't equal rape.

Q: What is the difference between sexual battery and rape?

Well, a stick or a finger would do injury, and sexual battery takes all this into account.

Q: The defendant said he raped her. Are you arguing with that?

No. But Weber's testimony said more than he said in his report. Sometimes medical examiners say more than they should in order to help prosecutors. Anyway his testimony and his report are inconsistent.

While there would be no argument about Brooks's self-incriminating words, Weber's words could be doubted and argued about. Quickly, however, the prosecutor turned his attention to the language of the expert himself.

Q: Are you saying Janine wasn't raped?

No. But you can be raped without being injured. There is still plenty of evidence to indicate that she was raped.

Q: Does the blood on her panties indicate the trauma associated with this rape?

Yes.

Q: Does it suggest the presence of brute force?

No. What we know is that someone had intercourse with her, caused a laceration, and it bled. Many people are, in fact, raped gently.

Q: Was Janine raped gently?

The bruise on her nipple may or may not have come from a bite. Other than the gunshot wound and the small tear in her vagina there is no evidence she was beaten or choked. There is evidence she was raped but not beaten up.

Q: She was kidnapped and forced to strip at gunpoint, then raped. . . .

The defendant said he had sex with her.

Q: The girl said she was a virgin?

Yes.

Q: Was this a pleasant situation to lose her virginity?

No.

Q: Is this the way virgins choose to lose their virginity?

Some might. She did not.

Q: Would this have been painful?

Yes.

In this sequence of questions and answers, Weber's speech is put aside and the focus is on the expert's use of the phrase "gentle rape." His introduction of this absurd idea rendered oxymoronic the very idea of rape itself, and it provided the prosecutor a chance to remind the jury again of Janine's violated innocence, the wounds she had suffered, and the pain spoken through those wounds.

The question of language and its adequacy in describing violence was critical throughout the trial. Brooks's defense insisted that his statement should be taken literally, that it be treated as an honest, full, and precise account of the events surrounding Janine Galloway's death, that the agent of her pain was the gun that "went off" on its own.[55] The prosecutor, in contrast, suggested that the words of that statement, especially the words "it went off" not be taken literally. As the prosecutor explained to the jury, "That's just how he happened to say it. That's just what his lawyer picked up on." Against the literalism of the defense was juxtaposed a theory of linguistic accident, of happenings rather than intentions, of words given meaning only by interpreters with purposes quite foreign to those of the original speaker.[56]

For the prosecutor what was not said in Brooks's statement was as revealing as what was said in it. "I want you to think about committing crimes and if you were telling the truth when you got to the part about the shooting you'd speak pages. 'I didn't mean to. I was going to let her go.' But none of that was ever said."

The defense responded that the statement was accurate and complete, and it appealed to a rather conventional idea of what makes a persuasive narrative.[57]

---

55. Brooks's defense lawyer told me that one of the classic mistakes that people make is to try to keep denying the statement or challenging the voluntariness of it even when it is clear that it is coming in. When they had Brooks admitting to the rape and the robbery and admitting to every other evil, criminal thing that he did and then they wanted us to say he was just trying to explain it away. As you know, my argument was that if we accepted everything else we should credit the statement in its entirety. Lawyers should find ways to turn statements like the one Brooks gave to their own advantage. That is what we were trying to do.

56. The defense accused the prosecution of rhetorical excess, of making a terrible thing seem needlessly worse than it was. "Part of this process is integrity. Things are bad enough. Some of these things were embellished. Things are bad enough. They don't need to be embellished."

57. See, for example, Wayne Booth, The Rhetoric of Ficiton, 2d ed. (Chicago: University of Chicago Press, 1983).

The first thing to look at is the statement itself. . . . It is long and detailed. It tells about everything that happened. It said that she was made to get into a car with a gun. The defendant didn't make things up. The statement tells about the crimes he committed in great detail. Those details are, in addition, corroborated by other evidence. Those details are the kind of things that no other person could have known. And every detail paints as bad a picture of the defendant as could be. Everything says it is true. And the prosecution wants you to believe everything but one sentence. Well they can't have it both ways. The whole statement is truthful.

Taking the statement literally would mean that the gun would become the personified agent of death. "The gun went off." Here agency is attributed to the weapon itself.[58]

The literal reading of the defendant's statement with its attribution of agency to the gun was bolstered by the testimony of a firearms expert.

Q: Is it possible for a gun to go off by itself?

Yes.

Q: Is it possible for a 357 Charter Arms to discharge inadvertently?

Yes.

Q: How can a revolver discharge accidentally?

It depends on the condition of the revolver and whether the safeties are operative. If the weapon is in poor condition the trigger pull might be much too tight so that when a person doesn't

---

58. As Cobb explains, "[P]ain is a manifestation of violence; but since there can be no description of violence that transcends subjectivity . . . we must understand pain by the way it is objectified via . . . 'the language of agency.' Pain is objectified, that is it is presented as located in that which inflicts pain, i.e. the weapon." "Domestication of Violence," 11.

intend it, it might fire. You might pull back the trigger accidentally after having the hammer back.

Q: Could the shooting in this case have been accidental?

Yes. There was one shot from close range. And the statement
of the defendant that the hammer had been pulled back and that
it went off. These things are all consistent with the conclusion
that the gun in this case could have gone off accidentally.

While the defense treated the gun as the agent of death in a
killing that Brooks himself did not control or intend, the prosecution
presented another version of the weapon and of the agency of violence
that was visited on Janine Galloway.

Guns are dangerous, but they have their place. We all know that
they don't just sit there looking to go off. The gun that snuffed
out her life didn't really do it. That defendant did it. He pulled
the trigger. . . . The mouth that marked her breast is that mouth
there. The sex organ that penetrated her is on that man right
there. The hand that fired the fatal bullet is on that man.

"Mouth," "sex organ," "hand," each a weapon used against Janine
Galloway; each an agent of the violence done to her, each a sign of
the pain unjustifiably imposed on her. As Cobb puts it, "The weapons
take on the attributes of the pain and require that the 'violated'
position themselves as victims of the weapons. . . . Pain and its objectification is accompanied by a loss of self, a loss of voice that both
signals the disintegration of the world of the person and confers the
attributes of pain on the object of the pain—and, in the process,
pain is read as power."[59] "Mouth," "sex organ," "hand," these are the
significations of a power brutally abused, a power able to silence
Janine Galloway, to render her screams unhearable. But they also
signify the dismemberment of Brooks's own body, a symbolic dismemberment in which each part of his body is linked with a discrete
injury to his victim.

---

59. Ibid., 11–12.

While the violence of Janine's death was, in the words of the defense, a tragic and accidental violence that knew no logic and for which no one could be held responsible, the prosecution portrayed the violence that took the life of Janine Galloway as the painful, humiliating violence of torture and slow death. But most of all it was an unnecessary violence. "If he wanted her to shut up he could have hit her with a big hand. When she woke up he would have been gone." This violence was, moreover, the willful, immoral, predatory gesture of an evil will transgressing against innocence itself. "One thing keeps coming back. It was all so unnecessary. If one person hadn't decided to use another for his lust she would still be alive. This is not the age of disposable people."

"It was all so unnecessary" and using another "for his lust" bring together two different narrative strands in the prosecution argument. The first is the portrait of violence outside the law with its implicit comparison to law's own violence, and the second is the story of race. With regard to the first, the violence outside law is senseless, random, almost inexplicable. Why did Brooks pick Galloway as his victim? Why that woman at that time? As the prosecutor put it, "We don't know whether he had staked out the Galloway house or whether he was just looking for anybody to rob." Thus the horrifying quality of Janine Galloway's murder was that it was a

> chance encounter between strangers, in which what...[was] casually exchanged happens to be death.... The radical disjunction, or discontinuity, between the immeasurably great value of what is being destroyed... and the miniscule, trivial, "perceived gain" that prompted the murder... leaves... a palpable, profound and almost physical need to reestablish sense and meaning in the universe.[60]

Galloway's murder, as described by the prosecution, was an instance of what Robin West has called "post-modern murders."[61] Such murders, West argues,

---

60. See Robin West, "Narrative, Responsibility, and Death: A Comment on the Death Penalty Cases from the 1989 Term," *Maryland Journal of Contemporary Legal Issues*, 1 (1990): 11.

61. Ibid.

strip the natural world of its hierarchy of values—life, love, nurture, work, care, play, sorrow, grief—and they do so for no reason, not even to satisfy the misguided pseudo-Nietzschean desire of a Loeb or Leopold to effectuate precisely that deconstruction. They are meaningless murders.[62]

If there is meaning in Galloway's death it is found only in a racial narrative in which "animal" passions of the young black male lead him to use another person to satisfy his "lust."[63] "How," the prosecutor asked, "did the defendant treat Janine—like some mother's baby, some daddy's little girl, or like something disposable?" The invitation in this question is to recover meaning by assigning responsibility and by asserting the difference between a violence that knows no law and a violence necessary to control or deter it, between the animal inability of black men to control their "lust" and respect the sanctity of human life and the human need for self-respect and self-control.

Garfinkel, in his famous discussion of the "conditions of successful degradation ceremonies," gives us a way of seeing how William Brooks and his heinous act can be accommodated to a general scheme of preferences and values.[64] Both Brooks and his act are treated as instances of a "type." The prosecutor's denunciation of Brooks as the type who would use another human being for his pleasure and then dispose of her invites the jury to identify with a "dialectical counterpart."[65] It is only, as Garfinkel argues, by the reference "it bears to its opposite" that the "profanity of an occurrence . . . is clarified."[66] As between meaninglessness and a racially coded meaning, the invitation is to reject the former and embrace the latter,[67] and to see

---

62. Ibid.
63. Omolade, "Black Codes," 16.
64. Harold Garfinkel, "Conditions of Successful Degradation Ceremonies," *American Journal of Sociology* 61 (1956): 422.
65. Ibid.
66. Ibid., 423. Indeed Garfinkel makes explicit reference to murder trials as examples of degradation ceremonies. "The features of the mad-dog murderer," he argues, "reverse the features of the peaceful citizen." Ibid.
67. West, "Narrative and Death," 12. West argues that such narratives create a palpable need to reassert responsibility and human agency for a momentous act and momentous deprivation; so that we can again feel in control of our destiny. They create a need to assign responsibility, not just liability and not just guilt. The defendant's ultimate responsibility for the murder is, in a

Brooks and his act as "inexplicably alien, horrendous and inhuman."[68] The jurors in the Brooks case accepted that invitation and rejected what the prosecutor had disparagingly called the "I didn't mean to" version of the death of Janine Galloway. As a result, they convicted Brooks of malice murder, and the trial moved into the second or sentencing phase.

Putting Violence into Discourse in the Trial of William Brooks: The Life and Death of William Brooks

The story of Janine Galloway's murder exemplifies one way in which violence is brought into legal discourse and suggests one set of comparisons between law's violence and its lawless counterpart. That story embodies what Stephen Carter calls "bilateral individualism."[69] In such a conception the status of victim is accorded

> to someone who loses something—property, physical safety—
> because of the predation of someone else. Victimization, then,
> is the result of concrete, individual acts by identifiable trans-
> gressors. . . . [Bilateral individualism] invents a reality in which
> the only victims of crime are those who have suffered at the
> hands of transgressors.[70]

In the penalty phase of Brooks's trial we see another way in which violence is put into legal discourse and a story about a different kind of violence. In this phase it was a narrative about violence that the defendant himself had endured that took center stage. Here again a racial narrative was constructed, only this time by the defense, a narrative of racial pain and racial victimization in which the rage of the young black male is portrayed as an understandable, if not justifiable, response to the constitutive violence of a world beyond his making.

In contrast to the direct, personal, decontextualized violence that

nutshell, essential to the coherence of those stories as human stories, and the coherence of these stories is essential to the meaningfulness of our lives.
68. Ibid., 15.
69. Carter, "When Victims," 421.
70. Ibid.

Janine suffered at Brooks's hands, the violence that was part of the
defendant's life story was more diffuse, spread out over a longer period
of time, and more systemic. In contrast to the violence that took
Janine's life, the violence that Brooks had endured made his life what
it is. In this alternative conception of violence and victimization both
become matters "of the sweep of history, not the actions of individual
transgressors. . . . In this vision of victimhood, the criminal behavior
of so many black males is itself a mark of victimhood, a victimhood
virtually determined from birth."[71]

If in the first phase of the trial the narrative of violence and
death was thick and the narrative of life thin, just the opposite would
be the case in the penalty phase. In this phase, Brooks's life became
the central object of inquiry, while the violence that might take his
life was, as Foucault would have suggested, left virtually invisible.[72]

Seeing the Tragic Life behind the Tragic Event: From Predator to Victim

In the penalty phase of the capital trial "the overall goal of the defense
is to present a human narrative, an explanation of the defendant's
apparently malignant violence as in some way rooted in understandable aspects of the human condition."[73] Thus Brooks's lawyer began
his opening argument in the penalty phase by saying,

> It is hard to get up in front of you. You reached a verdict on
> Saturday that is not what we had hoped, but I accept it. To this
> point, however, all you've heard about is one terrible incident.
> Now you must consider the larger picture of William Brooks's
> life as you decide about the most extraordinary and extreme
> punishments—life in prison and being electrocuted by the state.
> The fact of his conviction for murder is not enough. The state

---

71. Ibid., 426–27. The construction of this narrative is made all the more complex when, as in the Brooks case, the defense lawyer resists "bilateral individualism"
and argues that the defendant did not do what he is accused of doing (malice murder)
in the guilt or innocence phase of the trial, and then, in the penalty phase, shifts
the frame to the alternative conception of violence and victimization in order to
explain *why* the defendant did what the jury found him guilty of doing.

72. Michel Foucault, *Discipline and Punish*, trans. Alan Sheridan (New York:
Random House, 1977).

73. Weisberg, "Deregulating Death," 361.

must prove particular aggravating circumstances in this case. And even if those circumstances are established you still have to consider whether this person is so beyond redemption that he should be eliminated from the human community. To do that you must look at his whole life—good and bad. . . . We are going to tell the story of a life. In court we usually talk about just one incident. . . . Now we are going to talk about a life.

The invitation in this argument is to consider the person behind the crime, to put the crime in context. Through his rhetorical insistence that it is a "life" that must be talked about Brooks's lawyer reminds the jury of the reality of law's violence; he reminds them that there is now another life at stake, a life that can be extinguished through a legal gesture and a legal judgment with as much crushing finality as the life-destroying gesture of Brooks himself. Brooks's lawyer names that gesture "electrocution," and, in so doing, makes the violence of law at least momentarily visible by identifying its instrumentality. He urges each juror to take full responsibility for a life or death decision that is now unavoidable. "Each of you," he says, "is the Supreme Court today. It is your decision whether he lives or dies."

This is an anxiety-producing exhortation that is fraught with its own anxieties. As Scarry suggests, the effort to invent a language to represent violence and pain is shaped by the awareness of the jury's capacity to accept particular linguistic representations.[74] In the narration of the violence in Brooks's life and in the description of the context against which his crime might be judged, the defense has the difficult task of explaining that that narrative does not undo, or diminish, the seriousness of the murder itself. If it fails, or suggests that context overdetermines crime, it invites the jury to reaffirm the correctness of its judgment of guilt by imposing the death penalty.[75] What must be provided then is a narrative of violence and pain and a context for understanding both that explains but does not excuse, "that could respond to the need to assign responsibility . . . to the defendant, society, or history,"[76] and that helps the jury understand

74. *Body in Pain*, 10.
75. West, "Narrative and Death," 11.
76. Ibid., 14.

the sources and origins of the lawless violence perpetrated by William Brooks without suggesting that they should forgive that violence or recant their judgment.

> The defendant has hurt people and sinned against man and God. What you need to consider is what forces pushed him in that direction. But will any of this excuse what happened? Nothing excuses or justifies his crime. . . . Let me remind you what is not before you. This isn't about whether the defendant will be excused. There is no excuse for what William Brooks did. When you consider mitigating evidence it isn't to excuse or justify. He is responsible for what he did. That's why we are here, why we are at this point. That's been decided. . . . Mitigating evidence is offered to help you understand what he did and why, not to excuse or justify it.

Instead of excusing the crime the narrative of Brooks's life is presented as a reason for showing mercy.[77] Brooks's lawyer appealed to the jury to be better than the killer who showed no mercy to Janine Galloway, to follow "feelings of mercy and sympathy that flow from the evidence." "As Christians," he argued,

> we learn about the place of mercy and compassion. Here the law makes room for mercy and compassion. We are proud of our law because it allows us to show mercy. If you find mitigation that can be a reason to give life—anything about William Brooks's life and background, or about his life in prison that makes him worthy of not being killed. If anything you think merits mercy whether I've told you or not, you can vote for life.

This appeal to mercy suggests that law's violence can and should be different from the violence Brooks used against Janine Galloway, and that law can and should show compassionate concern for even the undeserving. It suggests that the question of whether law's violence, in the end, will be different rests in the hands of the jury. To

---

77. For an example of appeals to mercy in another context see Natalie Zemon Davis, *Fiction in the Archives: Pardon Tales and Their Tellers in Sixteenth Century France* (Stanford: Stanford University Press, 1987).

establish its difference and to legitimate law's violence the jury must show the very restraint that Brooks himself did not show; it must hear the call of mercy in ways that Brooks himself did not hear when Janine Galloway begged for her life. In making this argument Brooks's defense gave the state "its moral victory by acknowledging his crime" while, at the same time trying to "persuade the jury that it can accommodate the crime into the assumptions of a social order it wants to reaffirm."[78] At the center of those assumptions is the view that law must be different and better than those over whom it exercises the power of life.

The story of Brooks's life that might merit mercy was one of abuse, cruelty, and victimization. This story itself is a reminder not of law's victories but of its defeats, not of its capacity to protect, but of its frustrating limits. Brooks was the object of a lawless violence that showed no mercy. In contrast to the untroubled innocence of Janine Galloway's life, "the defendant's life," his lawyer contended, "was one nightmare after another." His family was torn apart by violence and abuse, violence first directed at his mother by an alcoholic father who was himself ultimately murdered on the streets of Columbus, Georgia, and then against Brooks by his stepfather.

In this narrative of violence and victimization directed against the perpetrator of violence, the defense faced the same task of representing pain, of putting pain into language, that faced the prosecution in its own efforts to speak about the pain of Janine Galloway. Here again the appeal was to wounds and weapons as the medium of pain's representation.[79] As the defense lawyer put it,

> The defendant carries scars on his back from the beatings he received from his stepfather who would take him in a room, lock the door and whip him on his back with a belt buckle. Gwen [Brooks's sister] used to come home and hear William screaming. When the beating was done, William would come out of the room, his back bloody from the beatings. Such beatings were a daily event.

The story of the violence done to Brooks was played against a domestic and familial life quite different from that of Janine Galloway.

---

78. Weisberg, "Deregulating Death," 362.
79. Scarry, Body in Pain.

While in her life home was a fortress against lawless violence, for Brooks it was the continuous scene of such violence. Whereas Janine's mother was called to the stand to speak about lost innocence, the disruption of domestic tranquility, and her singular, tragic inability to rescue her child from harm, Brooks's mother was called to testify to her continuous inability to do so.

Q: What happened after you moved to Columbus?

My husband began to drink heavily. And then he would try to hit me and we would have fights. He'd hit me and we would tussle. William saw all of this. He saw everything and he'd get very upset. Once he broke my nose and I had to go to the hospital. Another time he hit me and I began to beat him with the heel of my shoe. All the kids were there.

Q: Did you ever inflict injuries on your husband?

Well, once I scalded him with hot coffee once when we had a fight. And the children they saw it. They were all at the table.

Q: How frequent were the fights?

Every weekend. Pretty soon I had to leave every weekend and take the kids to my parents' house. . . . Later my father bought me a shot gun and told me to use it if he tried to beat me again. . . . Once my oldest daughter took the gun and shot him in the hand.

Three of William Brooks's sisters also testified about the violence he and they had experienced as they grew up. Brooks's sister Gwen provided the most vivid portrait of William's victimization.

Q: What was life like with your stepfather?

It was a kind of holy terror. He was abusive and when he wasn't being abusive he made us feel unwanted. He'd curse us and made us feel out of place in our own home. He'd always have a house full of young men drinking, smoking and being fresh.

He could get away with all that being abusive because my mother was at work.

Q: How did he treat William?

He really hated him. He beat him all the time with his belt buckle or with an extension cord. He was always hitting him and pushing him against the wall. More than once I'd heard my brother screaming when I came home. Once I pushed against the door in the room where the screams were coming from. My brother was lying on the mattress and there was blood all over the walls. William begged me to make him stop, but he threw me out of the room and started beating William again.

There is no lost innocence, no fall from grace, in this story because there was never an innocence to be lost. The violence directed against Brooks has its own particular instrumentalities—the belt buckle and the extension cord. It was brutal, continuous, and inescapable. Like many young black men, Brooks lived in a state of nature close to home, a state of nature made real in the pains imposed on him and the inscriptions on his body. What is made visible in this story is the specter of violence generating violence in which law is complicit by its inability to provide protection or defense.

But the rhetoric of law could neither fully contain nor explain the lawless violence to which the defendant was subject and the impact of that violence in precipitating or explaining what he did to Janine Galloway. For such an explanation the defense turned to an expert, a social worker experienced in issues of child development and in child abuse and neglect. As she put it,

William Brooks was subject to persistent and brutal abuse throughout his childhood. He saw explosive tempers all around him, and they became for him a model of how to behave.... To say the least, he grew up in the absence of a nurturing environment.... The abuse and neglect which he suffered caused fear, anxiety and anger. He was left alone to deal with these things. He needed but did not get professional help. Through no fault of his own the very volatile feelings inside him were left to fester. . . . He did not develop internal controls or mechanisms for dealing with his anger. He never found a place to put it.

The introduction of this testimony turned the penalty phase of the Brooks trial into a high culture–scientific expertise versus low culture–common sense contest in which what was contested was the extent to which violence constituted Brooks as a subject, the extent to which it shaped him and contributed to his own violent acts. The high culture–scientific discourse implied that the explanation for Brooks's behavior was complex and hard to disentangle from the violence which made him what he was. The low culture–common sense rendering searched for a more parsimonious explanation. Thus in the midst of his cross-examination of the social worker the prosecutor asked,

Q: Do you believe in the Christian principle of free moral agency? Do you believe that God gave us the capacity to choose right from wrong?

Yes, that can happen if one has a nurturing environment that would support that capacity and allow it to be used.

Q: Do you believe that Almighty God gave us the capacity to know right from wrong?

Almighty God gave us the potential. . . .

Q: How do you explain why some people who come from bad homes do well in life?

We all have different innate endowments and ability to tolerate frustration. One can't just look at people and know who will turn out good and who will turn out bad. You have to look carefully at the environment and especially at family dynamics.

Q: Are you saying that people are not responsible for what they do?

What William Brooks did was the product of interaction between himself and his environment.

Q: Can a child be spoiled?

Yes.

Q: Can someone be just plain mean?

No, not without reason. Children aren't born mean. Children are responsive to their environment.

In this denunciation of Brooks and counterexplanation of his actions, the prosecutor seeks to identify with the "dignity of the supra-personal values of the tribe" of a community of persons committed to the theological principle of free choice.[80] "Just plain mean" is presented as the community's commonsense response to a "scientific" discourse that seemed to make the explanation for violence disappear or to locate it outside the acting subject. For the prosecution what was at stake was the location of the responsibility for violence in a freely acting subject, what was at stake was the very idea of responsibility itself. As the cross-examination continued this theme reappeared.

Q: Was the defendant a time bomb? Was violence inevitable?

He had no way of expressing what was happening to him. His feelings were just festering inside him. He could have learned to channel those feelings and the violence if he'd gotten help.

Q: Suppose he confronted a young woman in her yard, twenty-three years old, a small woman, and he heard her mother coming. Would he be able to transport his victim to a place of seclusion so as to be able to continue his criminal enterprise?

One could not have predicted how he would act out. His anger was there. How it would be expressed could not be predicted.

---

80. See Garfinkel, "Degradation Ceremonies," 423.

. . .

Q: Whose fault was it that Brooks kidnapped Janine?

He would have to take responsibility for that.

Q: And for all his other voluntary acts?

He would be responsible.

. . .

Q: Isn't it true that heaven helps those who help themselves?

That capacity, like any other human capacity, needs to be activated by outside sources.

Q: Not even God could help him. It would take counseling.

The counselor would be an instrument of God.

. . .

Q: Aren't you saying that he wasn't responsible?

I'm not saying that. I'm not saying that he wasn't responsible for what he did. I am saying that things in his childhood caused problems and that he needed professional help that he never received.

The rhetoric of responsibility again provided the medium through which the prosecutor could construct a narrative about violence, about the life of William Brooks and his violent acts. Those acts have to be assigned individuated agency for law's response to have any pretense of efficacy. The narrative of violence begetting of violence, of an abused person enacting his abuse was characterized by the prosecution as a "Devil made me do it" defense. Such a defense "had" to be rejected. Ironically, perhaps, the language of compulsion is used to authorize or require the idea of responsible choice that the prosecution sought to defend. "We *have* to believe that God gave everybody the ability to know right from wrong, good from evil. . . . It is the American way to play by the rules, work hard. That's what he rejected. . . . The defendant, by his own volition, selected to live his life in dark places."

The prosecution denied that there was anything special about Brooks's life. He was a subjectivity constituted not by the violence of its origins and influences but by the violence engendered by its willed choices.[81] Brooks had to be judged and punished in the same way as anyone who made such choices should be judged and punished. For the defense, however, the story of Brooks's life was a story of difference not similarity. It was a life entirely contained by violence, a life unlike those imaginatively denoted by appeals to God's will or the American way.

> People aren't all the same [Brooks's defense lawyer argued]. Free will, yes, but we are not all the same. . . . Some people grow up in good ground, but William Brooks's seed was sown among the thorns. Yes, some sown among the thorns will grow up well. Some will survive, but even they aren't like those that are planted in the field. This little seed tried to struggle through the thorns. And the fact that some make it, well, that's life. You've got to look at where his seed was sown. "Just plain mean"—some people are just plain mean. When we see new babies do we see anyone who is just plain mean? When kids are two or five are they just plain mean? Do they exercise free will in deciding whether they are going to turn out to kill people? . . . People who are abused and neglected, it isn't surprising that they get in trouble. We know there's a road to that even though it doesn't make it okay. . . . It doesn't make it okay. . . . We are not saying if you are abused you can kill.

The narrative of Brooks's life was itself a narrative of violence and pain. The appeal to understand his suffering was, in turn, an appeal to see in it pain acting in a world known only as a source of pain. It was an appeal not to privilege and power, but to the

---

81. Meir Dan-Cohen, "Responsibility and the Boundaries of the Self," *Harvard Law Review* 105 (1992):959.

recognition of the ways that powerlessness and racial deprivations act out their powerful rage. The appeal here is to a shared, though not equally shared, responsibility for Janine Galloway's death. It suggests "an alternative understanding of societal responsibility" that challenges the prosecutor's "bi-lateral individualism."[82] Brooks, after all, was not "Ted Bundy. He didn't go to law school. He isn't somebody who had all that smarts. You've got to ask yourself, is this some poor kid who had never been taught values? You punish those people differently." In the rhetoric of law, punishment is the measure of all things. In this rhetoric the recognition of a different, of a violated, life required a different, less violent punishment.

Naming Law's Violence

In the penalty phase of a capital trial, law's own violence is put, as it always must be, precariously into discourse, and the disposition and use of law's ultimate power over life and death is made the subject of contention. In this moment the legitimation of that power is the most pressing because law enlists ordinary citizens and asks them to exercise its power over life and death. In so doing law seeks to make its violence our violence.

Yet even at this moment it is striking that so little is actually said about the nature of that violence. In contrast to the detailed presentation of the violence outside the law that both prosecution and defense present, neither presented a similarly detailed narrative of the prospective violence which the jury is being asked to authorize for William Brooks. That is, of course, not surprising as a tactic of the prosecution; one would expect him to foreground the violence done to the victim and the pain that she endured and to tread lightly on the terrain of law's own violence.[83] It is, however, not what one would have expected, at least initially, from the defense until one confronts the fact that in all death cases the defense confronts a "death qualified" jury, that is, a group of persons who as a condition of their service in a capital case must have already attested to their ability and willingness to impose the death penalty.[84] Given such an

---

82. Carter, "When Victims," 42.
83. Weisberg, "Deregulating Death," and West, "Narrative and Death."
84. I arrived in Georgia in time to watch the jury being selected for the Brooks trial. Immediately the specter of law's violence took center stage as the presiding

audience, with its known dispositions, to attack frontally and repeatedly the death penalty, to highlight its gruesome violence, would be
to undertake the burden of conversion.

Nonetheless, while neither prosecution or defense undertakes a
detailed explication of the nature of law's violence, the question before
the jury in the penalty phase of a capital trial like that of William
Brooks is what kind of violence are they being asked to do? And
how does that violence differ from the violence to which it is opposed?
The prosecution in the Brooks case consistently called that violence
"the death penalty" as if there was no means or mechanisms of
violence that would necessarily be deployed to bring about death.
The instrumentality, the weapon, the objectification of the pain of
the violence imposed found no expression.

The defense, not surprisingly, both named the weapon and the
act. What the prosecution called the "death penalty" the defense,
called the "most extreme and extraordinary punishment." Brooks's
lawyer insisted that what was at stake was the "elimination of life
by 2200 volts of electricity." What was at stake was not a penalty

---

judge, Judge Lawson, a stout, balding, serious-looking man, conducted voir dire.
Lawson provided each potential juror with a brief overview of the procedure to be
followed in the case. "The defendant," he said,

> is charged with one count of malice murder and if he is convicted the state will
> seek the death penalty. This trial will take place in two stages. In the first phase
> guilt and innocence is the only question. If the defendant is found guilty there
> will be a second stage or sentencing hearing. At the conclusion of the sentencing
> hearing the jury decides between life and death. The jury's decision is final. In
> this state the death penalty is authorized in particularly aggravated circum-
> stances. The death penalty can be imposed on more serious, more severe mur-
> ders. Aggravating circumstances mean more than being guilty of murder. But
> if the jury finds aggravating circumstances it is not required to impose the death
> penalty. Imposition of the death penalty is never mandatory. The defense is
> permitted to present mitigating circumstances, that is, anything in mercy and
> fairness having to do with the defendant or his background. Imposition of the
> death penalty is never mandatory. Finally, I would instruct you that you are
> to draw no inferences about the guilt or innocence of the defendant from the
> fact I have given you these instructions.

These instructions introduce potential jurors to the prospect of imposing a death
sentence before they have been empaneled and heard any evidence. Because the death
penalty is never mandatory, each of the potential jurors at the outset would have to
face the question of whether they could, should circumstances warrant, impose death
as a punishment. As part of what is called the process of "death qualification" Lawson
asked each of the jurors, "Are you conscientiously opposed to the death penalty?"
"If the state seeks the death penalty and you felt the death penalty was justified
would you be able to vote to impose it?"

abstractly called death, but whether law would "kill" William Brooks. The insistence that law's violence is a killing violence effectively blurs the distinction between the act of the criminal and the act of law itself.[85] And it suggests that the legitimation of law's violence cannot rest securely in any sanitized renaming of the death-doing, life-destroying instrumentalities of law itself.

The prosecution addressed the question of the legitimacy of law's violence by making explicit what had earlier in the trial been left unspoken. Here the violence on law's side of the boundary is overtly labeled purposive, measured, and necessary. "We have a right," the prosecutor claimed, "to be vindicated and protected." "We" is both an inclusive and a violent naming, a naming fraught with racial meaning. Who is included in the "we"? While this "we" reaches from this world to the next as a remembrance of and identification with Janine, at the same time, it makes the black Brooks an outsider in a community that needs protection from people like him. It excludes him by claiming law as an entitlement against him. Law's violence is necessary both to vindicate and protect "us" from him.

By speaking the language of "we" the prosecutor seeks to invest himself with the authority to speak for the jury and the community that it represents as well as to it. He reminds the jury that the trial that has brought them to the point of considering a capital sentence "has been conducted according to the rule of law." He identifies himself with the jury and the community while distancing himself and them from the defendant who he denounces. As Garfinkel puts it, in a successful degradation ceremony "the denounced person must be ritually separated from a place in the legitimate order. . . . He must be placed 'outside,' he must be made 'strange.'"[86] In this case law's violence could, the prosecutor claimed, properly be used to vindicate Janine's lost innocence and to protect those who, like her, lead innocent lives from those like Brooks who live in "dark places" and have "forfeited their place in the human community."

---

85. See Camus, "Reflections on the Guillotine."
86. "Degradation Ceremonies," 423. Garfinkel suggests that "[T]he denouncer must arrange to be invested with the right to speak in the name of those ultimate values. . . . The denouncer must get himself so defined by the witnesses that they locate him as a supporter of those values. Not only must the denouncer fix his own distance from the person being denounced, but the witnesses must be made to experience their distance from him also." Ibid.

And the prosecutor argued that this vindication and protection would be, again engaging the project of legitimating law's violence by differentiating it from violence of the kind that Brooks visited on Janine Galloway, a proportionate response to a horrible and horrifying violence:

> It fits the crime. Janine was taunted and tortured. It wasn't like TV. When it was all over she didn't get up and walk away. . . . When the defense says "mercy," think of what the defendant did to Janine. . . . Go back behind Dawson School when Janine was screaming, begging for her life and the defendant shot her and she was screaming and no scream came out. I want you to hear that silent scream when you hear him (the defense lawyer) say "mercy and mitigation."

But in the end, the most powerful authorization and the most unquestionable legitimation of law's violence rests with those to whom it would be applied.[87] Unlike Janine who did nothing to precipitate the violence that was done to her, Brooks had, by his own choice and acts, put himself in harm's way. "Some," the prosecutor argued, "by their own acts forfeit the right to breathe the air we breathe. If he had left Janine alone none of this would have happened. Mr. Brooks showed in what he did to her that he believes in the death penalty."

Juxtaposed to this argument was the defense's contention that the death penalty would be neither necessary nor rational *in this case*. To apply it would expose law's violence as excessive; to apply it would be, in essence, to reduce law's violence to the level of the violence which by their earlier verdict the jury had, in essence, condemned. Killing Brooks would be a vindictive desecration of someone who was already leading a life on the other side of an imagined, but real, line that separates the incarcerated from the free, those in law's custody from those allegedly beyond its confinement. In some sense Brooks was, as his lawyer suggested, already dead.

> What's at stake in this case isn't life as we know it. We are not talking about someone who can go home and play with his kids. We are talking about life lived inside a prison. I know the

---

87. Morris, "Persons and Punishment."

defendant is here because I hear the chains rattling. A life in chains and in prison, that is already an extreme and harsh punishment. . . . This is not about not being punished. You are choosing between two punishments. And you should remember that society has ways of punishing without killing people.

This questioning of the necessity of another killing dominated a defense argument that suggested that a violence dispensed excessively, unnecessarily is a violence no different from the violence used against Janine Galloway. For law's own violence to be different and better it has to meet the test of necessity and, in so doing, live with its own restraint. According to the defense this was a threshold that had not been, and could not be, met in the Brooks case.

We don't need to kill this defendant. The law doesn't require us to do so. There may be times when we need to but this isn't one. . . . No case requires the death penalty. There is no automatic capital punishment. There was no death penalty for the people who murdered those young, black children in Atlanta, or for the man who killed Dr. King or Medgar Evers. . . . No case has to bring the death penalty. . . . Society can be protected without killing William Brooks. . . . You don't have to kill. . . . Brooks's crimes were terrible, evil, and vile. But Janine Galloway's life can't be brought back. If we could bring Janine back I would electrocute William Brooks myself. . . . For everything there is a season. This is a time to punish, but not to kill.

While "You don't have to kill William Brooks" was the repeated refrain in the defense's argument against "electrocution," Brooks's lawyer's statement that "[I]f we would bring Janine back I would electrocute William Brooks myself" was quite extraordinary in marking the nature of law's violence. It served to identify the defense lawyer with the jurors; like them, he suggests he has no conscientious objection to the death penalty. Rather than seeking to turn them against the death penalty, this lawyer suggests that law's violence must be used in measured ways to achieve purposes that can be achieved by no other means. In this case, his statement serves to drive home the point that each use of law's violence must be justified on its own terms. In this case, he challenged the jury to maintain the legitimacy of law's violence by exercising restraint and by insuring that it is not used where it is unnecessary.

For William Brooks this was a persuasive appeal.[88] For him, January 1991, in fact, turned out to be a time to be punished, but not to be killed, a time to receive yet another life sentence rather than to be killed by electrocution.

Conclusion

Capital trials remind us that law's violent constitution does not end with the establishment of legal order. The law constituted, in part, in response to metaphorical violence traffics with literal violence.[89] In capital trials, we see the ways different kinds of violence first are made part of legal discourse and then are differentiated from one another.

First, of course, is the death of the victim. In constructing a narrative of violence and pain and in telling this story prosecutors, like the prosecutor in the Brooks case, construct a sociologically simple world of good and evil, and a morally clear world of responsibility and desert.[90] The prosecution seeks to create a binary opposition between the "angelic" character of the victim, who did not deserve to die, and the "evil" character of the perpetrator, who does not deserve to live. This is the dominant cultural motif for representing violence and victimization.

The second kind of violence and pain whose "reality" is put into discourse in capital trials is the violence done, in their childhood and throughout their life, to defendants like Brooks, the violence of an abusive home and family, the violence that crafts a life and a way of living. Inventing a language to accommodate and express this kind

---

88. When I later asked Brooks's defense lawyer to explain the verdict he suggested that

> [n]o jury is just going to let a guy walk away free when he's responsible for another person dying. . . . But this is the kind of thing that would cause a jury to compromise upon a penalty verdict. I don't think they were sure that he [Brooks] really maliciously intended this, but they could go and convict him of murder and then give him a life sentence as a compromise.

89. See Friedenberg, "Side Effects," 43; also Fitzpatrick, "Violence and Legal Subjection," 15.

90. Weisberg, "Deregulating Death," 361; also Dan-Cohen, "Responsibility and Boundaries."

of violence and pain involves contesting the dominant cultural conception of violence and victimization.[91] Defending a murderer like
Brooks requires the construction of a more complex narrative of
causation and accident, of mixed lives and mixed motives.[92]

The third kind of violence that is put into discourse in capital
trials is the violence of law itself. While the other kinds of violence
are presented as weapons and wounds and described in vivid, concrete, gory detail, law's violence is hardly presented at all. It is named,
when it is named, in the most general, abstract and impersonal ways.
As Foucault argues,

> Punishment . . . [has] become the most hidden part of the penal
> process. This has several consequences: it leaves the domain of
> more or less everyday perception and enters that of abstract
> consciousness; its effectiveness is seen as resulting from its inev-
> itability, not from its visible intensity; it is the certainty of being
> punished and not the horrifying spectacle of public punishment
> that must discourage crime. . . . As a result, justice no longer takes
> public responsibility for the violence that is bound up with its
> practice.[93]

In this process, capital punishment in particular becomes, at best,
a hidden reality.[94] It is a violence known by indirection. What we

91. Carter, "When Victims."
92. Weisberg, "Deregulating Death," 361.
93. Discipline and Punish, 9.
94. A year after my journey to Georgia, newspapers announced, "After Night
of Court Battles, a California Execution." Beneath this headline the New York Times
vividly reported the tangled maze of last minute legal maneuvers that immediately
preceded the death in California's gas chamber of Robert Alton Harris, the 169th
person to be executed since the Supreme Court restored capital punishment in 1976.
As in many previous executions, the hope for clemency or the possibility of a
stay of execution was in Harris's case pursued until the last minute. In the twelve-
hour period before Harris's execution no less than four separate stays were issued by
the 9th Circuit Court of Appeals. Finally, in an exasperated, and unusually dramatic
expression of Justice Rehnquist's aphoristic response to the seemingly endless appeals
in capital cases—"Let's get on with it"—the Supreme Court took the virtually unprecedented step of ordering that "no further stays shall be entered . . . except upon order
of this court." The Court scolded Harris's lawyers for "abusive delay which has been
compounded by last minute attempts to manipulate the judicial process" (New York
Times, 22 April 1992, sec. A). In so doing it displaced Harris as the soon-to-be

know about the way law does death comes in the most highly mediated way as a rumor, a report, an account of the voiceless expression of the body of the condemned rather than in a detailed recounting in the narratives of capital trials. However, even such highly mediated accounts convey the ferocity of death at the hands of the law, and, in so doing, arouse anxiety and fear.

The events those accounts describe suggest that law's violence bears substantial traces of the violence it is designed to deter and punish. In Foucault's words, it was "as if this rite that 'concluded the crime' was suspected of being in some undesirable way linked with it. It was as if the punishment was thought to equal, if not exceed,

---

victim of law and portrayed law itself as the victim of Harris and his manipulative lawyers. To defend the virtue of law required an assertion of the Court's supremacy against both the vexatious sympathies of other courts and the efforts of Harris and his lawyers to keep alive a dialogue about death. With this order the Supreme Court stopped the talk and took upon itself the responsibility for the execution of Robert Alton Harris.

Seldom has the Court's own role as a doer of death been so visible. Yet just as the Court's role was rendered unusually visible, Harris's death was rendered invisible. His execution was carried out, as is the modern custom, behind penitentiary walls, beyond public view. The *New York Times* reported that "In a last macabre twist, the A.C.L.U., which opposes capital punishment in all cases, received last-minute permission . . . to videotape [Harris's] execution. . . ." 22 April 1992, sec. A. In this way the penalty of death is linked to the privilege of viewing.

While executions have to be witnessed to be lawful, witnessing is carefully monitored. Who will be allowed to see what is for most of us unseeable is an important question in every execution. Robert Johnson, *Death Work: A Study of the Modern Execution Process* (Pacific Grove, Calif.: Brooks/Cole, 1990), 103–4. Silencing the condemned and limiting the visibility of lawfully imposed death is part of the modern bureaucratization of capital punishment, and part of the strategy for transforming execution from an arousing public spectacle of vengeance to a soothing matter of mere administration. Foucault, *Discipline and Punish,* chap. 1. The association of law and violence though rendered invisible in the bureaucratization of capital punishment is sometimes made visible elsewhere, for example, in the use of lethal force by police. It is, moreover, linguistically present in the ease and comfort with which we speak about enforcing the law. "'Applicability,' 'enforceability' is not," as Derrida puts it,

> an exterior or secondary possibility that may or may not be added as a supplement to law. . . . The word "enforceability" reminds us that there is no such thing as law that doesn't imply in itself, *a priori,* . . . the possibility of being "enforced," applied by force. There are, to be sure, laws that are not enforced, but there is no law without enforceability, and no applicabilty or enforceability of the law without force, whether this force be direct or indirect, physical or symbolic.

"Force of Law," 925.

in savagery the crime itself . . . to make the executioner resemble a criminal, judges murderers."[95] The bloodletting that such acts signal strains against and ultimately disrupts all efforts to normalize them, routinize them, and cover their tracks. While execution itself is effectively hidden from public view, the spectacle of law's dealings in death may be (re)located and made visible, if it is made visible at all, in capital trials like that of William Brooks. Under the force of this relocation we focus on the case rather than the body of the "condemned." As Foucault puts it, "[P]ublicity has shifted to the trial, and to the sentence; the execution itself is like an additional shame that justice is ashamed to impose on the condemned man"[96]

The Brooks trial, and others like it, expresses and embodies a deeply felt anxiety about the proper relationship of law and violence. This anxiety is reflected in the scrupulousness with which capital trials are themselves organized, regulated, and reviewed. It is also reflected in the enormous efforts put into the rationalization and justification of the apparatus of punishment, efforts that serve to efface the violence of law by renaming it. As Robert Weisberg recently observed,

> Anglo-American law has traditionally suffered a serious identity crisis over its awkward relation to violence. . . . Our system assumes that law is to hold a monopoly on violence, but this is a monopoly viewed as both necessary and discomforting. It is necessary because it is viewed as the alternative to something worse—unrestrained private vengeance—and it is discomforting because those who make and enforce the law would like us to believe that, though they may be required to use force, force is somehow categorically distinguishable from violence. . . . [T]he efforts of modern jurisprudence to finesse or deny the role of violence have not ceased.[97]

In all capital trials the juxtaposition of narratives about violence is disquieting, if not destabilizing. This is especially true of

95. Ibid.
96. Ibid.
97. See "Private Violence as Moral Action: The Law as Inspiration and Example," in *Law's Violence*, ed. Austin Sarat and Thomas R. Kearns, (Ann Arbor: University of Michigan Press, 1992).

the juxtaposition of the narratives of violence outside law with the linguistic representation of law's own violence. In these moments putting law's violence into discourse threatens to expose law as essentially similar to the antisocial violence it is supposed to deter and punish.[98] Benjamin argues that "in the exercise of violence over life and death more than in any other legal act, law reaffirms itself. But," he continues, "in this very violence something rotten in law is revealed, above all to a finer sensibility, because the latter knows itself to be infinitely remote from conditions in which fate might imperiously have shown itself in such a sentence."[99] The violence of law threatens to expose the facade of law's dispassionate reason, of its necessity and restraint, as just that—a facade—and to destabilize law by forcing choices between the normative aspirations of law and the need to maintain social order through force.[100] Violence threatens to swallow up law and leave nothing but a social world of forces arrayed in aggressive opposition. Where violence is present can there be anything other than violence? This question puts enormous pressures on events like the capital trial to demonstrate and affirm the difference between the violence of law and the violence that law condemns.

Here then is the site of the most intense efforts to finesse and deny the role of violence in law, to mark the differences between violence beyond law's control and that which law itself dispenses, and to transform law's violence into legitimate force. Capital trials are occasions for overcoming doubt and regaining stability. The cultural resources for doing so are both internal and external to law

---

98. See also Camus, "Reflections on the Guillotine." The imperatives of violence may be so overwhelming as to distort and destroy prevailing normative commitments. Two powerful examples are provided by Justice Powell in McClesky v. Kemp, 107 S. Ct. 1756 (1987) (holding that statistical evidence of racial discrimination may not be used to establish prime facie case of discrimination in death penalty cases), and by Justice Rehnquist in Payne v. Tennessee, 90-5721 (1991) (devising new understanding of the bindingness of precedent to overturn two decisions forbidding the use of victim impact information in death penalty litigation).

Unfortunately, except in the utopian imagination, there is no symmetry in the relation of law and violence. Law never similarly threatens violence. Even when we realize the way law itself often exaggerates the threat of violence *outside* law, we can never ourselves imagine that law could finally conquer and undo force, coercion, and disorder; its best promise is a promise to substitute one kind of force—legitimate force—for another.

99. "Critique of Violence," 286.
100. Sarat and Kearns, "Journey through Forgetting," 269.

itself. Random, unnecessary, irrational violence is vividly portrayed.
While the violence outside the law is unnecessary, irrational, indiscriminant, gruesome, and useless, law's violence, the violence of the
death penalty, is described as rational, purposive, and controlled
through values, norms, and procedures external to violence itself. In
capital trials, the force of law is represented as serving common
purposes and aims as against the anomic savagery lurking just beyond
law's boundaries.[101] Elaborate rituals and procedures, "super due process," give evidence of the care and concern with which law traffics
in violence. The case of the condemned is treated with a seriousness
equal to, if not greater than any other in law. Thus the procedures
and purposes of law are emphasized while its instrumentalities and
wounding effects are kept in the background.

Externally, law draws upon cultural symbols of race and danger.
Law's violence is, thus, "our" violence against "them." As Justice
Powell reminded us, the racialization of capital punishment and its
disproportionate use against black men and especially those who kill
white victims is not sufficiently disturbing in this culture to be "constitutionally significant."[102] It is the allegedly civilizing violence of
white order against savage disorder. Thus in the Brooks trial and in
others like it, the price paid for such efforts to alleviate anxiety is
very great. In addition to the actual violence that is all too often
unleashed and the linguistic violence done in the ritual naming and
in the process of rendering law's violence abstract, racialized social
conventions as well as flat narratives of purity and danger, responsibility and excuse, and innocence and guilt are regularly reaffirmed.

Yet the anxiety that surrounds the violence of law is not put to rest.
Capital trials place several narratives of violence side-by-side, one a
narrative of violence that has already taken life, one a narrative of
abuse and poverty that has shaped another life, and one the story of a
prospective killing. While the first is intended to justify and strengthen
the last, the last stands as an internal reminder of the artifice and arti-
ficiality of the very distinctions on which law's anxiety-alleviating

101. Susan Jacoby, *Wild Justice: The Evolution of Revenge* (New York: Harper
and Row, 1983). As Justice Stewart put it in his concurring opinion in Furman v.
Georgia, 408 U.S. 238, 309 (1972), "The instinct for retribution is part of the nature
of man and channeling that instinct in the administration of criminal justice serves
an important purpose in promoting the stability of a society governed by law."
102. See *McCleskey v. Kemp*, 1778.

legitimacy depends. Each narrative of lawless violence—whether of the kind that Brooks did or the kind that he suffered—is a reminder of the failure of law's own violence to guarantee security. Each narrative of lawless violence reminds us that law's violence constitutes us as anxious, fearful subjects caught between a fearful aversion to the former and a fearful embrace of the latter.[103]

---

103. Dumm, "Fear of Law."

Ordering Voice: Rhetoric and Democracy in Project Head Start

Lucie White

> It is not necessary to read far in the handbooks of rhetoric . . . to preceive an intimate and ideologically motivated link between the need to control the movement of tropes and contemporary exigencies of social control . . . [Yet] what is striking the more one reads in the treatments of order in discourse or the regulation of tropes is that the very terms that are supposed to produce or reflect order lead to a querying of its construction.
>
> —Patricia Parker, "Motivated Rhetorics"

Part of my job involves teaching basic courses to first-year law students. Many of these students have studied legal and social theory as undergraduates. Their life experience has taught them that the law denotes tangles of cultural meaning, as well as systems of rules. Yet when they enter law school, these students will often repress what they know of the law's complexity. Defiantly, they seek to return to a child's naive understanding, in which all of the law càn be reduced to the following formula: "Do X, or you'll be sorry."

To get these students to reclaim their fugitive mature consciousness of law, I remind them that much of the law that they will practice falls outside of their simple formula. Constitutional law, for instance, the law of dispute resolution, and the sprawling corpus of social law,

---

Throughout this essay, I use the term *voice* in the sense that Albert Hirschman elaborated in *Exit, Voice, and Loyalty: Responses to Decline in Firms, Organizations, and States*, 2d ed. (Cambridge, Mass.: Harvard University Press, 1978).

of public law, of international law—the law, in short, of the contemporary world—none of these bodies of law function like traffic rules,
commanding individual citizens when to stop and when to go. Rather,
much of this law is constitutive. It creates the social spaces within
which communities take shape. This law calls for a different basic
sentence, a different imperative, to account for how it works. To
frame such a formula, one might draw inspiration from an old rock
song: "Let's get together," by playing on *this* field. One everyday
example of how law works, in this fashion, to frame community can
be found in the popular Head Start preschool program for poor
children, which is both funded and structured by federal law.

The law that mandates Head Start and other social programs
does not seek to normalize individual conduct, at least not in a
transparent way. Rather, it frames space for social and political life.
My facetious formula is not really as innocent as it may sound,
however, for that formula conceals the force that law—even the law
of social programs, the law that coaxes community—may command.
In my students' formulaic understanding, the law's violence is all too
apparent: it dangles at the end of their imperative sentence, like a
sword. In the case of laws like Head Start's, however—the laws that
map out public programs—one has to search for the constraint. One
has to search for the ways that laws like Head Start's subtly order
the kinds of action that clients can invent. Two different projects
have been undertaken to search for this rhetorical ordering that is
effected by public law.

The first of these projects looks at the images that are embedded
in law's language, images of citizens, of the forum, of fair process,
the images through which law orders the rituals of citizenship. It
then looks for the hierarchies, the exclusions—the injustice, that those
images insinuate into human lives. Among the many works that have
pursued this thematic project, Carole Pateman's relentless feminist
deconstructions of liberal democratic rhetoric stand out.[1]

The second of these projects looks for the constraint implicit in
public law by tracing paths of action that the law's subjects have
taken, rather than by interpreting the regulative images that the law
projects. Here, the law's ordering force is not teased out of its imagery;

---

1. See, for example, Carole Pateman, *The Sexual Contract* (Stanford, Calif.:
Stanford University Press, 1988).

that order is detected by closely watching the action in different public law arenas, in real time. Rather than studying the images in the law's texts, this second critical project goes to the sites where law draws people together and studies how they move. It looks for the recurring plots and patterns that emerge through their action. Do different kinds of public law bring forth different degrees of solidarity, different tactics of subversion, different styles of play? Are some public law innovations—some approaches to gathering the group, or designing the forum, or governing the conversation—better than others—more consistent with our normative commitments and aspirations?

As Austin Sarat has documented in an ethnography of welfare recipients, in the experience of many poor people, "[T]he law is all over."[2] Poor people often look to the state to meet their everyday needs. And the state takes a special interest in keeping poor people under guard. Therefore, economically and politically subordinated groups often spend much of their time within the walls of law-framed institutions like welfare offices, public clinics, prisons, and, if they are lucky, Head Start centers. As a poverty lawyer, I have worked with many people who feel their lives to be boxed in at every juncture by the law. These people often feel their most capricious private gestures to be conscribed within the rules and spaces of law.

Yet at the same time, poor people often recognize that law does not constrain their every action in the same way. Though they come upon law-constituted institutions at many different moments in their day to day lives, these settings are not all cut from a single juridical mold. Rather, different law-framed spaces reflect different normative assumptions and consequently express different styles of institutional design. Those spaces in turn make different kinds of group action possible among poor people; different public law arenas both shape and confine community in different ways.

There are few accounts in legal scholarship of the street-level workings of public laws. There are few accounts of how these laws create spaces that both enable and obstruct real people in their work of improvising lives, families, and communities in what is often a hostile world. This essay seeks to add to such description. It follows the action that transpires over a two-hour period in the meeting of

2. Austin Sarat, "'. . . The Law Is All Over': Power, Resistance, and the Legal Consciousness of the Welfare Poor," *Yale Journal of Law and the Humanities* 8 (1990): 343.

a law-mandated Head Start parent council. It then asks how the law frames that action. Contrary to what the framing image evokes, however, the law in this instance does not impose clear boundaries around the action. It does not provide a code of rules that structures the forum and defines orderly speech, thereby ritualizing the action that is brought forth. Rather, the law figures in much more ambiguous ways.

As a texture of intersecting codes that mandate the gathering and regulate the speech within it, the law stands in a constitutive relation to the event and the actors who play it out. Yet the meaning of those codes—their force—is in turn constituted by the actors themselves, through the multiple interpretations they put forth as they probe the limits of their law-sanctioned roles. In the end, the law—the legal framework for the action—constrains the actors' performance. Yet the shape of that constraint is as much a comment on the actors' talent— on the boldness and rhythm and vision of their performance—as it is a reflection of the order that is prescribed by the law.

Given the complexity, the shifting ground, that close-up accounts of action inevitably reveal, it may not be possible to draw much programmatic wisdom from them. Such wisdom is likely to come intermittently, through the intuitions of those who are caught up in the action, as well as through the analyses of those who look on. When it does come, such wisdom will be subtle, situated, uncertain. Yet when "the law is all over," as it is for the "welfare poor," such pragmatic, ground-level knowledge may be called for to locate the changes in law-framed institutions that might make some difference in real lives.

Law in Action

The account that follows is based on field notes and transcripts of a routine monthly policy council meeting at a Head Start program in the rural South. I attended the meeting and interviewed the participants in the course of research on the informal community that women make around the Head Start program. Head Start is one of many government-sponsored local institutions in which law—federal and state statutes, administrative regulations, agency transmittals, memoranda, handbooks, and operating manuals—defines a site in which ordinary people are brought together to get something that they feel—or are told—that they need. In the case of Head Start, these people are mostly women whose household incomes fall below the federal poverty line; what they get is three hours a day of preschool instruction for their children and various health, educational, social, and vocational services for themselves.

The Law

Head Start's law is fairly explicit, both in ordering its subjects to come together at specific times and places, and in regulating what they say and do when they so convene. Therefore, Head Start offers a paradigmatic example of the law working first to gather people together and then to order the action that results. Project Head Start was initiated by President Lyndon Johnson in the spring of 1965, to provide "political ballast" for the embattled flagship of his War on Poverty, the community action program. Because Head Start fell under the Economic Opportunity Act of 1964,[3] the program was mandated to comply with the act's controversial gesture toward grassroots democracy. The statute required Head Start, as well as all of its other programs, to "be developed, conducted, and administered with the maximum feasible participation of . . . members of the groups served."[4]

The Head Start concept emerged from a presidentially appointed committee of child welfare experts, who envisioned the program within a deficit model of poverty, as a way to compensate for the assumed cultural deprivation of poor children. A dissenting group in the founding committee understood poverty more in terms of political subordination than cultural pathology. They saw Head Start as a grassroots political experiment that would engage poor women in collective action and thereby empower them to seek wider educational and social change. Through the influence of this dissenting group, parent involvement—not just in the classroom, but also in program management—became one of four official Head Start components, along with education, health and nutrition, and social services.[5] This

---

3. P.L. 88–452.
4. P.L. 88–452, sec. 202(a)(3).
5. Robert Cooke, "Improving the Opportunities and Achievements of the Children of the Poor," memorandum prepared by Planning Committee, Project Head Start, for the Office of Economic Opportunity, 1965.

parent governance focus was eventually written into the Head Start statute[6] and regulations.

After 1968, Head Start mothers organized to thwart an effort by President Nixon to transfer the program to the federal Office of Education. These women feared that the education bureaucracy would eliminate their self-governance rights.[7] In reaction to their protests, the Head Start Bureau, in 1970, issued a detailed regulation on parent governance,[8] which remains in effect today.[9] This law's primary author, Bessie Draper, is an African-American woman with a background in the civil rights movement. She was instructed to draft a parent governance regulation in order to "restore order" in the program, putting clear limits on the open-ended statutory mandate of "maximum feasible participation."[10] She worked with a private-sector management-consulting firm to produce a text that subverts these instructions as it carries them out.

The regulation begins by announcing that

[i]f Head Start children are to reach their fullest potential there must be an opportunity for Head Start parents to influence the character of programs affecting the development of their children. The organizational structure of every Head Start program must provide this opportunity.

It then admonishes "all parties" to approach the task of implementing its terms "in a spirit of mutual understanding and partnership." For

[s]uccessful parental involvement helps bring about changes in institutions in the community, and works toward altering the social conditions that have formed the systems that surround the economically disadvantaged child and his family. . . . Every Head Start program is obligated to provide the channels through

---

6. P.L. 90–222, sec. 222(a)(1)(B).

7. Author's interview with Mamie Moore, Atlanta, Ga., 28 March 1989.

8. Office of Child Development-Head Start, Transmittal Notice 70.2 for Instruction I-30, sec. B-2, 10 August 1970.

9. 45 CFR Sec. 1304.5–5 "Parent Involvement Plan content: Parents, area residents, and the program" and appendix B, "Head Start Policy Manual: The Parents."

10. Author's interview with Bessie Draper, former director of parent involvement in the Head Start National Office, Silver Spring, Md., 20 June 1990.

which such participation and involvement can be provided for and enriched. Unless this happens, the goals of Head Start will not be achieved . . . [There will be no] needed changes in social systems into which the child will move after his Head Start experience.

The regulation then mandates that each Head Start program set up a policy council, at least half of whose members must be Head Start parents elected by their peers. The remaining members shall be "community" representatives, generally chosen from social service agencies in the program's service area. Head Start staff may attend meetings on the council's invitation, but they cannot vote.

With the aid of four intricate charts, the regulation then enumerates the policy councils' powers. Each program's council must meet regularly. It must approve the program's annual budget, its criteria for hiring and firing, and all personnel decisions. It must also approve the program's criteria for selecting children, the siting of classrooms, major shifts in program policy, and the ground rules for the policy council itself. Head Start programs cannot get refunded without policy council approval of the grant application. Compliance with these requirements is monitored by federal officials and parents themselves.

The policy councils are required to conduct their business according to Robert's Rules of Order. As public bodies, the councils must also comply with additional procedural requirements that may be imposed by state and local public meeting laws. Finally, Head Start's parent governance regulation warns that

[i]t may not be easy for Head Start directors and professional staff to share responsibility when decisions must be made. Even when they are committed to involving parents, the Head Start staff must take care to avoid dominating meetings by force of their greater training and experience in the process of decision-making. At these meetings professionals may be tempted to do most of the talking. They must learn to ask parents for their ideas, and listen with attention, patience and understanding. Self-confidence and self-respect are powerful motivating forces. Activities which bring out these qualities can prove invaluable in improving family life of young children from low income homes.

The Scene

It is the hilly, red clay central region of Carolina, right on the imaginary line that separates the stubby farm plots of the northern Piedmont from the cotton plantations that extend to the south. This land was seized and settled by fiercely independent Scotch-Irish and German Protestants over two centuries ago. Some came south from the congestion of Pennsylvania, to carve modest farm plots out of the hills. And others pushed north from the cloying hierarchy of the coastal plain, to extend the cotton economy deep into the oak and maple woods. These folks' descendants still pride themselves for their small-farm self-reliance. They are the kind of people who go to church every Sunday and put up enough home grown vegetables in July to feed their families for the entire year. Yet many of the region's European settlers, particularly those who came up from the South, did not clear their land or plant their cotton with their own hands. Rather, this work was done for them by vast extended families of African slaves.

A major east-west highway dissects both the county and its only real town, connecting the large city that lies fifty miles to the west with the popular Atlantic beaches that lie a hundred and fifty miles due east. That town, which is called Robertsonville after one of its founders, is both the county's seat of government and the only place in the area where you can get a real selection of fast food. If you turn south off the highway at Hardee's and follow the road up the hill, you will reach the center of Robertsonville. An imposing post-bellum courthouse and jail, a standard feature in these small southern county seats, dominates the landscape. A plaque in the courthouse lobby, donated by a local citizens' group in the 1960s, commemorates the slaves in the county who remained loyal to their masters during the Civil War.

About a block from the courthouse, a sleek, brick and plate glass public library occupies a corner lot. A fire station stands nearby. Beside it, a bright blue sign, reassuringly emblazoned with a white *H*, points down a small road away from town. Several professionals' offices—doctors, dentists, lawyers—are clustered along this path. On the streets, you can feel that this is one of those places where white people are just about outnumbered, and where jobs are scarce. Indeed, almost half of the county's population is classified by the census as "black," and of this group, over a third live below the federal poverty line.

Groups of African-Americans, mostly middle-aged men, are gathered, "loitering," at just about every corner. No whites are visible, except inside their cars or behind the counters of the few white people's stores at the top of the hill—a farm supply depot, a drug store with a forlorn soda fountain, an insurance agency, and a white-ladies' dress shop displaying bold-colored women's fashions from a bygone era. Smaller black folks' stores encircle these shops, as the streets spread out in every direction from the courthouse, down the hill. Some of these stores display rap tapes and skin lighteners in their cluttered windows. Others sell tobacco, boiled peanuts, fried pork rinds, potato chips, soft drinks, and beer. You have to go to the next county to buy hard liquor without breaking the law.

Halfway down the hill, what looks like it used to be the local A & P is now the county department of social services, where poor people go for their food stamps and AFDC. Nearby, another large storefront, once a discount furniture store, has been transformed by flags and banners into the county's Republican headquarters for the fall election. People get their groceries down the hill, at two shopping centers on the main highway east of town. There, they can shop at Winn Dixie, Food Lion, KMart, Eckerds, and Pick and Pay. At these buzzing, brightly lit establishments that border expanses of asphalt, blacks and whites seem to mix easily, naturally, as they wait to hand cash, plastic, or food stamps to young white girls poised at state-of-the-art, optically sensitive, computerized cash registers.

At the west side of town, set just off the main highway, stands a pair of run-down buildings that look like they might have once been a public school. The larger building is an elegant red brick structure, built with the subtle artistry of depression era schoolhouses. It is a single story, with a dozen classrooms jutting from a hallway that runs to the left and right of the building's entrance and an auditorium extending to the rear. The building is in disrepair: there are several broken windows, and the white paint is peeling from its main door. Inside, the classrooms have poster-board signs on their doors: "Tax Advice," "Weatherization," "Homeless Outreach." These signs are the only clue that the building, once the county's all-black high school, is still in use. It now houses the remains of the county's War on Poverty.

The smaller of the two buildings is set off to one side of the first, closer to the highway. This structure has a fenced yard where harsh gray playground structures—swings, a slide, a jungle gym— sit beneath scattered pine trees in the grass. The building itself, of cheap, shoe box, 1960s construction, is a block of four classrooms with no interior hall. Each classroom has its own exit to the play yard and is linked to the opposite classroom by a stale-smelling bathroom with two tiny cabined toilets and a common sink.

In contrast to the forlorn appearance of the older, main building, this smaller structure is obviously in use. Three of the classrooms appear to be laid out for very small children. In each, a frayed red rug is spread on the floor in front of the blackboard. Off to one side are three small tables, each surrounded by eight little chairs. Waist-high shelves line the walls and extend into the room, dividing it up into alcoves just large enough to allow four or five children to play. These shelves are crammed with blocks, tattered puppets, board games, a few books, and an odd assortment of beat-up plastic toys. An old gray record player, with a stack of records beside it, sits on top of one of the shelves. Large signs, cut out from colored construction paper and taped to the walls, announce that one corner of the room is for "housekeeping," another for "science," a third for "manipulative skills," and a fourth for "reading." Along one wall is a wooden board with eighteen toothbrushes hanging from little metal hooks. Above each hook is a piece of masking tape with a name carefully printed on it in block letters—"Antoineisha," "Kayleisha," "Luscious," "Lafayette," "Mautavius." Childish paintings, in broad angry strokes of yellow and red and blue, are tacked up to bulletin boards. Each of these paintings is labeled in broad-tipped black marker, with one of these same names.

The fourth classroom is set up as an office and parent activity room. A small refrigerator and microwave are set on a counter in one corner. Two schoolteacher's desks are angled toward each other a few feet away. About twenty folding chairs are arranged in rows in the center of the room, facing two long tables set up end to end across the front of the room. Framing the blackboard are two bulletin boards. Tacked to one are notices to "employees," printed in small gray type. The second bulletin board, captioned "parents," displays a few photographs of awkward, proud women, and yet more notices, about "Child Abuse" and "HIB vaccinations" and "Bus Pick-up Schedules."

To one side of the gravel walkway that connects this classroom's exit to the parking lot and the highway beyond, stuck into the grass, is a wooden sign with profiles of two obviously African-American children crudely outlined in black paint. Below these figures, the words "County Head Start Program—from the parents, 1987" are somewhat uncertainly blocked out in red paint.

It is about six o'clock, just after sunset, on a warm, windy March evening. The lights are on in the Head Start office, which doubles on nights like this as the meeting room for parent groups. The program's monthly policy council meeting is about to begin. This Head Start program serves three rural counties that are strung together by the highway that heads to the beach. Because Robertsonville is right at the midpoint of this three-county string, the policy council meets here on the first Monday evening of each month. The policy council has one parent from each of the program's nine classroom sites, and eight community representatives, who work in places like food stamp offices, community colleges, and mental health centers.

The Actors

Carla Hanks

The program's director, Carla Hanks, has just arrived from the program's administrative office in Runyon County, which lies twenty-five miles down the highway to the west. Runyon is the westernmost county that is served by this Head Start. It has grown rapidly over the last decade, as the population of the large urban area to its west has spilled over into the surrounding farmland. Mrs. Hanks, who is in her early fifties, was raised as one of twelve children on a Runyon County farm. After graduating first in her class at a small rural high school, she commuted to the city to work at the phone company while raising her children. She also volunteered at the nursery school at her church. About a decade ago, an older cousin, who had become the Head Start director, gave her a job in the program. Carla, as she likes to be called, moved into the position of Head Start director when a conflict with the community action agency that sponsors this Head Start program forced her cousin to resign.

Carla Hanks's only clear childhood memory of African-Americans is an image of black children walking down a dirt road

to their schoolhouse as she and her sisters walked out to a hardtop
highway to catch their bus to the white school. In the early 1970s,
she worked briefly for a federally funded kindergarten program for
poor children. But by now, after working for over a decade in Head
Start, Carla feels comfortable with "her" parents, the great majority
of whom are African-American. And she has grown accustomed
to the impoverished conditions in which many of the Head Start
families live. Recently, Carla started taking classes at the local
Christian college, with plans to earn a bachelor's degree in business
and move on in her late-blooming career.

Jeanette Hastie

Moments after Carla enters the parent room and begins to set up for
the meeting, the Head Start van arrives in the school's gravel parking
lot, and six women get out. The driver, Jeanette Hastie, stands out
among these women because of her girth, which is enormous. She
struggles to free herself from the vehicle and moves slowly through
the play yard into the building. She talks in a wide, easygoing, country
lilt. Brought up by women kinfolk in a sharecropper's shack on a
plantation a few miles south, she "never realized till I grew up" that
her family was poor. After staying in school through the tenth grade,
she moved with her young husband to a little hamlet off the highway
twenty miles to the west. They soon established themselves in the
area. They now own a car wash and a beauty shop and rent out some
land. Several old Mercedes, all of them in running order, are positioned
like postmodern sculptures in their front yard.

Jeanette first found out about Head Start some fifteen years ago,
when her baby was getting up toward the age to start school. Head
Start has been around in these counties since 1965, but for some
reason Jeanette had not heard about it in time to send her older boys.
At first, Head Start was hard for Jeanette's baby, who was hardly
four when she started taking the big yellow Head Start bus twenty
miles down the highway to the old brick school. The baby seemed
to like Head Start a lot once she got used to it, though, especially
the songs, the apples she would get for snack, and the hugs. But
Jeanette still remembers her baby crying those first few mornings,
when she had to leave her mother to get on that bus.

It was her baby's fussing when the bus came that first got Jeanette into the habit of going to Head Start in the mornings on the bus. By then her two oldest sons had already been soured by the region's embattled, begrudgingly integrated public schools. Therefore, Jeanette didn't expect much on that morning when she first walked into the Head Start building, to see if she could help out in her baby's class. But from her first day in that classroom, Jeanette could tell that something about Head Start was different—different from the schools her sons had gone through, and different from the other programs that the government ran in these counties for blacks. The words for Head Start's difference elude her. It was something about how she felt when she worked there, something that made her feel good. Whatever it was, it hooked her. She started working in her baby's classroom every day. Then she got elected to the policy council and became its chair. She got up the nerve to take the five tests she had to pass to get her GED, and Head Start hired her to help out with its parent activities. With a regular job, she could go back to college at night to get her BA. She has been the program's "parent involvement coordinator" for about twelve years.

Sarah Grier

Of the five passengers who rode with Jeanette in the van, only one, Sarah Grier, is white. Sarah is tall and muscular, with a beet red complexion and long chestnut hair. She works with her husband in a roofing business. Weeks of working outdoors, asphalting and shingling the roof of the elementary school that is going up in a new subdivision in Runyon County, have leathered her face and hands. She is the policy council representative from one of the few classroom sites with a majority of white kids.

Corva Marshall

The four other parents in Jeanette Hastie's van are all dark-complexioned women of African descent. These women have rarely been farther from their homes than the city fifty miles to the west. Corva Marshall is the most talkative among them. A wiry woman with an intense gaze, she sets hair in a tiny shop that she rents with another woman in a block of offices just off Runyon County's courthouse square. Her work involves talking and listening as much as setting

hair. Corva knows that she has gotten very good at what she has
learned to do. Recently, she decided to start commuting to the city
in the evenings to take courses toward a BA in "human services," in
the hope that she might eventually find work as a high school guidance counselor. In such a job, she could listen to people full time,
forget about fixing their hair, and maybe occasionally do some good:

> I know I can't reach everybody, but if I just reach one or two
> persons . . . some of these people who are on the bitter end, on
> the end of their rope, whether it be to kill someone or to commit
> suicide. I just feel if that person has somebody that they can talk
> to, it might make a difference. I'm not going to say it will, but
> it might.[11]

Violet Soames

Violet Soames, the second of Jeanette's African-American passengers,
looks like Corva Marshall's alter ego. A large, soft, gentle figure,
already the mother of three, Violet, at twenty-two, is the youngest
member of the policy council. She has recently been assigned to do
thirty hours a week of filing at the local AFDC office as a condition
for keeping her welfare grant. She hopes that this work experience
will help her get an office job. Ms. Soames describes herself as a
"follower" rather than a "leader," at least in the context of Head Start:

> I'm not the material to be a leader. I'm a good follower. I guess
> because I been doing it for such a long time. . . . I can give good
> feedback. . . . [But] to put out to a group, I'm not that good. I'm
> [better] at putting into it, than putting out.[12]

Yet Violet's gentle eyes will sometimes flash without warning when
she explains how rich people have the power to

> make rules and regulations to tell you how can you live and
> what to do . . . but how [do] these people know these things and

---

11. CM 3, p. 32, 1. 14–19. This quotation, as well as all subsequent quotations
from Head Start parents, are taken from audiotaped interviews that I conducted in
North Carolina from March through June 1992, with funding from National Science
Foundation grant no. SES 9022787. The citations refer to the interview transcripts.
12. VS 2, p. 8, 1.37–39; p. 9, 1.13–20.

they never been on the bottom and to live that type of life that
I lives. It's easy for them to say what we should do. But if they
was out here living, as poor as I was, then they'd know it was[n't]
that easy. . . . If I was rich, then I would know how to speak on
the behalf of the poor people, because I been there. That's where
I come from.[13]

Yet invariably, after revealing this glimpse of her passion, Violet
Soames methodically wraps it back up and tucks it away. The other
women on the policy council describe Violet with affection, indeed
admiration. In another parent's words:

She's a lovely little girl and uninhibited. . . . She really has a nice
personality. . . . But she wasn't as capable as I thought. . . . You
have to have somebody that you figure can do the job. I figure
she could learn eventually, . . . [but] we don't have the time for
it right now. [Y]our council can get away from you while you're
learning.[14]

Sadie Washington

The eldest of the parents to disembark from the van is a seventy-two-
year-old woman whose great-granddaughter is enrolled in Head Start.
Sadie Washington taught school in Robertsonville for fifty years, seeing the system through the spasms of integration, before she finally
retired two years ago. Ms. Washington was born on a plantation in
the easternmost of the program's three counties. It was only through
the grace of god and the stubbornness of her father that she ever got
beyond the fifth grade in school. She remembers her family being
evicted just about every spring because her father insisted on keeping
his precocious daughter in school instead of pulling her out to pick
cotton, as custom required. Ms. Washington loses her composure as
she recounts these events to the white woman with the tape recorder
who eventually writes up the plot. Her voice straining to turn poison
to sadness, she tries to explain how white people seem determined to

13. VS 2, p. 10, 1.13–44.
14. SC 2, p. 17, 1.18–22; p. 18, 1.18–33.

keep black people down, even though "if you keep me down you're gonna have to stay here watching me."[15]

Unlike the other parents on the council, Sadie Washington has been to lots of meetings. Back before integration, she remembers the "ag men," the African-American Agricultural Extension Service agents who started showing up in the region during the New Deal, who "just knew the Robert Rules of Law upside down."[16] They would come to the segregated meetings of the African-American teachers' group, just to

> show their Robert's, parliamentary prowess, you know. . . . [T]hey would just show off. . . . [A]nd they were good. [W]hen we'd have these teacher meetings, my, you just had to tow the line. They would call you down on any kind of technical matter. . . . [S]ometimes it just pays to know how to rescind a motion and do all of those things, you know.[17]

She regrets that the young parents like Violet don't have a chance to learn it that way any more.

Janie Compton

The last parent to get out of the van got drawn into to the policy council unwillingly. The other members of the council were all elected by other parents at their children's Head Start sites. The significance of their victories varies, however, depending on the site from which each woman has come. A few of the centers boast good parent attendance at their monthly meetings and contested elections for the policy council. But in other centers only a handful of parents show up. Janie Compton comes from such a site. Janie has never felt inclined to follow the crowd. As a child, she aspired to "drive an 18-wheeler."[18] Reflecting on this decidedly unconventional ambition for a little girl growing up in the 1960s in the rural South, she explained, "I just live wild. I know you have to change a bunch of gears and that seemed like it would be fun."[19]

15. SC 2, p. 31, 1.47–50.
16. SC 2, p. 19, 1.50–51.
17. SC 2, p. 20, 1.15–17; p. 21, 1.10–12; p. 22, 1.36–38.
18. JH 1, p. 20, 1.49.
19. JH 1, p. 21, 1.7.

Janie was recently drafted by the staff to replace her center's prior policy council member, who failed to show up at a single meeting in the fall. "They just sort of pushed me on it," she explains.[20] The staff picked out Janie for this honor because she was one of only about five parents who regularly came to the center meetings. She explains her faithful attendance in the following terms:

> I go to find out about my kid. Keep up with what's going on. Make sure them teachers ain't getting out of hand. . . . I could care less whether they say, "Well, Janie don't go to no parent meetings." Because that ain't my main priority. My priority is seeing after my child and making sure he's getting what he deserves.[21]

Janie can't explain the source of this wisdom, but she is so convinced of its truth that she will often "force" her husband, an alcoholic who works pouring concrete, to go with her to these meetings. "[H]e wants to go sometime, but when he's just getting home he don't want to, but I force him to go."[22] She risks provoking his wrath because

> they're his kids too and he ought to want to go, because I went to Head Start when I was young [but] [h]e didn't get to go. . . . And . . . statistics say that people who go to Head Start come out better than the ones that don't. . . . So he ought to want to try to help. . . . See what's going on.[23]

She adds that when her husband actually gets to the meetings, "you can't even tell he didn't want to come. . . . He be running his mouth more than everybody else."[24]

After attending her first policy council meeting in February, Janie Compton felt "like a nut":

> [T]he policy council's supposed to vote, and they make the decisions for their kids for Head Start . . . [but] I don't really see the

---

20. JH 2, p. 3, 1.6.
21. JH 2, p. 7, 1.35–47.
22. JH 2, p. 8, 1.8–13.
23. JH 2, p. 8, 1.22–33.
24. JH 2, p. 8, 1.45–50.

need for me being there. I'm just lost when they're sitting there. . . . [I] don't know what's going on. . . . [T]hat lady that was sitting beside me, she kept saying "I'm motioning for everything. Say something so my name won't be on the minutes." I didn't know what I was motioning for. . . . I may motion to get my head cut off![25]

Linda Bradshaw

Several other women come to the meeting in their own cars. Linda Bradshaw is a community representative who works for the community action agency that sponsors Head Start. Perhaps in part because she is an African-American woman who came from the country, she lacks the elusive look that marks most of the people who work for the government in these parts.

Caroline Sutherland

The council's other African-American community representative, Caroline Sutherland, will not show up for the meeting, but she did send a letter to Carla Hanks to be read at the proper time. Ms. Sutherland is a food stamp supervisor from the program's easternmost county. When she was hired by the agency as a file clerk in a burst of affirmative action some twenty years ago, she was a single mother with two little boys in Head Start. Yet to move up in her job she had to forget what the world looked like from that lonely place. Today Caroline Sutherland is proud of what she has accomplished in life. Her younger son is a doctoral student in biochemistry at a prestigious university. Although her pay is not great, she supervises a whole office of food stamp workers, both white and black.

When Ms. Sutherland comes to policy council meetings, she speaks in favor of the decisions that she thinks Carla wants the group to make. And she keeps her eye on the parents, to make sure they don't get too taken by this sharing of power. She announces this mission quite bluntly, through her stiff posture, her tailored hairdo, and the way she has ironed every wrinkle of African rhythm out of her measured speech. The parents say that they welcome Caroline's

___

25. JH 1, p. 37, 1.19–20; p. 42, 1.30–33; JH 2, p. 1, 1.42–43; p. 2, 1.8–35.

presence when she comes to the meetings, because she speaks well and knows how to keep the meetings on track.

The Sandwich Meal

As soon as Carla arrives at the Head Start center, she unloads the portable file box that protects her policy council documents. Then she goes to work spreading food on the formica counter that spans the back of the room. There is a package of sliced ham, marbled with flecks of iridescent, pinkish fat. She peels apart the slices, arranging them on a paper plate that she has ringed with wedges of American cheese. There is a plate piled with iceberg lettuce, a pot of potato salad, some mayonnaise, a loaf of bread. At the far end of the counter are some quartered apples, a tin of Sara Lee brownies, and a plastic jug of instant, presweetened iced tea.

As Jeanette and her passengers enter, they head for the formica counter and then carry their sagging paper plates to the table. The conversation pulsates, as women chat boisterously with their friends, and then, catching themselves, strain to make small talk with strangers. Linda Bradshaw takes a seat beside Violet Soames; like giddy high school freshmen, they trade insider gossip about Runyon County's social service establishment, where Violet has just landed her workfare job. Sarah Grier sits at the foot of the table and silently consumes her ham sandwich. Jeanette and Corva stand by the angled desks and chat politely about Corva's four-year-old Head Start son. Meanwhile, Carla Hanks strolls through the room like a dutiful hostess entertaining her husband's business associates, seeking to put everyone at ease.

In her teal blue rayon pantsuit, Carla Hanks cuts a commanding figure. Her graying hair is subtly frosted and stylishly coiffed; her aging eyelids are painted the same shade of blue as her pants. With the cautiousness of not-quite-tamed young cats, the women at the table approach Carla Hanks with friendly conversation and then abruptly withdraw. Carla is certainly down-to-earth enough, but she is white. Her boss, and Linda's, the executive director of Runyon County's community action program, is the sheriff's wife.

The Meeting's Agenda: Electing a New Chair

Over the last three or four years, Carla Hanks has had a big problem getting parents to come to policy council meetings. The Department

of Health and Human Services, which administers Head Start, monitors local programs to make sure the policy councils really meet.
Every program must record monthly attendance on standardized
forms. Every few years, auditors from the HHS Regional Office in
Atlanta come to Runyon County to review these forms, and to make
sure that there are written notes from each policy council meeting
to back up the typed minutes preserved in the files. Programs are
declared "out of compliance" if they fail to leave such a trail. The
consequences of this judgment have varied wildly over the quarter
century history of the Head Start program, depending on the prevailing mood in the White House.

The record on the Runyon policy council would more than satisfy
the current corps of federal monitors. For these records paint a grim
picture of "maximum feasible participation": a harried staff caught
up in webs of regulation, welfare pathology, and pulling teeth. Repeatedly over the last three years, meetings have been convened and then
aborted for lack of a quorum. Repeatedly, attendance rosters show
agency representatives outnumbering parents, two or three to one.
The agendas, which are mailed out a week before each meeting,
include this plea at the bottom of the page:

> * * *   PLEASE COME TO THE MEETING. WE MUST
> HAVE A QUORUM IN ORDER TO CONDUCT BUSINESS
> AND COMPLY WITH THE LAW.   * * *

But for some reason there is a good showing of parents tonight;
the only ones who are absent are from the program's easternmost
county, an hour's drive away. After the meeting, however, several
parents confess that they came only because Jeanette Hastie had called
the day before, urging them to attend. As Janie Compton explains:

> It's just not worth going. I don't know what's happening. . . . [Carla
> Hanks] knows that the people there don't really know what they're
> doing. . . . [But] [t]hey don't care. They just want you [to] be
> there . . . [so they can say] that this school participated. . . . I wasn't
> going to the meetings [but] Jeanette kept hounding me. I even told
> her I didn't have a babysitter. Then she called me back and told
> me to bring the kids with me. If I would have brought three kids,
> wouldn't nobody heard nothing.[26]

26. JH 1, p. 28, 1.47–48; p. 29, 1.19, 22, 27–28, 45; p. 30, 1.35–39; 43–44.

Violet Soames is also less than enthusiastic about attending policy council meetings. She compares the policy council to the tenant group she belongs to at the public housing project where she lives. The tenant group was convened by the project's management to "better [the tenants'] lifestyles . . . get up activities for the children . . . [and] keep drugs and guns and stuff out of the community."[27] In that group, unlike Head Start, Violet finds herself acting like a leader rather than a follower. She can "put out" ideas, suggesting "what would be good."[28] She feels able to take such an active role because "I live out there and I know what goes on a day-to-day basis. And I can suggest what would be good."[29] But at Head Start meetings she feels uncertain and falls into a follower role. She explains the difference between these two settings:

> [At Head Start] I don't know the day-to-day faces and the staff. . . . [W]e don't mess with hands-on experience on the budget. All we do is just look at what she gives us. You know, we have to go for what we see.[30]

Then she notes that the tenant group itself "fell" recently, because

> the people's not motivated. It takes a lot to get people to come out and get it motivated, and start doing things. [You] can't get them to come out to the meetings, but if you plan things, they be out there to help.[31]

In an attempt to build a sense of unity among the newly-elected policy council, Carla took the group to a cottage on one of the state's famed beaches for a weekend training session and retreat. During this weekend, she and Jeanette walked the parents through the quaintly impenetrable charts in the regulation that defines the policy council's powers. They also got a short course on Robert's Rules of Order, the protocol that they were told to use at policy council meetings if they dared speak. Several of the parents had never heard of Robert's Rules

---

27. VS 2, p. 4, 1.13–15.
28. VS 2, p. 9, 1.19–20, 43–44.
29. VS 2, p. 9, 1.43–44.
30. VS 2, p. 10, 1.1–2; p. 11, 1.25–30.
31. VS 2, p. 4, 1.27–30; p. 5, 1.3–5.

before the training; they were puzzled that some white man should be telling them how to talk, apparently from beyond the grave. A handful of parents had learned the rudiments of parliamentary procedure through groups that they had joined at church or school. Only Sadie Washington considered herself an expert in the arcane grammar of Robert's Rules.

The policy council elected its officers at its first formal meeting, two weeks after the trip to the beach. From Carla's perspective, the election went according to plan. From a skeptic's perspective, however, it looked like a cliché of gender and race domination. Everyone witnessing the event would have to agree, however, that it happened very quickly. First, the nominating committee that Carla had both appointed and coached announced its slate. Then the council elected that slate unanimously, by voice vote. The chairman that this process selected, Jimmy Stedman, was a white male. Indeed, he was the only male on the council, and along with Sarah Grier, one of just two whites. Not only did he look the role of a "redneck," complete with beer belly and hillbilly drawl, but he talked the line as well, complaining in private about all the "welfare mothers" in the program, who were "too lazy" to stop getting pregnant, or to get a job. Perhaps to balance the ticket, the nominating committee had listed Violet Soames as vice chair.

Jimmy Stedman hasn't been in town for many policy council meetings because he works on the road. In his absence, Violet has been called on to step in as chair. She has been exquisitely uncomfortable in the chairman's role. She typically whispers her every statement to Sadie Washington before repeating it, properly corrected, to the group. After Jimmy had been absent for several months, Carla Hanks urged him to resign. Finally, in late February, just a week before this meeting, he complied. Carla did not want to see Violet take over his position, because she was convinced that Violet would never catch on to the job. Therefore, she searched through the council's bylaws, to assure herself that she wasn't required to elevate the vice chairman if the chair resigned.

Enter, the Tardy Whites

Evelyn Calhoun

A few minutes after everyone has finally settled at the table, two white women enter the room. Evelyn Calhoun is fortyish, heavyset, single, with cropped hair and gray oxford clothing. Among the African-American women of Robertsonville, Evelyn Calhoun is regarded, and respected, as a tough white woman, that rare kind who can do her own laundry and isn't afraid to stay alone at night. Evelyn heads special education services for Robertsonville's public schools. Having just been appointed as a replacement community representative, this is Evelyn's first policy council meeting.

Laura Scott

Evelyn's companion, Laura Scott, is a veteran of community rep, having served on the council for two and a half years. Laura belongs to the region's social elite. She is married to a prominent farmer and is the grandmother of two lovely, well-polished young boys. Laura came of age at a time when the young ladies of Robertsonville didn't go to college. But she is smart and ambitious; as soon as her only child, a daughter, married and left home in the early 1980s, Laura worked her connections to get hired on the staff of the county's newly funded family literacy program. This program was brought to the county with the syndicated blessing of Nancy Reagan and Barbara Bush. It has since joined forces with the local welfare office, to require AFDC mothers to take classes that teach them to read to their kids.

Evelyn and Laura hastily make their ham sandwiches and attempt to mingle with the parents, whose plates are long empty and who are getting impatient for the meeting to start. The brownies are getting passed around one last time, and the conversation has finally died down.

Rick Little

Abruptly, a slight, blue-jeaned, bearded white man enters the room. A rustle passes through the group as the women try to place this vaguely familiar face. Rick Little is Jimmy Stedman's best friend: they went to Head Start together last fall to enroll their sons. Rick Little has come to some of the previous policy council meetings to watch his friend. He quickly occupies the empty chair between Corva Marshall and Evelyn Calhoun. When he senses that the room is silent, he blurts out the reason for his presence: the parents at his center chose him to join the council when Jimmy resigned. The women nod, murmur for a moment, and then settle down for the meeting to start.

The Vote

Violet Soames looks uneasy as she feels the group's collective expectation. Sadie Washington repositions her chair so she sits squarely in Violet's line of vision, poised to guide her young colleague through the murky waters of Robert's Rules. The first item on Violet's agenda is to elect her own replacement, the new policy council chair. In little more than a whisper, Violet calls the meeting to order. She asks the secretary, Linda Bradshaw, to read the minutes from the last meeting. With what she takes for a nod from Ms. Washington, Violet then prepares to declare the minutes approved as read. Just as these words are forming in Violet's mouth, Evelyn Calhoun breaks in to ask if anyone has any corrections or additions before the minutes are approved. Dazed by the interruption, Violet repeats Evelyn's question on Sadie's cue. Then, without further prompting, she calls for a motion and a vote. The minutes are approved.

Violet goes on to announce that the group must elect a new chair. Carla rises from one of the desks on the sidelines and strides toward the council's table. In her low-key but all-knowing voice, she explains that the bylaws call for a new election when the policy council chairman resigns in the middle of the year. Violet Soames will step down as interim chairman as soon as her replacement is elected. Violet laughs gently, in a gesture of acquiescence and relief.

Carla then picks up a letter from Caroline Sutherland, the food stamp supervisor and single parent who was unable to attend this meeting, and begins to read. Caroline has nominated Rick Little to replace Jimmy Stedman as chair. Almost without a change of demeanor, Sadie Washington harbors a smirk.

Violet looks briefly toward Sadie before asking for nominations from the floor. As if Violet's formulaic question had spoken her name, Ms. Washington immediately raises her voice. She names Corva Marshall, the tall thin woman who washes hair. Violet asks for more nominations, but no one speaks. The group prepares for a voice vote. Violet poses a question to Carla in a barely audible voice: "I thought that was supposed to be secret, okay?"[32] The day after the meeting, Violet affirms that she had thought "it was supposed to be a written

---

32. PC 3-2-92, p. 10, 1.1.

[vote]," but she is unable to recall that she raised the question at the meeting.[33] Janie Compton recalls the moment, however, with some bitterness:

> we should have voted it on paper or something. . . . Violet thought that it should be too, because she asked me. . . . Violet said it to Carla. [But] they said, "No. Just get it over. Let them go ahead and raise their hands." . . . I can't see where Carla even had the right to say whether it was confidential. [W]e're the policy council. We should have voted whether we want to raise our hands. [I]t ain't none of her business.[34]

Carla seems prepared for Violet's query. For, in Janie's recollection, she promptly quips, "No, go ahead. We need to hurry up and get it done. . . .[I]t ain't but three meetings left, two meetings left, so it don't matter."[35] Janie is enraged by this response. To her, it seems a clear signal that Carla

> didn't think that the vote was important. . . . I think she know that the people there don't really know what they're doing. . . . [S]he's supposed to be there just to help them, but she more or less tell [them what to do] and they go along with what she's saying because they don't know and they don't want to be the one to make a mistake.[36]

Yet Violet nods when Carla announces that there need not be a secret vote. Sadie Washington glances toward the ceiling in relief.

Violet then tries to call for the vote. "Okay, those that . . ." As her voice trails off in uncertainty, Linda Bradshaw intrudes to reframe Violet's sentence. With the condescension that befits a social services bureaucrat, Linda pronounces that "all in favor . . ." is the correct locution. Violet gets Linda's message and starts her sentence anew. "All . . . those in favor of Corva Marshall raise your hand."[37] Sadie

---

33. VS 2, p. 19, 1.36–50.
34. JH 2, p. 23, 1.38–40; p. 24, 1.4, 8, 19–22, 35–36, 40–41.
35. JH 2, p. 24, 1.7–8; p. 28, 1.25–27.
36. JH 2, p. 28, 120–21; p. 29, 1.1–5.
37. PC 3-2-92, p. 10, 1.5–9.

Washington's hand goes up; no one else moves. Taking a command
from her elder's eyes, Violet remains silent. The three white women on
the Council, Sarah Grier, Laura Scott, and Evelyn Calhoun, glance at
each other and shift in their seats. No one casts an eye toward Rick
Little, the young white man. Corva Marshall jerks up her own thin
hand. Linda Bradshaw does the same. Sadie peels her gaze off of Violet
Soames and looks down the table toward the whites. Once freed from
the hypnotic force of Sadie's gaze, Violet slowly raises her own hand.
Sarah Grier impulsively mimics Violet's move. Abandoned by their
white colleague, Laura and Evelyn search each other's eyes for what to
do. Laura then shifts her eyes toward the young white man, who is
looking down toward his hands. Violet remains silent, her own hand
straight up in the air. Laura and Evelyn exchange one more I-wish-I-
were-elsewhere glance. Then, in almost perfect synchrony, they put up
their hands. Sadie's breath bristles as it finally escapes from her lungs.
She settles back in her chair.

Violet then raises her voice again. Forgetting to count her own
hand, she tallies the vote: "Six."[38] She then asks for all those in favor
of Rick Little. Before Violet has finished her sentence, Janie Compton
has already raised her hand. Rick Little stays quiet, looking at his fin-
gernails. Violet then announces the result: "I let it be known that
Corva Marshall will be the chairman, chairperson. Is that correct?"[39]
For the first time in the meeting, Sadie Washington smiles.

The Next Day

Violet Soames

Violet Soames feels great relief when her tenure as interim chairman
of the policy council is finally over at the end of this meeting.

> [T]his is the first time I ever been in a meeting where they go by
> the Robert's Rules of Order. . . . Gosh, [chairing the meeting] was,
> eh! Because I didn't know. [It was like] getting in your car and
> driving. [T]he red light means stop. [Y]ou already know that. You
> know, so you don't have no fear, because you know that what it

38. PC 3-2-92, p. 10, 1.10.
39. PC 3-2-92, p. 10, 1.12-13.

means is stop. And green means go. . . . And I'm glad I ain't gotta
do this no more . . . [u]ntil I know it better.[40]

Although somewhat resentful that she had received no training or
preparation for her role prior to chairing the meeting, she was relieved
that Sadie Washington and Linda Bradshaw had stepped in to help her:

> I felt good. It was good that Ms. Washington was there that she
> can help me, because I didn't know. And the other lady [Linda],
> she know because she's one of the community reps. She's on the
> [community action] board so she knows how it went. And Ms.
> Washington been dealing with Head Start, they say, for years and
> years, so she knew how things went, so I was glad that they both
> were there to help me.[41]

She thinks that the new bylaws required a written ballot, but "we
hadn't gotten the new bylaws . . . distributed out yet . . . and the school
term is going to be over in about two months."[42] She has no memory
of raising the question of a secret ballot at the meeting. The transcript
shows that she didn't protest when Carla squelched the notion of a
written ballot because it would take too much time.

Corva Marshall

Corva Marshall takes her new responsibilities as policy council chairman very seriously. She knows that many Head Start parents don't
understand what the policy council can offer them. At the beginning
of the year, she had no idea what was going on at these meetings. But
slowly, by coming and listening, she has started to feel less afraid. Now
she is starting to ask questions when she doesn't understand something,
without worrying whether or not they sound stupid.

> A lot of times . . . we might think they sound stupid, but a question
> is a question to me. I don't think there's no limits on how smart

---

40. VS 2, p. 3, 1.28–29; p. 7, 1.26–44; p. 8, 1.6–7.
41. VS 2, p. 21, 1.14–32.
42. VS 2, p. 20, 1.1–2; 6–7.

or how dumb a question is. If you don't know, you just don't know.[43]

She is starting to understand what goes on behind the scenes to make federal programs like Head Start work. She respects the staff more, because she "see[s] what a person has to go through in order to do a particular job."[44] She is starting to comprehend the budget, and to see how the people at the HHS office in Atlanta control a lot of the choices that Carla and the parents supposedly make. She is starting to get the hang of Robert's Rules, and to see that when parliamentary procedure is used

> it helps things to go a little bit more smoothly. . . . [T]hat type of procedure keeps things in a business atmosphere. [W]ithout it things tend to get out of control . . . and really I find that a lot of things don't get concluded. . . . [I]t kind of lingers on.[45]

Therefore, when "it's actual hardcore business"[46] that the group needs to conduct, Corva endorses the use of Robert's Rules of Order, even though she knows that it "bothers some people . . . because they don't understand it."[47] In short, Corva Marshall thinks that the policy council is great, and she wants to do everything she can to get more parents to take advantage of the unique opportunity that it offers. Echoing the rhetoric of the government pamphlets that promote Head Start's parent involvement component, Corva Marshall explains how:

> the parents fail to realize that this is an opportunity, at least once in their child's history throughout school, that they can really be involved. . . . [T]hey don't realize how much this is help-ing them. And if they start at an early age with their child . . . [it's] going to get into them and they're going to continue to follow through with it as the child goes throughout the school years.[48]

---

43. CM 3, p. 13, 1.1–4.
44. CM 3, p. 2, 1.11–13.
45. CM 3, p. 17, 1.22–24; p. 18, 1.47–48; p. 19, 1.5–6, 16–18.
46. CM 3, p. 19, 1.31–32.
47. CM 3, p. 18, 1.29–31.
48. CM 3, p. 5, 1.25–29; p. 9, 1.7–8.

Indeed, like its original advocates, Corva Marshall sees parent involvement as a catalyst for social change, for "if enough parents get involved and protest a certain situation, that's the only way you are going to get any change most of the time."[49]

Sadie Washington

Sadie Washington considers the meeting one more day's work. After some coaxing, she explains to her white listener what was really going on at the meeting. She describes how, after Violet called for the vote on Corva Marshall, she could feel the white people around the table looking around to see who was going to raise their hands.[50] When she sensed this conspiracy brewing among the whites, she called upon a subtle power of her own—her eyes: "I just looked them down all of them and so their hands came on up."[51] She recalls the effect: "Evelyn Calhoun put her hand up at first, and then she brought it down, and she [put it back] up. And when she did Laura Scott did."[52] Had the vote been taken by secret ballot, she feels certain that Rick Little would have won. She distinctly recalls that "there was a black hand that went up for him."[53] She speculates about the "mind-set"[54] that was behind that vote:

> There are black people who feel there are things that we're not supposed to do. . . . [I]t's that plantation mentality. . . . It comes from way back. . . . They say, "You're not supposed to do that." . . . [W]hen I was growing up your doll was supposed to be white. Because they made the little black dolls with lips that protruded and hair bunched up. Little Topsies, you know. And that was to squash our pride. . . . [I]t's just that mentality from way back . . . that we figure that the whites will do it better.[55]

She feels that she had to use her power to shape the white people's votes because white people deny how racism works. They do not see

49. CM 3, p. 10, 1.17–20.
50. SC 2, p. 7, 1.14–17.
51. SC 2, p. 7, 1.25–26.
52. SC 2, p. 8, 1.29–31.
53. SC 2, p. 9, 1.49.
54. SC 2, p. 10, 1.10.
55. SC 2, p. 10, 1.11–13, 17; p. 11, 1.1–8; p. 12, 1.16.

why it is so important for African-American people to hold positions
of power, especially in organizations like Head Start, in which the
rank-and-file membership is almost entirely black.[56] Sadie Washington
knows that Corva Marshall's election as policy council chair will
"kind of boost to her courage."[57] For "if you haven't ever had any
experience in doing anything, how are you going to learn to do it?"[58]

Janie Compton

And what of Janie Compton, the one person at the meeting who cast
her vote for the white man? According to Sadie Washington, Janie
is a clear case of the plantation mentality. It is this mind-set that
explains why she would vote for the white man instead of Corva
Marshall, who is one of her own people. Janie, however, explains
her action in a somewhat different way. In her view, there should
have been a secret ballot. The policy council members should have
decided how they wanted to take the vote. Carla Hanks had no right
to decide the matter, or even to inject her opinion into the council's
debate. Janie voted for Rick Little because, in her words, he "would
have done good"[59] as policy council chair. In her view, he was simply
more qualified than Corva Marshall to do the job. Perhaps Sadie
was right that this was the plantation mind-set, but to Janie Compton,
Rick Little, unlike either Violet Soames or Corva Marshall, "can get
serious and he'll run the meeting better."[60] Indeed, with Violet as chair

> they might as well just let Miss Washington chair the meeting . . .
> because she was telling Violet everything anyway. That's wasting
> our time for her to talk and tell her what to say when she done
> already said it. . . . Violet didn't know nothing about it, so Miss
> Washington was telling her what to say.[61]

Yet Janie's high regard for Rick Little's innate abilities was not
the only reason that she broke ranks with the group. Her vote was

---

56. SC 2, p. 13, 1.30–37.
57. SC 2, p. 14, 1.17.
58. SC 2, p. 13, 1.20–23.
59. JH 2, p. 22, 1.29.
60. JH 2, p. 22, 1.35–36.
61. JH 2, p. 22, 1.35–47.

also an act of rebellion against the pressure that she felt to conform. She couldn't quite express why, but to Janie Compton, taking a stand against this pressure was a matter of principle, even if it meant casting her vote for a white:

> some of the people was raising their hands by what the others was raising, because when it first start out [there were] just two or three hands up in the air. As I looked around and all the hands kept going up, I guessed they thought I was going to go up too, but I say, "No, my vote is my vote, and I want to vote for Rick."[62]

In Janie's opinion, Sadie Washington's interventions were not helping younger people like Violet Soames learn the ropes. These were not selfless efforts to empower a new generation of African-American community leaders. Rather, to Janie, Sadie Washington's under the table coaching of Violet Soames was a power trip; it was an indirect way to control the agenda, thereby keeping everyone else down.

> Miss Washington do all the voting. . . . [S]he always be the first one to vote, because she been there since [she] was a kid. She know everything. She know the ropes. [S]he don't let nobody use their mind. . . . I said look at these idiots. They ain't got no mind of their own. . . . Everybody's hand went up but mine.[63]

So Janie Compton cast her vote against Carla Hanks and her eagerness to override the group process at a crucial point. She voted against Sadie Washington, and the power that she wielded with her whispers and her eyes. She voted against the fear that shaped the votes of Laura Scott and Evelyn Calhoun. She voted against all the bad faith that she felt in that room, all the manipulation that was going on. She wasn't going to let any of them tell her what to do. To Janie Compton, a vote for Rick Little was not a symptom of her plantation mentality. Quite the contrary. It was the only way she could think of to reject that colonial mind-set. Her vote for Rick Little was the only way she could think of to exercise her law-framed

62. JH 2, p. 23, 1.44–50.
63. JH 2, p. 25, 1.11–15, 32–34; p. 26, 1.4–5, 42–43.

franchise in a principled way. It was the only way she knew of to speak her mind in a world with no heroes and too much history.

Law's Rhetoric

Caged Voices

Head Start is a "poverty" program. The subjects that its law calls together have annual incomes below the poverty line. Among those our law classifies as poor, a greater than random portion are likely to identify themselves with historically subordinated ethnic and cultural groups. For many of these peoples, social power seldom feels as fluid and multidirectional as postmodern political theorists maintain. Rather, the powers that work in these people's communities often seem to work in just one direction, and that is against them. Power seems to work with a single-minded efficiency, to keep them down.

One need not be an astute geographer of culture to appreciate the sense of such perceptions. For Head Start policy councils convene in the very heartlands of domination. They convene in those settings where power has long been marshaled, in countless routine ways, to maintain historic patterns of domination. From the perspectives of those whose lives are enmeshed in this history, there is little reason to think that Head Start's law will disrupt long-settled expectations. There is little reason to hope that Head Start's law was written—or can be worked—to shake up a skewed, but stable, balance of social and political power.

On a first reading, the law of Head Start seems to challenge this truth. It seems to stake out an enclave of community in which entrenched structures of social power are disrupted. On a first reading, the law of Head Start seems to enlist the state's power to support the social citizenship of historically disfranchised groups. At least in its precatory language, the law of Head Start seems to contradict the expectation that the law's power will always work against the poor. Head Start Transmittal 70.2, for instance, presents a striking exception to the "typical" administrative rule: its language evokes images of robust republican deliberation and sweeping societal change. It envisions the policy council as the center of a widening circle of political mobilization. It suggests that poor women, emboldened by the schooling they receive in Head Start policy councils, will move on into larger institutions to bring about systemic change. It chides the staff to stay quiet at policy council meetings, so that poor women can find the space to speak. And it commands the agencies that run Head Start programs to share their managerial power, or risk losing their funding.

The law's rhetoric may seem to proclaim that for once the state is really serious about empowering the poor. But these promises do not constitute the entire meaning of Head Start's law. There is also another rhetoric—an order embedded in the institutional and procedural blueprints that the law sets out. This order undercuts the promises that the law's imagery seems to hold out. What looked, from afar, like a vast field for the play of citizenship, seems on closer inspection to be more like an English garden. For while it makes bold public gestures toward empowerment and transformation, the law also lays out an intricate circle of pathways to channel its subjects' supposed powers. Its rhetorical grammar thus systematically confines whatever transformative passion that its imagery might call forth.

Many features of the law's order work together to cage the voices that its subjects are invited to raise. Three examples will give some sense of the subtle and diverse methods of its work. The first is the way that the law defines the ends that the policy councils are convened to serve. Unlike Enlightenment rhetoric, which defined the purpose of the democratic project as the radically open-ended self-realization of Man, Head Start's rhetoric presents the goal of its self-governance mandate in stingy, instrumentalist terms. Parents are not brought together to explore and enact a provisional, emergent social identity. Rather, they are put through the paces of democratic interaction in order to fit themselves into prescribed roles, conceived to further the needs of their children, their neighborhoods, or the society at large, rather than to realize their own human possibility.

Like their children, whose Head Start experiences too often center on endless choral readings of the alphabet, rather than free play, policy council members are encouraged to recite the formulas of parliamentary process, rather than to talk together about the actions that they might take. Just as their children's Head Start curriculum too often aims at conditioning three- and four-year-old children to behave as though they were in school, the policy council drills parents in the protocols of public meetings, so they will know how to behave at the PTA. And just as their children are trained to perform for parents and teachers, rather than to please themselves, policy council members are coached in the role of "good citizen," not so they can exercise their own franchise, but rather so they can provide good "role models" for their children and good public relations for the program.

It should come as no surprise, then, that the parents on the Runyon policy council, in spite of great differences in outlook and temperament, all agree that the point of their participation has little to do with their potential political power. When asked what difference their participation makes, they do not talk about shaping the program's policies. Indeed, it is rare that they speak of their work in terms of making decisions, or debating alternatives, or offering suggestions, or even asking questions. Instead, they are more likely to talk about the council's purpose, and their own duties as policy council members, in the same instrumentalist categories that permeate Head Start's law: the council will teach them more about the program, so they will somehow become better parents for their children.

A second way that law confines the voices of policy council members is through the way that it describes the councils' power. The law presents this power as a list of discrete, indeed fragmented obligations that the group must discharge. The most expansive of these prerogatives, the council's power to supervise financial and personnel decisions, are granted as vetoes, rather than as options to initiate action. Transmittal 70.2 lays out the councils' powers in a bewildering matrix of boxes, rather than prose that lay people can read.

This grid creates legally enforceable rights. Yet it orders a lockstep process, in which there is no time for parents to explore what they think about the staff's decisions, or to formulate agenda items on their own. With their rights and duties ordered in this way, it should come as no surprise that the typical policy council meeting plays out as a random sequence of votes to approve staff decisions, with very little discussion between the invariably unanimous vote counts.

A third way that the law conscribes the parents' voices is through the protocols that council members must use when they speak. Like many other quasi-public bodies, policy councils are required to use parliamentary procedure when they conduct business. For most civic groups, this process works more or less transparently, to facilitate efficient meetings without obstructing the flow of ideas. It gives every group member the same formal chance to have her say. It gives meeting an imprimatur of "legality," defining the group's official actions and bringing discussion to closure. And in contested matters, parliamentary procedure helps to choreograph conflict, keeping passions from getting out of hand.

But for many Head Start parents, Robert's Rules of Order come from a foreign cultural world. For them, this protocol does not transform conflict into well-ordered discussion; it intimidates the group into silence. A few will figure out how to make formal motions and then speak the ritual sentence repeatedly, on cue. Occasionally a woman like Sadie Washington will come to the council already schooled in the intricacies of Robert's Rules. Then she can use this superior knowledge to seize agenda-setting power. But neither the rote recitation of procedural motions nor the silence that these performances interrupt constitute the kind of give-and-take conversation that might make a group's decisions feel like their own.

The ways that the law conceives the policy council's purpose, constructs its power, and constrains its conversation are but three of the features of the law's order that undo the promise of democracy that its precatory imagery seems to hold out. The law seems to promise a process in which the group is granted the power to rewrite the premises on which it was convened. But that law then works to ensure that this limit of democratic power is never reached. The law works to preclude fluent deliberation, full-throated contestation, or evenhanded play. It works to ensure that conversation will never take off at the meetings that it mandates. Thus, as Violet Soames observes, women find themselves unable to "put out" ideas at policy council meetings. It just isn't the same as the sheltered places, like church meeting halls and neighbors' front porches, where people can speak their minds, in their own rhythms, and feel at home.

Replaying the Frame

The image of Sadie Washington, Corva Marshall, and Janie Compton as caged creatures, trying to speak their own voices within an ornate, but constricting framework that is constituted by the law—this picture of law-made structures encircling, indeed entrapping, human actors— is a very comforting image to rely on as we seek to understand the interplay of law, social citizenship, and political power. First of all, the image is familiar. Second, it is cognitively friendly. It is an easy image to picture, and to hold in mind. The image may seem too simple to illuminate the complex workings of law and human action. Yet, like the lone horse-drawn wagon that caught the young boy's eye on Dr. Seuss's Mulberry Street, this simple image will tolerate all of the embellishment that our theory-building intellects are likely to dream up.

The image of frame and agents gives us two solid conceptual fixed points when we try to map the movement between action and law. Indeed, sometimes this image works nicely as background, for instance, when we want to examine one term of the structure/agent dyad as though it could stand alone. Thus, the previous section of this essay presumed this basic image, in order to expose the subtle, voice-muting features of Head Start's law. Yet for all of its attractions, the image of frame and agents does not help very much when we try to comprehend the movement of law, citizenship, and power. This image does not help us make sense of the action, when the women in Runyon County's policy council gather to do business. The capricious twists and turns of their stories strain the power of this image to help us understand how the law, in real-time contexts, actually works.

Accounts of events like this policy council meeting show that the metaphor of a frame or structure casts the law as too rigid, too set and too singular, both in its meanings—as those meanings emerge through in action—and in its effects. Such accounts also show how the other term in the structure/agent image—the concept of people acting "inside" a frame of law—imposes too much confinement upon the site or scope of the action, while at the same time depicting that action as radically—implausibly—free. Yet even as such accounts thus debunk a well-worn master image of the law in action, they do not thereby call forth an obvious replacement. These stories do not suggest a single image that captures in a few evocative brush-strokes the cumbersome truth of Anthony Giddens's observation that meanings emerge in relations of power where "even the most autonomous agent is in some degree dependent, and the most dependent actor . . . retains some autonomy."[64]

---

64. Anthony Giddens, *Central Problems in Social Theory: Action, Structure, and Contradiction in Social Analysis* 93 (Berkeley and Los Angeles: University of California Press, 1979), quoted in Maureen Mahoney and Barbara Yngvesson, "The Construction of Subjectivity and the Paradox of Resistance: Reintegrating Feminist Anthropology and Psychology," *Signs* 18, no. 1 (Autumn 1992): 46.

Instead of a rigid legal framework confining autonomous human actors, the story of Runyon County's policy council calls forth a world in which both the framework and the actors take their meaning from the other's play. Thus, the subjects who animate the story are not autonomous agents who find themselves confined, for the moment, within a space that law ordains. Rather, each actor's unique sensibility as subject has been shaped through a lifelong encounter with the law's normative, ritual, and repressive force. Her self is always subject to revision, both by her new experiences, and by the new stories that she tells about the old ones. Yet at the same time, that self has always already been inscribed with the order of law. And that legal order is itself continually recast as its subjects repeatedly act out what it means. It is this recursive movement—this ongoing, mutual enactment of the two conceptual fixed points of law in action through the other's play—that becomes palpable as we collect and report accounts of law and action. Yet even though we can get the feel of this movement by studying stories, that movement defies representation in a single, simple, stable epistemic frame.

In Runyon County's policy council meeting, we get a few hints of how each actor's being—that sum of the passions and moral intuitions that seem to ground her action—has been shaped, in part, through prior encounters with law. We know, for instance, that as a young child, Sadie Washington saw the law repeatedly join forces with her father's landlords, to evict him and his family for sending his daughter to school. Yet the same young girl saw the law come into her community in the 1930s, through the New Deal workers who taught people how to hold meetings and distributed food. We cannot say exactly how these divergent experiences left their trace on the Sadie Washington who came to the policy council meeting. Yet perhaps it should not surprise us that this woman seemed to approach Head Start's law as though its meaning—its moral value— were up for grabs. We do not know what encounters with law might have colored the aspirations, the expectations, and the fears of Janie Compton, or Violet Soames, or Corva Marshall. But the story shows quite clearly how these women perceived, and thereby reordered, the law's framework in very different ways.

To Sadie Washington, that framework was a labyrinth. It offered a landscape of countless, half-hidden spaces through which a clever actor could maneuver against the plodding forward march of entrenched social and political power. For Violet Soames, the same law seemed more like a straitjacket. The limited scope of the policy council's powers and the formality of its procedures worked to stifle her intuitions and ideas in the Head Start setting, but without causing her any enduring moral harm. For Corva Marshall, the law of Head Start was neither a maze nor a straitjacket. Instead, it was like one of those dangling baskets that rescue pilots use to lift stranded people from stormy seas. By trusting the law enough to climb within it, Corva Marshall had figured out a way to lift herself toward a better life.

Finally, to Janie Compton, Head Start's law presented a moral and existential threat. It might look benign or even appealing. But like a pod from the horror movie, it would seek first to trap you, and then to transform you into an agent of its own power. Violet Soames could avoid what she saw as the law's danger by simply keeping still. By assuming a pose of passivity while in the law's ambit, she could not be reduced to passivity by the force of the law. For Janie Compton, however, the law's danger was not so easy to evade. The only way she could escape the risk that law might corrupt her will was to reject the consensus that she saw the law working to produce. For her, the law did not invite Violet's style of disengagement; rather, it sparked a burst of resistance.

Sadie Washington, Violet Soames, Corva Marshall, and Janie Compton appear to have much in common. They have lived through the same turbulent local history, and they share the same markers of social identity and political power. Yet these four women have interpreted the legal structure through which they are brought together in very different ways. By acting upon those divergent understandings, these women have both upset and reshaped what that law is. They have redefined its meaning and realigned its force, albeit in marginal, multiple, and apparently random ways. Through their diverse readings of the law's meaning, these women have subverted— or at least queried, to return to Professor Parker's formulation—the law's pretense to authorize social and political order in the community that it constitutes among them. And as they have jointly opened up the meaning of the law, these women have also reworked who it is that they might become.

In closing, we might return to the questions that motivated this account of a single policy council meeting in a small town. We sought to explore the constraints imposed by constitutive law. Our excursion was part of a larger search for the distinctive qualities of community and possibilities for politics that different regimes of public law might bring forth. We encountered a group of women who looked very much alike, at least according to crude indicia of social identity like gender, race, and class. Yet we saw these women read widely divergent meanings into what looked like a single body of law. We found a subversive value in the multiple meanings that these women could draw forth from the ostensibly monolithic order of law. But we also suggested that the very multiplicity of their collective project might render it marginal, if not entirely inconsequential, in political and moral terms. Their varied projects, though all undertaken in the same law-framed space, seemed too diffuse, too random—too solipsistic— to support a democratic politics with any power in their repressive social world.

Could any changes in the law's constitutive language enable these women to find common meaning in the multiple readings that they perform? Or are these women's responses to the law's order shaped much more by their own private histories—and quirks—than by any cues from the text? Is a convergence of vision among multiple actors inevitably purchased, as it was in this story, through one person's manipulation of the others' franchise? And finally, can we pose such questions without losing the movement, without lapsing into the constraining language of actors and frame? If we try to stay close to that movement, to that ground where stories can surprise us, will a democratic politics in the interest of social justice forever elude our reach?

Constitutional Discourse and Its Discontents: An Essay on the Rhetoric of Judicial Review

Lawrence Douglas

> It is rooted in an essential function of language itself, a function that is wholly realistic, and is continually born anew; the use of language as symbolic means of inducing cooperation in beings that by nature respond to symbols.
>
> —Kenneth Burke, *A Rhetoric of Motives*

To speak of the rhetoric of law suggests two meanings of the concept of rhetoric. The first conjures the craft of the lawyer—the ability to twist and manipulate words for the purposes of winning a court case or a jury's favor. This notion of rhetoric finds its earliest elaboration in Plato's *Gorgias*, where Socrates dismisses rhetoric as a superficial art of "making great matters small and small things great."[1] It is no more than the "knack" (elsewhere, "pseudo-art") of "pandering," of championing the pleasurable over the true; and when Plato writes, "[T]he orator does not teach juries ... about right and wrong. ... it is enough for him to have discovered a knack of convincing the ignorant that he knows more than the experts,"[2] his prose rings remarkably modern, suggesting that the courtroom pyrotechnics of a Barry Slotnik were not without their counterpart in Pericles' Athens.

I am grateful for the helpful comments of Owen Fiss, Carol Greenhouse, Felipe Gutteriez, Sandy Levinson, Robert Post, Austin Sarat, and Kim Lane Scheppele.

1. Plato, *Gorgias*, trans. Walter Hamilton (New York: Penguin Books, 1960), 44.
2. Plato, *Gorgias*, 38.

The second notion of rhetoric is anticipated in the work of Aristotle, who saw rhetoric as an invaluable constituent of argumentation in circumstances in which the meaning rather than the truth of an event was at issue.[3] Whether a specific period constituted a city's golden age, or a particular culture was in decline, were matters susceptible to neither syllogism nor empirical confirmation. As subjects of debate and colloquy, these were issues in which the truth of an asserted position was ultimately a function of its power to persuade—and here persuasion understood not as crass manipulation, but as a forceful and meaningful rendering into language.

The Aristotelian vision of rhetoric thus draws an implicit distinction between *manipulation* and *persuasion*. The former implies a willful twisting or utilization of words toward an end that remains untouched by the discursive means of its expression; the latter implies a practice of communication that contains norms embedded within the very discursive performance that lead a speaker toward a specific model of the proper and convincing utterance.[4]

The Aristotelian view of rhetoric has been most influentially applied to contemporary understandings of the law by James Boyd White. In a number of thoughtful monographs and articles,[5] White has articulated the view that language cannot be seen as a neutral medium for the expression of legal meaning; rather, the law "acts upon" language, creating a distinctive discourse.[6] The discourse created by the dialectic between law and language in turn serves to constitute a specific vision of "community," a particular normative view of the social world—an idea that lies at the heart of White's concept of "constitutive rhetoric."[7]

While White's principal scholarly works have been directed toward revealing the legal and rhetorical understandings contained

3. Aristotle, *Rhetoric*, trans. W. Rhys Roberts (New York: Modern Library, 1984).

4. See, for example, Kenneth Burke, *A Rhetoric of Motives* (Berkeley and Los Angeles: University of California Press, 1969).

5. See, for example, *When Words Lose Their Meaning: The Constitution and Reconstruction of Language, Character, and Community* (Chicago: University of Chicago Press, 1984) and *Heracles' Bow: Essays on the Rhetoric and Poetics of Law* (Madison: University of Wisconsin Press, 1985), as well as "Law as Rhetoric, Rhetoric as Law: The Arts of Cultural and Communal Life," *University of Chicago Law Review* 52 (1985): 684.

6. "Law as Rhetoric," 690.

7. "Law as Rhetoric," 692.

in traditional literary texts, more recently he has offered readings of
the critical exegetical text of legal study in America: the Supreme
Court opinion.[8] This essay attempts to follow the lead of White,
among others,[9] in the study of the distinctive discourse and rhetoric
of the high court. Specifically, this essay attempts to recover the
Supreme Court's rhetorical response to the instabilities contained
within the project of judicial review and within its own role as privileged expositor of constitutional meaning.

As we shall see, the distinctive rhetoric of judicial review both
bears the traces of the Court's difficult, though largely self-assumed,
position as reader of the Constitution, as well as gives expression to
the Court's claim to be able to offer legitimate readings of fundamental
law. By focusing on two exemplary cases—*Marbury v. Madison* and
Adamson v. California—we will read how the Court's own discursive
response to its problematic role as constitutional expositor has come
to define less a clearly and consistently elaborated logic or theory of
legitimation, and more a tight and richly woven rhetoric of reading
in which the instabilities within the Court's own hermeneutic project
are ceaselessly concealed and revealed, displaced and declaimed. Yet
these endlessly recapitulated acts mustn't be understood in the Platonic sense as mere instrumental attempts to shore the Court's claim
to power. Rather, they serve to constitute, and lie at the heart of,
the Court's unusual rhetoric of legitimation.

Justice Jackson's Curious Rhetoric of Legitimation

Authority and Interpretation

Consider Justice Jackson's talismanic phrase, "We are not final because
we are infallible, but we are infallible only because we are final." The
statement makes its appearance in Jackson's concurrence in *Brown v.
Allen*,[10] a case that attempts to articulate the availability and scope
of habeas corpus relief on federal constitutional grounds to state
prisoners. Agreeing with the majority's denial of the writ in the instant

---

8. See, for example, James Boyd White, *Justice as Translation: An Essay in
Cultural and Legal Criticism* (Chicago: University of Chicago Press, 1990).

9. See, for example, Robert Ferguson, "The Judicial Opinion as Literary Genre,"
Yale Journal of Law and the Humanities 2 (1990): 201.

10. 344 U.S. 443, 540 (1953) (Jackson concurring).

case, Jackson writes separately to express the intensity of his belief
that the writ be issued only in extraordinary and clearly demarcated
instances. To grant broad habeas powers to federal courts would, in
Jackson's mind, permit federal judges simply to supplant the judgments of state courts. Such an arrangement is objectionable, Jackson
reasons, for it both upsets the delicate balance of federalism, and,
more critically, creates the suggestion that the only difference between
the judgments of the respective courts is their respective personnel.
"Reversal by a higher court," he writes, "is not proof that justice is
thereby better done": "There is no doubt that if there were a super–
Supreme Court, a substantial proportion of our reversals of state
courts would also be reversed."[11]

The strong implication of this statement is that such reversals
would not be justified in any juridical sense; they would simply be
a measure of the idiosyncratic quality of judicial decision making.
Thus, although Jackson's statement focuses upon the relationship
between semiautonomous judicial institutions, read more generally
his point seems to unite Alexander Bickel's concerns regarding the
countermajoritarian nature of the Court with fears about the finality
of high-court judgment.

In the classic elaboration of the countermajoritarian difficulty,
Bickel argued that judicial review is problematic because it replaces
the preferences of a democratically elected, representative body with
those of a nondemocratic body.[12] This countermajoritarian problematic is linked by Bickel to its corollary—the problem of finality. To
the extent that the Supreme Court renders decisions that are final—
that cannot be changed except through the Court's own willingness
to reconsider its opinion or through the cumbersome process of formal
amendment—the invocation of the power is deeply problematic, at
least from the perspective of a system that contemplates majoritarian
correction as critical to its normative theory of government. Bickel's
elaboration of the countermajoritarian difficulty should not, of
course, be read as a general refutation of judicial review; rather it
is an attempt to articulate principles of self-limitation in order to
reconcile the practice with a prescriptive understanding of democ-

11. Ibid.
12. Alexander Bickel, *The Least Dangerous Branch* (New Haven: Yale University
Press, 1962).

racy.[13] Bickel's familiar and important arguments about "the passive virtues" must be understood as attempts to narrow the scope of judicial review and thus save the Court from egregious displays of countermajoritarianism.[14] Stated differently, Bickel attempts to articulate norms to guide the prudential exercise of judicial power so as to legitimate the Court's place in the American system of governance. The Bickelian project is centrally one of legitimation.

Here, however, it is important to understand that the concept of legitimation, as employed by constitutionalists such as Bickel, refers not simply to the requisite level of compliance to Court rulings so as to avoid open rebellion.[15] As Weber importantly observed, the problem of legitimation describes less a simple relationship between ruler and ruled, and more a complex and heterogeneous interaction between actors and the subcommunities in which they perform.[16] The

---

13. For a contrasting argument, see Henry Steele Commager, *Majority Rule and Minority Rights* (Oxford: Oxford University Press, 1943). Commager's countermajoritarian argument attempts to refute the case for judicial review rather than narrow the scope of its application.

14. Bickel's theory of adjudication seems, however, to presuppose a radical skepticism about interpretation's ability to contain the Constitution's power to generate meanings. If, for example, one were able to show—bracketing, for the moment, the question of how one would demonstrate such a proposition—that constitutional interpretation was 1) a bounded affair 2) an exercise that required a precise hermeneutic training, then the countermajoritarian difficulty would largely dissolve. One might still express reservations about empowering a nonelected group to overturn preferences of an electorate, yet the practice would be justified in terms of the criteria it has established for itself.

The concern about finality, as articulated most clearly in a recent book by Harry Wellington, both complements and represents the obverse of this problem. Here anxiety is not about the text's power to generate meanings; rather, the fear is of the damage to constitutionalism by radically limiting this very force. In a sense, then, the concern about finality is a fear that the Court will perform the textually bound act of reading counseled for by countermajoritarians all too well—it will suppress the Constitution's legal fecundity. In this regard, the concern about finality seems to demand exactly what the countermajoritarian problematic counsels against—judicial review that redeems the text's ability to generate new constitutional meanings. See Harry Wellington, *Interpreting the Constitution* (New Haven: Yale University Press, 1990).

15. At times, however, the Court itself seems to edge toward such an apocalyptic rhetoric of legitimation—notably, for example, in Scalia's concurrence in *Webster v. Reproductive Health Services* 492 U.S. 490 (1989) (Scalia concurring). "We can look forward to at least another Term with carts full of mail from the public, and streets full of demonstrators, urging us—their unelected and life-tenured judges who have been awarded those extraordinary undemocratic characteristics precisely in order that we might follow the law despite the popular will—to follow the popular will." (544).

16. Max Weber, "The Types of Legitimate Domination," in *Economy and Society,*

legitimation problematic embraces norms of appropriate conduct and understandings regarding the proper parameters of power and action. And as Weber himself demonstrated, these norms reflect themselves in discursive commitments, as actors engaged in a practice must develop competence in the rhetorics or professional grammars that legitimate their performances.

In this light, Justice Jackson's statement seems highly anomalous. One would expect a Supreme Court justice writing in an official opinion to attempt to engage in a Bickelian effort at legitimation. Jackson's statement, however, merely restates, indeed exacerbates, the problems about judicial review that so preoccupied Bickel. Indeed, Jackson seems to assume that the Court's powers of constitutional exposition cannot be fully grounded. According to Jackson, the Court's right to offer authoritative readings of the Constitution does not proceed from the peculiar hermeneutic strengths of the Supreme Court; rather the privilege and burdens of reading contrive to create and sustain an artificial notion of authority. In this regard, Jackson's statement both anticipates and encapsulates Robert Cover's notion of the jurispathic—the idea that the Court's readings of the Constitution *perform* not because of their interpretive excellence but because of their position in a hierarchy.[17] In fact Jackson's statement remains more radical still, for it expresses the notion that legal adequacy and interpretive adequacy are wholly separable. Just as legal authority cannot be reduced to interpretive authority, interpretive authority cannot be justified except by fiat—by its connection to legal authority.

The aphorism seems, then, to challenge any logic of legitimation that would justify the exercise of judicial review by appeal to the interpretive acumen of the Supreme Court. Indeed, Jackson seems to have offered—in the middle of a high-court opinion—a pithy and deep critique of the Court's right to engage in the project of constitutional exposition. He has revealed the deep artifice of the Court's

---

ed. G. Roth, trans. Edward Shils and Max Rheinstein (Berkeley and Los Angeles: University of California Press, 1978). For a neo-Weberian treatment of the subject, see Jürgen Habermas, *Legitimation Crisis,* trans. Thomas McCarthy (Boston: Beacon Press, 1975).

17. "The Supreme Court, 1982 Term—Foreword: Nomos and Narrative," *Harvard Law Review* 97 (1983): 4. Cover's argument need not, however, focus specifically on the Supreme Court, though he articulates the concept of the jurispathic by using the Supreme Court as the model of a jurispathic institution.

power to read the Constitution—a power that does not have to demonstrate its superiority in the crucible of rival readings, but that exists by fiat. The potency of the Court's readings are not born of the Court's interpretive skill or art; rather they exist by dint of the Court's position in an architecture of governance.

Interpretation and Legitimation

Such an argument, of course, need not undermine an institution's claims to legitimacy, as legitimacy and hermeneutic prowess *can* be entirely separable. Congress offers precisely such an example.[18] When Congress debates the constitutionality of a piece of legislation, the legitimacy of its readings will not critically hinge on how brilliantly this branch of government reads the Constitution. We might wish that Congress reads the Constitution well; its *authority* to read and the *legitimacy* of its readings, however, do not depend upon, nor are they a measure of, the excellence of such readings. The legitimacy of constitutional exposition by Congress instead derives from the logic of representative governance; and it is this normative understanding of democracy that confers upon the legislative branch the authority to offer constructions of the Constitution. Thus if applied to Congress, Jackson's comment would not be particularly critical, as legitimation and hermeneutic strength are discrete and largely independent variables.

Not so with the Court. As we have noted, the countermajoritarian difficulty and the problem of finality bar the Court from borrowing from Congress's logic of legitimation. Instead, the Court's institutional legitimacy has always been closely associated with its hermeneutic function: its task of constitutional exposition. Here it is important to proceed slowly so as not to confuse the argument. By associating legitimacy with textual interpretation, I do not mean to suggest that it is critical for the Court to be able to demonstrate that the power of judicial review is clearly contained in the four corners of the constitutional document. As Bickel demonstrated, the textual justification for judicial review is neither a sufficient nor necessary condition for the legitimation of the project: not sufficient, because

---

18. See Commager's classic defense of majoritarianism in *Majority Rule and Minority Rights*.

a practice that upsets the normative ordering of a democracy ought not be sustained even if originally contemplated by the founders; not necessary, because a practice that performs a critical function in sustaining a healthy polity ought to be upheld regardless of its questionable constitutional pedigree.[19] So formulated, it is important to distinguish *justification* from *legitimation*, as the former focuses upon the adequacy or sufficiency of the reasons for believing judicial review to be part of the original design of the Constitution, while the latter considers the norms that guide the practice's invocation. Thus acceptance of a textual justification for judicial review does not solve the legitimation problem, as the question remains: how do we limit the judicial act such that it remains within the proper bounds of its justified power? Given concerns about countermajoritarianism and the finality of judicial review, what "bounds" or "disciplines" the performance of the judicial function?

Here, then, is where interpretation becomes critical, as it is this function that has been traditionally understood as defining the limits of the Court's legitimate practice. According to this reasoning, the Court's project of constitutional exposition must be limited to offering readings of the written text. The failure to remain faithful to this project of hermeneutic recovery erodes the Court's legitimacy.[20] Various commentators, of course, have tried to separate interpretation from legitimation, and much recent debate has focused on whether the act of interpretation can ever meaningfully constrain judicial action,[21] but even these attempts continue to presuppose a close asso-

----

19. Bickel, *Least Dangerous Branch*, chap. 1.

20. See, for example, Ely, "The Wages of Crying Wolf," *Yale Law Journal* 82 (1973): 920. In this much-cited piece, Ely attacks *Roe* not as a bad interpretation of the Constitution, but as no interpretation at all. This critique, we shall see, closely tracks Black's critique of Frankfurter in *Adamson*.

21. In its most general terms, this debate focuses on whether constitutional interpretation is or can ever be a "bounded affair." Commentators as jurisprudentially diverse as Robert Bork and Ronald Dworkin have attempted to suggest that such bounds can be discovered within the enterprise of interpretation. Others have rejected these claims. Some scholars, schooled in poststructuralist understandings of language, have attacked the proposition that any text can "fix" or determine or police the range of interpretations it can sponsor. Still others have focused less on the nature of interpretation per se and instead have limited their claims to the nature of constitutional exposition, questioning the coherence of any project that would claim the ability to read an open-textured multiauthored document. And a final loose group has attempted to defend the proposition that interpretation is a bounded affair, but has suggested that such bounds reside neither in the text nor in the process of reading

ciation between high-court legitimacy and the project of constitutional interpretation.

In this light it would seem that Jackson has boldly challenged the assumptions upon which the Court's legitimacy is predicated, iconoclastically suggesting that fiat rather than reasoned reading accounts for the Court's power. As one commentator has observed:

> Hermeneutical mediation comes to an end whenever one party arrogates to itself a sovereign prerogative, that is, the capacity to determine the meaning of legal . . . texts in a unilaterally binding fashion.[22]

This, however, seems to be precisely what Jackson tells us the Court routinely does. The delicate balance between reading and legitimacy has been upset; hermeneutic strength reveals itself to be no more than a contrivance of power. Ostensibly Jackson has created a volatile situation that, one would think, could be stabilized only through a fresh infusion of a rhetoric of legitimation to repair the harm done by his self-inflicted wound of candor.

This, however, misses the genius of Jackson's statement, for it fails to consider the aphorism as, *itself*, a rhetorical move—an attempt to resolve the tensions between interpretation and legitimation not by an act of mystification or fetishization,[23] but by an even more provocative move: by an act of confession. Jackson's comment gives expression to a critical and unusual strand of the Court's rhetoric of legitimation—that the power to read authoritatively can be justified by expressing a radical uncertainty about its very possibility. An expression of the impossibility of justifying the discourse is thus a chief feature of the discourse itself.

---

per se but are embedded in, and thus implicitly enforced by, the interpretive community before which the Court must offer its readings. The material on this subject is large. For a useful overview, see Steven Winter, "Indeterminacy and Incommensurability in Constitutional Law," *California Law Review* 78 (1990): 1441.

22. Fred Dallmayr, "Hermeneutics and the Rule of Law," in *Legal Hermeneutics: History, Theory, and Practice*, ed. Gregory Leyh (Berkeley and Los Angeles: University of California Press, 1992), 17–18.

23. Much of the literature associated with critical legal studies examines the manner in which legal discourse obfuscates and fetishizes its power relations. For a particularly trenchant analysis from a distinctly British perspective, see Peter Goodrich, *Languages of Law* (London: Weidenfeld and Nicolson, 1990).

Read in this manner, Jackson's statement suggests that the tension between interpretation and legitimation can be best managed, if not resolved, by a public declamation of the impossibility of such a resolution. If we are correct in suggesting that such a position is a critical discursive feature of the rhetoric of high-court legitimation, it is critical to examine the foundations of this rhetorical practice to understand why it remains ever haunted by the specter of its own instabilities.

The Marshallian Dilemma

At the foundation of a well-formed belief lies the belief that it is not well-founded.
                                        —Wittgenstein, *On Certainty*

Exposition as Reading: The Marshallian Innovation

If the instabilities in constitutional discourse are brilliantly revealed and thereby stabilized in Jackson's famous aphorism, then nowhere are they more provocatively concealed and contained than within the legal opinion that created the rhetorical practice: *Marbury v. Madison.*[24] Marshall's interpretive deviousness has been the subject of considerable writing, but even those commentators who have explicitly considered his opinion as an exemplary exercise in legal manipulation have wholly failed to consider his reading of the Constitution in light of the rhetorical understanding it contains.[25]

The facts of the case, often ignored, have the overdetermined quality of a nightmare. In one of the last acts of his presidency, John Adams pushed through the Organic Act of the District of Columbia, creating forty-two justices of the peace. The forty-two new justices were selected on 2 March 1801; Senate confirmation followed a day

---

24. 5 U.S. (1 Cranch) 137 (1803).

25. The classic commentary on Marshall's cunning is found in Robert G. McCloskey, *The American Supreme Court* (Chicago: University of Chicago Press, 1960), 26–53. For a more recent consideration of the political exigencies facing Marshall at the time of the opinion's composition, see James M. O'Fallon, "*Marbury,*" *Stanford Law Review* 44 (1992): 219. See also, Robert Lowry Clinton, *Marbury v. Madison and Judicial Review* (Lawrence: University of Kansas Press, 1989).

later.[26] John Marshall, as the departing secretary of state under the Adams administration, was responsible for signing, sealing, and delivering the forty-two commissions. Though Marshall was able to complete the first two tasks, the delivery of the commissions created a problem. On 4 March 1801, the last day of the departing administration, Marshall had to perform a duty mandated by the judicial position he had assumed thanks to yet another last-minute act by Adams during his tenure as a lame duck. As the new chief justice of the United States Supreme Court, Marshall had to swear in the new president, his Republican political adversary, Thomas Jefferson. The job of completing his unfinished work—the delivery of the commissions—he left to his brother, James, who "finding that he could not conveniently carry the whole, returned several of them" to the secretary's desk.[27] The new secretary of state, Madison, refused to deliver the commissions; Marbury, a would-be recipient, filed a writ of mandamus in the Supreme Court, and thus *Marbury v. Madison*.[28]

In bringing his suit directly to Marshall's Supreme Court, Marbury no doubt expected to find a sympathetic audience. More importantly, Marbury was following the jurisdictional mandates of the Judiciary Act of 1789, which, in addition to establishing inferior federal courts as authorized by Article III of the Constitution, decreed that the Supreme Court "shall have power to issue . . . writs of *mandamus* . . . to . . . persons holding office*, under authority of the United States."[29] As is familiar to any student of the Court, Marshall concludes that Marbury has a right to his commission, that a right violated implies a remedy; that as a general matter a writ of mandamus would be the proper remedy; but that in this case, such a writ cannot issue from the Supreme Court as the congressional act that authorized the Court to use this power was, itself, unconstitutional and therefore without legal effect. Thus at the very moment Marshall seems to be checking the power of the judiciary, he, in

---

26. These were not the so-called "Midnight Appointments"—that term refers to the judges appointed through the Circuit Court Act passed on 13 February 1801. To remain true to the temporal trope, the justices of the peace would have to be considered the "four A.M. appointments."

27. 5 U.S. (1 Cranch) 137, 146.

28. Even though Marshall was intimately associated with the facts of the case, the Court's difficulty in recovering these facts reminds us that stonewalling by the executive branch is no recent phenomenon. Ibid., 138–42, passim.

29. Ibid., 148.

fact, radically expands it; and it is this expansion—namely, the articulation of the power of judicial review—along with its supporting
argument that makes *Marbury* the most famous case in American
constitutional history.

It is important, however, not to exaggerate the degree to which
Marshall's articulation of a power of judicial review marked a radical
departure from the then-prevailing norms of judicial practice. That
contemporaries of Marshall voiced dissent against Marshall's argument in favor of judicial review is no doubt clear;[30] nevertheless, an
abundance of historical material suggests that the founders were at
least familiar with the concept of judicial review and that many were
accepting of it.[31] Indeed, Hamilton's argument for judicial review in
Federalist 78 anticipates many of Marshall's arguments—in certain
respects, with greater sweep and vision.[32]

This being the case, it is nevertheless important to note how the
actual bounds of the power of judicial review were enlarged upon
by Marshall in a manner that marked an important departure from
then-prevailing understandings. In an important recent work, Sylvia
Snowiss has argued that Marshall's critical achievement lay not in
articulating the principle of judicial review, but in dramatically
reshaping its meaning.[33] At the time of the founding of the Republic,
Snowiss argues, judicial review was a familiar doctrine, but one with
a specific meaning and a decidedly narrow scope. To borrow language
that became fashionable only a century later in Thayer's famous
article about judicial review[34] but that more aptly applied to the

---

30. Often cited in this regard in Gibson's dissent in Eakin v. Raub, 12 Sergeant
and Rawles (Pa.) 330, 354 (1825). In this dissent, Gibson does not challenge the
proposition that an unconstitutional legislative act is void; rather he challenges the
Court's right to make this determination. He does not, however, offer an unconditional
attack on judicial review—he implicitly argues that it should extend only to cases in
which acts have been passed in violation of constitutionally mandated procedures of
enactment (e.g., in absence of a quorum).

31. See, for example, *The Records of the Federal Convention of 1787*, ed. Max
Farrand, 4 vols. (New Haven: Yale University Press, 1966), 1:97–98, 2:298–300.

32. *The Federalist Papers*, ed. Clinton Rossiter (New York: Mentor, 1961), 464–
72. Marshall's argument, however, differs importantly from Hamilton's with respect
to the question of the Constitution's writtenness. Hamilton views the Constitution
as fundamental law but does not specifically link judicial exposition of this law with
its written quality. Marshall's innovation lies in uniting the two.

33. Sylvia Snowiss, *Judicial Review and the Law of the Constitution* (New
Haven: Yale University Press, 1990).

34. James Thayer, "The Origin and Scope of the American Doctrine of Con-

jurisprudence of the founding, the power was meant to be invoked only "in a very clear case."[35] This idea—that the judicial check on the legislature be limited to circumstances of "concededly unconstitutional" acts—contained, according to Snowiss, two critical tenets. The first was the idea that the concept of facial unconstitutionality was in no way necessarily linked with the idea of a *written* constitution. Schooled in common and natural law traditions, jurists at the time believed in the existence of fundamental laws upon which a polity was predicated, and any facial violation of these fundamental laws—whether written or not—was void. The second point is thus a corollary of the first: schooled on such assumptions, jurists at the time did not associate judicial review with a project of *reading*. Techniques of statutory construction—of reading and construing written instruments so as to ascertain and fix meaning—were never considered appropriate for the purposes of judicial review. In fact, as Snowiss argues, the power to declare legislative acts unconstitutional was not considered a *judicial* act in the proper sense—it was considered more an extraordinary extra-judicial declaration, and as such, the functional equivalent of challenging sovereign prerogative.[36]

This is not to suggest that before Marshall techniques of statutory construction were never used on the Constitution for the purposes of fixing the document's meaning;[37] rather, it is to say that such techniques were never used for the purpose of attacking the constitutionality of challenged legislation. Thus Marshall's critical innovation lay not in creating judicial review, but in transforming the act into one of *reading* a *written* document.[38] In so doing, Marshall assimilates judicial review

---

stitutional Law," *Harvard Law Review* 7 (1893): 129. Thayer, in fact, saw himself as attempting to reintroduce a pre-Marshallian, viz., prelapsarian, standard of judicial review.

35. Hylton v. United States, 3 Dall. (3 U.S.) 171 (1796), (Chase concurring), 175. Chase implicitly acknowledges that the Court had the power to strike down unconstitutional acts of Congress, though he argues that such a power should be invoked only in circumstances of facial unconstitutionality.

36. Snowiss, *Judicial Review*, 51.

37. Snowiss, *Judicial Review*, 125. Thus Calder v. Bull, 3 Dall (3 U.S.) 386 (1798), presents an example of a case in which the Court engaged in an act of constitutional interpretation, but not for the purposes of striking down a legislative act. Irdell, in a famous opinion, specifically seems to argue that judicial review would be inappropriate in circumstances other than enforcing *express* limitations upon legislative power.

38. Marshall continued to use the prevailing "clear mistake" language. In

into a standard project of statutory construction, a practice with which
he and many contemporary jurists were familiar.[39] How he does this—
that is, how he associates the judicial check upon the legislature with
a process of expounding the meaning of a written text—remains exemplary of the problems of linking high-court legitimacy with the hermeneutic strengths of the institution.

Imaging the Constitution

In a blithe moment, Marshall writes, "The question whether an act
repugnant to the Constitution can become law of the land is . . .
deeply interesting . . . but, happily, not of an intricacy proportioned
toward its interest."[40] Happiness comes from simplicity—to permit
ordinary legislation to trump the Constitution is to render the latter
document a dead letter, for the Constitution, by design, is to act as
a curb upon legislative power. This point supports the idea that the
Constitution *is* different from ordinary legislative acts, but it leaves
unanswered *how* this difference is manifest. Is it accounted for by
the simple fact that the document was authored in a sweaty convention hall rather than a grimy legislative assembly?

Obviously not. The Constitution's *constitutionality* is, for Marshall, identified with five discrete points: First, the Constitution establishes "principles" that "are deemed fundamental"; second, these
fundamental principles have been inscribed in *writing*; third, these
fundamental principles inscribed in writing have been authored by a
national collectivity; fourth, these written principles are of a legal
character; and therefore, fifth, they can be read by courts.[41] Thus different from ordinary legislation, the Constitution expresses the collective meanings of "We, the People," a rhetorical figure that the

---

Fletcher v. Peck, for example, Marshall wrote, "The question, whether a law be void
for its repugnancy to the constitution, is, at all times, a question of much delicacy,
which ought seldom, if ever, to be decided in the affirmative, in a doubtful
case. . . . The opposition between the constitution and law should be such that the
judge feels a clear and strong conviction of their incompatibility with each other."
10 U.S. (6 Cranch) 87 (1810).

39. For a discussion of then-prevailing techniques of statutory construction, see
H. Jefferson Powell, "The Original Understanding of Original Intent," *Harvard Law
Review* 98 (1985): 885.

40. *Marbury*, 176.

41. Ibid., 176–78.

document enshrines as its author. That the Constitution's *constitutionality* is a function of the unusual terms of its authorship is an argument that Marshall makes all the more powerfully and explicitly fifteen years later in *McCulloch v. Maryland*, noting that the Constitution "derives its whole authority" from the "people" in whose name it is "ordained and established."[42]

To say "We the People" is a rhetorical figure is not, then, to call it "mere" rhetoric—at least not as understood in the Platonic sense that we identified at the beginning of this essay. For if "We the People" were read as merely a synecdochal device used by a group of men collected in Philadelphia to add a patina of deeper authority to their document, then it would no longer be possible to distinguish the Constitution from ordinary legislation. One could argue that the Constitution's continuing power to trump ordinary legislation is a function of the extraordinary historical circumstances associated with its composition, circumstances that permitted the Philadelphia drafters to become for all time and place "We the People"; unfortunately, this view does not survive closer scrutiny.

However one might praise the founders' philosophic acumen and skills of statesmancraft (recall Jefferson's proclamation in Paris that the document was drafted by "an assembly of demigods"), it is difficult to justify why their understandings should continue to control contemporary constitutional meanings. Of the fifty-five men (only thirty-nine of whom actually participated in the drafting of the document), all were white, and with the exception of the Catholic Daniel Carroll of Maryland, all were Protestant. If the familiar rhetoric of the "Founding Fathers" suggests a collection of sagacious septuagenarians, it is worth recalling that Charles Pinckney was twenty-nine, Alexander Hamilton thirty, and Madison, thirty-six. The average age of the founders was forty-three, a figure itself somewhat inflated by Benjamin Franklin's venerable eighty-one years.[43] All this simply calls into question the soundness of the view that the Constitution creates a system that authorizes a small group of white men to monopolize the universe of constitutional meanings.

Although one can plausibly argue that Marshall was not partic-

---

42. McCulloch v. Maryland, 17 U.S. (4 Wheat.) 316, 403 (1819).

43. Catherine Drinker Bowen, *Miracle at Philadelphia* (Boston: Atlantic Monthly Press, 1986).

ularly animated by these concerns (though Jefferson clearly was),[44] he nevertheless redeems the Constitution's claim to fundamental legal supremacy by taking the authorial rhetoric of "We the People" seriously. He reads "We the People" not as a figure for the Philadelphia drafters; rather, the founders are read as conduits, performing a function that must be understood as oracular or Mosaic. The Constitution thus upsets the classical model of signifying—it is no longer the metaphor that stands for the concrete; it is now the concrete authors who become a mere figure for the powerful metaphor of "We the People." "We the People" thus must be read as "deep" rhetoric: a powerful figure capable of generating legal meaning independent of its connection to the men in Philadelphia.

This, however, both redeems the meaning-generating force of the Constitution and creates deep hermeneutic problems. As Marshall writes in *McCulloch*, "[W]e must never forget, that it is a *constitution* we are expounding"[45]—a statement that recognizes the Constitution's dependence on interpretation, at the same time that it begs the question. How does one interpret a document with an unspecified potential for meaning whose very author is a trope created by the text? Moreover, how is it possible to create a case for the Supreme Court as privileged reader? In this regard, the rhetorical and interpretive problem facing Marshall is quite different from the task of interpreting other texts fecund with potential meaning, such as poems. In Marshall's case, it isn't sufficient to show that he can offer one among many plausible readings of a refractory document—he must create a case, *through reading*, for arrogating interpretation to the prerogatives of a putatively privileged institution. It is not enough to offer *an* interpretation; Marshall must offer *the* interpretation.

Marshall's Rhetoric of Reading: Intentionalism

In the face of this hermeneutic quandary, Marshall seems at moments to engage in a variety of intentionalist reasoning. For example, when

---

44. Troubled by the idea that one generation could monopolize the constitutional meanings of future generations, Jefferson favored generational constitutional conventions. *The Writings of Thomas Jefferson*, ed. A. E. Lipscomb and A. E. Bergh (Washington, D.C.: Thomas Jefferson Memorial Association of the United States, 1903), 15:41–42. It is this argument that Madison attempts to refute in *Federalist 49*, arguing, "Notwithstanding the success which has attended the revisions of our established forms of government . . . it must be confessed that the experiments are of too ticklish a nature to be unnecessarily multiplied" (315).

45. 17 U.S. (4 Wheat.) 316, 407 (1819).

it comes to offering a textual argument in support of judicial review, Marshall speaks of "the intention of those who gave this [judicial] power."[46] How, however, can we reconcile Marshall's talk of "intention" with his repudiation of a flat synecdochal reading of "We the People"?

To answer this, it is important to distinguish between intentionalism as a *theory* of meaning—which posits that a text's meaning has, in some relatively determinate sense, been "fixed" by its author(s)[47]—and intentionalism as a *strategy* for gaining meaning—which encourages the consultation and examination of extratextual sources (diaries, letters, minutes, etc.) for the purposes of "getting at" the meaning encoded in the text.[48] Thus whereas intentionalism as a strategy necessarily implies commitment to intentionalism as a theory, the obverse need not obtain.

In jurisprudential terms, intentionalism has been most powerfully associated with its strategic sense—the idea, associated with exponents from Justice Sunderland[49] to Edwin Meese,[50] that the meaning of ambiguous constitutional clauses can be gained by examining ratification debates or other documents or sources that might clarify the intent of the framers. "Intentionalism as strategy" has, however, been the subject of several important recent critiques such as that provided by H. Jefferson Powell, who argues, through a careful canvasing of historical material, that the intent of the framers was that their intent not control constitutional meanings.[51] To the extent one is committed to intentionalism, this commitment would oblige the student of the Constitution not to privilege intent. Cast differently, one can remain an intentionalist only by a selective fidelity to the strategy. Often

46. *Marbury,* 179.

47. See, for example, E. D. Hirsch, *Validity in Interpretation* (New Haven: Yale University Press, 1967), and *The Aims of Interpretation* (Chicago: University of Chicago Press, 1976).

48. For an outstanding example of this strategy as applied to the study of literature, see Elias Canneti, *Kafka's Other Trial* (New York: Schocken, 1982). Canneti offers a new reading of *The Trial* based on an imaginative examination of Kafka's *Letters to Felice.*

49. "The whole aim of construction . . . is to discover the meaning, to ascertain and give effect to the intent, of its framers and the people who adopted it." United States v. Curtiss-Wright Export Corp., 299 U.S. 304 (1936).

50. See, for example, Meese's "Address before the D.C. Chapter of the Federalist Society Lawyers Division," in *Interpreting Law and Literature: A Hermeneutic Reader,* ed. Sandford Levinson and Steven Mailloux (Evanston: Northwestern University Press, 1988).

51. "Original Understanding of Original Intent."

overlooked in the enthusiasm that greeted Powell's piece is the fact
that the technique he uses *is* intentionalist—that is, though his argument renders intentionalism as a strategy problematic for the student
of the Constitution, the argument does not touch intentionalism as
a general theory of meaning—and, in fact, implicitly relies on the
coherence of this theory for the force of the historical argument.

This is not to suggest that all jurisprudential critics of intentionalism focus on its adequacy as a strategy. Paul Brest, for example,
has attempted to point out the philosophical instabilities contained
within the theory of intentionalism as it applies to multiauthored
documents.[52] Such arguments, however, run the risk of proving too
much. As the literary critics Winsatt and Beardsley once noted,[53] the
interesting question is not whether a text *contains* the meanings of
its author; the question is whether authorial intent *exhausts* the universe of textual meaning.[54]

Thus theory-intentionalism does not answer the question of *reading*, it simply displaces it. This we see in Marshall's opinion. That
Marshall eschews strategy-intentionalism is one of the most striking
features of his opinion: had he been interested in canvassing the
framers' intent, presumably he could have asked them directly—they
were, after all, his contemporaries. This point could not have been
raised more dramatically than in *Marbury*, as the very defendant in
the action, James Madison, was the principal architect of the Constitution. Of course if Powell's history is reliable, Madison would not
have responded to Marshall's queries—he, too, deemed the extratextual intent of the framers irrelevant for the purposes of interpreting
the text.[55] Alternatively, had Madison demonstrated a willingness
to reveal the meaning he attached to Article III, Marshall plausibly

52. "The Misconceived Quest for the Original Understanding," *Boston University Law Review* 60 (1980): 204.
53. "The Intentional Fallacy," in *The Verbal Icon: Studies in the Meaning of Poetry* (Lexington: University of Kentucky Press, 1954).
54. Or as Walter Benn Michaels has observed, at the time of its composition, the Constitution had to mean something, and that meaning was presumably that of its authors. "The Fate of the Constitution," *Texas Law Review* 61 (1982): 765.
55. "As a guide in expounding and applying the provisions of the Constitution, the debates and incidental decisions of the Convention can have no authoritative character." Letter from James Madison to Thomas Ritchie, 15 September 1821, quoted in Powell, "Original Understanding of Original Intent."

might have feared that Madison, as a party to a litigation in 1803, might have been less than faithful to his specific intent in 1787.

More importantly, one could argue that Marshall, schooled in accepted canons of statutory construction, was unwilling to exploit his privileged access to the framers' extratextual intent for the purposes of construing constitutional language. This attempt to rehabilitate Marshall's opinion, however, fails to make sense of his careful avoidance of entirely appropriate techniques of construing legal documents. If Marshall had entirely sound reasons for eschewing a direct interrogation of the framers for the purpose of establishing intent, he might, perfectly consistent with accepted canons of statutory construction, have considered other legislative acts passed by a similar, if not identical, group of individuals, as relevant for the purposes of reconstructing the framers' intent. Or to apply this reasoning to the instant case, saddled as he was with the task of attempting to make sense of the jurisdictional architecture of Article III, one might have thought that Marshall would have seized upon the Judiciary Act of 1789, drafted and passed by many of the selfsame individuals who participated in the Philadelphia convention, as a valuable document for the purposes of parsing the meaning of the text authored two years previously.[56] Although one might argue that this implicitly and facilely assumes that individuals' (i.e., the framers') political commitments remain stable over time, in this particular case it is difficult to find why this assumption should be viewed as problematic. Thus one of the critical ambiguities contained in *Marbury* is the fact that Marshall declares unconstitutional the very legislative act that arguably would have been of greatest utility in guiding him through a reading of Article III.

Marshall himself returns to this very problematic in *McCulloch*. Upholding the Bank of the United States, a creature of federal law, Marshall writes,

> The power now contested was exercised by the first Congress elected under the present constitution. . . . It would require no

---

56. The Judiciary Act of 1789 passed with the support of at least sixteen members of Congress who also participated in the Philadelphia convention, including James Madison. None of the framers who were members of the First Congress voted against the Judiciary Act. See *1 Annals of Congress 50, 964.*

ordinary share of intrepidity to assert that a measure adopted under these circumstances was bold and plain usurpation, to which the constitution gave no countenance.[57]

But it is precisely such an act of extraordinary intrepidity that Marshall commits in *Marbury*.

Reading the Deep Rhetoric of "We the People"

Here again it is possible to rehabilitate Marshall's reasoning by returning to the rhetoric of "We the People." Remaining faithful to the rhetorical figure that the document names as its author would seem to require, as noted earlier, reading the document in a manner such that the group classically enshrined as the founding fathers—that is, the men gathered in the east chamber of the Pennsylvania statehouse— are not permitted to exhaust the universe of constitutional meanings. In this spirit, Marshall, in other contexts and cases, focuses his intentionalist arguments not upon the group that authored the text, but upon those that rendered it *authoritative*—the ratifiers. This point emerges both in *Marbury* and in later opinions such as *McCulloch* when Marshall writes, "From these conventions [i.e., for ratification] the constitution derives its whole authority."[58] Of course, this move alone would be enough to give some theory-intentionalists fits, as the ratifiers' relationship to the original text ultimately was interpretive. For theory-intentionalists such as E. D. Hirsch, the act of privileging the ratifiers' intent—even if the ratifiers were responsible for the document's *authority* and thus *power* to signify—already upsets the entire scheme of meanings that underlies theory-intentionalism, as it permits interpreters to usurp authors as the sponsors of textual meaning. In any case, one could argue that Marshall avoids relying on the Judiciary Act of 1789, as this at best would represent the intent of the framers to the exclusion of the ratifiers.

Here, however, it is critical to distinguish two possible conceptions of representation. The first can be understood as isomorphic: In this view, the constitutional commitments of the "people" are elaborated

57. U.S. (4 Wheat.) 316 (1819). See also William W. Van Alstyne, "A Critical Guide to *Marbury v. Madison*," *Duke Law Journal* (1969): 1, 32–33.
58. McCulloch v. Maryland, 17 U.S. (4 Wheat.) 316, 403 (1819).

and articulated by their representatives; indeed, these commitments cannot be said to enjoy any discursively prior existence.[59] What is crucial about this isomorphic reading of the Constitution is the hermeneutic it implicitly sanctions: If "We the People" find complete representation in the discursive commitments of the framers/ratifiers of the Constitution (indeed, if the people's constitutional understandings *exist* only by dint of this act of representation), then an intentionalist reading of the document would legitimately focus exclusively on the framers'/ratifiers' intent, sanctioning precisely the kind of parsing of legislative history that Marshall conspicuously avoids.

A second understanding of representation, however, needs to be considered, the semiotic.[60] In this view, the function performed by the ratifiers remains one of representation, but much in the same way that a name re-presents a referent: the signifier *stands* for the signified, but does not *embrace* or *exhaust* it. Thus, if one reads "We the People" as not a mere synecdoche for the drafters or ratifiers, but as an authorial body neither entirely represented, nor spoken for, by the framers/ratifiers, then Marshall's interpretive strategy begins to look coherent, born of something other than political exigency.

That Marshall's understanding of the relationship between the framers/ratifiers and "We the People" can best be seen as semiotic rather than isomorphic is made clear by considering Marshall's demonstrated ease with consulting legislative history for the purposes of parsing the meaning of ordinary (i.e., nonconstitutional) statutory acts. Isomorphic representation is the very model of ordinary legislative politics: legal meanings are articulated by elected representatives, and these meanings control the process of statutory construction by courts.[61] Thus in other cases such as *McCulloch*,[62] Marshall

---

59. Such a theory of representation implicitly informs John Hart Ely, *Democracy and Distrust* (Cambridge: Harvard University Press, 1980). In this work, Ely presupposes a close correspondence between what the legislature says and what the people mean. In fact, his entire theory of judicial review is limited to correcting those instances in which this correspondence seems to have been disrupted. Bickel, however, takes a somewhat more ambivalent position regarding isomorphic representation in *Least Dangerous Branch*.

60. For a similar account of the distinction between isomorphic and semiotic representation, see Bruce Ackerman, "The Storrs Lectures," *Yale Law Journal* 93 (1984): 1013, 1025–1030.

61. See, for example, Richard Posner, *Law and Literature: A Misunderstood Relation* (Cambridge: Harvard University Press, 1988), 245–50.

62. 17 U.S. (4 Wheat.) 316 (1819). Marshall did, however, sidestep deciding

THE RHETORIC OF LAW

demonstrates no discomfort with the project of reading legislative enactments in light of congressional intent. But this "weak" rhetorical project fails when applied to the Constitution. As we have already noted, the deeper legal pedigree of the Constitution derives from its nature as deep rhetoric, a chief feature of which is the document's positing of its own author. The intent of the framers/ratifiers cannot be coextensive with, and exhaustive of, the meanings of the document's named author(s).

Thus it is possible to explain why Marshall eschews consulting the intent of the framers/ratifiers with such remarkable insouciance. And all the while remaining an avowed intentionalist, at least as this term refers to a theory of textual meaning. But to the extent that Marshall redeems the Constitution's *constitutionality* by taking seriously the rhetorical figure that the document names as its author, he continues to beg the daunting problem of interpretation. For if the relevant set of intentions for the purpose of interpreting the Constitution are the "peoples'," and if the peoples' intentions resist representation in a simple isomorphic form, then how is one to read the deep constitutional rhetoric of "We the People"?

Rhetoric of Reading: "Plain Import of the Words"

Had Marshall been satisfied to limit judicial review to the then-prevailing standards (i.e., as an extrajudicial power to be invoked only in instances of facial violations of fundamental law), then his deep rhetorical understanding of the Constitution would not have presented any particular problems. Judicial review would have been used to protect the constitutional meanings of "We the People" against legislative encroachment only in circumstances in which a violation was so transparent that there was no need to consult extratextual intent for the purposes of parsing the text.

But this is precisely the concept of judicial review that Marshall abandons. Indeed, his critical innovation, first articulated in *Marbury* and then further elaborated during his tenure as chief justice, is to link the project of constitutional exposition with a hermeneutic function. The intent of "We the People" must be recovered through *reading* the constitutional text.

---

cases based upon impermissible or corrupt legislative intent. See Fletcher v. Peck, 10 U.S. (6 Cranch) 87 (1810).

Here Marshall makes a brilliant and problematic move: For the purposes of *reading*, Marshall treats the Constitution like any other piece of law, a written text containing specific commands, which, he argues, courts are uniquely schooled in the art of interpreting. "It is," he reminds his reader, "emphatically the province and duty of the judicial department to say what the law is."[63] Moreover:

> If two laws conflict with each other, the courts must decide on the operation of each. . . . This is the very essence of the judicial duty. . . . Those who controvert the principle that the constitution is to be considered, in court, as a paramount law . . . subvert the very foundation of all written constitutions.[64]

Here, however, Marshall seems to hark back to the clear-mistake rule. Reading, he seems to suggest, is no different from the traditional concept of limiting judicial review to instances of facial unconstitutionality—even though the reading he offers of Article III thoroughly belies this claim. Thus in creating the case for judicial review as constitutional exposition through reading, Marshall offers a highly misleading notion of the Constitution's ability to signify with specificity, one that contradicts his vision of the document as rhetorical figure; still, this move is absolutely essential in order to establish a case for its readability.

Nowhere is this point more poignantly—and crassly—made than in his examination of the jurisdictional architecture contemplated by Article III, an examination he ends by quoting the Constitution: "In all other cases before mentioned, the Supreme Court shall have appellate jurisdiction."[65] The full stop, however, is Marshall's, not the Constitution's. The Constitution continues, "with such exceptions and under such regulations as Congress shall make." Thus it would not seem absurd to suggest that if the Judiciary Act of 1789 did indeed expand the original jurisdiction of the Supreme Court, such a change was sanctioned by the "exceptions clause." Marshall, to his credit, explicitly refutes the idea that the language of Article III supports such a reading. It would, he argues, effectively destroy the jurisdictional

---

63. 5 U.S. (1 Cranch) 137 (1803), at 177.
64. Ibid., 177–78.
65. Ibid., 174.

architecture of Article III. While commentators have drawn attention
to the logical problems with this reading of Article III—that, for
example, Marshall overlooks the possibility that the exceptions clause
contemplates the expansion of the Court's original jurisdiction by
"excepting out" matters from the Court's appellate jurisdiction—these
commentators themselves have ignored the rhetorical implications of
Marshall's subtle act of constitutional redaction.[66] Marshall's failure
to end his citation of Article III with as much as an ellipsis, however,
supports more than the classical image of Marshall as devious jurist,
willing to rewrite constitutional text in order to consolidate the claims
of readership. Rather, Marshall's rhetorical project supports and mandates the bold act of excision. If the power of *writtenness* to constrain
interpretation is to be taken seriously, then any textual—i.e., written—pronouncements that might inadvertently serve to undermine
the coherence of this power must be redacted out. Or stated differently, if writtenness supports judicial review based on reading, then
any writing that undermines this project must be literally read out
of the text.

Of course, a less intrepid and more faithful reader might have
reached the opposite conclusion: that a fidelity to the document *qua*
writing required remaining faithful even to those stretches of writing
that might seem to weaken the text's power to direct interpretation;
Marshall, however, violates the very written text he wishes to defend
in order to defend the idea that the Constitution's writtenness constrains ordinary legislation—and, by extension, that the document signifies in a manner specific enough so as to support a project of reading.

This point resonates with Marshall's more general effort to render
the Constitution interpretively legible. Arguing by means of a series
of rhetorical questions, he writes:

> The Constitution declares that "no bill of attainder or ex post
> facto law shall be passed." If, however, such a bill should be
> passed . . . must the court condemn to death those victims whom
> the Constitution endeavors to preserve?[67]

Marshall's choice of the ex post facto prohibition as a paragon of
constitutional clarity was clearly strategic: his contemporaries on the

---

66. See, for example, Van Alstyne, "Critical Guide," 30–33.
67. *Marbury*, 179.

whole agreed that ex post facto laws were exemplars of facial uncon-stitutionality.[68] In fact, several delegates to the Philadelphia conven-tion opposed the inclusion of the ex post facto prohibition in the Constitution for the simple reason that such laws so clearly violated fundamental law that it was superfluous to say so in writing.[69]

In the case of *Marbury*, however, the ex post facto analogy seems inapposite as the Judiciary Act of 1789 could hardly be said to constitute a facial violation of Article III. But even if one accepts Marshall's point, his rhetorical victory is Pyrrhic, for if the Consti-tution always operated on such a level of specificity, it would cease to be the Constitution. Its *constitutionality* is a property of its open-textured discourse; yet, to create a case for its readability, this very nature as rhetorical figure must be denied.

But this only serves to create greater instabilities. For if the prerogatives of readership can be defended only by rendering the text legally transparent, this begs the question why the document's author (itself, as noted, a powerful figure) did not explicitly lodge the power of reading in the Court. Marshall, of course, argues the power is there implicitly—as we have already noted, he reconstructs intent by carefully scrutinizing the legal meanings of the word *case* and by approvingly citing the oath requirement.[70] These arguments have met with varying degrees of skepticism and support,[71] but clearly many of Marshall's contemporaries believed that judicial review was meant to protect fundamental law—whether written or not—and thus the case for review was in no sense dependent on being conferred through a written instrument. For Marshall, however, the failure to supply a convincing textual argument is more serious, for, as we have seen, he links judicial review with exposition. Thus, if the Constitution's

---

68. Yet in *Fletcher v. Peck*, Marshall had to face the discomfiting reality that the question whether a law was indeed ex post facto could require precisely the kind of probing interpretation that *Marbury* dismisses with a rhetorical question. 10 U.S. (6 Cranch) 87 (1810).

69. "There was no lawyer, no civilian who would not say that ex post facto laws were void," declared Oliver Ellsworth during the Federal convention. "It cannot then be necessary to prohibit them." Quoted in Snowiss, *Judicial Review*, 42.

70. *Marbury*, 180.

71. We have already observed that an early and influential critique was offered by Gibson in Eakins v. Raub, 12 S. & R. 330, 345-57 (Pa. 1825); Van Alstyne in "Critical Guide," however, finds Marshall's parsing of the meaning of *case* plausible, particularly as it would apply to issues of federalism (i.e., review of state court verdicts).

meanings are recoverable through reading, then why is the very power to read one that can be discovered only through a complex hermeneutic deduction?

But if tensions exist at the heart of Marshall's opinion, they do not reflect his defects as a jurist. Indeed, these tensions cannot be resolved; they can merely be dodged or displaced; and the genius of Marshall's opinion lies in its rhetorical dancing—how in order to justify the supremacy of the Constitution he must conjure an image of textual fecundity that then must be subverted in order to create a case for the Court's power to read.

Marshall's opinion thus confers a blessing and a curse. It makes possible, and offers the first contribution to, the discourse of judicial review but it fails to link persuasively the judicial project of constitutional exposition with a bounded hermeneutic that privileges the Court as reader. Indeed, Marshall's reading of the Constitution is predicated upon an understanding of the nature of the text that undercuts his claim to arrogate the powers of reading to the Court— and in fact challenges the coherence of any hermeneutic that claims to be able to read the deep rhetoric of "We the People."[72]

Deep Rhetoric Revisited:
The Black-Frankfurter Debate

O body swayed to music, O brightening glance,
How can we know the dancer from the dance?
    —William Butler Yeats, "Among Schoolchildren"

The Rhetoric of Fundamental Value Analysis

The Marshallian dilemma—the tension between the Constitution as deep rhetoric and as readable text—remains a source of deep instability within high-court practice, and its fault lines continue to define constitutional discourse as such; indeed, the rhetoric of constitutional jurisprudence since Marshall must be understood in light of the suc-

---

72. Bickel argues that in this respect, Marshall's opinion remains a non sequitur. Marshall's most dramatic failure, Bickel argues, is his inability to support the Court's privilege as *exclusive* reader through a reading of the text. Thus, Bickel makes recourse to an extratextual theory of democracy to fashion a normative argument in support of judicial review. *Least Dangerous Branch*, 1–33.

cessive and ever-evolving attempts to solve, or at least displace, this
intractable problem.

To consider how the Marshallian dilemma is rhetorically played
out in latter day Supreme Court jurisprudence, let us consider the
1947 case of *Adamson v. California*.[73] *Adamson* can be considered
exemplary not only because of the excellence of the rhetorical performances it contains; more importantly, it offers in paradigmatic
fashion a full range of the arguments associated with what has come
to be known as the Court's "fundamental values" jurisprudence. This
jurisprudence, vehemently assailed by some students of the Court,
while passionately defended by others, lies at the heart of doctrinal
holdings extending from matters of reproductive rights[74] to issues of
criminal procedure.[75] The basic assumption of these doctrinal commitments is that the Constitution protects values fundamental to the
traditions of our social order—even if such values find no clear articulation in "the four corners" of the constitutional document. Fundamental values jurisprudence thus poses in stark relief the Court's
continuing struggle to associate the legitimacy of its institutional
function with a project of *reading* the Constitution. For if legitimation
remains coupled with bounded interpretation, and if fundamental
values are not recoverable through reading, then a jurisprudence
dedicated to their articulation and defense would seem to except itself
from the Court's logic of legitimacy.[76]

In *Adamson*, the Court is asked to pass on the constitutionality
of a California statute that permits a prosecutor to comment on the
accused's failure to testify in circumstances in which the accused
refuses to take the stand in his own defense.[77] The case comes on
appeal to the Supreme Court following the defendant's conviction for
first degree murder. The Court remains laconic about the facts of the
case; a few isolated details—a stolen diamond ring, the severed tops
of a pair of stockings—offer obscure images of a female victim and
a robbery that ends in a brutal killing. The defendant, we are told,

73. 332 U.S. 46 (1947).
74. See, for example, Planned Parenthood v. Casey, nos. 91–744 and 91–902
(1992).
75. See, for example, Rochin v. California, 342 U.S. 165 (1952).
76. As we have noted, such is the argument advanced by Ely in *Democracy
and Distrust*. See also Robert Bork, "Neutral Principles and Some First Amendment
Problems," *Indiana Law Journal* 47 (1971): 1.
77. These provisions were also contained in the state constitution.

never took the stand before the jury that sentenced him to death; whatever words the prosecutor uttered about this failure to testify remain in the case unreported, though presumably inferences were drawn.[78] On appeal, Adamson argues that the California statute violated his right against self-incrimination as guaranteed by the Fifth Amendment as applied against the states via the Fourteenth.

Had Adamson been tried in a federal court, the prosecutor's commenting on the silence of the accused would have constituted, so the Court is willing to assume, a Fifth Amendment violation. Whether it violates the Fourteenth Amendment's due process clause is, however, another issue. Does the putative federal right run against the states via the due process clause of the Fourteenth Amendment? The question is not one that can be mechanically solved by a consideration of a provision as textually specific as the ex post facto prohibition. Here the Court must decide an issue of life or death through an act of deep interpretation. The sociolegal issue—the vulnerability of the accused to his past—thus resonates with the constitutional issue—whether the past utterances of the Constitution (i.e., the first eight amendments) are concealed in the more recent words of "We the People": the Fourteenth Amendment. In both cases, the Court must consider how much of the past can properly be contained in the silence or words of the present.

Frankfurter's Due Process as Floating Signifier

In a famous concurrence, Justice Frankfurter supports the Court's finding that the Fourteenth Amendment does not contain a right against self-incrimination. He begins his concurrence by noting that his reading of the Fourteenth Amendment is supported by seventy years of doctrine. During this time, forty-three separate jurists had resolved constitutional issues by offering a similar reading of the text; only one judge resisted this interpretive trend: nameless, he is dismissed by Frankfurter as an "eccentric exception."[79] Quantity of doctrinal support is strengthened by appeals to quality; Frankfurter

---

78. The prosecutor argued in his summation that if he were a defendant who knew himself to be innocent, it would take "twenty or fifty horses" to keep him from testifying. James F. Simon, *The Antagonists* (New York: Simon and Schuster, 1989), 177.

79. 332 U.S. 46, 62 (1947).

reminds us that the judges who dismissed the arguments for incorporation included "those whose services in the cause of human rights and the spirit of freedom are the most conspicuous in our history."[80]

As opposed to Marshall, Frankfurter's relationship to constitutional text is highly mediated. Absolved of the burden of offering a *naked* reading of the "open-textured" constitutional clause, Frankfurter can anchor his reading in the slow accretion of doctrine, replacing Marshall's hermeneutics of naked reading with a hermeneutics of *rereading*.[81] The problem of reading the Constitution's deep rhetoric is thereby displaced, shifted onto the successive layers of interpretations that offer *texture* to the "open-ended" Constitution. Thus the act of constitutional exposition becomes in this manner a promiscuous act of self-reading, a deeply self-referential process whereby a fixation on the ever-evolving body of precedents shifts the burden of reading away from the exposition of the original text.

Nevertheless, the image of the original text (or in this case, the Fourteenth Amendment, an addition and redaction of the urtext) that emerges from this act of rereading is remarkably rich and deeply rhetorical. Expounding upon his theory of the Constitution, Frankfurter concludes that the due process clause is more than a mere "summary of the specific provisions of the Bill of Rights" such as the "prescriptions in a pharmacopoeia."[82] This argument resonates with Marshall's constitutional understanding: due process cannot be read as a laundry list not simply because such a reading is wrong—that is, a misreading of the putative intent of the document—but because it is impoverishing of what we expect the Constitution to be. This conclusion can be seen to complement Frankfurter's preceding arguments that reason from history, text and structure, but it also undermines them. For if due process is to be read as a trope, a figure that stands for unspecified standards of "decency and fairness," then the very project of exposition that Frankfurter engages in to demonstrate the correctness of his reading is called into question.

This point goes to the very heart of his argument against incorporation. An incorporationist reading, Frankfurter argues, does

---

80. Ibid., 62.

81. For an elaborate and thought-provoking attempt to associate the project of constitutional exposition with a project of re-reading the Court's own readings, see Ronald Dworkin, *Law's Empire* (Cambridge: Harvard University Press, 1986).

82. *Adamson*, 68.

violence to due process. As it first appears in the Fifth Amendment, due process stands beside other procedural guarantees such as double jeopardy and the right against self-incrimination, and thus would appear to signify an independent procedural norm; to turn around and claim that in the Fourteenth Amendment it simply stands as an overdetermined signifier of the other guarantees of the Bill of Rights violates the stability of language. In a tone edging toward disdain, Frankfurter writes, "[I]t ought not to require argument to reject the notion that due process of law meant one thing in the fifth and another in the fourteenth."[83] Such a proposition is dismissed out of hand. Yet seven years later Frankfurter joined the Court in handing down a decision that implicitly made precisely this point.

In *Bolling v. Sharpe*,[84] a companion decision to *Brown*, the Court was called upon to consider the constitutionality of the District of Columbia's segregated school system. *Bolling* presented a discomfiting challenge to the logic of *Brown:* As the equal protection clause of the Fourteenth Amendment (the textual basis for the constitutional ruling in *Brown*) applied only to the states, it wasn't clear how one could argue that the District of Columbia's segregated schools constituted a constitutional violation. Faced with the "unthinkable" prospect that the Constitution "would impose a lesser duty on the Federal Government" than on the states,[85] the Court engaged in a famous act of interpretive contortionism, reading an equal protection component into the due process clause of the Fifth Amendment.

Striking, then, is the implicit image of due process contained in the *Bolling* decision. According to the unanimous Court, the due process clause of the Fifth Amendment contains an equal protection component, whereas the due process clause of the Fourteenth Amendment obviously does not: *Bolling* thus stands for precisely the proposition that Frankfurter wants to dismiss as absurd—namely, that identical constitutional language can have different meanings in different contexts. Yet if Frankfurter agrees with Marshall that what distinguishes a Constitution from other legal texts is the power of its signs to generate meanings in a manner different from normal legislation, then it seems plausible that identical words *could* stand

---

83. Ibid., 66.
84. 347 U.S. 497 (1954).
85. Ibid., 500.

for different things.[86] To embrace the deep rhetoric of the Constitution only then to turn around and insist on a stable and fixed meaning of open-textured signifiers such as due process is to repeat the problematic interpretive move we located in Marshall's *Marbury* opinion. Once one accepts the Constitution as deep rhetoric, it no longer is possible to contain these meanings—even through a rhetorical flourish such as Frankfurter's.

Black's Self-Signifying Text

This concern is precisely what animates Black's dissent. Black labors to limit the due process clause's power to generate meanings lest the Court's legitimacy as privileged reader be eroded: thus his charge, repeated throughout his dissent, that Frankfurter's opinion relies on a "natural law formula."[87] The crux of the indictment is that subjective preference has replaced reading; philosophical choice has overthrown hermeneutic necessity. In this regard, Black accuses Frankfurter not simply of offering a weak or bad interpretation of the Fourteenth Amendment, but of offering no interpretation at all. The "canons of decency" standard has no text, no material that can *guide* or *direct* a reading; and consequently, confers upon the Court "boundless power."[88] The rhetoric of boundlessness, however, means to raise the specter of its negation. For an institution whose legitimacy is predicated upon bounded readings, boundless power suggests no power at all. Accordingly, like Marshall, Black attempts to contain the floating signifier of due process by anchoring it to written constitutional guarantees. Specifically, Black's strategy recalls Marshall's attempt to associate judicial review with the interpretation of self-applying standards such as the prohibition against ex post facto laws—only now in Black's hands even the most open-textured language of the Constitution is to be rendered self-applying. Judicial review is to be limited to the exposition and defense of a fixed and self-signifying text.[89]

---

86. Much work in contemporary legal and literary hermeneutics focuses on the proposition that meaning is never a facial or stable property of words or texts, but rather a function of the contexts in which words signify. See, for example, Steven Knapp and Walter Benn Michaels, "Intention, Identity, and the Constitution," in Leyh, *Legal Hermeneutics*.

87. *Adamson*, 68.

88. Ibid., 69.

89. Even Black had to acknowledge the limits of this jurisprudence in such cases as *Bolling v. Sharpe.*

But Black's effort collides with Frankfurter's most persuasive argument: to consider due process as merely a shorthand statement of other specific clauses in the same amendment is "to charge Madison and his contemporaries with writing into the Bill of Rights a meaningless clause."[90] Here Black must either argue that the words *due process* mean different things in different places, or he must accept that the words as they appear originally in the Fifth Amendment perform nothing more than an uncertain rhetorical function, summarizing, like some stirring peroration, the words that immediately precede them.

In either case, Black must violate the very canons of reading that he wants to defend. In the first case, due process can contain the right against self-incrimination only if read precisely in the manner he dismisses—as an indeterminate signifier whose meaning changes from context to context. In the second case (in which due process is read as peroration), the concept can be tethered to something written only by misreading the writing to which it is to be tethered—and here *misreading* suggests not the powerful variety of the strong poet, but the trivial brand associated with weak students. In both cases, Black is forced into an impossible hermeneutic position: uncomfortable with a project of constitutional exposition predicated upon deep reading, he attempts to turn judicial review into a trivial hermeneutic act, but in order to support even this weak interpretive project, he must offer a vision of the constitutional text that defeats it.

Black thus looks to the text to constrain the affair of reading, but ultimately his meta-interpretive or normative concerns define his relationship to the text. The Fourteenth Amendment *must* be read as he urges not because the signifiers require such a construction but because only such a reading, in his mind, can support the Court's claims to legitimacy.

That Black's strategy should enter the literature of law as "interpretivism" though it is an attempt to do just the opposite—to contain the Constitution's power to generate meanings by anchoring indeterminate text to mechanical processes; while Frankfurter's refusal to embrace literalism should be associated with something called "noninterpretivism"[91]—is a final irony of this colloquy and underscores

90. *Adamson,* 69.
91. See, for example, Thomas Grey, "Do We Have an Unwritten Constitution?"

how impoverished the American legal academy's understanding of hermeneutics was until relatively recently. Neither strategy, however, ultimately can conceal the instabilities upon which it is founded. Frankfurter must use a literal reading to defend the rhetorical sweep of the Constitution; Black must rely on a rhetorical reading to anchor due process in bounded literalisms. But the conundrums to which these two great justices fall prey are not idiosyncratic lapses of rhetorical or interpretive ability. The tension between the Constitution as readable law and the Constitution as deep rhetoric subverting the strategies of reading is endlessly repeated in constitutional jurisprudence.

Constitutional Colloquy as Rhetorical Device

Are we then to conclude that the very ferocity of the colloquy between Black and Frankfurter, and the vehemence with which they advance and defend mutually and self-contradictory techniques of textual exposition, undermines the Court's strong claim that judicial review can be legitimated by appeal to a theory of reading? But this returns us to our point of departure, Justice Jackson's aphorism. There we encountered an attempt to justify the Court's power to read by a public declamation of the futility of such justifications; in *Adamson* we find a similar rhetorical strategy, one, however, advanced not in terms of the specific arguments of the respective justices, but on the level of *form*. In this regard, I mean to call attention to one final unusual rhetorical feature of the high-court opinion: that as a document, it presents rival readings of the Constitution side by side in the form of majority and dissenting opinions.

It is not within the scope of these concluding remarks to canvass the history of the dissent. Marshall, we will recall, abolished the practice of seriatim opinions, thus enhancing the Court's capacity to speak in one voice. The practice of filing dissenting or concurring opinions, however, persisted, its roots extending back into common law jurisprudence. Still, to appreciate how rhetorically anomalous the dissent remains, consider Robert Cover's attempt to distinguish legal narratives from their counterparts in literature. Cover reminds

---

Stanford Law Review 27 (1975): 703. Grey has since recanted the use of these misleading appellations.

us that legal narratives differ from other narratives in that they deal in a field of pain and death.[92] This connection to death exhausts and destabilizes for Cover any attempt to consider law as simply another rhetorical system. Thus, to borrow from J. L. Austin, a legal narrative can be understood as a performative, a speech act whose intrinsic meaning cannot be grasped independently of certain actions it allows the speaker to accomplish.[93] If this action includes the putting to death of persons—as it does in *Adamson*—then the gravity of the performance would seem merely to highlight the rhetorical burden that the legal narrative must shoulder.

This notion, however, calls attention to an ostensible anomaly— that the law presents its efforts at constitutional exposition in a rhetorical form that orchestrates this performance through measured subversion, namely, by presenting a majority opinion along with its systematic refutation in the form of a dissent. This point is vividly illustrated by Black's vituperative in *Adamson*, which assails the Court's abandonment of precedent, the perversion of original intent, and the forsaking of every sound principle of legal argument. The project of offering bounded readings of a canonical text thus is presented in a rhetorical form that permits and indeed invites a vehement attack upon the interpretive adequacy of the constitutional command issuing from the Court.

If this weren't so familiar, it certainly would be astonishing. A professor, for example, who ended every lecture with a point-by-point trashing of every point she had made would be presumed to be launching a postmodern critique of the concept of authority. One can, of course, attempt to explain the phenomenon of the dissent in light of standard arguments. The first is associated with the notion of the dialogical: through a public expression of disagreement, the Court makes good on its dedication to reasoned argument. The second is Talmudic: as legal doctrine evolves through a succession of readings, the dissent creates a rival narrative of origins that can be drawn upon in moments of "constitutional redemption,"[94] when the present

92. Robert Cover, "Violence and the Word," *Yale Law Journal* 95 (1986): 1601. See also, Austin Sarat and Thomas R. Kearns, "Making Peace with Violence: Robert Cover on Law and Legal Theory," in *Law's Violence*, ed. Sarat and Kearns (Ann Arbor: University of Michigan Press, 1992).

93. J. L. Austin, *How to Do Things with Words* (Oxford: Oxford University Press, 1962).

94. Cover, "Supreme Court," 33–40.

is redeemed by a renarrativization of the past. The third is strategic: through the specter of its possibility, the dissent is meant to shape the opinion of the Court.[95] And the fourth is transcendental: the presence of a dissent creates a powerful argument against a species of legal positivism that would radically deny the existence of constitutional meanings independent of the doctrinal articulations of the Court.

As plausible as these accounts are, they fail to appreciate the provocative role the dissent plays in the Court's rhetoric of legitimation. In this light, the dissent (as well as its increasing proliferation)[96] must be understood as more than a mere symptom of the instabilities contained within earlier strategies of textual containment (such as we've observed in *Marbury* and *Adamson*). Rather, the genius of the phenomenon is that it, itself, is just such a strategy, a critical constituent of a rhetoric of legitimation that empowers the Court's project of constitutional exposition not simply through orchestrated persuasion (the opinion of the Court), but through a public declamation of the Court's *awareness* of the impossibility of ultimately demonstrating the correctness of its readings and privilege of readership.

In this sense, the very genre of the high-court opinion seems to make manifest what Jackson must confess—that the Court is fallible. Again, the reader seeks to legitimate his interpretive authority through a confessional act. The excruciating burden of reading in an authoritative fashion is grounded through a complex display of the impossibility of the hermeneutic task. The Court can be trusted to read in a bounded fashion only by publicly (that is, before its own interpretive community)[97] demonstrating that the boundaries are not to be located in the act itself, but in the Court's declaration of its recognition of this. The conventional act of rhetorical persuasion (the opinion of the Court) thus proceeds in lockstep with a second legitimating strategy, one that on the level of genre reveals the instabilities within the project of constitutional exposition founded upon

---

95. See, for example, David M. O'Brien, *Storm Center: The Supreme Court in American Politics* (New York: W. W. Norton, 1990).

96. See, for example, Joseph Goldstein, *The Intelligible Constitution* (New York: Oxford University Press, 1992). Goldstein's work focuses on what he reads as the escalating divisiveness and particularism in high-court opinions. See also, Percival E. Jackson, *Dissent in the Supreme Court* (Norman: University of Oklahoma Press, 1969).

97. For a discussion of the Court's interpretive community, see Owen Fiss, "Objectivity and Interpretation," *Stanford Law Review* 34 (1982): 739.

reading. Thus, the attempt to anchor a concept of authority in a genre that by its very terms seems to deconstruct its possibility is perfectly consistent with the qualities of constitutional discourse we have already considered. The high-court opinion offers, on the level of genre, another response to the discursive commitments and instabilities of *Marbury*.[98]

Conclusion

Jackson's confessional, Marshall's hermeneutic dance, Frankfurter's embrace of deep reading, Black's interpretive anxiety, and the rhetorical form that unites these separate stances—all are discursive responses to the same dilemma: To deny the Constitution's power to generate meanings is to render the Constitution moribund and judicial review trivial. To embrace the deep rhetoric of the Constitution and to link judicial exposition with a project of deep reading is to subvert the Court's claim to speak as the privileged reader of the text. The discourse of constitutional exposition is reconstituted by, and terrified of, legal fecundity.

---

98. How critical is this unusual rhetoric of legitimation to permitting the Court to fulfill the interpretive task with which it finds itself burdened? Do we make sense of the behavior and words of the Court as we would understand the words and deeds of a neurotic, a person for whom anxiety is, but need not be, a condition of existence? This question assumes added relevance in light of poststructuralist understandings which suggest that 1) textual instabilities can never be contained through a specific hermeneutic or by recourse to theory; and 2) hand-wringing about interpretive strategies and theories is superfluous as interpretation is bound not by theory but by the practices of an interpretive community. See, for example, Stanley Fish, *Doing What Comes Naturally: Change, Rhetoric, and the Practice of Theory in Literary and Legal Studies* (Durham, N.C.: Duke University Press, 1992).

The Alchemy of Style and Law

Barbara Johnson

> My turn. The story of one of my madnesses.
> —Arthur Rimbaud, "The Alchemy of the Word"

> I have always dreamed and attempted something else, with the
> patience of an alchemist, ready to sacrifice all vanity and all
> satisfaction, as once they burned the contents and the rafters of
> their homes, to feed the furnace of the Great Work. What? it's
> hard to say . . . a book . . . the Orphic explanation of the Earth . . .
> whose rhythm would be impersonal and alive all the way down to
> its pagination . . . the Text would speak on its own, without the
> voice of an author.
> —Stéphane Mallarmé, "Autobiography"

From my two epigraphs, it can be deduced that my subject is the
relationship between madness and the existence of the impersonal
book, between verbal alchemy and autobiography, between dream
and sacrifice.

I hasten to reassure you that I am about to abandon the domain
of the poetic. I promise that I will not mix genres. I am here to
present a paper on the rhetoric of law.

The title of my paper, "The Alchemy of Style and Law," is meant
to be heard as an echo of the title of a book by Patricia Williams,
The Alchemy of Race and Rights, subtitled *Diary of a Law Professor*.[1]

What is to be understood by the word *alchemy*? Rather than
answer that question directly, I would like to bring in a quotation

---

1. Cambridge: Harvard University Press, 1991. Subsequent references are incorporated in the text.

from Walter Benjamin concerning the difference between a commentary and a critique:

> The history of works of art prepares their critique, and this is why historical distance increases their power. If, to use a simile, one views the growing work as a funeral pyre, its commentator can be likened to the chemist, its critic to an alchemist. While the former is left with wood and ashes as the sole objects of his analysis, the latter is concerned only with the enigma of the flame itself: the enigma of being alive.[2]

This curious conjunction of an image of death (a funeral pyre) with a concept of life (the "enigma of being alive") will return in an unexpected way in the present essay. But for the moment, I would like simply to suggest that if "the work" in question is the entire edifice of American law, then it seems to me that Patricia Williams is undertaking its critique in exactly this sense.

Is my own title meant to suggest that style is to race as law is to rights? Am I, in other words, asserting a connection between race and style? No, if it means asserting a one-to-one correspondence between a race and a style—saying, for instance, that an author's race can be identified from his or her style, as though style were a natural and continuous and un-self-different emanation of a racial identity. But yes, if it means asserting that the intractability of racial misunderstanding or inequality might have something to do with style—both because conflict might arise from not recognizing the effects of different styles, and because certain styles are privileged over others. The ideology of style is a powerful reinforcer of hierarchy. This, at least, is one of the central tenets of Patricia Williams's critique. It is not that Patricia Williams's style can be identified as black or female, but that her writing possesses a logic that makes perceptible the realities of difference subordinated behind the rhetoric of neutrality and impersonality into which students of the law are inevitably inducted. In other words, the style of Patricia Williams is not the sign of her identity but the enactment of her critique.

It is not easy to give a capsule description of the style of Williams's

---

2. Quoted in Hannah Arendt's introduction to Walter Benjamin, *Illuminations,* ed. Hannah Arendt, trans. Harry Zohn (New York: Schocken Books, 1969), 5.

book. It is not autobiography, or legal theory, or editorial, or allegory, but it partakes of all of these. It is a breakthrough book for the possibilities of a fully conscious historical subject of discourse who does not coincide with—indeed, has been subtly or overtly excluded from—the position defined as neutral, objective, impersonal. Williams analyzes the exclusions and costs of adopting that voice, the ways in which it has shaped distributions of power and privilege, the ways in which it has erased, oppressed, even killed. In a telling example, she describes the three successive edits to which one of her essays was subjected. The essay discussed effects of privatization on public accountability by narrating her experience of being kept out of Benetton's by a white sales clerk who would not press the buzzer to open the door when he saw her waiting outside. In the first edit, her anger was erased. In the second, the name of Benetton's was removed for fear of libel. In the third, all mention of her race was deleted because editorial policy forbade descriptions of physiognomy, and anyway, "any reader will know what you must have looked like when standing at that window." "This is just a matter of style," she was told. She concludes:

> Ultimately I did convince the editors that mention of my race was central to the whole sense of the subsequent text; that my story became one of extreme paranoia without the information that I am black; or that it became one in which the reader had to fill in the gap by assumption, presumption, prejudgment, or prejudice. What was most interesting to me in this experience was how the blind application of principles of neutrality, through the device of omission, acted either to make me look crazy or to make the reader participate in old habits of cultural bias.(48)

Again and again Williams punctures the mask of neutrality and impersonality assumed by others, showing, for instance, that when she interrogates the racism of some of the questions written by her impersonal and neutral colleagues for their law exams, they respond by taking it "personally." Again and again, the personal comes out from its hiding place whenever the ideology of neutrality is questioned.

The reader of *The Alchemy of Race and Rights* never forgets that its author speaks from a crossroads of discourses. Yet her analysis deconstructs the premises that would turn a black female law professor into an oxymoron. When she walks into a classroom, a clothing store, a street, an academic conference, everyone around her bristles with expectations, preconceptions, desires, fears, curiosities, defenses. This book is an attempt to keep just to one side of those expectations, to analyze them, to reread the social order in terms of them. The book is *not* written in function of known and expected polarities of black and white, private and public, male and female, academic and emotional, self and other. It is precisely a way of complicating, demystifying, confounding, rethinking such polarities. This is surely what explains the insistent allegorical presence of *polar* bears. Those bears, so white, so innocent, so caged, so violent, cannot be read in any simple way. Indeed, animals in Patricia Williams's text function consistently both as parables—beast fables—and as very real victims trapped in human systems of control. When she quotes a description from the *Economist* of the proper degree of socialization required to ensure the docility of pigs urged down a chute to oblivion, she does not need to transform the text's language at all for it to stand as a monstrous allegory. If academic writing or legal codes are defined through their exclusions and disconnections, then what Patricia Williams does is to find, explore, elaborate, and restore the connections among the bill of sale for her great-great-grandmother, the lawyer who bought her and impregnated her, the contemporary homeless man on the street, the advertising industry, the academic conference circuit, a basketball camp in Hanover, New Hampshire, Christmas shopping, the critical legal studies movement, and the United States Constitution. The madness of juxtaposition mimes the structure of the social text.

This daring, groundbreaking style is not without risks. In one of the more exquisitely ironic passages, Williams quotes a rejection letter from a law review that has sent back an essay with extensive comments. That is, she quoted it in the manuscript of her book, where I had read and noted it as a good example of how ordinary frames of reference obscure what Williams is doing. But when, in preparing to write this paper, I turned to the page in the published book on which I expected to find the letter quoted, I found the following:

> [A note to the reader: Logically, what should follow here is the actual letter of rejection; but the editors of Harvard Univer-

sity Press, on the advice of the Press's lawyers, informed me
that I could not reprint it, even anonymously, without the
authors' permission, which in the circumstances has not been
forthcoming.](214)

Williams then concocts a fake letter to substitute for the original. In
my frustration at not being able to quote the letter myself, I will
here try to rephrase the gist of it and then offer my own commentary.

The editors see Williams's style as an evasive tactic. They note
that she speaks of the high costs of daily traversing racial and gender
boundaries, describes herself as schizophrenic and drowning, but yet
also claims that it is "not just intelligent, but fashionable, feminist,
and even postmodern" to be so. They complain that her calm and
self-confidence impede their sympathy. They ask her whether she
wouldn't be willing to take the risks of real self-exposure and write
a more convincing piece.

Apart from the generally condescending and patronizing tone of
this rejection letter, I think it stands as an exemplary misreading.
The editors expect certain things that are highly revealing: that calm
is the opposite of engagement, that to be convincing about anxiety
one must demonstrate a loss of control. What seems to bother the
editors is the *combination* of control and panic. They almost *want*
the panic. There is nothing unfamiliar about the sight of a crazy
black woman ("What's so new about a schizophrenic black lady pouring her heart out?" Williams quotes her sister as asking early in the
book). What is unfamiliar is a black woman writing calmly about
panic, situating her own discourse as intelligent, fashionable, feminist, and postmodern—having the kind of self-consciousness about
style and reception, about genre and metadiscourse, that instates a
complex narrative voice as something other than a symptom. The
editors want to privatize the nature of Williams's writing, to see her
control as a symptom rather than an accomplishment (they ask
whether she is afraid of being perceived as unstable). Williams knows,
in contrast, that impersonality, neutrality, and abstraction can themselves be the very *sign* of anxiety, but that that anxiety is not a
private matter. She makes very clear the costs, the fragility, the
victory, the sacrifice involved in her calm. But she extends the significance of all of that outward into the social construction of selves
and others, into the crossroads and contradictions she—and not only
she—traverses every day.

Patricia Williams repeatedly documents the revisions, erasures, and displacements her writing undergoes in its encounters with the rules of legal style and citation. Let me now digress a moment to describe my own small encounter with the ideology of law review style. This fall I was asked by the Harvard Law Review to write a commentary on an essay left unfinished at the death of its author. The essay is entitled "A Postmodern Feminist Legal Manifesto," and the author, Mary Joe Frug, a law professor at the New England School of Law, was murdered, presumably by a stranger, on a Cambridge street. Interestingly, in presenting Frug's essay for publication, the editors of the *Harvard Law Review* have preceded it with the following note:

> The following commentary is an unfinished work. Professor Frug was working on this Commentary when she was murdered on April 4, 1991. The Editors of the Harvard Law Review agreed that, under the circumstances, the preservation of Mary Joe Frug's voice outweighed strict adherence to traditional editorial policy. For this reason, neither stylistic nor organizational changes have been made, and footnotes have been expanded but not added.[3]

What can be said about this departure from usual editorial procedures? It seems that it is only when the author is dead that a law review sees value in the preservation of "voice." Does the respect paid to Frug's text here have any relation to the long tradition of idealizing dead women in Western poetry? That is, is it possible for a woman to have authority only on the condition that she be dead? How does this preservation of voice as writing relate to the long philosophical tradition that, from Plato onward, tries to devalue writing as inert and secondary while voice conveys living human intentionality? It seems as though there are two no-win models for authorship here: an interactive editorial process through which a living author participates in the progressive erasure of her own words and a textual respect that can occur only if the author is dead.

I had just finished writing the above remarks when I learned that, at the 1992 Harvard Law Review Banquet, the annual "spoof" issue included a parody of Mary Joe Frug's essay entitled "He-Manifesto Of

---

3. *Harvard Law Review* 105 (1992): 1045.

Post-Mortem Legal Feminism," authored by "Mary Doe, Rigor-Mortis Professor of Law." It seems that to some of the members of the Law Review Editorial Board who had opposed the publication of Frug's unfinished manuscript, the author was not quite dead enough. The banquet, to which Frug's widower had been invited, was held on the first anniversary of Mary Joe's murder.

Frug's essay concerns ways in which legal rules combine to maternalize, terrorize, and sexualize the female body so that heterosexual monogamy is a woman's safest life choice. Not only was her essay itself unfinished at her death; she got up to go out for her fatal walk in the middle of a sentence. Here is the sentence:

Women who might expect that sexual relationships with other women could

Then she gets up, she goes out, she dies. The sentence dangles in the middle of the essay, which continues for another nine pages.

Now my assignment is to read the text. Critics of contemporary literary theory have attacked the concept of the death of the author, especially of Paul de Man's statement that "death is a displaced name for a linguistic predicament,"[4] but here I precisely *encountered* Mary Joe Frug's death as a linguistic predicament. In my commentary, I wrote about this sentence, calling it "the lesbian gap," and asking, "How does this gap signify?" I sent my commentary to the *Harvard Law Review* for its round of editorial responses. When it came back from its first reading, the editors had changed "How does this gap signify?" to "What does this gap mean?" This is not at all the same question. "*What* does the gap mean" implies that it *has* a meaning, and all I have to do is to figure out what it is. "*How* does the gap signify" raises the *question* of what it means to mean, raises meaning as a question, implies that the gap *has to be read*, but that it can't be presumed to have been intended. The law review responded as if to question the mode or possibility of meaning was to speak a foreign language. In every successive revision that my text underwent, the *how* was again changed to *what*. From this I learned that legal

---

4. This statement occurs at the end of an analysis of autobiography in "Autobiography as De-facement," *The Rhetoric of Romanticism* (New York: Columbia University Press, 1984), 81.

thinking is a resistance to opening up meaning as a question, as a nongiven, as a bafflement, as the possibility that what is intended and what is readable might not be the same. The ideology of law review style attempts to create a world saturated with meaning, without gaps, and, indeed, doubtless without lesbians. It is no accident that the double gap occurs at the point at which the text would have spoken of that which Queen Victoria defined as impossible. How can two absences add up to anything legally recognizable? If lesbianism here stands as that which escapes the regime of the phallus, and if, as the privileged signifier of patriarchal relations, the phallus stands as the guarantor of meaning, then it seems all too fitting that Mary Joe Frug's text should exit the sayable precisely at this point.

"Style is the man," proclaimed Buffon in his acceptance speech to the French Academy. And Patricia Williams begins her book, "Since subject position is everything in my analysis of the law, you deserve to know that it's a bad morning." The connection between style and subject position, between subject position and subjective discourse, is both manipulated and parodied by this opening. For if subject position *is* everything in Patricia Williams's analysis of the law, it is not because of her moods. The apparatus of confession appears, but is not the place of subject position. To get at what is, I cite Lacan's rewriting of Buffon: "Style is the man, the man I am addressing." If style is thus constructed out of the other, whom might we say Patricia Williams is addressing? In a review in the *New York Times Book Review,* Wendy Kaminer criticizes Williams's style for its failure of address:

> Describing her encounters with students and deans or strangers on the street, recalling her family history and analyzing recent criminal cases, she darts from conversation to discourse. The result is an alternately engaging and tedious book with valuable insights, weighed down by the baroque, encoded language of post-structural legal and literary theory.
>
> How did it become de rigueur to protest oppression in a language of elites? If Ms. Williams believes that "theoretical legal understanding and social transformation need not be oxymoronic," why doesn't she simply say that scholars can be activists too? How socially transformative are academics talking to one

another in a code that may take several years of graduate school to crack? Secret words and grueling initiation rites make sure that the power to critique power will not be freely shared. Ms. Williams defends her emotive, first-person theorizing, but that's not what troubles me. The first person invites us in but the language shuts us out, and her diary finally seems less personal than private, self-enclosed. Readers outside a small circle of post-structural theorists may be not only befuddled, but too alienated by her exclusive discourse to stay with it. And that could be their loss as well as hers.[5]

While I do not think that the issues Kaminer raises here are nonissues, I want to focus on her assumptions about Williams's intentions. The reviewer clearly thinks she knows that Williams's language is the language of protest, and that what she means to say is that scholars can be activists too. This implies that Williams's main goal is to recommend action. But the quotation that is said to be equivalent to "scholars can be activists," is "theoretical legal understanding and social transformation need not be oxymoronic." That is, Williams is talking about rhetoric, not directly about reality. Her object of analysis is first and foremost *language* and other forms of nontransparent representation, and the ways in which they allow certain things to be sayable and other things erased. The reviewer assumes that Williams is addressing—should be addressing—readers outside the academy, outside the circle of theorists. But does this mean that the academy should not be addressed? Do most legal theorists write for the general public? If an argument has public implications, must it conform to a rhetoric of the common reader? Isn't part of Williams's point that the articulations agreed upon in academic and elite circles have so pervasive and yet hidden an effect on social structures that it might be well to meet them on their own ground? Of course, Williams's writing is generally no more likely to be welcomed by the legal academy than by the general public. In her repeated encounters with the way in which editorial boards and other institutions of style attempt to dictate what and how she writes, Williams lays bare the network of constraints and censorships that attempt to produce

5. *New York Times Book Review*, Wendy Kaminer, "Citizens of the Supermarket State," *NYTBR*, May 26, 1991, 10.

"plain, readable prose." In other words, what Kaminer seems to call for as a transparently readable style may be produced through just as much displacement and erasure as a style that displays its discontinuous multilayeredness.

When Kaminer complains that "[T]he first person invites us in but the language shuts us out," I don't think she is wrong. This effect of being at once open and closed, at once revealing and concealing, *is*, I think, strategically and explicitly intended by Williams. In one of her opening moves, she presents a conversation between herself and her sister, a dialogue in which neither sister hears, understands, or responds directly to the other, in which Williams gives a very clear statement of her intentions in writing this book, but in the embedded, self-parodic form of half a dialogue of the deaf. Communication is here represented as fundamentally missed. Williams describes her project as one of "writing in a way that reveals the intersubjectivity of legal constructions, that forces the reader both to participate in the construction of meaning and to be conscious of that process," but the moment the sister seems to catch on and pay attention, alert, ears pricked, nose quivering, Williams can only say to her, "My, what big teeth you have." The "intersubjectivity of legal constructions" is based not on a model of transitive communication, but on a dialogue of profound discontinuity.

What Williams means by subject position, in other words, involves the ways in which *she* displays herself *as constructed by others*. Her style becomes the style of the other addressing *her*. Almost half the book is taken up with reports of the ways in which she is read. She offers rejection letters, student evaluations, departmental memos, newspaper reports of talks she has given—the book is filled with scenes of reading like the following:

A man with whom I used to work once told me that I made too much of my race. "After all," he said, "I don't even think of you as black." Yet sometime later, when another black woman became engaged in an ultimately unsuccessful tenure battle, he confided to me that he wished the school could find more blacks like me. I felt myself slip in and out of shadow, as I became nonblack for purposes of inclusion and black for purposes of exclusion; I felt the boundaries of my very body manipulated, casually inscribed by definitional demarcations that did not refer to me. (9–10)

The following quotation from Gayatri Spivak stands, I think, as a fitting definition of the notion of subject position as it is wielded by Williams:

> Quite often when we say "subject position" we reduce it to a kind of confessional attitudinizing. We say, "I'm white, I'm black, I'm a mulatto, I am male, I'm bourgeois." A subject position is not, in fact, a confessional self-description either in praise or in dis-praise. . . . This is because the position of the subject *can be assigned* . . . and "assigned" means, I think, that it can and must become a sign; not for the person who speaks, but for the person who listens, not for the person who writes, who can say what she likes about who she is, but for the person who reads. When, in fact, the responsible reader reads the sign that is the subject position of the speaker or the writer, it becomes the sign, let us say, of an ethno-politics, of a psychosexual reality, or an institutional position, and this is not under the control of the person who speaks. She cannot diagnose herself; we are given over to our readers.[6]

What Williams has accomplished in *The Alchemy of Race and Rights* is the writing of the giving of herself over to her readers and her reading of those readings.

Let us look again at Williams's parodic use of the question of subject position in the opening of her first chapter.

> Since subject position is everything in my analysis of the law, you deserve to know that it's a bad morning. I am very depressed. It always takes a while to sort out what's wrong, but it usually starts with some kind of perfectly irrational thought such as: I *hate* being a lawyer. This particular morning I'm sitting up in bed reading about redhibitory vices. A redhibitory vice is a defect in merchandise which, if existing at the time of purchase, gives rise to a claim allowing the buyer to return the thing and to get back part or all of the purchase price. (3)

---

6. Gayatri Spivak, "A Response to 'The Difference Within: Feminism and Critical Theory,'" in *The Difference Within: Feminism and Critical Theory*, ed. Elizabeth Meese and Alice Parker (Amsterdam: John Benjamins, 1989), 208.

The mix of genres and expectations has already begun: parodic self-description, parodic direct address to the reader, irrationality, official legal definition of a contract violation. The case Williams quotes further disconcerts expectation: it is an 1835 decision from Louisiana, the merchandise in question is a human being, a slave named Kate, and the vice in question is craziness. It seems the merchandise was crazy and ran away, and that the seller knew she had the vice when he sold her. The seller counters with the argument that she is not crazy but stupid, a defect against which he did not warrant. Two things leap out of this case as a first example in a book of legal theory: the law in question involves the structure of a catch-22: if you run away, you are crazy; but wouldn't you have to be crazy *not* to want to run away from slavery? The law, in other words, can make a stance of sanity impossible. Legally. Second observation: Williams's own "irrational thought" mirrors the "craziness" of the slave. What rationality is, is clearly going to be constantly in question in this book. Williams goes on:

> As I said, this is the sort of morning when I hate being a lawyer, a teacher, and just about everything else in my life. It's all I can do to feed the cats. I let my hair stream wildly and the eyes roll back in my head.
>
> So you should know that this is one of those mornings when I refuse to compose myself properly; you should know you are dealing with someone who is writing this in an old terry bathrobe with a little fringe of blue and white tassles dangling from the hem, trying to decide if she is stupid or crazy. (4)

This opening resembles nothing so much as the beginning of another text in which subject position, rationality, and madness come together:

> Everything which I have thus far accepted as entirely true and assured has been acquired from the senses or by means of the senses. But I have learned by experience that these senses sometimes mislead me, and it is prudent never to trust wholly those things which have once deceived us.
>
> But it is possible that, even though the senses occasionally deceive us about things which are barely perceptible and very

far away, there are many other things which we cannot reasonably doubt, even though we know them through the senses—
as, for example, that I am here, seated by the fire, wearing a
winter dressing gown, holding this paper in my hands, and
other things of this nature. And how could I deny that these
hands and this body are mine, unless I am to compare myself
with certain lunatics whose brain is so troubled and befogged
by the black vapors of the bile that they continually affirm that
they are kings while they are paupers, that they are clothed in
gold and purple while they are naked; or imagine that their
head is made of clay, or that they are gourds, or that their body
is glass? But this is ridiculous; such men are fools, and I would
be no less insane than they if I followed their example.[7]

The author, of course, is René Descartes. In his synopsis of the six
Meditations, Descartes describes the usefulness of the progress of
methodical doubt as the peeling away of uncertainties:

Although it is not immediately apparent that so general a doubt
can be useful, it is in fact very much so, since it delivers us
from all sorts of prejudices and makes available to us an easy
method of accustoming our minds to become independent of
the senses. (71).

Williams's book is, among other things, a meditation on the madness
of accustoming the mind to become independent of the senses, the
ways in which such a dissociation *underwrites* rather then eliminates
prejudices.

It can hardly be an accident that Williams's opening mirrors
and inverts Descartes's gestures of instatement of the self-present
thinking subject in his dressing gown, holding "this" paper, concluding *both* that what I cannot doubt is that I am, *and* that I who
am (rational), am not mad. Williams relocates the human subject
within the framework of historical, legal, and corporeal intersubjectivity. She charts the exclusions and omissions that have gone into
the construction of the impersonal, neutral, authoritative—indeed,

7. René Descartes, "First Meditation," in *Philosophical Essays*, trans. Laurence
Lafleur (Indianapolis: Bobbs-Merrill, 1964), 76.

Cartesian—legal subject, just as Descartes himself does, and she makes readable her own mobile subject position as a floating signifier:

> I pause for a moment and gaze out the train window. My life, I think, has become one long stream of text, delivered on the run to gatherings of mostly strangers. It is a strange period in my life, watching the world whiz by, these brazen moments of intimate revelation to no one in particular in my declared challenge to the necessary juxtaposition of the personal with the private. In some odd way, it is as though the question with which I began—Who Am I—has become reconstituted into Where Am I. (16)

Where Descartes's search for certainty leads him to conclude, I think therefore I am, Williams demonstrates again and again that I am where I am thought by, and think, the other.

Reading the Law

Adam Thurschwell

In every era the attempt must be made anew to wrest tradition
away from a conformism that is about to overpower it.
—Walter Benjamin, "Theses on the Philosophy of History"

I have felt warranted heretofore in throwing out the caution that
continuity with the past is only a necessity and not a duty.
—Oliver Wendell Holmes, Jr., "Law in Science
and Science in Law"

1

"Poetry makes nothing happen," mourned W. H. Auden, reflecting
in verse on the death of William Butler Yeats on the eve of the Second
World War.[1] Even the mythmaking of as great a national poet as
Yeats could not heal Ireland's communal madness; much less could
it stave off the coming global catastrophe. One hears in Auden's
lament an echo from the side of literature of an accusation generally
leveled *at* literature—that it has no place in the conduct of the world's
affairs. The poet's impotence, according to the familiar story, lies in

This essay originated as a comment presented at a symposium titled "Deconstruction
and the Possibility of Justice" held at the Benjamin N. Cardozo School of Law in
New York City in October 1989. I thank the organizers of the symposium for giving
me the opportunity and incentive to put these ideas in a semblance of coherent form.
I also want to thank several individuals whose criticisms and encouragement greatly
improved this final product: Ellen Hertz, Adam Bresnick, David Cole, Jonathan Elmer,
Scott Rhodes, and Pam Thurschwell.
    1. W. H. Auden, "In Memory of W. B. Yeats," in *Selected Poetry of W. H.
Auden*, 2d ed. (New York: Vintage Books, 1970), 53.

the gulf between the purely linguistic nature of literature and the hard world out of which it grows: even the most political of poets trades simply in the language of fiction and figure, not the cold facts of political-legal-economic reality. The flip side of this dismissal is the claim that the poet's participation in the governance of the worldly city would be actively dangerous, because the fictional and seductive character of literary language leads the people away from, rather than toward, the true and the good. It has thus been a home truth of political and legal theorists from Plato to Posner[2] that within the realm of political and legal practice "the literary" is at best an irrelevant distraction and at worst a pernicious, irresponsible contaminant. As Judge Posner has been only the most recent to argue, literature thrives on ambiguity, fiction, and the free play of the imagination, values that at least appear to be anathema to the univocal interpretations and sober—in Posner's loaded term, "mature"—attitude required by the sovereign's need to decide and act.

Of course, precisely because it *is* poetry, Auden's categorical assertion of poetry's impotence remains subject to an ironic reading that calls into question the statement's literal force, a reading that in fact overtakes the pessimism of the literal statement as the poem's extraordinary concluding stanzas shift from elegy into triumphal cadences.[3] The conventionally "literary" status of the declaration—it occurs in a poem, not a statute, treatise, judicial opinion, or similar example of what is sometimes called "serious" discourse[4]—licenses

---

2. See generally Richard A. Posner, *Law and Literature: A Misunderstood Relation* (Cambridge: Harvard University Press, 1988).
3. The poem concludes with an urgent call to poetry's redemptive powers:
Follow, poet, follow right
To the bottom of the night,
With your unconstraining voice
Still persuade us to rejoice;

With the framing of a verse
Make a vineyard of the curse,
Sing of human unsuccess
In a rapture of distress;

In the deserts of the heart
Let the healing fountain start,
In the prison of his days
Teach the free man how to praise.
4. On the well-known distinction between "serious" and "non-serious" discourse, see J. L. Austin, *How to Do Things with Words*, 2d ed. (Cambridge: Harvard University Press, 1975), 104–5. Interestingly, Austin's distinction recalls Auden's dictum—

the reader to interpret it as meaning something other than what it seems to say: that poetry does (or, more true to the poem's hortatory conclusion, *should*) "make something happen." This seductive possibility of turning the tables on lawlike assertoric pronouncements, combined with the growing recognition that law, like literature, is primarily made of language and interpretation, has perhaps inevitably raised the question of the applicability of literary modes of reading to the study and practice of law. Thus, even taking Auden's caution at its (literal) word, law professors and literature professors are beginning to ask whether, if not poetry, then *poetics*—that is, the theory and practice of literary reading—might not "make something happen" within the sphere of law and legal practice.[5]

Four general competing positions have emerged in the wake of this question, which can be rendered schematically as follows (making allowances for the reductiveness of any such typology).

First, there are those who take the view that literary readings and insights have no place within the law. Richard Posner, for example, considers law and literature to be separate disciplines with almost no relevance to each other.

Second, there are those who believe that literary insights can enhance and improve the law. James Boyd White exemplifies this perspective. He views law and literature as cultural practices that share the common experiential "integrative" and "constitutive" functions of establishing and maintaining the forms of culture and community in which they are embedded.[6] White thus argues that the introduction of literature and literary study into the law provides

---

Austin distinguishes the poetic use of language from "serious" uses in part on the basis that in poetry there is "no attempt to make you do anything, as Walt Whitman does not seriously incite the eagle of liberty to soar." Ibid.

5. For a consideration of this question from another deconstructive perspective, see Anselm Haverkamp, "Rhetoric, Law, and the Poetics of Memory," *Cardozo Law Review* 13 (1992): 1369.

6. As White explains, humanistic and literary texts

are not propositional, but experiential and performative; . . . not purely intellectual, but affective and constitutive, and in this sense integrative, both of the composer and of the audience, indeed in a sense of the culture in which they work. Texts of this sort . . . offer an experience, not a message, and an experience that will not merely add to one's stock of information but change one's way of seeing and being, of talking and acting.

White, "What Can a Lawyer Learn From Literature?" *Harvard Law Review* 102 (1989): 2014, 2018 (book review of Posner, *Law and Literature*); see also White, *Heracles' Bow: Essays on the Rhetoric and Poetics of Law* (Madison: University of Wisconsin Press, 1985).

new forms of experience that may illuminate and improve the law's own forms of community and ethical life produced by statutes and legal opinions.

Third, there are those (within the legal academy, primarily members of the Conference on Critical Legal Studies [CLS]) who believe that literary theory undermines the very foundations that give law its legitimacy. Using various literary theorists' demonstrations of the rhetorical and social constitution of literary and philosophical works' claims to conceptual "purity," CLS criticizes the law's similar ideological pretensions to having a firmer foundation for its edicts than mere rhetorical and social construction.[7]

Finally, straddling all of these far-from-consistent political and epistemological positions there is Stanley Fish, a critic who has been among the most successful in synthesizing a global theory of literary interpretation with a similarly broad perspective on the law. In a remarkable balancing act, Fish manages both to endorse White's affirmative view of the law as rhetorically constitutive of community and CLS's critical demonstration of the ideological nature of the law's claims to a more than rhetorical foundation, while simultaneously adopting as his own the Posner-like claim that literary theory has no proper place within the law itself. Although (as he is well aware) Fish's theoretical maneuvering irritates all sides of the debates about law—all the more so because of the seamlessness of his arguments— his work simply extends in rigorous fashion a philosophical tradition that has venerable antecedents within the law itself, the tradition of American pragmatism.

Fish's neopragmatism represents the late flowering of the anti-metaphysical and practical spirit that emerged at the end of the last century in the thought of Charles Sanders Pierce, John Dewey, and William James and, within law, of Oliver Wendell Holmes, Jr., as well. Consistent with the philosophy of his contemporaries, Holmes rejected "the eternal" as a basis for law and adopted (in the "less theological" times in which he wrote) historical and scientific rather than formalist or dogmatic modes of explanation.[8] And like his con-

---

7. This overview omits one other perspective on law and literature: the view of literature as a repository of substantive values that can be used to criticize and improve the law. For an effective critique of the politics of this position, see Brook Thomas, "Reflections on the Law and Literature Revival," *Critical Inquiry* 17 (1991): 510.

8. Holmes, "Law in Science and Science in Law," *Harvard Law Review* 12 (1899):

temporaries, Holmes's philosophical positioning was motivated by the spirit of reform: to sweep away the outgrown rules of law that continued to exist as "mere survivals" and, more generally, to combat any orthodoxy that pretended to authority on some basis beyond the realm of practical human knowledge and experience. This pragmatic turn, in the words of another scion of the tradition, "has helped free us, gradually but steadily, from theology and metaphysics—from the temptation to look for an escape from time and chance."[9]

Within the American legal tradition since Holmes, the pragmatic critique has exerted its steady (if only intermittently effective) pressure whenever lawyers and legal academics have attempted to justify legal outcomes on some basis that purports to stand beyond the contingent vocabulary and social desires of the day, from the legal realists' social-scientific critique of Langdellian formalism to Critical Legal Studies' contemporary attack on the "interest" and "policy"-based analysis that grew up in the wake of the realists. Where the realists once criticized the law's pretense to formalism as masking (or obstructing) the service of legitimate social interests and policies, CLS, citing recent social and linguistic theories, now challenges the law's reliance on such "interests and policies" as itself an ideological pretense that unduly limits human freedom and forms of community. Fish's contribution to this ongoing history is to take Critical Legal Studies to task in its turn for its faith that contemporary critical theory can help free us from artificial constraints imposed by law's ideology, a faith in an "outside" of language that Fish views as yet another instance of succumbing to the theological "temptation to look for an escape from time and chance."

In this essay I attempt to articulate what is at stake in Fish's debate with CLS over whether a self-consciously literary and rhetorical theory of law can (or should) "make something happen" within law's practical sphere, through a reading that begins and ends with Fish's essay "The Law Wishes to Have a Formal Existence."[10]

---

443. Of course, as Brook Thomas points out, Holmes was a "transitional subject." Thomas, *supra* at 519. Holmes's pragmatism was conditioned by the tenor of his time, and today Fish would unquestionably reject his scientific faith in "accurately measured social desires instead of tradition" as yet another disguised form of the theological dogma he sought to oppose. Holmes, "Law in Science," 452.

9. Richard Rorty, *Contingency, Irony, and Solidarity* (Cambridge: Cambridge University Press, 1989), xiii.

10. Published in *The Fate of Law*, ed. Austin Sarat and Thomas R. Kearns (Ann

The rhetorical reading of Fish's essay I propose in turn compels a detour through the work of the literary theorist Paul de Man. While one goal of this essay is thus to suggest points of similarity and difference between the views of Fish and de Man on rhetoric and law, my hope is to demonstrate a relationship that goes beyond mere analogy or comparison—specifically, I hope to show that de Man's work articulates the rhetorical performance that Fish's essay enacts. If this critical reading of Fish falls short of endorsing CLS's quasi-theological hopes for theory, my own more modest hope is that it at least exposes and explains a certain critical capitulation to the story the law tells about itself that inheres in Fish's position. This capitulation, which is also a form of positivism (in a sense that requires explanation), seems to me to be characteristic of neopragmatic philosophy generally and to be the troubling point of divergence between neopragmatism's largely self-satisfied liberalism and the left's dissatisfied radicalism (which is not to deny that the left suffers from its own unanalyzed capitulations). As the epigraphs are in part intended to suggest, the ultimate burden of this essay is to persuade the reader that this capitulation does not have to be endorsed even if it cannot finally be refuted in theory or even, perhaps, avoided in practice.

By way of anticipating this final point, it is worth noting that the theological impulse from which pragmatism attempts to free us possesses a remarkable resilience, even in the antitheological and antimetaphysical climate that prevails in the academy today. Hidden from sight, it emerges at odd times in texts that are otherwise militantly opposed to theological and metaphysical styles of thinking: for example, at the conclusion of Holmes's essay "Law in Science and Science in Law," when he cites George Herbert's praise of acting in "God's cause" in support of pursuing the unattainable ideal of making science "everywhere supreme."[11] If a theological impulse lurked behind

---

Arbor: University of Michican Press, 1991), 159–208 (reprinted in Fish, *There's No Such Thing as Free Speech... And It's a Good Thing, Too* [New York: Oxford University Press, 1994], 141–79). Further page references to the *Fate of Law* version appear in parentheses in the text.

11. Holmes's essay concludes:
Very likely it may be that with all the help that statistics and every modern appliance can bring us there will never be a commonwealth in which science is everywhere supreme. But it is an ideal, and without ideals what is life worth? They furnish us our perspectives and open glimpses of the infinite. It often is

Holmes's exaltation of science, one can similarly wonder who or what pulls the strings of theology's opponents today. Fish himself has observed (at a time when the affinity of his own work for "poststructuralist insights and positions" was perhaps less clear) that

> it seems to me that structuralist and poststructuralist insights and positions have been anticipated by theological modes of reasoning even though "theological" is a term of accusation in structuralist and poststructuralist rhetoric.[12]

The recurrence of these theological "modes" is generally attributed to a nostalgia for firm foundations, and it is these foundational longings that neopragmatism has been so successful in undermining. But it is worth remembering that religion has traditionally also served to provide another comfort, which is not the same as foundationalism, that somewhere, somehow, there is—or there will be—more than *this* world of suffering and injustice. Neopragmatism would extinguish theology's promise of a "more than this" from legal theory and practice along with its foundationalism, but it is far from certain that it can succeed in the former even when it succeeds in the latter. Within the legal academy, for example, Drucilla Cornell, while avoiding any trace of foundational thinking, still elicits from her readings of Emmanuel Levinas and Jacques Derrida an "allegory of messianism" in which she finds a new ethic of legal interpretation and a call to heed "the disjuncture between law and the ideal and to affirm our responsibility to make the promise to the ideal, to aspire to counter the violence of our world in the name of universal justice."[13] It is

---

a merit of an ideal to be unattainable. Its being so keeps forever before us something more to be done, and saves us from the ennui of a monotonous perfection. At the least it glorifies dull details, and uplifts and sustains weary years of toil with George Herbert's often quoted but ever inspiring verse:
"Who sweeps a room as in Thy cause,
Makes that and the action fine."
Holmes, "Law in Science," 462–63. Brook Thomas provides an interesting gloss on this passage from a different perspective (using it to illustrate Holmes's adoption of science as a new god), and also points out Holmes's misquotation of the Herbert poem (substituting "in Thy cause" for "for Thy laws"). Thomas, "Reflections," 522.

12. Fish, "Structuralist Homiletics," in *Is There a Text in This Class?* (Cambridge: Harvard University Press, 1980), 181.

13. Cornell, "Post-structuralism, the Ethical Relation, and the Law," *Cardozo Law Review* 9 (1988): 1587, 1628.

true that this "promise to the ideal" remains suspended in its impossibility, since any articulation of the ethic in legal form—any attempt
to translate the absolute call to responsibility into a general and
enforceable standard—instantly constitutes the very violence that the
ethic aspires to counter. But if the call (and the promise and the
hope) of "universal justice" can therefore technically "make nothing
happen" within the sphere of law, this in no way diminishes its force.
Like poetry, its effectiveness depends not on achieving some specific
result but on its exemplary power as performance. Even within law,
the call "survives / A way of happening."[14]

2

Stanley Fish presents a hard case for those who align themselves with
the progressive critique of the law. His work is received by the legal
Left—archetypically, the Conference on Critical Legal Studies—with
a frustrating mix of admiration and rejection, reactions that "The Law
Wishes to Have a Formal Existence" can only exacerbate. The debate,
as usual, is over the value of theoretical insight to progressive practice.
Despite his explicit agreement with the left critique of the traditional
essentialist and proceduralist arguments for law's determinacy, Fish
steadfastly refuses to acknowledge that any emancipatory consequences flow from this insight.[15]

---

14. Auden, "In Memory of W. B. Yeats." Compare Haverkamp, "Rhetoric, Law,"
1651, on the "endurance" of poetics. For Haverkamp, the most poetics can achieve
(at least without compromising its integrity by subordinating itself to the law's system-
maintaining purposes) is to "endure (without 'hopes')" and bear witness to the violence perpetrated by the law in the name of its systemic self-maintenance. He may
well be right that "[t]here is no 'theory hope' in poetics," at least in Fish's sense of
the term. Nevertheless, beyond its elegiac function and even beyond its role in
"exposing [legal] rhetoric's own self-destructive momentum" (ibid), poetics also has
a role to play in "exposing" the affirmation or promise that is no less constitutive
of the legal-rhetorical act than its violence and negativity, an exposition that I attempt
here.
15. The term *left* has a specific idiosyncratic meaning in Fish's work. Fish's
polemics are not limited to the political legal left (such as members of CLS) but are
directed at any commentator who views the insight into the rhetorical constitution
of law as having consequences for legal practice. Thus, Fish groups some liberals,
such as James Boyd White, with the CLS critics, while others, such as Owen Fiss,
are grouped with the "right" defenders of the traditional foundationalist view of the
law. Compare Fish, "Law Wishes," 62–66 (criticizing White for "anti-foundationalist

Thus, in "The Law Wishes to Have a Formal Existence" Fish once again brilliantly demonstrates the law's failure to legitimate itself on its preferred terms of formalism, autonomy, proceduralism, neutral principles, or any of the other talismans used to ward off incursions from the (allegedly) unprincipled and unreliable realms of morality and politics. He again shows, in the first two sections of his paper, that the "formal existence" wished for by the law is a false hope and empty claim. Yet what he takes away with the left hand Fish gives back with the right, by celebrating the self-delusion he exposes. For Fish, the fact that "the law is at once thoroughly rhetorical and engaged in the effacing of its own rhetoricity" ("Law Wishes," 195) is as much a sign of the law's genius as of its duplicity.

Despite the close affinity of Fish's rhetorical analyses to CLS's own delegitimation/"trashing"/*Ideologiekritische* arguments, Fish's ultimate thesis—that the antifoundationalist insight is impotent in practice—has typically been interpreted as entailing a necessary resignation to the status quo. Fish regularly protests, with some force, that his position does not *necessarily* have these reactionary consequences[16]—indeed, his often-repeated claim is that his position has no (theoretical or necessary) consequences at all. The parenthetical qualification is crucial because Fish is also always careful to specify that theories—including his own—*do* in fact have consequences, but only insofar as they are (always and inevitably) actually practices. Fish simply holds that the notion of theory as an "independent and abstract calculus" that "stands apart from and can guide practice" is incoherent because there is nothing "apart from" practice; he does not deny that the practical activity of doing theory has practical consequences (in fact he insists on it). Fish succinctly poses the distinction as that between "being a form of" and "informing" practice:

---

theory hope") with Fish, "Fish v. Fiss," in *Doing What Comes Naturally: Change, Rhetoric, and the Practice of Theory in Literature and Legal Studies* (Durham, N.C.: Duke University Press, 1989), 120 (criticizing Fiss for the characteristic rightist error of "objectivism"). As Fish explains, he "uses right, center and left to denote places in the intellectual rather than political landscape." Fish, "Dennis Martinez and the Uses of Theory" in *Doing What Comes Naturally*, 380, 582 n. 22.

16. See, e.g., Fish, "The Anti-Formalist Road," in *Doing What Comes Naturally* 27 ("I do not argue against radical change, but against the possibility that radical change, of either a feared or desired kind, will be brought about by theory").

There is a world of difference between saying that theory is a form of practice and saying that theory informs practice: to say the one is to claim for theory no more than can be claimed for anything else; to say the other is to claim everything.[17]

Nevertheless, despite his protestations and qualifications, Fish's texts are consistently read—at least by the left—as ruling out the possibility of meaningful progressive change.[18]

17. Fish, "Consequences," in *Doing What Comes Naturally*, 315, 340, 336, 337.

18. In the face of the common epistemological assumptions Fish shares with most of his left critics and his regular claims to having been misunderstood, other possible explanations for the persistent reading of Fish as an apologist for the status quo can be entertained. One could make a persuasive case, for instance, that this reading is fostered by the cheerful tone with which Fish characteristically dispatches issues and arguments that are freighted with the greatest political, ethical, and moral weight. Thus, Fish's response to the proposition that "the law is at once thoroughly rhetorical and engaged in the effacing of its own rhetoricity" (i.e., that the law is fundamentally deceptive, a lie): "Exactly, I would reply, and isn't it marvelous (a word intended non-evaluatively) to behold" ("Law Wishes," 195). The parenthetical attempt to control the reception of the term "marvelous" does little to deflect the affective (if not the cognitive) force of the statement.

Of course, one who responds to Fish's tone in this way naturally hesitates to argue merely from this personal reaction that Fish's intellectual position entails substantive conservative positions. One attempting such an argument could justly be accused of making an ad hominem argument, mistaking Fish's personal, subjective feelings—characteristically expressed in the nuances of literary tone—for theoretical consequences of his argument. The fear of being so accused in this case is only increased by the fact that Fish's arguments are, at least on their face, exclusively epistemological rather than political, and that he specifically and forcefully abjures any political consequences. More fundamentally, arguments from literary tone are inherently suspect within a "serious" academic discourse over the meaning of non-literary texts. Since tone is fundamentally inessential to serious academic discourse, it would evidently be unjust to hold Fish responsible for his tone in the course of an academic dispute or argument; it is his *ideas*, not his presentation of them, that are properly at issue in such a debate. One can certainly criticize tone where one disagrees with the implicit value judgments being expressed, but the responsible reader, the reader committed to serious academic discourse, should confine his or her personal reactions to tone to (at most) passing observations or comments (for example, in footnotes).

Fish himself, on the other hand, might recognize the force of such an argument from tone; as a partisan of rhetoric over philosophy, he is committed to acknowledging the force of an utterance's "persuasive accent" as well as its semantic content (assuming the two can be distinguished) regardless of whether the text in question is designated as "literary" or "philosophical." See Fish, "Rhetoric," in *Doing What Comes Naturally*, 471, 473-74. *Accent*, in Fish's use, plays a role similar to tone; both terms refer to individual or idiosyncratic inflections of discourse that contribute only indirectly to meaning. In any event, to the extent that tone is something that can be criticized, my critique of Fish in this essay may be nothing more than a critique of his tone.

Fish, on the other hand, criticizes CLS for its claims that theory can indeed "inform practice." The CLS partisans want to seize the insight into the rhetorical constitution of law as an opportunity

> to struggle against being demobilized by our own conventional beliefs . . . [,] to unfreeze the world as it appears to common sense as a bunch of more or less objectively determined social relations and to make it appear as (we believe) it really is: people acting, imagining, rationalizing, justifying.[19]

Fish objects that this hope is necessarily futile because it forgets even while stating the radically local nature of all such insights. We cannot "make [the world] appear as . . . it really is"; we could only do so "if by some act of magic the insight that one is historically conditioned is itself not historically achieved and enables one (presumably for the first time) to operate outside of history."[20] For Fish, attributing liberatory consequences to the antifoundationalist insight illegitimately turns it on its head. Fish calls this error "'anti-foundationalist theory hope' (the hope that by becoming aware of the rhetoricity of our foundations we gain a (non-rhetorical) perspective on them that we didn't have before)" ("Law Wishes," 198); its peculiar form is the forgetting of what one knows in the act of enunciating it.

Rather than attempting to adjudicate between Fish's and CLS's positions, which risks losing sight of the possibility that both sides are right, my approach here is to try to articulate what is at stake by examining Fish's rhetorical self-positioning in the debate. In particular, one can read Fish's paper with an eye toward the question of whether, if the hopeful act of forgetting that he calls "anti-foundationalist theory hope" is indeed an error, it is one that anyone, including Fish, can avoid. Fish argues in "The Law Wishes to Have a Formal Existence" that every practice "depends for its emergence as a practice—as an activity distinct from other activities—on a certain ignorance of its debts and complicities," that is, on the delusive belief that it excludes that which in reality constitutes it ("Law Wishes," 204). Thus, although Fish's own antifoundationalist position is largely constituted

---

19. Gordon, "New Developments in Legal Theory," in *The Politics of Law*, ed. David Kairys, rev. ed. (New York: Pantheon Books, 1990), 420.

20. Fish, "Anti-Professionalism," in *Doing What Comes Naturally*, 215, 228.

in polemical contrast to the left's delusively hopeful position, the possibility cannot be ruled out that Fish himself unknowingly commits the same error—in a form that admittedly is not immediately evident—in the very act of denouncing it.

3

In any event, the intended practical effects of "The Law Wishes to Have a Formal Existence" are very clear. The third section of the paper is a focused and forceful argument against introducing philosophical or rhetorical analysis (of the type that Fish himself practices, and is practicing in this very argument) into practical legal discourse. Thus, he asserts that although it may well be true that "the law is not 'best read in its own terms,'"

> that does not mean that the law is best not *practiced* in its own terms, for it is only by deploying its own terms confidently and without metacritical reservation that it can be practiced at all. (205)[21]

The distinction made in this passage between "practice" and "reading"—here signifying "self-reading" or critical self-consciousness, a synonym for what Fish means by "theory"—organizes the entire thrust of his argument in the paper's final section and provides the linchpin for Fish's claim that the law is best left ignorant of its rhetorical, philosophical, political, and social complicities (complicities whose existence Fish conclusively demonstrates in the first two sections of the paper). Recalling with Fish that "'[f]orgetfulness'... is a condition of action, and the difference between activities—between doing judging and doing literary criticism or doing sociology—is a difference between differing species of forgetting,"[22] one can ask what Fish forgets in arguing for and relying on this distinction.

Fish himself displays a great deal of confidence in the sturdiness of the distinction between "legal practice" and "reading the law" (i.e., legal theory). In the paper's final section, Fish characterizes the "pri-

---

21. Fish is quoting from and discussing Peter Goodrich's book, *Legal Discourse: Studies in Linguistics, Rhetoric, and Legal Analysis* (New York: St. Martin's, 1987).
22. Fish, "Dennis Martinez," 397.

mary business" of legal practice as concerned not with the "remaking of culture" or "change" or "challenge," but with "winning and deciding cases" ("Law Wishes," 196, 200–201). He concedes that "challenge and change are often the byproducts of the resourcefulness legal actors display," but he claims that "they are not the motives for which legal action is usually taken" (201). Indeed, Fish goes so far as to assert that "one could always engage in that business [of using legal practice to discover and revise cultural values,] but to do so would not be to practice law as the institution's members now recognize it" (199).

In the context of Fish's polemic with CLS, this narrow rendering of the scope of legal practice serves to undergird a rigorous distinction—corresponding to that of *practice* and *reading*—between the *internal* perspective of the legal practitioner and the *external* perspective of the moral philosopher or critic. The left critics' mistake

is to conflate the perspective from which one might ask questions about the nature of law (is it formal or moral or rhetorical?) with the perspective from which one might ask questions in the hope that the answers will be of use in getting on with a legal job of work. (200)

In short, the "legal job of work" consists in "winning and deciding cases"; "remaking culture," "change," and "challenge" are jobs for moral philosophers, political activists, and rhetoricians, not lawyers.

Coming after the first two sections of the paper, this argument is striking because it suddenly resurrects an inside/outside distinction between the practice of law and rhetoric/philosophy/morality, etc. within (or rather around) legal discourse that the earlier sections have effectively demolished. There is no contradiction, however, because Fish is not arguing that morality or rhetoric or philosophy *can* actually be kept outside of legal practice, but only that legal practice *should* remain ignorant of this inevitable contamination. The law's wish for a formal existence cannot be granted, but we should nevertheless humor it by pretending that it has.

The distinction between "reading the law" (i.e., the philosophical/moral/rhetorical perspective) and "practicing the law" therefore returns in an imperative and normative mode. Fish makes it clear that it would be a very bad thing indeed if moral philosophy and rhetorical analysis were to infect properly legal discourse.[23] The language he employs to underscore the importance of maintaining the law's self-ignorance is as striking as the return of the distinction itself: the prospect of incorporating rhetorical analysis into legal discourse makes Fish "nervous" ("Law Wishes," 198); it would be "inept and irresponsible," perhaps even "dangerous" (200), dangers the left critics ignore when they urge the expansion of legal discourse to include extralegal and self-critical modes of argument.

Fish is explicit about this danger:

> Were the law to deploy its categories and concepts in the company of an analysis of their roots in extralegal discourse, it would not be exercising, but dismantling, its authority; in short, it would no longer be law. (203).

Fish's anxiety, in other words, is provoked by a threat to the law's identity. A legal practice informed by the rhetorician's or philosopher's

---

23. In this he evidently agrees with Richard Rorty, who has expressed similar views about the danger of allowing "Barthian readings" into the teaching of law:
> I confess that I tremble at the thought of Barthian readings in law schools. . . . I suspect that civilization reposes on a lot of people who take the normal practice of the discipline with full "realistic" seriousness. However, I should like to think that a pragmatist's understanding of knowledge and community would be, in the end, compatible with normal inquiry—the practitioners of such inquiry reserving their irony for after-hours.
> Letter to Sanford Levinson, 28 April 1981, quoted in Levinson, "Law as Literature," *Texas Law Review* 60 (1982): 373, 401 n. 117.
The difference between Fish and Rorty is that where Fish would protect legal discourse by quarantining the dangers of self-consciousness and irony within professions (political/moral philosopher and rhetorician) that are not connected to the structures of legal authority and power, Rorty believes that legal practitioners themselves can (and should) reserve their critical self-consciousness "for after hours." Indeed, in *Contingency, Irony, and Solidarity,* Rorty raises this notion to a programmatic level, "arguing"—if that is the right word, since Rorty's argument amounts to the suggestion that with respect to one area of life we should stop bothering to argue—that one should reserve one's critical self-consciousness for one's private affairs while accepting the fundamental public values imparted in the tradition and structure of the liberal state as givens.
    Anselm Haverkamp shares the neopragmatists' apprehensions about introducing poetics into the law, but for symmetrically opposed reasons. Where Fish fears that the law would be corrupted beyond recognition by the introduction of exegetical self-consciousness, Haverkamp worries that poetics' integrity—its resistant and elegiac functions—would be compromised by being caught up in law's systems-maintenance activities. See Haverkamp, "Rhetoric, Law" 1652–53.

"critical self-consciousness" (201) "would no longer be law," because such a self-critical stance would open the door to the "dismantling" (as opposed to the exercise) of the law's distinguishing characteristic, its "authority." The law could no longer maintain the illusion of its autonomy and formality that is essential to its authority; it could no longer tell in good faith its "two [contradictory] stories . . . and then [make them] into the single story that assures the continuity of the tradition" (193). As this reference to tradition indicates, the law's identity has a temporal dimension—it is the identity of a history or a tradition. And, as Fish also expresses it, this "history" of the law's continually renewed "victory . . . in the shape of *keeping going*" would be threatened by the infusion of self-critical discourse (179); this history, we can infer, might even be brought to an end. In short, permitting rhetorical analysis and moral philosophy into the sphere of legal discourse would be a self-crippling act.[24]

The point Fish wants to make here is that CLS's attempt to incorporate extralegal, theoretical insights into legal practice—to "practice the law" by "reading the law"—is self-defeating, because legal practice

---

24. It is worth noting that the constellation of anxiety, identity, self-knowledge, and authority displayed in Fish's account of the law recapitulates the categories and narrative structure of *Oedipus Tyrranus*. In Fish's cautionary tale, the law plays the role of King Oedipus, who, ignorant of his impure identity (as the law remains ignorant of its own rhetorical impurities), issues an edict banishing the defiler of his kingdom (as the law seeks to banish rhetoric), not realizing that he himself is the edict's proper object. Upon gaining self-knowledge of his impurity, Oedipus becomes subject to his own edict (as would the law in Fish's scenario) and must abandon his throne and kingdom (just as the law's accurate self-knowledge would cause it to abdicate ["dismantle"] its claim to authority). This conjunction provides an alternative interpretation and pathos to the allegorical figure of blind Justice. Nor is this tragic figure of law merely fortuitous; as we will see, the allegory of legal interpretation teaches, in part, the same lesson as *Oedipus:* that an uncontrollable, blind, and violent fatality inheres in the radical disjunction between the law's powers of self-knowledge and its force as act.

Fish admits that the self-delusive process of law he describes "is a spectacle that could be described (as members of the Critical Legal Studies Movement tend to do) as farce." He views the law differently, however: "as an amazing kind of success."

[T]he history of legal doctrine and its applications is a history neither of rationalistic purity nor of incoherence and bad faith, but an almost Ovidian history of transformation under the pressure of enormously complicated social, political and economic urgencies, a history in which victory—in the shape of *keeping going*—is always being wrested from what looks like certain defeat. . . . ("Law Wishes," 179).

Against both CLS and Fish, I am suggesting here that the fundamental literary form of law is neither comedy nor historical narrative, but tragedy.

cannot accommodate such insights and still remain legal. "The law . . . is not philosophy; it is law, although, like everything else it can become the object of philosophical analysis, in which case it becomes something different from what it is in its own terms" ("Law Wishes," 205). The law's autonomy (which grounds its claim to authority) is indeed, as CLS claims and Fish himself demonstrates, a delusion; but to expose the law to this truth in the hope of improving its condition would, so to speak, kill the patient rather than cure it. The law could not "still remain operative as law"; it could not continue to "adjudicate disputes" or provide "prompt remedies and decisions." Moreover, despite his claim of his position's indifference to political perspective, Fish's implicit political judgment of this outcome is clear—he is plainly apprehensive of the specter of the law's "victory" turning to defeat.

Fish's critique of CLS's hopes for theory may well be persuasive on its own terms—it is possible that for some, the law would lose its authority if it no longer maintained the fiction of its distinction from politics, rhetoric, and moral philosophy (although for others, one can speculate, it might gain an authority it has never before deserved). But beyond the self-chosen scope of his analysis, if one entertains the possibility that "the goals of law" could aspire to something more than performing a "legal job of work," "deciding cases," or "winning an argument or crafting an opinion," then Fish's critique becomes problematic on other grounds. The possibility of this "something more" is, of course, the traditional progressive hope for the law, a possibility that is ruled out in advance by Fish's narrow and wholly technical conception of legal practice. Without yet attempting to move beyond an immediate and (perhaps) naive notion of the nature of this "something more," it is clear enough that what Fish's conception omits is the aspect of law that CLS and other progressive critics of law always foreground, the relationship of law to justice.

If the purpose of law is to establish justice—that is (we can say provisionally), to concretely realize in the world the ideal of the good embodied in the law[25]—then "to dismantle the authority of the law" is a legitimate and *legal* endeavor; not because as a technical matter

---

25. See Robert Cover, "Violence and the Word," *Yale Law Journal* 95 (1986): 1601, 1604: "Law is the projection of an imagined future upon reality."

of linguistic philosophy the law makes claims to determine interpretation it cannot fulfill, but because the law, to cite only one example, permits and enforces such grotesque disparities of wealth and power in this wealthiest and most powerful of nations that thousands of people are left to live and die on city streets. Measured against the demand for justice, the law's authority is illegitimate and deserves to be exposed. CLS thus invokes critical theory not for its own sake, or for the sake of finding some utopian point beyond context, but for the possibility it holds out of achieving a more just world. This hardly demonstrates that CLS's hopes for theory are justified, but it does call into question the terms of Fish's critique.

Fish, in short, omits from his account of legal practice—he forgets—that the law's consequential and performative aspect (its impulse toward realizing itself as justice) is no less constitutive of law than "winning and deciding cases" or "prompt remedies and decisions." One sees this very clearly in the one place in the paper where justice is discussed. Fish asserts that the statement, "'I do not think the law ought to be separated from justice,' . . . amounts to a denial of the law's independence" ("Law Wishes," 192–93). In other words, justice for Fish is on par with the other foreign influences (like morality and interpretation) that may well be law's constitutive outside but that must nevertheless be denied and ignored by legal practitioners if law is to "still remain operative as law."

By treating law simply as a system for producing outcomes— that is, by omitting from his analysis the projective and performative relationship of law to justice—Fish disguises what may be called (as a first approximation) a dispute about the nature of law as a theoretical error on the part of CLS. When he praises the "victory" of law "in the shape of *keeping going*," when he defines the "primary business" of law as "winning and deciding" rather than "challenge," "change," or the "remaking of culture," he is not identifying immutable characteristics of the law that the left has overlooked but is simply advocating a particular view of the law—the view of the law as a system for producing outcomes—that the left rejects in favor of the view that the law is intended to serve justice. Fish's antifoundationalist agenda, moreover, is symmetrical, if opposed, to the agenda of the left's "anti-foundationalist theory hope." If the left's version of anti-foundationalism preaches the political lesson that we can transcend the distorted values and beliefs that constitute our present legal context,

Fish's version preaches the opposite (but equally political) lesson that the law cannot transcend the givenness of present values and beliefs. The left may forget that law cannot afford to sacrifice the illusion of its formal existence and still maintain its identity as law, but in defending the preservation of that illusion Fish forgets that law's impulse toward realizing itself concretely as justice is no less constitutive of this identity.

Thus, although Fish is himself an astute critic of legal positivism in other forms, his view of the law may also be called "positivism" because it privileges legal decisions insofar as they are "properly" legal (i.e., made by legal actors in the course of legal proceedings) and shelters them from political or ethical critique, by designating a proper sphere of legal discourse from which such critiques are excluded. As Fish explains,

> Although much of legal theory is an effort to draw a direct line between some description of the law's workings and the rightness (or wrongness) of particular decisions, it has been my (anti-theoretical) point that "rightness" is automatically conferred on any decision the system produces, that is to say, any decision that follows from the persuasive marshalling of certain arguments. As soon as an argument has proven to be persuasive to the relevant parties—a court, a jury—we say of it that it is right, by which we mean that it is now the law (nothing succeeds like success), that it is *legally* right. Of course, we are still free to object to the decision on other grounds, to find it "wrong" in moral terms or in terms of the long-range health of the republic. In that event, however, our recourse would not be to an alternative form of the legal process but to alternative arguments that would be successful—that is, persuasive—within the same general form. (206)

Of course, Fish is careful not to give this proper sphere any predetermined substance; his point, as this passage makes clear, is that the "form" of argument that is proper to law only comes into view after the fact, and depends solely on whether the argument has "succeeded," that is, convinced the relevant decision maker. He can therefore plausibly continue to claim that his analysis has no normative consequences for what *particular* forms of argument should or will prevail in legal disputes—this cannot be determined in advance but only retrospectively, because the only criterion is "success." Nevertheless, if he avoids endorsing any particular form of the legal process, Fish's commitment to the process itself—whatever its outcomes and whatever its ultimate form—is clear enough. He insists that, if one has moral or other (nonlegal) objections to a legal decision, the proper response is not to resort to "alternative forms of the legal process" but to attempt to put one's arguments in the "same general [i.e., legal] form."

Even if Fish's refusal to endorse any particular form of legal process reduces his commitment to law's "general form" to a rhetorical gesture, this gesture—which, it is worth remarking, in no way follows from his general analysis of law—is sufficient to mark him as a positivist in the classical sense of identifying law on strictly procedural grounds (albeit retroactively). And even empty rhetorical gestures, particularly those made in defense of the general form of the legal process, can have unintended and highly political consequences, by, for example, encouraging those self-styled traditionalists who would deny access and the law's imprimatur to social values that supposedly fail to meet the formal characteristics recognized as properly legal under the prevailing status quo. (The values left standing at the law's door by these requirements are becoming increasingly familiar as feminists and others analyze the limitations imposed by routinely accepted norms of legal discourse on what constitutes a "legitimate" legal argument.) But Fish is a positivist in a distinct and more fundamental sense than this gratuitous endorsement of formal legality, as his critique of the archpositivist H. L. A. Hart best illustrates.

Fish criticizes H. L. A. Hart's positivist account of law in his essay "Force," by showing (as he also does in "The Law Wishes to Have a Formal Existence") that legal rules can never be sufficiently clear and perspicuous to eliminate the need for interpretation that is based on principles that stand beyond these legal rules.[26] Fish shows, against Hart, that the law requires interpretive judgments even to decide "clear" cases. Yet this critique is at the same time curiously sympathetic to the concerns motivating Hart's positivism, and Fish in fact ends up reassuring rather than criticizing these concerns: he

---

26. Fish, *Doing What Comes Naturally*, 503–24.

concludes that Hart's worry—that without rule-bound interpretation law will be indistinguishable from the exercise of raw, unprincipled (social and political) force—is unfounded, because "[f]orce ... is already a repository of everything it supposedly threatens—norms, standards, reasons, and, yes, even rules."[27] Fish's point in "Force," in other words, is the complement to his point in "The Law Wishes to Have a Formal Existence": in the latter essay he shows that law is made of the same stuff as morality, politics, and interpretation, while in "Force" he shows that morality, politics, and interpretation are made of the same stuff as law. Accordingly, despite his effective critique of Hart's limited rule-determined view, Fish himself rein-scribes law within an expanded positivism, one that incorporates the social, ethical, and political values excluded by Hart in a conven-tional, rule-bound form that is ultimately indistinguishable from Hart's legal rules. There is thus no question but that for Fish, "justice," despite its pretensions to stand beyond the (merely) conventional system of the law, can only be another name for more of the same—more conventions, more rules, more law.

Fish's critique of Hart—the demonstration that social and polit-ical values and commitments (including the values subsumed under the term *justice*) are possessed of the same sheer positivity as law's rules and conventions—represents one version of neopragmatism's attempt to synthesize a rigorous historical immanentism with the rejection of naive realism, (i.e., the belief that there is an outside of language with which linguistic propositions can be compared to deter-mine their truth value). The rejection of realism permits Fish to criticize Hart's "naive" assumption that rules and past precedents exist apart from the language in which they are recounted in the judicial opinions that cite them (the assumption that underlies Hart's overriding concern that these authorities may "not be followed"); and the immanentism allows him nevertheless to reassure Hart that no judgment is genuinely unconstrained, since all judgments are ulti-mately made of, and therefore constrained by, the same historically given assumptions, values, and conventions as legal rules. One can wonder whether a truly language-centered epistemology can tolerate the normative and rhetorical weight that neopragmatism grants to the concepts of history and the historically given, a question to which

27. Ibid., 522.

I return in the next section through a closer look at Fish's Hart essay. For now, however, it is at least clear that one cannot dismiss Fish's positivism as simply the result of a politically conservative perspective, since it is so tightly bound to his deepest epistemological commitments.[28] It would be an even more serious mistake to conclude that Fish's forgetting of justice represents a naive failure of insight on his part, if only because Fish himself describes with precision the process by which this forgetting occurs—albeit attributing the forgetting to the process of law rather than to his own interpretation of this process.

Thus, in the paper's one passage on justice, Fish explains how the constitutive significance of justice (in the emphatic sense of the substantive realization of the good) is "forgotten" by the law:

> what Justice Marshall says ["I do not think the law ought to be separated from justice"] amounts to the denial of the law's

---

28. Fish's skirmishes with self-styled conservative academics have been much publicized. Specifically with respect to law, not a single one of Fish's frequent attacks on CLS comes close to matching the contempt he displays in dispatching Richard Posner's view of law and literature. See Fish, "Don't Know Much About the Middle Ages: Posner on Law and Literature" in *Doing What Comes Naturally*, 294–329. In this essay Fish not only defends the propositions that the theoretical program of CLS may be influencing current legal practice and that "the actions of literary critics can have consequences as far-reaching as any court," but asserts that

[g]iven the *structural* interdependence of [law and literary criticism]...it is incumbent upon those who find [Posner's] views not only wrong, but supportive of wrong views now being put forward in other (sometimes high) places, to challenge them in the strongest possible terms. (Ibid., 308, 306, 310–11)

These statements are, at a minimum, in some tension with the positions I am attributing to Fish in "The Law Wishes to Have a Formal Existence." More recently he has departed even further from the tone I criticize in footnote 18, *supra*, in the course of reformulating and defending the notion of "political correctness":

"Political correctness" is simply a perjorative term for the condition of operating on the basis of a partial vision, and since that is the condition of all of us, we are all politically correct.... That is what it means to be partial, or, in an older and preferable vocabulary, fallen.... This is at once our infirmity and our glory. It is our infirmity because it keeps us from eternity, and it is our glory because it sends us in search of eternity and keeps us from premature rest. (Fish, *There's No Such Thing*, 79)

The religious vocabulary and uplifting message of this passage strongly recall the similarly, spiritual and hortatory conclusion of Holmes's "Law in Science," see note 11, *supra*, and come close to the position I advance in this essay. Apart from the question of fairness to Fish, I point this out to emphasize that analyzing his texts in terms of what they *do*—their rhetorical performance—is a far more fruitful and interesting approach to them than trying to analyze his personal political positions.

independence, but the fact that he, the most respected jurist in American history, said it makes his pronouncement a *legal* one and therefore one that can be invoked as a legal justification for departing from the rule of law. (193)

The law, in other words, absorbs the emphatic concept of justice (with its reference to the realization of a normative ideal external to law) into its internal rhetorical system as just another rhetorical ploy for maintaining the illusion of its formal autonomy. "Once again, . . . the legal establishment reaffirms its commitment to a formal process it is in the act of setting aside" (id). Justice (a projected and sought-after state of the world) is replaced—and effaced—by "justice" (a linguistic signifier with rhetorical functions within a conventional rhetorical system). And it is precisely this act of forgetting that seals the law's self-deceptive claim to formal autonomy.

Of course, Fish's point here is that *the law*—not he himself—forgets the law's constitutive relationship to justice. In Fish's terms, insofar as he is a reader rather than practitioner of law, he is capable (as the law is not) of recognizing and characterizing the law's (self-) deceptive rhetorical operations, including the effacement of the con-stitutive role of justice. Nevertheless, Fish's own omission of justice from his account of legal practice repeats at the level of reading this same rhetorical ploy. Identifying law's "primary business" and "goals" with "winning an argument or crafting an opinion," rather than with the remaking of cultural values or the achievement of a just world, demarcates law as a set of technical and formal rhetorical practices without regard to the meaning of these practices outside the sphere of their conventional usage. Despite his acute awareness of the self-deception inherent in the banishment of justice from the sphere proper to law, he repeats the same gesture in his account of legal practice. Far from being the result of mere naïveté or political leanings, the impulse to forget the constitutive role of justice—and thus to seal law within an identity (whether formal, rhetorical, or procedural)—seems to exert a coercive power strong enough to cause as sophis-ticated a reader as Fish to fall victim to it even as he is calling it by name.

If one resists a little while longer the impulse to judge Fish rather than to read him and instead returns to his text, one can begin to answer the questions posed by this puzzling repetition by locating its source in his dispute with the left. The crux of this dispute is Fish's claim that the introduction of rhetorical and philosophical discourse into the law would have the effect of destroying the law's identity. As we saw above, according to Fish, were rhetorical analysis a properly legal method, the law could no longer maintain the illusion of its autonomy and formality that is essential to its authority. Of course, as we also saw, since Fish himself demonstrates that the law's formal identity is necessarily illusory, he can only assert its possibility in an imperative mode. The first two sections of his paper are devoted to demonstrating the necessary failure of the law's attempts to establish its formal self-identity; the third section defends the proposition that the illusion of the law's identity nevertheless *must*—not *can*—be preserved.

Paul de Man has described the structure of this rhetorical dilemma as characteristic of "positional speech acts":

> Something one has failed to do can become feasible again only in the mode of compulsion; the performative correlate of "I cannot" is "I [or you] must." The language of identity and of logic asserts itself in the imperative mode and thus recognizes its own activity as the positing of entities. Logic consists of positional speech acts.[29]

The "language of identity" that de Man refers to in this passage is that of logical self-identity, the principle of noncontradiction, not the specific self-identity of law that is the subject of Fish's essay. Nevertheless, de Man's discussion of what he calls "positional speech acts" and the "positional power" of language is immediately relevant to the questions that are raised, directly and indirectly, by Fish's paper—specifically, *Allegories of Reading* states the aporia between reading and self-knowledge that Fish's text performs. De Man takes up the same questions of rhetoric, law, reading, and knowledge that emerge from Fish's reading of law, and, like Fish, he also demonstrates both the necessity and impossibility of the law's claim to hold a formal, mechanical, and determinate method of deciding particular cases. But by linking this impossibility to the law's performative functions,

---

29. Paul de Man, *Allegories of Reading* (New Haven: Yale University Press, 1979), 124. Further references to this work appear in parentheses in the text.

de Man demonstrates something else as well: the radical disjunction
of law and justice. "Justice," de Man says, "is unjust" (*Allegories*,
269). Elucidating the meaning of this statement—and, no doubt, inevitably passing (unjust) judgment upon Fish as well—is the burden of
the remainder of this essay.

4

Allegories of Reading is, among many other things, a meditation on
the defeat of self-knowledge at the hands of language, a defeat that we
seem to have encountered in Fish's apparent failure to recognize in his
own text the same rhetorical self-delusion that he identifies at work in
the rhetoric of law. Law in fact plays a critical part in the development
of *Allegories of Reading*, particularly in the chapter on Rousseau's
Social Contract. But since de Man's ultimate aim is an account of reading, rhetoric, and figural language, not an account of law—he uses
"law" (along with "selfhood," "love," and other ostensible chapter
topics) to allegorize certain rhetorical aspects of language and not as
subjects of study in their own right—it would be precipitous simply
to apply or compare de Man's discussion of law to Fish's account. As
I hope to show, *Allegories of Reading* is in fact extremely useful for
understanding Fish's text and its substantive assertions about the law,
but the articulation of de Man's work with Fish's occurs, at least initially, at the level of Fish's rhetorical performance. As the conclusion
of the preceding section was intended to suggest, it is de Man's notions
of positing and language's positional power that provide an initial
glimpse into the rhetorical processes that Fish's text simultaneously
describes and exemplifies.

   "Positing" and "positional speech acts" for de Man name a performative power of language—its power to engender, as opposed to
reflect, the true. Positing is understood in opposition to knowing,
the passive representation of self-subsistent entities and truths. In the
speech act terminology that de Man employs, knowledge corresponds
to language's constative function, because it does not enact or create
the truth it states—as would, for example, the utterances constituting
the christening ceremony that officially names a ship—but merely
reflects a truth whose source lies elsewhere.

   To know . . . is a transitive function that assumes the prior existence of an entity to be known and that predicates the ability

of knowing by ways of properties. It does not itself predicate these attributes but receives them, so to speak, from the entity itself by merely allowing it to be what it is. To the extent that it is verbal it is *properly* denominative and constative. It depends on a built-in continuity within the system that unites the entity to its attributes, the grammar that links the adjective to the noun by predication. The specifically verbal intervention stems from predication, but since the predicate is nonpositional with regard to its properties, it cannot be called a speech *act*. We could call it a speech *fact* or a fact that *can* be spoken and, consequently, known without necessarily introducing deviations. Such a fact *can*, on the one hand, be spoken ... without changing the order of things but it does not, on the other hand, *have to be* spoken ... since the order of things does not depend on its predicative power for its existence. Knowledge ... depends on this non-coercive possibility and in fact enunciates it by ways of the principle of the self-identity of entities, "the self-identical A." (*Allegories*, 121–22)

"Positing," by contrast, names "genuine *acts* of speech" (122)—acts in which the entities and attributes posited are not independently subsistent but are predicated by the language in which they are formulated. Posited entities *"have to be* spoken," because they exist only insofar as they are the subjects of acts of language. They can therefore also be called fictional, in the specific sense that their (illusory) being is wholly dependent on the acts of language that give rise to them.

The distinction between knowing and positing can be clarified, and its significance for Fish's account of law can begin to be understood, by reference to the specific linguistic phenomenon that is the topic of Fish's paper. Although Fish does not name it as such, the formal self-identity wished for by the law is a posited entity. This self-identity cannot be achieved in fact; yet, as Fish shows, the law posits it with every decision. The law is constantly in the process of creating its illusion of formality and autonomy by means of the various rhetorical devices at its disposal. Fish describes this process and catalogs these devices in the second section of his paper, using the example of contract law. He shows that the formalism to which consideration doctrine aspires is made rather than given; it is achieved, belatedly, by the very decisions that purport to refer to and rely on it as their anterior foundation and ground of support. The rhetorical structure peculiar to the law's positional power is thus that of self-suspension: the law's claim to formality "is upheld by the rhetorical structure it has generated" ("Law Wishes," 187). In other words, the law's formality and self-identity are self-posited fictions; although the law believes that its existence is formal and cites its formal features (e.g., consideration doctrine) as the justification for its acts, in fact this formalism is always in the process of being posited by the very acts that it is claimed to justify.

As this discussion already suggests, the act of positing stands in an antithetical relationship to the possibility of knowing. De Man shows that the relationship between knowing and positing is in fact self-destabilizing. The possibility of knowing depends on the ability of the formal, grammatical structure of language to model already-existing entities and their properties, a homology that presupposes that entities have the self-identical structure attributed to them by the law of noncontradiction: "Knowledge . . . depends on this non-coercive possibility (of representing self-subsistent truths about entities) and in fact enunciates it by way of the principle of the self-identity of entities, 'the self-identical A'" (*Allegories*, 122). But since the existence of "the self-identical A" is itself nothing more than a logical postulate, its own claim to truth remains indeterminate. The possibility that the principle of noncontradiction is itself merely a posited fiction cannot be ruled out. This (impossible to rule out) possibility of the fictional status of the principle of noncontradiction overturns any confidence we might have that we can know the world, at least in the strong sense of a guaranteed homology between propositional statements and nonlinguistic truths; the possibility always remains that what we (think we) know is just a fiction generated by the language that we use (or rather, by which we are used).

> We cannot say that we know "das Seiende" nor can it be said that we do not know it. What can be said is that we do not know whether or not we know it because the knowledge we once thought we possessed has been shown to be open to suspicion; our ontological confidence has been forever shaken. (*Allegories*, 123)

De Man goes further and claims that not only the possibility of knowledge, but the possibility of signification in general, is undermined by the positional structure of language. Knowledge is a subject-object relationship governed by the representational or mimetic capacity of language, but signification depends only on the existence of a formal code capable of systematically producing units of meaning, that is, a grammar or syntax: "it is the alignment of a signification with any principle of linguistic articulation whatsoever, sensory or not, which constitutes the figure."[30]

Fish demonstrates that the law wishes to operate as just such a formal code, since it seeks to justify its authority on the basis of the formality, generality, and mechanical nature of its decision-making processes. But, as he also shows, the law's claim to formal autonomy and authority is undermined by its constitutive relationship to its "outside." The law's self-deception, its need to tell "two [contradictory] stories," is precisely its effort to maintain the illusion of a formal and mechanical decision-making process despite the regular disruption of this process by the moral, rhetorical, and political concerns that form the real substance of its decisions. The law's stratagems for maintaining the fiction of a self-enclosed, formal identity—for example, the reduction of justice to "justice"—are thus effective only at the level of fiction: insofar as they are in fact acts, the law's positings also undermine the (fictional) identity that they purport to establish.

De Man adds that the curious properties of positionality do not even allow for the assurance of knowing that the performative takes precedence over the constative functions of language.

[T]his deconstruction seems to end in a reassertion of the active performative power of language. . . . This would allow for the reassuring conviction that it is legitimate to do just about anything with words, as long as we know that a rigorous mind, fully aware of the misleading power of tropes, pulls the strings. But if it turns out that the same mind does not even know whether it is doing or not doing something, then there are considerable grounds for suspicion that it does not know *what* it is doing. (*Allegories*, 131)

Fish shows how law, as a self-positing system of rhetoric, indeed

---

30. De Man, "Shelley Disfigured," in *The Rhetoric of Romanticism* (New York: Columbia University Press, 1984), 114.

does not know what it is doing or even that it is doing (in the sense of positing) anything. The law mistakenly believes that it is not doing anything: as we have seen, it mistakes a fictional, posited entity (its formal self-identity) for one that has a substantial reality independent of its rhetorical machinations. More important, the law does not know what it is doing: in "providing prompt remedies and decisions," it is also exercising its all-too-literal power to reshape the world it seeks to exclude from its rhetorical confines. And, to the extent that the law justifies its acts by reference to its wholly posited and fictional formal autonomy rather than the substantive political or ethical norms that constitute it—that is, a vision of justice—one can call these acts a blind exercise of power.

What de Man says of Rousseau's social contract can then also be said of the law:

> it is a complex and purely defensive verbal strategy by means of which the literal world is given some of the consistency of fiction, an intricate set of feints and ruses by means of which the moment is temporarily delayed when fictional seductions will no longer be able to resist transformation into literal acts. (*Allegories*, 159)

Law, as Fish shows, indeed transforms justice and morality into rhetorical feints and ruses in defense of its fictional formality and autonomy. As we also know, these feints and ruses are themselves inevitably transformed into literal acts, most literally in the form of legal decisions that mobilize the power of the state, but also by the institutionalization of particular perspectives and modes of discourse that determine the ideological shape of the social world.

Fish's discussion of contract law in the second part of his paper brilliantly demonstrates this aspect of the law's constitutive and purely linguistic power. As Fish explains, the ostensible goal of contract law, and the doctrine of consideration in particular, is to rigorously "separate the realm of legal obligation from the larger and putatively more 'subjective' realm of moral obligation." The law attempts to achieve this goal "by providing *formal* (as opposed to value-laden) criteria of the intention to be legally bound." Thus,

> There are all kinds of reasons why one might make promises or perform actions conferring benefits on another and all kinds of

after-the-fact analyses of what the promise signified or what the action contemplated. But if there is something tangible offered in return for something tangible requested [i.e., consideration], the transaction is a legal one and the machinery of legal obligation kicks in. ("Law Wishes," 179)

The purpose of this formalism is to permit courts to adjudicate disputes in a mechanical fashion without interjecting their own views of fairness or justice.

[T]he act of contracting (or so it is claimed) becomes purely rational as the parties play out their formal roles in response to a mechanical requirement, the requirement of consideration. This in turn requires the court to be similarly mechanical (formal) lest it substitute for the bargain of two free agents rationally made a bargain it would have preferred them to make. (180)

The danger here is clear: the law may become the dictator of private choices and moral judgments. The separation the law seeks from morality, in other words, runs in both directions; the law wishes to keep itself immune from extrinsic influences, but it also wants to avoid extruding beyond its proper sphere and into the realms of moral and political choice. As Fish puts it, the danger is that "the court would pass from being an instrument of *the* law into an instrument of *a* morality" (181).

It comes as no surprise that the law's efforts to remain neutral vis-à-vis competing moral visions is entirely futile. Rather than achieving neutrality, consideration doctrine

finally makes sense not as an alternative to morality, but as the very embodiment of the morality of the market, a morality of arms-length dealing between agents without histories, gender or class affiliation. Whatever one thinks of this conception of transaction and agency, it is hardly one that has bracketed moral questions; rather it has decided them in a particular way, and, moreover, in a way that is neither necessary nor inevitable. (182)

Law institutes a dominant but entirely contingent system of social values and moral discourse, simultaneously naturalizing it (by effacing its contingent and value-specific nature under the formalist rubric of "consideration") and enforcing it (state-sanctioned violence is only the grossest of its enforcement mechanisms), and then claims to have been doing something else (i.e., simply to have been following a mechanical or similarly constrained procedure). In this sense, the performative force of law's rhetorical feints and ruses are indeed transformed into the literal acts of world making that de Man calls positional. Law, however, forgets the constitutive role of its performative force, although it is precisely this force that provides law's formalist rhetoric with its literal meaning.

For de Man, language (including the language of law) thus carries a potent performative power: "Words cannot be isolated from the deeds they perform;...[n]ot only because they represent or reflect on actions but because they themselves, literally, are actions." However, as we have seen, "Their power to act exists independently of their power to know."[31] Language fragments cognition into the pattern of mutually self-destructive moments that we have seen at work in Fish's account of the law: 1) the positing of the knowable entity (for Fish, the formal self-identity of the law), 2) the forgetting of the (merely) positional status of this entity, and 3) the blind performative consequences that are the literal force of the positional act, blind because they are radically severed from knowledge (and therefore from intention or control) by the coercive forgetting that language interposes between act and cognition.[32] The linguistic act's force is

---

31. De Man, "Shelley Disfigured," 102, 103.

32. What follows from this is the peculiar conclusion that the same potency of language that produces meaning—in the form of effective speech acts—also destroys the possibility of meaning—in the sense of fully cognized or intentional speech acts, that is, speech acts saturated with, or exhausted by, the subject's intention. This point is developed at length—with considerably more philosophical sophistication than I can do justice to here—by Rodolphe Gasché. See "'Setzung' and 'Übersetzung': Notes on Paul de Man," *Diacritics* 11 (Winter 1981): 36, 49–57. In brief, he delimits de Man's distinctive contribution to speech act theory by tracing the idealism that grounds Austin's notion of the "total speech act" and contrasting it with de Man's nonidealist notion of a linguistic performativity that disrupts, rather than presupposes, the "infinite activity of the self-positing self." Gasché argues that

> Austin's concept of the act as pure doing is like the Fichtean *Thathandlung* linked to the notion of presence. The Fichtean *Act* is an inversion of the self upon itself, a reflection of the self upon itself (prior to all subject-object separation) by means of which it acquires (itself) its present being....Positing [in Austin's sense], then, as the act through which the self asserts itself in its being before all intentionality, or as the act that precedes the speech act's becoming

beyond the reach of the cognitional and meaning-giving powers of the subject of knowledge, whether that subject is institutional, as in the case of law, or human. And, since its force is literal, it can also be called violent.

Given their linkage to the institutions of state power, the notion that legal speech acts have a literal and violent force is not difficult to accept. But it should be kept in mind that the legal speech act is not unique but merely exemplary of a specifically linguistic violence in which *all* linguistic utterances participate, because all utterances possess, by virtue of the fact that they are speech *acts*, the certainty of producing (unknowingly and uncontrollably) effects—semantic and otherwise—that exceed the semantic entity posited by the utterance itself as its final destination. These entities may be truth values associated with propositions (in the case of constative utterances), illocutionary effects (in the case of performatives narrowly defined), or, as Fish shows in "The Law Wishes to Have a Formal Existence," formal identities, mechanical-deterministic structures, and "victorious histories."[33] In each case what I am calling (following de Man) the

---

an act of denomination or of communication, is dependent on the conception of spirit as a subject, or of language as the predominant manifestation of the subject's subjectivity. (Ibid., 53)

De Man's "more radical notion of positing," on the other hand,

far from permitting texts to close upon themselves (from becoming selves, reflexive and autonomous entities) temporalizes them, historicizes them. The performative, then, is characterized by its power of dissociation. In particular, by the dissociation of the cognitive from the act within what Austin called the total speech act. (Ibid., 57, 56)

Thus, "This allegorized notion of the performative [is] a disjunctive which generates time and history" (ibid)—albeit very different notions of "time" and "history" than those implied in Fish's celebration of the "history" of the law's continually renewed "victory . . . in the shape of *keeping going*" ("Law Wishes," 179), as I will attempt to show in the next section.

33. A more complete explanation of de Man's concept of linguistic violence would require an account of the relationship between de Man's and Austin's concepts of linguistic performativity that unfortunately lies beyond the scope of this essay. For one such account that touches on these issues, see Gasché, "'Setzung' and 'Übersetzung.'" See also Jacques Derrida's "Signature, Event, Context," in *Margins of Philosophy* (Chicago: University of Chicago Press, 1982), in which Derrida demonstrates how what he calls the structural "iterability" of every utterance keeps the utterance's illocutionary effect (or meaning) from ever being fully determined by its context. Derrida's concept of iterability is closely related to de Man's assertions of language's potential for violence. It is this structural "untetheredness" of utterances from any context or intention, and the accompanying certainty that every utterance is fated to have (from the perspective of its intention or context) absolutely random

linguistic violence is measured by the radical disjuncture that separates the event of semantic production from the semantic content
produced.

To mean, to signify, language must parse itself into units (semantic and grammatical), and what is lost to the meanings and significations thus generated, what cannot be comprehended by these
meanings and significations, is the act of parsing itself. This uncom-
prehended act, which shadows every semantic entity, is the blind (and
therefore violent) force that disjoins intention from consequence (linguistic or "real world"); in the vocabulary of naive realism, it is what
guarantees that concept, word, and proposition will never be adequate
to the extralinguistic thing or truth they represent. Moreover, since
what we call the world apart from the law is similarly made up of
rhetorically posited entities, with regard to the specifically linguistic
violence isolated by de Man there is no distinction to be made between
a literal and a purely linguistic or figural violence; linguistic violence
is as literal as it is figural.[34]

Linguistic violence, although literal, is not, it should be clear,
identical to the physical force we ordinarily associate with the term
violence. Linguistic violence and physical violence may be intimately
related, however, as, again, examples from law illustrate. One need
look no further than the familiar story of the marital-rape exemption.
Until recently, under the laws of most jurisdictions the legal term
rape was held not to apply to a case in which a husband forced sex
on his wife. To be a wife was not to be subject to rape by one's
husband. The physical violence perpetrated in the name of this particular legal fiction need hardly be recounted here. What should be

---

effects, that for de Man is a critical part of what he means by linguistic violence.
De Man also emphasizes, however, the impossibility of the utterance correctly reading
itself *as an act.* Thus de Man isolates an unavoidable gap between the utterance's
posited meaning and its performative force as the fundamental structure of the linguistic act.

34. I am leaving aside the separate question of the law's access to the mechanisms
of state violence, which would at least appear to distinguish the law's *institutional*
violence from that of other institutions (in particular, literature and literary criticism).
Even this seemingly absolute distinction fails to hold up under scrutiny, however.
Fish, for example, argues for the *"structural* interdependence" of legal-linguistic performativity and other, nonlegal spheres of linguistic performance in his essay "Don't
Know Much," 306. He shows convincingly (in the course of criticizing Posner's rigid
distinction between legal and literary interpretive activity) that "the actions of literary
critics can have consequences as far-reaching as any court." Ibid., 308.

noted, however, are the propositions and semantic equivalences that this legal definition necessarily assumes—i.e., posits—as true: that *woman* equals "property of some man (father or husband)" and that "sexual access is a property right." The *linguistic* violence of the marital-rape exemption is this semantic reduction of woman to property, a linguistic act that in a real sense was what enabled and justified the *physical* violence perpetrated against women under the cover of the exemption.

What is equally important for our purposes here, although perhaps more difficult to see, is the sense in which the violence of this semantic reduction is necessarily unknown and unknowable—that is, is forgotten—by the linguistic act itself. It was certainly true that many of the legal opinions discussing and justifying the marital-rape exemption were explicit and self-conscious about its archaic family-property basis. And it is equally true that the violence embodied and perpetrated by the proposition "a wife cannot be raped by her husband" can be identified *now* (and therefore, in de Manian terms, cognitively known). Nevertheless, from the perspective of the proposition itself, the *violence* of the positional semantic reduction of woman to property is invisible; indeed, the proposition "a wife cannot be raped by her husband" means, in essence, that raping one's wife-property is *not* violent. And because this semantic violence was invisible, its consequences—legal, social, historical—were not and could not have been predictable or controllable. The marital-rape exemption is an example in which the positional semantic violence is (at least from our current historical perspective) very clear, but the same violent disjunction of act, meaning, and consequence inheres in every legal act and every linguistic proposition. Language and law (because law *is* language) have to posit such semantic relationships, because it is exactly these (posited, reductive, "fictional") relationships that allow law to act and language to mean (and law that does not act is not law and language that does not mean is not language).

Accordingly, because it inheres in language itself as a medium, the structure of this linguistic forgetting and violence cannot be dismissed as a contingent failure or error. To overcome this violent forgetting, to restore the relationship among word, act, and knowledge such that the linguistic act is brought back within the sphere of cognitive intention and control, would require the possibility of a pure cognition whose representational equilibrium is undisturbed by the disruption of thought from act interpolated by the linguistic medium. But although language necessarily posits this possibility of pure cognition, because this possibility is itself founded on a positional act—the positing of the truth of the principle of noncontradiction and the real existence of the self-identical entity—it is open to radical doubt. Cognition, too, is a positional—and therefore actively forgetful—linguistic act. The "articulated language of cognition [emerges] by the erasure, the forgetting of the events this language in fact performed."[35]

Cognition is itself therefore no more reliable, or subject to cognitive control, than any other act of positing, because the cognitional act that would overcome the disruption of cognition and linguistic act is already implicated in the very disruption it is attempting to overcome. Cognition certainly takes place; we succeed in making sense of the world around us, from the lowest level of cognition to the most sophisticated interpretive acts. De Man's point is not that cognition is impossible, but that, despite its appearance and claims, the knowledge it attains is achieved by means that render it as lacking in certainty, meaning, necessity, and finality as the events upon which it intends to bestow these qualities: "the initial violence of position can only be half-erased, since the erasure is accomplished by a device of language that never ceases to partake of the very violence against which it is directed."[36]

Thus, even when cognition imposes meaning on language's positional acts, the imposition of this meaning is itself a performative act that stands beyond this meaning and unmoors it from the possibility of any certainty or finality. The act always remains "in advance" of the meaning it posits. To take yet another illustration from law, when a judge interprets a past precedent as having a certain meaning in the context before her and therefore requiring a certain outcome, she cannot know how future judges will assign meaning to her own judicial act of interpreting this precedent when they in their turn attempt to interpret its meaning. Her interpretive act is part of the meaning of the past precedent (indeed, that is exactly what declaring that a past precedent requires a particular outcome means), but this part of its meaning is not accessible to the judge

---

35. De Man, "Shelley Disfigured," 118.
36. De Man, "Shelley Disfigured," 118–19.

herself in the moment of interpretation. The interpretive act, precisely because it is an *act* or *event*, unmoors the meaning she declares from the very certainty and finality that this declaration (and every act of judgment) necessarily announces, since the act itself adds a layer to the meaning of the past precedent that, so to speak, arrives too late to be taken into account by her own interpretation. It is this disjunction of interpretive act from interpretive meaning that obstructs the possibility of controlling or knowing with certainty what consequences—judicial, legislative, social-political, revolutionary—a judicial decision (or any other act of interpretation) will set in motion. Nor can this uncertainty be overcome by the judge's knowledge that this is in fact her situation, since all attempts to control the future reception of her judgment—by, for example, couching it in ever more precise language or exhaustively explaining her reasoning—will also consist of linguistic acts that similarly remain in advance of, and therefore unknown by, the meanings they posit.

Knowledge always arrives too late, because as an event itself cognition always exceeds the meaning it imposes on the events it subsumes and cognizes. We can know, but we cannot know what we *do* when we know, and it is precisely this excess of linguistic act over posited meaning that inserts in every moment of every tradition, legal and otherwise, a structural openness that defeats the possibility of any final and definitive interpretation of its moments or of the tradition itself; this excess "becomes precisely the challenge to understanding that always again demands to be read."[37]

As the example of the judge's interpretation of past precedent suggests, the positional structure of the interpretive act bears directly on the question of the interpretation of traditions and histories (legal and otherwise). The question of tradition and history in turn leads back to the issue of Fish's neopragmatic positivism, at the heart of which, I suggested earlier, are inadequate conceptions of history and

---

37. De Man, "Shelley Disfigured," 122. Use of the metaphor of knowledge's "late arrival" in this context should not be confused with Hegel's dictum about the owl of Minerva flying only at fall of dusk, since the two figures are intended to convey fundamentally opposed conceptions of the relationship of knowledge to history. For Hegel, the belated flight of knowledge is the sign of an historical epoch's completion in the form of its comprehension by self-conscious spirit, while here the "late arrival" of knowledge signifies the essential falsity of any such claim of completion (including, of course, any claim to having comprehended in thought a definable historical period, such as Romanticism).

the historically given. Against the background of the de Manian schema, we can now return to this point and to Fish's discussion of the law's reliance on past precedent to decide present cases in his essay on H. L. A. Hart, "Force." In particular, as a more focused reading of this essay demonstrates, Fish's conception of history fails to do full justice to his own insights into the performative and constructive nature of language, which track, but only up to a certain point, de Man's account of the positional structure of linguistic-interpretive acts.

In "Force," Fish shows that the classical view of precedent (he cites Hart) "as a means of controlling an indeterminate present by reference to an already determined (and therefore determining) past" gets the process exactly backward; in fact, "The truth about precedent . . . is the opposite of the story we tell about it."[38] Hart's account of following precedent has the "agent who must decide [consider] 'whether the present case resembles the plain case [i.e., the settled precedent] 'sufficiently' in 'relevant' respects.'"[39] Fish criticizes Hart's implicit assumption (positing) of the independent self-identity of the plain case (the assumption that "the plain case resembles itself, establishes its own configurations in relation to which later cases are either like it or unlike it"), and correctly points out that "[r]esemblance and its opposite . . . are not immanent in the object but emerge from the perspective of the differential criteria that inform perception."[40]

It then follows, according to Fish, that it is the "differential criteria" of the present act of interpretation that determine the shape of the past precedent, rather than the past precedent controlling the present interpretive act:

What this means is that resemblance (or difference) is always a constructed (i.e., interpretive) phenomenon and therefore it can always be constructed again. In fact, that is what happens in the citing of precedents; the so-called plain case doesn't sit still, silently measuring the distance or closeness between it and the present case. Indeed, the demands are made from either direction, for it is the interests and concerns of the present case that generate the pressure for comparison and dictate its terms; and it is in

38. "Force," in *Doing What Comes Naturally*, 514.
39. Ibid. (quoting Hart).
40. Ibid.

light of the interests and concerns flowing from the present case that the "plain case" will then be constituted.[41]

In short, "precedent is the process by which the past gets produced by the present so that it can then be cited as the producer of the present."[42] Fish thus shows that the act of interpreting a past precedent—which in the traditional view is based on the (cognitive) act of receiving the case's plain meaning—is in fact a positional act that effaces its own positionality behind the guise of cognition. More specifically, he points to the curious fact that the positional structure of the interpretive act reverses what we ordinarily consider the natural temporal order.

This temporal reversal applies equally to the positional status of the history or tradition as a whole. For example, Fish shows, as he also does in "The Law Wishes to Have a Formal Existence," that this self-deceptive positional structure undergirds the law's "continuity":

> It is in this way that the law achieves what Ronald Dworkin calls "articulate consistency," a way of thinking and talking about itself which creates and recreates the continuity that is so crucial to its largest claim, the claim to have an unchanging center that founds its authority. Articulate consistency is not a fact, but an achievement, something that is forever being wrested out of diverse materials which are then retroactively declared always to have had its shape.[43]

He thus shows that the law's continuity—that is, its history conceived as a coherent tradition—is itself posited rather than actual.

Fish does not, however, carry his insight consistently through to its conclusion—that even the *present*, historically given "norms, standards, reasons, and, yes, even rules"[44] that he cites as constraints on the act of interpretation are themselves merely posited entities, fictions, that emerge retroactively from the very interpretive acts they are said to constrain. Such a notion is anathema to Fish—the assertion of the possibility of being unconstrained by context is the error he

---

41. Ibid.
42. Ibid.
43. Ibid., 514–15.
44. Ibid., 522.

denounces as antifoundationalist theory hope. He would insist that in fact legal interpretation *is* constrained, not by past precedent but by the present interests and beliefs that determine its interpretive context.[45] "Present interests and beliefs," however, are indistinguishable from the "past precedents" that he acknowledges are fictions posited retroactively by the interpretive act itself.

Fish mistakes the temporal distinction—past precedents versus present context—as fundamental, even though, as he himself shows, the temporal order of past and present is itself simply a misleading linguistic effect produced by an act of interpretation that establishes a (linguistic) relationship between two (linguistic) entities—the "present" case and the "past" precedent. What determines the relationship between the two entities is not their temporal order—this is a derivative effect—but the positional structure of the relationship, that is, the "process by which the past gets produced by the present so that it can then be cited as the producer of the present."[46] And the linguistic nature of this process changes not at all if one substitutes "present interpretive act" for "present case" and "present context" for "past precedent."

Thus, although it is always possible to demonstrate, *after the fact*, that any interpretive act was determined by some "contemporaneous interpretive conventions" or "present interests and beliefs" this order of cause and result could always be reversed—as Fish does in the case of present decision and past precedent—by showing that these "contemporaneous interpretive conventions" have no independent (extralinguistic) existence but are simply entities posited in the act of interpretation itself. "Contemporaneous interpretive conventions" and "present interests and beliefs" are neither contemporaneous with nor present to the interpretive act they purportedly constrain. They are fictions imposed retroactively to endow it with the appearance of necessity peculiar to causal explanation, or to insert it in an (equally fictional) historical tradition, or otherwise to bring its *force as act* into conformity with a static and therefore knowable entity, whether that entity consists of a physical or social law, history or tradition, formal identity, or similar device of knowledge. Nor is it possible to dismiss this retroactive structure as merely the

---

45. See, e.g., "Dennis Martinez," 384–98.
46. Ibid.

sign of the inevitable limitation of our knowledge and not a truth about reality. Such an attempt to save the real existence of causality, history, necessity, and similar concepts by pointing to the linguistic limitations on our knowledge of the real world merely confirms de Man's fundamental point, by acknowledging that the possibility of knowledge of these concepts can only be saved at the expense of conceding their posited status—we cannot assert (or even deny) their real existence.

Contemporaneous interpretive conventions and present interests and beliefs are posited fictions. This means that interpretive acts are as radically untethered from the constraints of present constitutive norms of meaning or context as Fish shows "present cases" are from "past precedent." It should be clear that this does *not* mean that interpretive acts are free (or potentially free) in any subjective sense of the word—that interpreters are free to choose their interpretations, that they are free of obstructions to clear understanding, and so on— since it is precisely the possibility of such subjective knowledge and control that is foreclosed by the positional structure of interpretation as act. But it does mean that the privilege granted by neopragmatism to "present" values, conventions, norms, and interpretive communities (as well as to the historical narratives in which these entities are necessarily inserted) is entirely illusory, since the constraint they exercise on interpretation, thought, and imagination is conjured retroactively by the act of historical interpretation itself to bring the force of these (linguistic) acts into conformity with the form of knowledge. It is this privileging of a historical "present"—and therefore also a past history of similar historical "presents" and the historically given values, beliefs and interests that they hand down to us as our putative birthright and burden—that marks the positivist tendency of neopragmatism.[47]

---

47. Drucilla Cornell has also criticized Fish for holding the positivist view that "law is only an expression of the *present* power of an actual existing community" and has emphasized the future-oriented, "fictional" moment in the interpretive act of following precedent. Cornell, "Institutionalization of Meaning, Recollective Imagination, and the Potential for Transformative Legal Interpretation," *University of Pennsylvania Law Review* 136 (1988): 1135, 1162–63 n. 95; see also, e.g., ibid., 1140 ("For Fish, antifoundationalism is positivism"); 1172 ("[The judge] posits the very ideals she reads into the law. By so doing, she is remembering the future as she recollects the past. . . . She does not just perpetuate the past; she, at least in part, makes it what it is to become"). See also Cornell, "Time, Deconstruction, and the

Fish is too true to his antifoundationalist epistemology to fall into the worst of these tendencies—uncritically mouthing liberal pieties in the name of philosophical-historical argument, to take one increasingly common example—and he has taken note and responded to other criticisms that have perceived a tendency to stasis lurking in his analysis.[48] But even so, the neopragmatic bias that equates antifoundationalism with historicism exerts a pull in his work that consistently draws him back toward a rhetorical privileging of *present* interests and beliefs, norms and conventions, and interpretive communities (as well as the monolithic histories, like the law's "history of victory," that these figures presuppose), and away from the insight into the structural excess of act over meaning that inheres in every interpretive positing of every such allegedly present moment.[49]

Challenge to Legal Positivism," *Yale Journal of Law & Humanities* 2 (1990): 267; Cornell, "'Convention' and Critique," *Cardozo Law Review* 7 (1986): 679, 687.

48. See Fish, "Change," in *Doing What Comes Naturally.*

49. For example, one can see the effects of this tug-of-war in Fish's recent critique of the notion of "Reason" as the neutral and ahistorical "center of liberal thought." See Fish, *There's No Such Thing,* 17–18. Fish's critique incorporates a deManian insight into the posited status of all explanatory devices of reason but fails to recognize that this same insight also undermines his own (and other neopragmatists') unselfconscious use of the notions of history and historically given conventions and interpretive communities.

"Reason," Fish asserts, is the name assigned to the liberal doctrine that the competing claims of different historical and ideological agendas can be adjudicated by a neutral mechanism—"the cool light of rational inquiry"—which floats above the fray of partisan interests below. Of course, as he points out, in order to decide *particular* conflicts Reason must inevitably stoop to the giving of (lower case plural) "reasons," which only appear as rational (and indeed intelligible) to a disputant by virtue of assumptions implicit in "the personal and institutional history which brought [the disputant] to [the] dispute" in the first place. Nevertheless, Fish asks, why is it not possible to "go deeper," to "put those underlying assumptions on the table so that *they* could be scrutinized and assessed?" Ibid.

His response replicates (in language that substitutes the more familiar terminology of "assumption" for the deManian "position") the structure of the deManian argument provided in the text *infra*: You can certainly "scrutinize and assess" such assumptions, he says, but if you do so

you will examine and assess them with forms of thought that themselves rest on underlying assumptions. At any level, the tools of rational analysis will be vulnerable to the very deconstruction they claim to perform. You can never go deep enough, for no matter how deep you go, you will find reasons whose perspicuity is a function of just those factors—institutional history, personal education, political and religious affiliations—from which Reason supposedly stands apart. (Ibid., 18)

What remains *invulnerable* in Fish's own deconstructive discourse, however, is the

This excess is precisely *not* historical, since it opens within each "present" moment of a tradition a floodgate of potential rereadings and historical interpretaions that run directly counter to the moment's received meaning and to the history in which it is embedded. And it is this structural excess that opens every present to a future that is neither determinable nor determined by this present or its history. But this excess *is* historicizing, since (as Fish's examples of the law's past precedent and "articulate consistency" illustrate) it is in such acts of language that histories, traditions, and temporal sequences are posited in the first instance. In this specific sense, one can say that the linguistic act (figuratively) *precedes* the historical. In short, if there is a true present, it is the nontemporal "present" of the act *as act* and not of its imposed historical meaning. This "present" is therefore not a category of history at all.

None of which means that one can shrug off history or the historically given as mere ideological constructs that can be seen through in theory and then discarded in favor of some deeper truth as, at least on Fish's reading, CLS would like to do. Neopragmatism is right, if for reasons that it only partly understands, that the metaphysical-eschatological dream of overcoming history cannot be realized. First, from the metaphysical-eschatological perspective, the same disjunction of linguistic act from interpretive meaning that opens the space for reinterpretation of any given history also condemns every new interpretation—every demonstration of the contingency and inadequacy of a received understanding of the tradition—to the same structure of fictionality and forgetting as the old.[50] In this sense, we

---

"perspicuity" of a particular quality of "just those factors"—the quality that guarantees it is they (and not some other factors) that you will inevitably find underlying your reasons, "no matter how deep you go." As his list of examples (and all of his writings) make clear, this quality is "historicity," the strict identification of an entity's essence with a limited temporal and contextual moment.

Neopragmatism assumes and posits the perspicuity of historicity no less than liberalism assumes and posits the perspicuity of Reason. One can therefore cite as a corollary to Fish's claim that "Reason is a political entity, and never more so than when its claim is to have transcended politics," that neopragmatism is also a political entity, and never more so than when its claim is to be without any political consequences. One can also say, consistent with Fish's assertion that "liberalism, bereft of its formal center, does not exist," that neopragmatism, bereft of its own fictional center—the privileged category of the historical—does not exist. Ibid., 19.

50. It should be kept in mind that this applies with equal force to interpretations, like de Man's and the one offered here, that attempt to "see through" the concepts

are stuck with our (posited, fictional) histories, and, as Fish rightly insists, no amount of knowledge or antifoundationalist insight can save us from this fate. It also bears repeating—again as Fish and other neopragmatists point out—that forthright recognition of this all-too-human predicament only appears as skeptical or relativist or nihilist if one persists in clinging to the impossible dream of escaping beyond history (a dream that, at a deeper level, is the desire of thought to escape beyond language).

Apart from this fate, however, there is another sense of history that continues to call out for the work of historical interpretation and reinterpretation even after the fictionality of all such histories is exposed. This other history (de Man called it, in a different context, "the materiality of actual history")[51] is very different from the stories that historicism reveres under the same name. As we saw above, historicism's histories "have to be told," since, although fictional (in the specific sense elaborated here), they are necessarily posited as actual by every interpretive act of historical knowledge. The materiality of actual history, by contrast, carries none of this necessity and in fact resists being told at all, because it is the story of precisely those linguistic acts of violence, and of the victims of those acts, that are the noncognitive—and therefore unrecognizable and unrecountable—side of the interpretive act. Within the law, it is the story of the losers in the law's "history of victory." Losers like the raped wife, whose story of violation was not a story that could be heard, in court or elsewhere, because the same acts of language that equated being a wife with not being subject to rape by one's husband, and thereby subjected her to the very literal violence of wife rape, at the same time deprived her of the vocabulary needed to name this violation *as* violation, by making "wife rape" a contradiction in terms. The violence of the linguistic act is in fact indistinguishable from this silencing of its victims, a point to which I will return in the next section.

Of course, as we saw above, by virtue of the same positional linguistic structure this silencing can never be total, since the door

---

of "historicity" and "history" in general. De Man, of course, had no illusions that his account was immune from the misleading linguistic forces he identified. See, e.g., "Shelley Disfigured," 122.

51. De Man, "Anthropomorphism and Trope in the Lyric," in *The Rhetoric of Romanticism*, 262.

necessarily remains open to reinterpretations of the tradition that may begin to grant the victims their voice. Nevertheless, from the perspective of the posited present conventions that are both the perpetrator of the violence and the privileged focus of the neopragmatic analysis, the victims' stories just as necessarily appear voiceless. Accordingly, neopragmatism can forget the actual history of violence and take historicism's official story of the present at face value. Indeed it can only forget the victims' actual history, because knowledge only arrives and only can arrive, always belatedly and by virtue of the retroactive operation of the positional act, in the posited form of an official story.

Neopragmatism privileges the cognitive moment and its retroactively imposed official story, but cognition only declares, after the fact, *what had to be*; it cannot say *what must have been* or *what must be* (much less what must be done). And if it is true that the "other history" of the victims exerts none of the cognitive force (in the sense of both violence and necessity) of the official story of the victors, this may simply illustrate the limits of a neopragmatic approach to law (and to history in general). There may yet be, in other words, another force—although *force* is no doubt the wrong word here—exercised by the victims' actual history that has a role to play in the rhetorical performance that is law. Toward an answer to this question, I return to reading Paul de Man's reading of *law* and *justice.*

5

De Man articulates his speculations about language in a specifically legal context in the chapter of *Allegories of Reading* devoted to Rousseau's *Social Contract.* According to de Man's elaborate rhetorical reading, the *Social Contract* (and its earlier notes and drafts) are organized around a series of relationships between mutually dependent but incompatible terms—between public and private happiness, the general and particular will, private property and the property of the state, and the individual as private citizen and as participant in the sovereign authority, among others—that express (or, more precisely, allegorize) the inevitable undoing (or deconstruction) of figures of metaphorical and organic totalization by the metonymic relationships that compose these figures. This series converges toward a concept

of "legal text" that embodies the two aspects of law with which we
are concerned here: the law as a formal system of mechanical decision
making and the law as performative, the active vehicle of justice.[52]

De Man identifies the "first characteristic" of the legal text as its
"generality" (*Allegories*, 267). By generality, he means the laws independence from individual, partisan perspectives—that is, its universality—but also its ability to function apart from the particularity
of its application to specific individuals or cases. This autonomous
ability is in turn equated with law's aspect as a code or grammar,
in opposition to the particularization of the law's application, which
is equated with reference.

> From the point of view of the legal text, it is this generality
> which ruthlessly rejects any particularization, which allows for
> the possibility of its coming into being. Within the textual model,
> particularization corresponds to reference, since reference is the
> application of an undetermined, general potential for meaning
> to a specific unit. The indifferrence of the text with regard to its
> referential meaning is what allows the legal text to proliferate,
> exactly as the preordained, coded repetition of a specific gesture
> or set of gestures allows Helen to weave the story into the
> epic. . . . The system of relationships that generates the text and
> that functions independently of its referential meaning is its gram-
> mar. (*Allegories*, 268)

De Man emphasizes that to the extent the law is general, it is purely
formal, "a logical code or machine" (*Allegories*, 268), and reiterates
the necessary disjunction between the law's formal, "grammatical"
origins and its future application: "Just as no law can ever be written
unless one suspends any consideration of applicability to a particular
entity including, of course, oneself, grammatical logic can function
only if its referential consequences are disregarded" (*Allegories*, 269).

"On the other hand," de Man points out, "no law is a law unless
it also applies to particular individuals."

---

52. 'The structure of the entity with which we are concerned (be it as property,
a national State or any other political institution) is most clearly revealed when it
is considered as the general form that subsumes all these particular versions, namely
as legal *text*" (*Allegories*, 267).

> [Law] cannot be left hanging in the air, in the abstraction of its generality. Only by thus referring back to the particular praxis can the *justice* of law be tested, just as the *justesse* of any statement can only be tested by referential verifiability, or by deviation from this verification. For how is justice to be determined if not by particular reference? (*Allegories*, 259)

The answer to this question is less obvious than it appears, because it turns out that the law's "particular praxis," its role as the vehicle of justice, is incompatible with the requirement of its generality. De Man illustrates this point with a quote from Rousseau:

> Why is the general will always right, and why do all citizens constantly desire the well-being of each, if it were not for the fact that no one exists who does not secretly appropriate the term *each* and think of himself when he votes for all . . .? Which proves that the equality of right and the notion of justice that follows from it derive from the preference that each man gives to himself, and therefore from the nature of man. (*Allegories* 269, quoting Rousseau)

The individual acquiesces in the general will (expressed in the law's generality) only to the extent that she "secretly" treats the law as tailored to her own, particular benefit. As de Man puts it, "The preceding passage makes clear that the incompatibility between the elaboration of law and its application (or justice) can only be bridged by an act of deceit" (*Allegories*, 269), the secret appropriation of the law's generality for the particularized purposes of the individual. "To secretly appropriate the term 'each' is to steal from the text the very meaning to which, according to this text, we are not entitled, the particular *I* which destroys its generality; hence the deceitful, covert gesture '*en secret*,' in the foolish hope that the theft will go unnoticed" (*Allegories*, 269). The need to apply to individual cases destroys the formality and mechanical determinacy that provide the law with its generality and, therefore, with its authority. No wonder Fish omits the question of justice from his definition of legal practice; rather than demonstrating the "victory" of the law "in the shape of keeping going," the more inclusive definition leads to the disheartening conclusion that the law continually suffers defeat at its own hands, caught

between its equally necessary but incompatible needs to be formal
and general and to be realized by applications in particular cases.
De Man states this aporia in linguistic terms:

> There can be no text without grammar: the logic of grammar
> generates texts only in the absence of referential meaning, but
> every text generates a referent that subverts the grammatical
> principle to which it owed its constitution. What remains hidden
> in the everyday use of language, the fundamental incompatibility
> between grammar and meaning, becomes explicit when the lin-
> guistic structures are stated, as is the case here, in political terms.
> (*Allegories*, 269)

This incompatibility manifests itself in the legal sphere in the divergence between what the law *does* and what it *says*, "between political
action and political prescription . . . or, in linguistic terms, between
the constative and the performative function of language" (*Allegories*,
270). Fish himself demonstrates that the law's assertion of its "formal
existence" is self-deluded to the extent that this formalism is actively
produced rather than given. As his example of contract law shows,
the same rhetorical operation that seals the law's claim to formal
autonomy and value neutrality simultaneously institutes and enforces
a particular, value-laden moral order (in the case of contract law,
the morality of the market). "The legal machine, it turns out, never
works exactly as it was programmed to do" (*Allegories*, 271), because
the law's claim to formal operation is constantly disrupted by its
application in concrete cases.

De Man's dictum, that "[w]ords cannot be isolated from the deeds
they perform; . . . [n]ot only because they represent or reflect on
actions, but because they themselves, literally, are actions,"[53] is itself
most literally instantiated by the case of legal language. The legal
word is defined by its linkage to the power of the state. If, however,
this performative power is severed from the formality and generality
that supply law with its claim to legitimacy, if it in fact destroys the
law's claim to formality and generality, then it cannot be distinguished
in principle from unmotivated acts. Moreover, since it can no longer

---

53. De Man, "Shelley Disfigured," 102, 103.

appeal to law's legitimacy, the exercise of state power triggered by legal interpretation cannot in principle be distinguished from violence or violation; de Man cites Rousseau for the proposition that "to found a State ... is to kill, to annihilate, and 'to mutilate, so to speak, the human constitution in order to strengthen it'" (*Allegories*, 271, quoting Rousseau).

The extent to which de Man treats such (apparently) metaphorical violence as literal was suggested in the preceding section. I will return to his reading of Rousseau, but the significance of de Man's problematics for law can best be understood by means of a brief detour through the work of a more traditional legal academic, Robert Cover. Cover, more than any other recent commentator, similarly emphasized legal language's intrinsic connection to violence. In his essay "Violence and the Word," Cover argues that legal interpretation is primarily characterized by the literal institutional acts of violence that accompany and constitute it. "Legal interpretive acts signal and occasion the imposition of violence upon others,"[54] whether that violence is realized by the Supreme Court's denial of a death row inmate's final appeal or by an interpretation of a lease in a municipal housing court that forces a tenant out of her home (or, alternatively, deprives the landlord of money or rights that would otherwise be hers). "[T]he relationship between legal interpretation and the infliction of pain remains operative even in the most routine of legal acts."[55]

Cover notes the surprising fact that although legal interpretation's institutional connection to violence is obvious, it has gone unmentioned by the vast majority of those who have commented on the subject.[56] Like Fish, they overlook what law *does*—violence—in favor of the story law tells about itself.[57] Law's violence recedes from these readers' view because they see law as the bearer of legitimate force—a legitimacy that is grounded on the narrative power and meaning

54. Cover, "Violence and the Word," 1601.
55. "Violence and the Word," 1607.
56. "Violence and the Word," 1601.
57. I do not mean to obscure the significant differences between Fish and most other legal commentators, who take law's claim to formality and autonomy at face value. Fish's position is quite different, for example, from that of Owen Fiss, who defends law's formality and autonomy on its own terms. Compare Fiss, "Objectivity and Interpretation," *Stanford Law Review* 34 (1984):739, with Fish, "Fish v. Fiss," in *Doing What Comes Naturally* 120.

engendered by the legal tradition. The significance of this narrative power is the primary point of Cover's "Nomos and Narrative."[58] According to Cover, the law does not exist as an abstract and independent set of principles, but as a text inserted in a narrative epic. It does not exist apart from the story it tells to the community of those who view themselves as the bearers of and actors in that narrative. In the epic of the Western democracies, the law claims to embody the norms of the community within a formal system whose operation guarantees the production of legitimate legal rulings and the continuing orderly creation, in Cover's sense, of a nomos, a world of legal meaning.[59] It is this "continuity of the tradition," to use Fish's words, that provides legal violence with the meaning that permits it to appear as legitimate force and that deflects attention from its violent performative effects. Legal violence is effaced by legal meaning.

The institutional violence that legal interpretation effects is accompanied, however, by a meaning-destroying violence that disrupts this strategem of effacement and legitimation. Thus, beyond the law's institutional violence, Cover also identifies a specifically semantic legal violence. Expanding on his observation in "Nomos and Narrative" that "there is a radical dichotomy between the social organization of law as power and the organization of law as meaning,"[60] Cover demonstrates that the violence of legal interpretation destroys meaning as much as it creates it:

> Taken by itself, the word "interpretation" may be misleading. "Interpretation" suggests a social construction of an interpersonal reality through language. But pain and death have quite other implications. Indeed, pain and death destroy the world that "interpretation" calls up.[61]

The linguistic violence inherent in legal interpretation gives the lie to its claim to speak in the name of the whole community, as Cover's example of the sentencing of a prisoner best illustrates.

In analyzing the role of violence in the sentencing hearing, Cover

---

58. Cover, "The Supreme Court, 1982 Term—Forward: Nomos and Narrative," *Harvard Law Review* 97 (1983):4.
59. Ibid. (on the "jurisgenerative" function of law).
60. "Supreme Court," 18.
61. "Violence and the Word," 1602.

emphasizes the differential perspectives of the judge and the prisoner. It is the prisoner who is the object of the law's violence, and the judge whose task it is to provide this violent act with an interpretive meaning that elevates it above mere violence.

> Therefore, any account which seeks to downplay the violence or elevate the interpretive character or meaning of the event within a community of shared values will tend to ignore the prisoner or defendant and focus upon the judge and the judicial interpretive act. Beginning with broad interpretive categories such as "blame" or "punishment," meaning is created for the event which justifies the judge to herself and to others with respect to her role in the acts of violence.[62]

Cover notes that the sentencing of a convicted criminal defendant is widely understood in terms of these interpretive categories, not only by judges and other legal actors but by prisoners as well. He therefore asks whether it might not be the case that the interpretive act achieves the cementing of the community that is its fundamental claim to legitimacy, even to the extent of including the prisoner within this "community of shared values."[63]

The radical divergence between law as interpretation and law as act will not permit this happy resolution, however:

> For as the judge interprets, using the concept of punishment, she also acts—through others—to restrain, hurt, render helpless, even kill the prisoner. Thus, any commonality of interpretation that may or may not be achieved is one that has its common meaning destroyed by the divergent experiences that constitute it. Just as the torturer and the victim achieve a "shared" world only by virtue of their diametrically opposed experiences, so the judge and prisoner understand "punishment" through their diametrically opposed experiences of the punishing act.[64]

The performative force of the legal statement is radically severed

---

62. "Violence and the Word," 1608.
63. "Violence and the Word," 1608.
64. "Violence and the Word," 1609.

from its interpretive meaning; the judge and the prisoner cannot be brought together in a common understanding because the legal act casts the prisoner out from those for whom the legal interpretation has meaning. The language of the judge is not the language of the prisoner; and here the prisoner stands, allegorically, for all of the losers in the law's "history of victory" whom the law violently silences. The structure of Cover's scene reveals the structure of this linguistic violence at work in the law: law destroys the possibility of achieving the community of shared meaning in the act of announcing its achievement. Justice is indeed unjust.

Cover's work confirms and illuminates the disjunction between legal act and legal meaning that de Man also identifies. There is more, however, to de Man's account of the force of law than the negativity of the disjunction between law and justice. De Man continues his rhetorical analysis of the *Social Contract* by observing that the rhetorical structure of law is prospective: its rhetorical mode is that of the promise. "All laws are future-oriented and prospective; their illocutionary mode is that of the *promise*" (*Allegories*, 273). The law declares how the world should be rather than how it is, and is therefore indeed a forward-looking rather than descriptive. And since the law is authorized and empowered to bring about its projected state of the world, its declaration can accurately be characterized as a promise, a promise that purports to be made good with each application of the law to particular cases.

As we have seen, this promise is in fact broken with each application. The promise of justice achieved that the law makes with each legal act is in each case violated by the performative violence of that same act. But since this promissory structure is intrinsic to law's functioning, its continual failure must continually be forgotten, or it could no longer "remain operative as law" (as Fish puts it). The law therefore deceives itself and its subjects by positing as already established the community of meaning that it is in fact always already in the process of destroying.

This paradoxical and deceptive structure is represented in Rousseau by the dilemma posed by the need for the law to speak "'in the name of the people of today and not the past'" (*Allegories*, 273, quoting Rousseau). The laws should express the present general will of the people, since the people as sovereign are the law's ultimate authors. But without the institutional guidance of an already-constituted law to shape and teach the people the meaning of the general good, it would seem that there can be no general will to express. Rousseau asks, "How could a blind mob, which often does not know what it wants because it rarely knows its own good, carry out by itself as huge and difficult an enterprise as the promulgation of a system of Law?" (*Allegories*, 274, quoting Rousseau).

His famous solution to this paradox was to posit an individual who can somehow articulate in advance the people's (yet unformed) general will:

> For a people to appreciate the sound maxims of politics and to follow the fundamental rules of political reason . . . , effect should become cause, and the social spirit that the institutions are to produce should preside over their elaboration. Men should be, prior to the laws, what they are to become through them. (*Allegories*, 274, quoting Rousseau)

Rousseau named the individual who claims to speak for the people in advance of their existence, the "lawgiver." Given the impossible conditions the lawgiver is required to meet, and given the magnitude of the task of forging a unified general will out of the multitude of different individuals and divergent interests that made up the masses, Rousseau recognized that the lawgiver would have to have "recourse to an authority of another order":

> It is this that has, in all ages, obliged the founders of nations to have recourse to the intervention of Heaven and to attribute to the gods what has proceeded from their own wisdom, that the people might submit to the laws of the State as to those of nature and, recognizing that the same power which formed man created the city, obey freely, and contentedly endure that restraint so necessary to the public happiness.[65]

The lawgiver in other words is the worst kind of impostor—the false prophet.

As de Man rightly points out, "The metaphorical substitution of one's own for the divine voice is blasphemous," and the deceitful

---

65. Rousseau, *The Social Contract*, ed. C. Frankel (New York: Hafner Publishing Company, 1947), 38.

regime the lawmaker establishes is therefore of necessity one of "unjust justice." But de Man also notes that the necessity for this deceit is matched by the equally "implacable necessity" of its "eventual denunciation, in the future undoing of any State or any political institution"[66] This parallel necessity of deceit followed by exposure and downfall follows from de Man's linguistic schema. According to de Man, the lawgiver's recourse "can only be [to] God" because

> the temporal and causal reversal that puts the realization of the promise before its utterance can only occur within a teleological system oriented toward the convergence of figure and meaning. (*Allegories*, 274)

Only God's promises, in which figurative language and meaning indeed "converge," have the self-effecting performative force required by the lawmaker's task (a "convergence" of language and referential meaning exemplified by the biblical statement, "God said, 'Let there be light,' and there was light"). Since we saw in the preceding section, however, that this "convergence of figure and meaning" is precisely what is blocked by the positional disjunction of linguistic act from semantic meaning, the lawgiver's God-like declaration is necessarily deceitful and false. But as we also saw in the preceding section, this disjunction is at the same time what inserts in every such declarative act the inextinguishable possibility of a new interpretation that runs counter to, and therefore exposes, the deceitful force of the declaration's original meaning. Thus it is the positional structure of the lawgiver's act that at once gives it its effective force, makes it (of necessity) false and deceitful, and yet also guarantees its eventual exposure, "denunciation" and "future undoing."

Rousseau accurately perceived that only a false prophet can give effect to the law, and de Man foresaw—promised, one could also say, or even prophesied—every such prophet's ultimate downfall. The temporal reversal that the lawgiver pretends to effect emblematizes the structure of the legal-linguistic act of interpretation, which, in Fish's words, "is the process by which the past gets produced by the

---

66. "The metaphorical substitution of one's own for the divine voice is blasphemous, although the necessity for this deceit is as implacable as its eventual denunciation, in the future undoing of any State or any political institution" (*Allegories*, 274–75).

present so that it can then be cited as the producer of the present"
(Fish, "Force," in *Doing What Comes Naturally*, 514), but which also
(as we saw in the preceding section) is how this present is itself
produced in acts of language which always remain beyond its reach.
And, as we have also seen, if this process of production is necessarily
deceitful and violent, it is at the same time what promises the possibility of ever new interpretations and a future beyond the violence
and deceit of this posited present. Just as the lawgiver claims to speak
in the name of a community that does not and cannot yet exist as
if it were already in existence, the judge who renders a legal decision—
whether passing sentence on a prisoner or any other act—claims to
speak in the name of a present community of shared values whose
real existence is at once promised and infinitely deferred, because the
act of decision is always already in the process of destroying it.

Again, it would be an error to view this structure as confined
to the linguistic-interpretive acts of the law proper. The "judge who
decides" is, like Rousseau's lawgiver and Cover's prisoner, merely an
exemplary figure for a performative structure that inheres in the linguistic act of interpretation as such. And this structure controls readers of the law no less than legal practitioners. One can hear the
lawgiver's decree, for example, in the concluding lines of "The Law
Wishes to Have a Formal Existence."

Fish asks,

> Assuming, for the sake of argument, that I am right about the law
> and that it is in the business of producing the very authority it
> retroactively invokes, why should it be so? Why should the law
> take *that* self-occluding and perhaps self-deceiving form? (207)

His answer is that that is what "we" want it to do, that the law is
something "we" believe in and that answers to "our" desires:

> The short answer is that that's the law's job, to stand between us
> and the contingency out of which its own structures are fashioned.
> In a world without foundational essences—the world of human
> existence, there may be another, more essential one, but we know
> nothing of it—there are always institutions (the family, the
> university, local and national governments) that are assigned the
> task of providing the spaces (or are they theaters) in which we

negotiate the differences that would, if they were given full sway, prevent us from living together in what we are pleased to call civilization. And what, after all, are the alternatives? Either the impossible alternative of grounding the law in perspicuous and immutable abstractions, or the unworkable alternative of intruding that impossibility into every phase of the law's operations, unworkable because the effect of such intrusions would be so to attenuate those operations that they would finally disappear. That leaves us with the law as it is, something we believe in because it answers to, even as it is the creation of, our desires. (207–8)

"The law as it is, something we believe in": who, we? Not the homeless; women dying from back-alley abortions; strikers who have lost their jobs to replacement workers—the list could be extended indefinitely, and every legal reform that removes one group only adds another in its place. The existence of this "we" is as fictional as Fish himself shows the existence of the "law as it is" to be; but even if Fish's "we" is (and can be) nothing more than a hopeful rhetorical gesture—and there is no more deliriously hopeful gesture than the assertion of a "we"—it remains no less true that of such rhetorical gestures (the founding of a state, the creation of a rule of law, the justification of injustice) is history made.

De Man's conclusion is both more and less hopeful than Fish's happy ending. The essay ends with a parody of Heidegger:

> Die Sprache verspricht (sich) [language promises (itself)]; to the extent that it is necessarily misleading, language just as necessarily conveys the promise of its own truth. This is also why textual allegories on this level of rhetorical complexity generate history. (Allegories, 277)

Although de Man in this passage has taken leave of the law proper for his more general interest in language, his aphorism remains instructive for the instant reading of law. "Die Sprache verspricht": language—in this context, the language of law—promises, and what it promises is its fulfillment in the establishment of justice. But, "Die Sprache verspricht (sich)"—language promises (itself)—again, in this context, law promises (itself). Or, as I would even more liberally translate it, law promises justice but delivers only more law. And thus is its unbroken "history of victory"—in the shape of "keeping going," and nothing more—generated.

Law's promise of justice is never fulfilled, indeed it cannot be fulfilled and can therefore be considered bad faith and illegitimate, but by that same token must be made again and again, each time a legal decision is rendered and a legal actor appeals to a (not yet existent) community of meaning that would finally make good on law's promise and end once and for all its fatal violence. But if it is true that this promise can never finally be made good, it is also true, as Jacques Derrida reminds us, that "a promise is not nothing, it is not only marked by what it lacks."[67] Law remains suspended between its meaning-destroying violence and its impossible, necessary promise of justice.[68]

Does this aporetic structure shed any light on the Fish-CLS debate over literary theory and legal practice with which this essay began? Certainly Fish forgets (even while repeating) the violence and hope that are intrinsic to law's fundamental linguistic structure, but since such forgetfulness is installed in the deceitful structure of the interpretive act as such, some form of this forgetfulness is, as we have seen, unavoidable. Thus, to claim that recognition of this aporetic structure provides an opening in the "struggle against being demobilized by our own conventional beliefs"[69] would undoubtedly be to claim too much, at least if the hope is that convention itself can be transcended once and for all. And it would also certainly be irresponsible to suggest that Paul de Man would himself have subscribed to a liberatory reading of his theories.[70]

---

67. Derrida, "Le Tour des Babel" in *Difference in Translation*, ed. J. Graham (Ithaca: Cornell University Press, 1985), 191.

68. Or, as Walter Benjamin put it, between law as mythic violence and law as the divine violence that brings all violence to an end. Walter Benjamin, "Critique of Violence," in *Reflections*, trans. Edmond Jephcott (New York: Harcourt Brace Jovanovich, 1978). See also Jacques Derrida, "Force of Law: The Mystical Foundation of Authority," in *Deconstruction and the Possibility of Justice*, ed. Drucilla Cornell, Michel Rosenfeld, and David Carlson (New York: Routledge, 1992), for a superb reading of this Benjamin essay that bears directly on many of the points I make here.

69. Gordon, "New Developments in Legal Theory," 420.

70. Nevertheless, I would also take issue with the view that de Man's writings are devoid of political—or more specifically, ethical—import. Susan Handelman, for example, in her very interesting and helpful essay on some similarities and differences in the thought of Jacques Derrida and the philosopher and theologian Emmanuel

Nevertheless, it would be wrong to see in the deconstructive reading of law offered here merely paralysis or an endorsement of Fish's apolitical self-positioning, much less an affirmation of the resignation, skepticism, and nihilism so often attributed to deconstruction by its critics. If deconstruction risks being given these interpretations, it is because the price of avoiding that risk—complacency, self-willed blindness, intellectual fear—is too high, and because, more fundamentally, the risk cannot be avoided. There exist, side by side in every interpretive act, both the violent positing of a fictional present and its fictional history masquerading as truth—language in the guise of a

---

Levinas, opposes de Man's attitude toward language to Levinas's overtly ethical and religious view. Employing a familiar interpretation of de Man's work, she claims that whereas Levinas understands reading as "partak[ing]" of the ethical structure of the other than being," de Man "appropriated the epistemological critique of Derrida as mainly a cognitive problem and thus understood the problem of interpretation as undecidability or impossibility." Handelman, "Parodic Play and Prophetic Reason: Two Interpretations of Interpretation," in *The Rhetoric of Interpretation and the Interpretation of Rhetoric*, ed. Paul Hernadi (Durham: Duke University Press, 1989), 167. One goal of this essay is to begin to bring these "two interpretations of interpretation" closer together by eliciting from de Man's superficially epistemological attitude something like Levinas's idea of (in Handelman's words) "the 'saying' as the otherness which is the excess of meaning in all language and the very *prophetic dignity of language*" (Ibid., 166). Of course, Handelman herself quotes de Man (as reported by J. Hillis Miller) as saying "For me, the most important questions are religious questions" (Ibid., 167).

There remains the question of de Man's association with a collaborationist Belgian newspaper during a two-year period of the Nazi occupation (1940–42), an association which included at least one article in which he himself espoused overtly and virulently antisemitic views. Those who cannot separate de Man's later work from the biographical and historical weight of his youthful writings may balk at the suggestion that the late work shares a theological impulse—even a subterranean and unconscious impulse—with the work of a noted Jewish theologian. It would be too simple to respond that the biographical facts are irrelevant to interpretation of the late work, particularly its susceptibility to the charge of nihilism (although the relationship of the biography to this tendency is also far more complex than most of de Man's critics allow). Rather than an apology for or obfuscation of de Man's negativity, I have attempted, to borrow Benjamin's terms, to "subject this . . . negative part" of his corpus to a "shift of point of view (but not of criteria!)" in the hope that "it too will reveal a new positive element." Walter Benjamin, "N: [Re the Theory of Knowledge, Theory of Progress]," in *Benjamin: Philosophy, Aesthetics, History*, ed. Gary Smith (Chicago: The University of Chicago Press, 1989), 46. Benjamin referred to his redemptive reading practice as effecting an "historic apocatastasis"—a secularized version of the doctrine of the final restoration of all sinful beings to a state of blessedness in God. (Ibid.) The reading offered here may not redeem the sinful man— nor is it intended to—but I hope at least to have made plausible the possibility that the work is not beyond redemption.

false prophet—and the redemptive opening of a "true present," which, though not itself historical, holds out hope and promises justice to those silenced by the actual history of this violence. Nothing, however, stands in the way if deconstruction's critics (or its proponents) attend only to the fatality and positional violence of the interpretive act and ignore its promise of redemption, because this redemptive moment—which is not even a moment, and which can only be said to exist allegorically—as the pure *act* that remains *in advance* of the imposed meanings and semantic violence that follow in its train, cannot itself be known. It therefore also cannot be said or used, and nothing—no thing, no knowable entity, no theoretical construct or political program or ethical commitment—follows from it as a consequence, logical, causal, or practical. Yet the pure act of language is at the same time what breaks open the fatality of imposed meaning for the original saying and naming of its violence *as* violence (even while joining these new semantic acts to the same structure of violence and deception as the old).

The violent necessity with which the linguistic act imposes its official story of the present and its "history of victory" is thus in each case called into question by the same retroactive force that gave it effect. This questioning is itself without necessity or force; it cannot break the cycle of deception and imposed meaning to which it is joined. But it also can never be totally silenced. Listening carefully, deconstruction (in its best incarnations) answers by imposing on itself the "responsibility without limits"[71] and endless task of naming the violence and its victims, not in the name of the fatal violence itself, but in the name of the hope and possibility of justice that is inseparable from the violence.

Thus if the deconstructive reading of law has anything to give to the legal practitioner, it is a call for responsibility to the victims of legal violence. This call may seem no more than another empty rhetorical gesture, since, as we have seen, the linguistic violence of the law is general and inheres in even the most trivial of legal acts. But it should rather be seen as a demand to uncover the not-yet-visible violence perpetrated by precisely those legal acts and rules which appear "at present" most trivial, uncontroversial or nonviolent, like the marital-rape exemption of another day. Beyond this endless

---

71. Derrida, "Force of Law," 19.

and necessary process of critique and self-critique, however, it is clear enough to whom the call to responsibility refers: criminal defendants (and their victims, whom the law has failed), the poor, racial and sexual minorities, and all the rest who bear most directly the first brunt of the law's literal and rhetorical force—the list is familiar, since the law's long history has modified it hardly at all. It is in their names that the law's impossible promise of justice is made, and it is on their backs that its never-satisfied but constantly renewed promissory note—the law's hopelessly hopeful "we"—is inscribed. "Only for the sake of the hopeless are we given hope."[72]

Of course, nothing prevents one from ignoring this call to responsibility and hope, and responsibility *for* hope, if only because, as Fish demonstrates, the law's (rhetorical) victory in the shape of keeping going is assured from the outset. Victory, however, is not everything. As Robert Cover warned in his allegory of the primal scene of legal violence, the sentencing hearing, "any account which seeks to downplay the violence or elevate the interpretive character or meaning of the event within the community of shared values will tend to ignore the prisoner or defendant and focus on the judge and the judicial interpretive act."[73] Stanley Fish's reading of law in "The Law Wishes to Have a Formal Existence" ignores the prisoner and the other victims of law's violence in favor of the law's official story; in the courtroom drama of the sentencing hearing, he sits with the judges. The deconstructive reading calls on us to stand with the prisoners.

72. Walter Benjamin, "Goethes Wahlverwandtschaften," in *Gesammelte Schriften*, Band I, 123 (Frankfurt am Main: Suhrkamp, 1991), 201 (quote translated in Theodor Adorno, "A Portrait of Walter Benjamin," in *Prisms* 227, trans. Samuel and Shierry Weber [Cambridge: MIT Press], 1967), 241.
    73. "Violence and the Word," 1608.

Contributors

Lawrence Douglas is Assistant Professor of Law, Jurisprudence, and Social Thought at Amherst College.

Robert Ferguson is George Edward Woodberry Professor in the Department of English and Comparative Literature and Professor of Law at Columbia University.

Peter Goodrich is Corporation of London Professor of Law at Birkbeck College, University of London.

Barbara Johnson is Professor of English, Afro-American Studies, and Comparative Literature at Harvard University.

Thomas R. Kearns is William H. Hastie Professor of Philosophy and Professor of Law, Jurisprudence, and Social Thought at Amherst College.

Austin Sarat is William Nelson Cromwell Professor of Jurisprudence and Political Science and Professor of Law, Jurisprudence, and Social Thought at Amherst College.

Adam Thurschwell is Assistant Professor of Law at Oklahoma City University School of Law.

James Boyd White is Hart Wright Professor of Law, Professor of English Language and Literature, and Adjunct Professor of Classical Studies at the University of Michigan.

Lucie White is Professor of Law at the University of California at Los Angeles.

Index